To John

Understanding the Chinese

A personal A-Z

Alan Macfarlane

with best wishes from

Alan Macfarlane

CAM RIVERS PUBLISHING

First published in Great Britain in 2020 by
Cam Rivers Publishing Ltd
33 Trumpington Street
Cambridge CB2 1QY

www.cambridgerivers.com
press@cambridgerivers.com

Series Editor: Zilan Wang
Editor: Sarah Harrison
Project Manager: Qin Yuchen
Typesetting by Wang Yichen
Cover design by MUYE

ISBN:978-1-912603-52-7

Table of Contents

Preface 14

1. The return of China 24
2. How has China achieved an economic miracle? 35
3. The largest, oldest and most diverse civilisation 42
4. Ignorance and Prejudice 50
5. Misunderstanding 64
6. Why China is so easy, yet difficult, to understand 82

Understanding the Chinese A-Z 89

Advanced technologies 92
Alphabets 93
Administrative levels 96
Ancestors 98
Animals 99
Animal calendar 101
Animal symbols 103
Architecture 105
Armies 108
Bamboo 111
Bargaining and haggling 112
Belt and road 114
Books 115
Boxer rebellion 117
Bribery 118
Calligraphy and painting 120
Canals and waterways 122

Change - patterns of 124
Childrearing 125
Chopsticks 127
Cities 129
Clash or harmony of civilisations 131
Clocks 134
Clubs and associations 136
Colours 138
Confrontation and harmony 140
Confucius 142
Conservatism 143
Custom 145
Disasters 147
Divination 150
Dominant Superpower 152
Earthquakes and floods 155
Eating 157
Education 160
Elements 163
Emotional warmth 164
Face and honour 167
Fashion 170
Fat and thin civilisations 173
Festivals 175
Finger-nail guards, bound feet and manual labour 178
Flowers and plants 179
Galactic Empire 181
Gaokao and education 182
Gender 184

Ghosts 185
Gifts 187
Ginkgo and durability 188
Glass 189
Green energy 190
Guanxi 192
Gunpowder and fireworks 194
Health and health care 197
High level equilibrium traps 199
Hong Kong 202
Humour 204
Industrial revolution 207
Industrious and industrial 209
Intellectual property 210
Investment and saving 212
Inward and outward looking civilisations 214
Islam 216
Joint responsibility 220
Journey to the West 221
Kung-fu and martial arts 224
Landward and seaward 226
Law and justice 227
Love and marriage 232
Mah Jong and other games 235
Mandarins 236
Mandate of heaven and democracy 238
Mao Tse-tung 239
Markets and marketing 242
Memory and forgiveness 243

Mills	244
Minorities	246
Missions and missionaries	248
Modernity	250
Money and cities	255
Mongols and Manchus	255
Mountains and rocks	257
Nightmares	260
Nobility	264
Opera	266
Opium	267
Opium Wars	268
Overseas Chinese	270
Paper	272
Physical infrastructure	273
Poetry and poets	275
Politeness and etiquette	278
Population patterns	279
Porcelain	285
Poverty reduction	286
Printing	288
Professions and professionals	289
Public and private	290
Qin Emperor	292
Rapid change	294
Rare earths	296
Reinvention of traditions	297
Responsibility	298
Rice	299

Scholars	302
Self-respect	303
Science and civilisation	305
Sex	310
Shamanism	311
Shenzhen	313
Shock of the future	316
Silk and Silk Roads	319
Sin and guilt	322
Sino-Japanese relations	323
Social media and digital communication	325
Socialism with Chinese characteristics	326
Soil	328
South China Sea	329
Surveillance	330
Taiwan	335
Tibet	336
Tai Qi	339
Taxation	341
Tea	344
Tea ceremonies	346
Team games	347
Temples and shrines	348
Terracotta army	349
The Great Divergence	351
Toilets	353
Torture	354
Traditional Chinese medicine	355
Triads	356

Universities and academies 358
Urbanisation 361
Vast and integrated 365
Violence and war 367
Wall(s) of China 369
Water management and hydraulic civilization 371
Westernization 373
Witches 374
Xanadu 376
Yangtze 378
Yin and Yang 379
Zen – Chan (Chinese) Buddhism 382

7. A unique civilisation 387
8. The future of China: some guesses 418

Twenty books and ten films which I recommend 431
Acknowledgements 433

Preface

I do not recall being interested in, or knowing much about, China before my 50th year in 1991. I had never studied Chinese history or read any serious books solely devoted to China. Though the Gurungs, whom I had worked with for many years, were reputedly from northern China, there was no real chance to work in China and I was preoccupied with Nepal and England. When a prospective Ph.D. student of mine in the mid 1980s wanted to work in China, I dissuaded him because I had heard it was more or less impossible to do so at that time.

I was aware, I think, after the fall of the 'gang of four' and the gradual opening up in the 1980s that something was changing dramatically in China, but after 1989, China seemed to close up again a little for a year or two.

Nevertheless, I began to become interested in China, following my first visit to Japan. Our visits to Japan in 1990 and 1993 gave us our first encounter with the Far East and with a culture heavily influenced by China. Separating out what was specifically Japanese and what the Japanese owed to China became a growing interest.

After the first two visits to Japan, my friend Gerry Martin suggested that we should go for a tourist trip to China in 1996. Gerry had visited Hong Kong and Singapore a number of times to set up engineering firms there and knew much more about China than I did. He was aware that something dramatic was occurring. He and I were both interested in the origins of the Scientific and Industrial revolutions, so the puzzle of why science and the industrial revolution first emerged in the West and not China was already interesting us.

I had read various 'European miracle' books which referred to China – E.L. Jones, David Landes and others – which suggested that China had been the foremost civilisation in the world in many ways up to the fifteenth century, but after that had hit some kind of ceiling. I had read Max Weber's influential *Religion of*

China, which elaborated the Marxian idea of an 'Asiatic Mode of Production', which proved a block to modernisation.

The portrayal of China from Montesquieu, through Adam Smith and David Hume, to Tocqueville and later was the model I had in my mind. And around that time the model was given a modern rendering in Mark Elvin's *The Pattern of the Chinese Past* (1973). I was also starting to read Jonathan Spence's books, watch 'The Outlaws of the Marsh' and gingerly learn a little more. I also read R.H. Tawney's *Land and Labour in China* (1932) and F. H. King's *Farmers of 40 Centuries* (1911). Yet I was still without any real feeling for China.

By early 1996, I had a three-way model – the West, Nepal, Japan. I sensed that adding China would make it even richer but how to encompass not just a country but a huge civilisation – the largest and the longest in history?

We went for our first tour of China for two weeks in 1996. It was basically an escorted trip, though we managed to get away occasionally from the tourist route into remote areas and people's homes. A combination of these experiences, long conversations with Gerry who was both knowledgeable and perceptive, and my comparative experiences of the West, Nepal and Japan meant that it was a surprisingly fruitful trip.

During the next six years I read much more about China and ran some comparative seminars with a focus on China. I was also involved in a television series for Channel 4, 'The Day the World Took Off', in which China played a large part. Then in 2002, my wife Sarah and I were invited to join a historical investigation in northern China. At the same time my first mainland Chinese Ph.D. student was admitted to Cambridge and my first book to be translated into Chinese was under way.

The subsequent seventeen years have given my wife and I an opportunity to visit China almost every year. The dates of our visits, which coincided with the period of maximum growth in China, are shown in a diagram at the end of chapter 4. We have travelled all over China, the only areas we have not visited are the extreme north-east and north-west, and Tibet and Inner Mongolia. We have visited all the great cities and many remote villages, particularly in the south and western minority areas. We made these tours with a succession of my Chinese Ph.D. students and friends who introduce us to their families and answered our questions about what we were encountering. I have taken many hundreds of hours of film, and Sarah has kept detailed diaries of our visits.

I have also given many lectures in Chinese universities, book fairs, government offices, publishing houses. I have been a visiting Professor at Tsinghua, Peking and Sichuan Universities where we have run comparative projects, particularly on education, with Chinese scholars. We have been involved with summer schools in Cambridge for school children, university students, government officials and bankers .

I became the 'keeper' of a memorial stone to the poet Xu Zhimo at King's College, Cambridge in 2009 and more recently we have built a memorial Chinese garden in his memory. Over the last six years, I have been working with my former student Zilan Wang to try to build a cultural bridge between China and the West. We have held many exhibitions of Chinese arts, music, literature and poetry in Cambridge. All these are to try to explain the essence of China to the West, and in return we have taken choirs, artists and academics to China to help the Chinese learn a little about us.

Numerous visitors from China have worked with us and my friendships with Chinese students and academics in Cambridge has deepened my understanding. We have also set up a small firm, Cam Rivers Publishing, which specialises in translating books Chinese books into English and vice versa. We have recently opened an arts gallery and shop opposite the Fitzwilliam Museum in Cambridge.

For some years I wanted to explain what I had learnt about China and the West. Faced with the size and variety of China, and the fact that I have to work second-hand because I do not read or speak Mandarin, I found it very difficult to see how to do this. My first attempt, which placed China within the context of three other civilizations which I knew better was my *China, Japan, Europe and the Anglo-sphere; a comparative analysis* (2018). After all our experiences and conversations, I wanted to explain more than I could in the short synthesis in that book.

*

I am fully aware that in writing this book I am attempting the impossible. There is no way to write an uncontested book about 'China' or 'the Chinese'. Every assertion or generalization can be disputed, highly qualified or shown to be only a partial truth.

Firstly, China is so huge that no observation is true across it. Even within a single Chinese province, often the size of a European nation like France, there are huge variations. So, to be accurate, every generalization should properly be in the form 'In south-western Yunnan, among the Boolong people...' This would be tedious in the extreme, but for strict accuracy it would be necessary.

Secondly, China is socially highly differentiated in the past and even more so nowadays. There were huge differences between the Mandarin literati and the peasants, the city dwellers and country dwellers, men and women, the young and the old. This is particularly true recently with the massive shift to the cities and the growth of wealth differentiation. So each remark should take the form 'Among elderly, educated, rich, city dwellers...' as opposed to 'young, uneducated, poor, rural dwellers...' Again, it would lead to an encyclopedia rather than a book.

Thirdly, China, though having a deep continuity, also changes constantly and sometimes very rapidly. What was true in 1989, is definitely not true in the same way thirty years later in 2019. It is essential to look at China in the long arc of its history since at least the unification in 221 B.C., this is magnified hugely. What is true of the later Qing in the nineteenth century is not true of the early

Qing of the second half of the seventeenth century and even less so of the Ming in the fifteenth, the Song in the twelfth or Tang in the eighth. So every observation should be date specific as well 'During the southern Song, on the east coast, among the literati...' and so on.

Fourthly, as I will explain in more detail, China, like all civilisations, is not based on a single coherent logic. It contains many contradictions and oppositions, clashes and unresolved tensions. Let me just give a string of assertions that could be made about the Chinese or China, both of which are supportable. If I were setting my students an exam paper on China, it might take the form.

Choose three of the following and comment on them.

1. The Chinese regard themselves as the centre of the world, the Middle Kingdom, and are supercilious about foreign 'barbarians'.
OR
The Chinese feel inferior, backward and lack self-confidence in relation to the West.

2. Chinese women are tough, dominate their men and run much of life.
OR
Chinese women are second-class citizens, repressed and humiliated.

3. China is unchanging and continuous.
OR
China is constantly changing and has gone through many huge alterations and is currently changing faster than anywhere else in the world.

4. Chinese marriage was traditionally arranged, so love was not relevant.
OR The Chinese were obsessed in their literature and opera with romantic love and its difficulties.

5. The Chinese are pragmatic, rational, this-worldly, with their feet on the ground.
OR
The Chinese are highly superstitious, their life filled with omens, ghosts, powerful invisible forces over which they have little control.

6. The Chinese are highly religious for most of their history, their country filled with temples and shrines, their people constantly performing rituals in the family and village, keen adherents to ancestor cults, Daoism and Buddhism.
OR
The Chinese do not know what true religion is, they have no word for 'God', do not have a Creator and all-seeing God or heaven and hell in the western sense.

7. The Chinese have a great reverence for nature – for rocks, trees, mountains and rivers.
OR
The Chinese treat their natural environment with merciless neglect, polluting rivers, cutting down forests, levelling mountains, destroying the fertility of the soil.

8. The Chinese were regarded by many foreigners who worked closely with them as scrupulously loyal, very honest and trustworthy.
OR
Others saw them as shifting their loyalty easily, cunning and constantly telling lies to cover up their dishonesty.

9. The Chinese are a puritanical people in relation to sex, their costumes are generally modest and attitudes to the body on the whole have very little emphasis on sexuality.
OR
The Chinese are a lascivious and highly sexualised people as shown in the 'pillow books' of erotic art and literature, their concubines, and their general absence of guilt over sexual misbehaviour.

10.The Chinese are one of the most peaceful, non-aggressive peoples in their world. Their Confucian and Buddhist philosophies extol harmony and the need to avoid causing suffering.
OR
The Chinese past is one of huge violence, both against their minorities, neighbouring countries, internal rebellions and in their incredibly savage legal system.

One could go on like this for pages and conclude that, like Japan, China is a both/and civilization. The usual binaries, which a western observer assumes do not work, for, like quantum theory, things are in a shifting, fluctuating and intermediate state as represented in their symbols of yin and yang.

*

Given the impossibility of saying anything that cannot be contested about the Chinese, I have found myself blocked from writing about them seriously for some years. I could leave it at that, either just documenting our tours with films and diaries, detailed ethnography with minute description, or perhaps abandoning any attempt to communicate what we have learnt through our many contacts with China.

Instead I have decided to throw caution aside and tried to generalize. I have followed Albert Einstein's suggestion that 'It is better to be roughly right than precisely wrong'. I have done what my whole training in history and anthropology warned me against, that is generalizing from a limited experience without presenting immense evidence for each conclusion in the form of either primary data or citing numerous other experts.

If you are a reader who is averse to intuitive synthesis, 'Guessing before demonstrating' in Henri Poincaré's description of how science proceeds, to the broad picture which is bound to have flaws, then this book is not for you.

Likewise, if you are a reader who feels it is not helpful to approach a huge civilisation like China from a personal point of view, explaining my own take on things and how it has been challenged by China, again the book will not be your kind of book. My aim is to encourage the reader to cross the bridge into China as my companion. To do this I often need to explain who I am, what I think and what I am comparing from my own experience with what I have found in China.

This is again a risky strategy and not one that is often adopted in cross-cultural work. I did use it in a modified way in trying to understand *Japan Through the Looking Glass* (2007). There I moved from the known, my own life, to the unknown in the hardly conceivable world of Japan. The book seemed to be helpful to people who read it, so I have deployed the same approach, but on a larger scale to deal with the more complex case of China.

So this is very much, as the subtitle suggests, a personal A-Z. It is a voyage of discovery, the Chinese seen through the eyes of an elderly, white, middle-class, male, British, academic, with all the biases, but perhaps with some of the benefits, of such a position.

Ultimately you can read the book as a provocation to learn more. If you feel uneasy or unpersuaded by my suggestions, it is now relatively easy to pursue any of the topics on the internet or in the vast literature on China. If China as portrayed challenges your preconceptions, as it has challenged mine, that will be all I can hope for.

*

This book was originally written in late 2018 and early 2019. Since then I have been seeking the advice of experts and re-writing parts, completing the present draft in the middle of 2019. The book is being published in early summer 2010. Many things have occurred already since it was written. Some of these, in particular the riots in Hong Kong and the COVID 19 virus outbreak are, relevant to this account. If I were writing the book today I would alter a few entries to a small extent. I have decided, however, since history is constantly unfolding, to leave the text in the form it had reached in mid 2019.

The recent events, especially the virus, which has apparently been contained in China, but is spreading rapidly in Europe and the U.S. as I write, makes this book even more relevant I believe. There are a number of people in the West who are tempted to revert to the nineteenth century stereotypes of the Chinese which I outline in the preliminary chapters. This leads them to blame a China which they know nothing about. So, it is even more important to explain the deeper nature of China and the Chinese for a western audience.

The recent events have made the tensions between the two dominant superpowers, the U.S. and China, even more dangerous. I hope, therefore, that my explanations of the nature of Chinese economic, political and social systems will diminish a little of the potentially disastrous friction.

Recent events have also revealed even more clearly the differences between the group-based nature of China, and the individualistic West. Reading the book through now, I am interested to see that most of the predictions and analyses within it seem to be confirmed by recent events. They will be further illuminated by what happens in the months ahead.

Ivy Farm Barn, Near Cambridge
27th March 2020

1. The return of China

What, exactly, is happening in China, and why, is largely unknown to most people outside China,many are like the sailors who landed on what they thought was an island. Only when they lit a fire did the whale shake itself and reveal its true nature. All of our present is already deeply affected by the fate of China. Our future will be even more so. This book will attempt to explore what China was and is, and how it differs from the West.

One thing that many of us do know without being able to go into detail is that China is growing very fast in every way – economically, culturally, politically and socially. It is predicted to become the dominant world power within the next generation. Already the richest three provinces have a combined wealth greater than Russia or India. The city of Shenzhen alone has an economy larger than Hong Kong or Taiwan. China is already affecting the lives of all on this planet and it will increasingly do so.

I am curious to know how this huge revolution has happened. I know that forty years ago, at the time of Chairman Mao's death, China was a relatively poor, isolated, drab country. Just forty years later it has achieved the most dramatic industrial revolution in history, twice as fast as that in the West in the nineteenth century, and on a scale ten times larger than that of Japan. It has done so in a peaceful and calm way, with surprisingly little of the terrible side-effects of the industrial revolution of the West. I wonder how and why this happened?

One way to look at what has happened in a succinct way is through a few diagrams which illustrate the extraordinary events of the last forty years.

For almost all of history, China was the largest and most powerful economy and civilisation in the world. For a brief two centuries, from about 1820, it was overtaken by the West as a result of the industrial revolution and the desire for trade. It is now returning to its previous position.

This basic fact is shown in the following two diagrams and subsequent graphs. The first shows the way in which the economic centre of gravity started to shift westwards from 1820, but then started to move back very rapidly from 2000.

Exhibit 3

By far the most rapid shift in the world's economic center of gravity happened in 2000–10, reversing previous decades of development

Evolution of the earth's economic center of gravity[1]

AD 1 to 2025

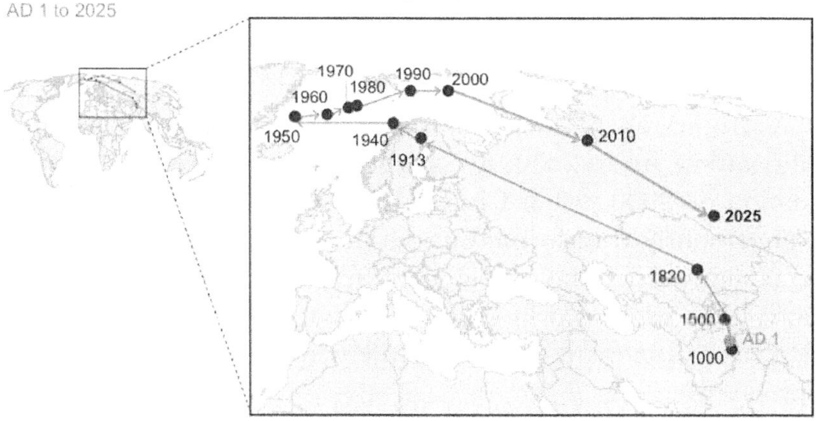

1 Economic center of gravity is calculated by weighting locations by GDP in three dimensions and projected to the nearest point on the earth's surface. The surface projection of the center of gravity shifts north over the course of the century, reflecting the fact that in three-dimensional space America and Asia are not only "next" to each other, but also "across" from each other.

SOURCE: McKinsey Global Institute analysis using data from Angus Maddison; University of Groningen

Another way of putting this visually is as follows. Only taking the story up to 2008, and thus missing the extraordinary continued growth of China in the last ten years, this shows how China started to shrink relatively from 1820, and only started to become a major actor from about 1980.

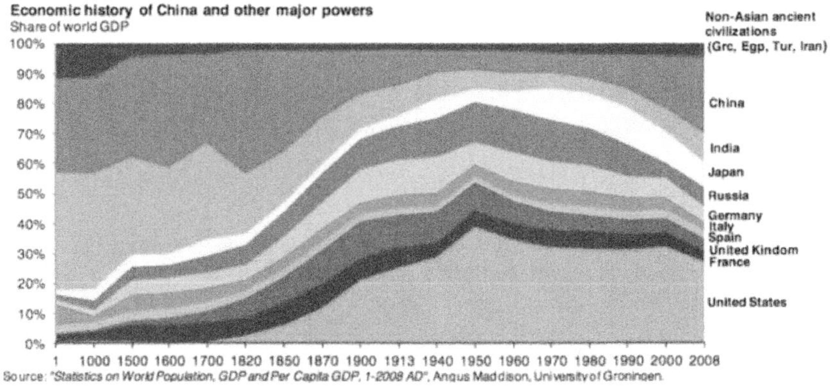

A projection of how this relative economic development will continue up to 2050, if it is roughly correct, shows how the situation of 2008, when China is relatively still quite small, will be enormously transformed in the next generation. It will have an economy twice the size of the United States, and nearly one third of the whole world. Much may intervene to strop this, but this graph alone is enough to show why some in the West are apprehensive.

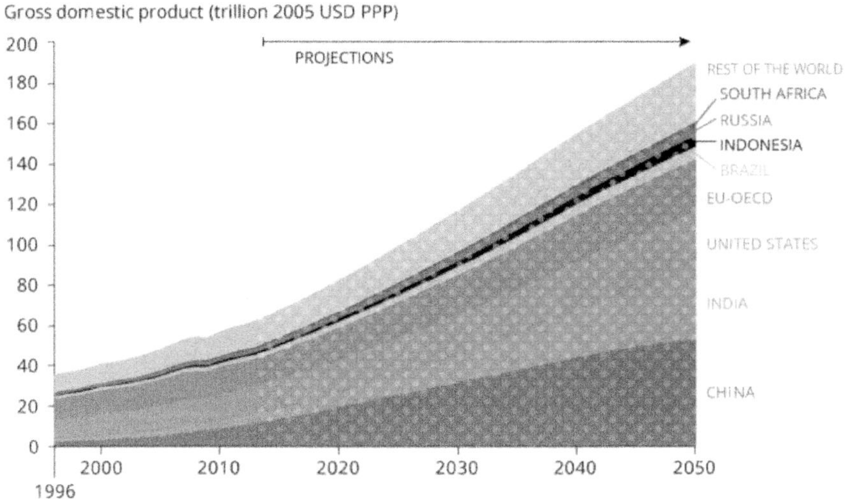

Another way to show the situation is in a diagram of how China by 2017 had become one of the two mega-powers, with Japan relegated to a distant third.

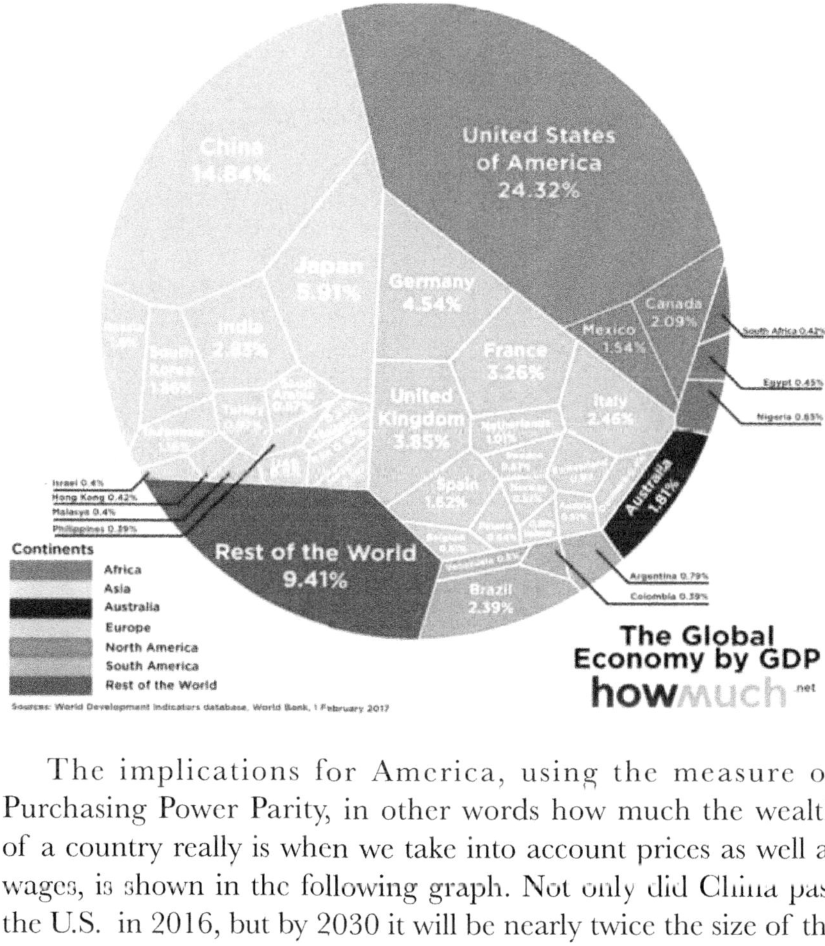

The implications for America, using the measure of Purchasing Power Parity, in other words how much the wealth of a country really is when we take into account prices as well as wages, is shown in the following graph. Not only did China pass the U.S. in 2016, but by 2030 it will be nearly twice the size of the U.S.

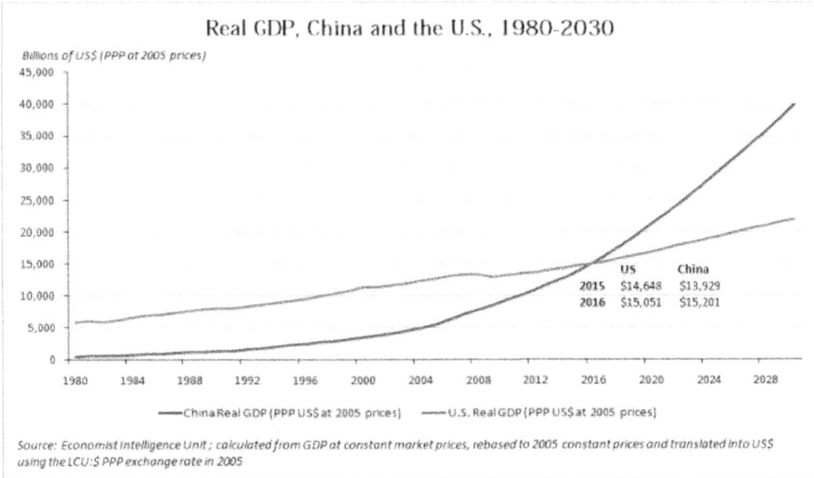

It is worth pointing out that the growth in overseas Chinese trade has been to the whole world, and that the exports to the United States are a small part of this, as shown in the following diagram.

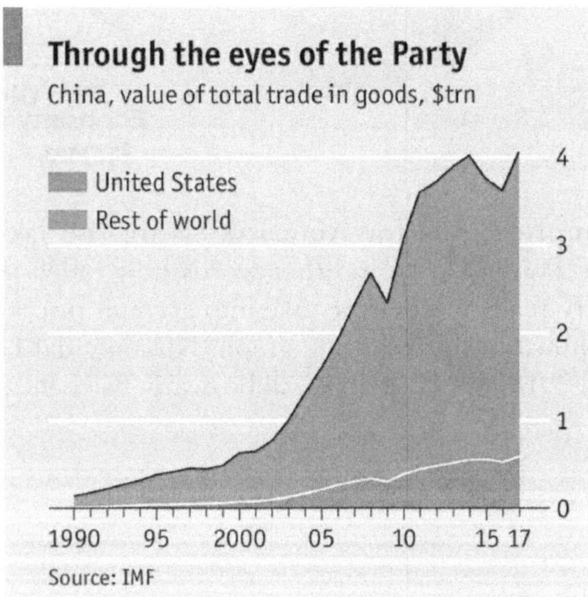

Economist.com

This is what is happening in terms of the balance of economies, but it is also worth looking to see how it has happened. The first graph below shows that the take-off started around 1978, with Deng Xiaoping's reforms. Two significant events were the privatization of farms, and the opening of the first Special Economic Zone in Shenzhen. The rapid increase started with the opening of the Shanghai SEZ in 1992. It is interesting to note that the entry into the World Trade Organization in 2002 came quite far into the 'take-off'. Some have alleged that it was joining this organization (with the implication that the Chinese have somehow cheated) which enabled the event. This diagram shows that this is false.

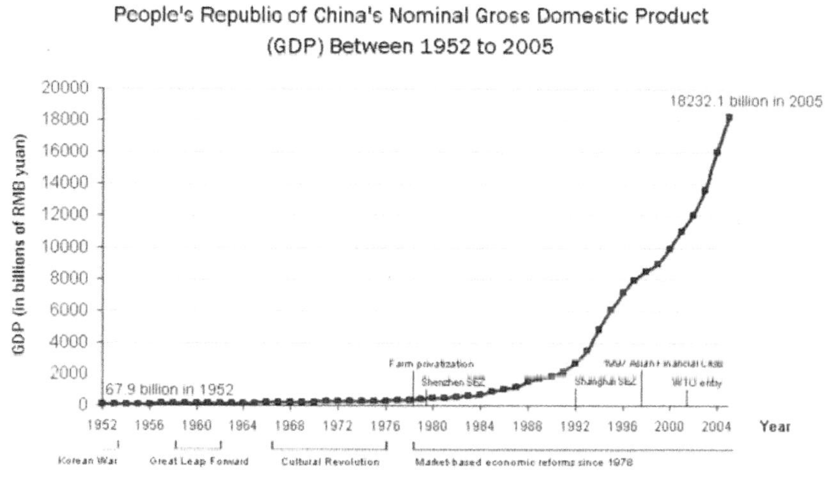

Clearly this growth is the result of a number of years of rapid growth in gross domestic product. This can be shown in the following diagram. This shows some astonishing peaks in 1985, 1993-5, 2005-2007, and a serious drop in the year of the Tiananmen Square demonstrations (1989) and the year after. The recent six years have seen rates of between six and seven per cent, but because the Chinese economy is several times larger than it was even fifteen years ago, this is a massive growth.

Figure 3. Chinese Real GDP Growth: 1979-2017

(percent)

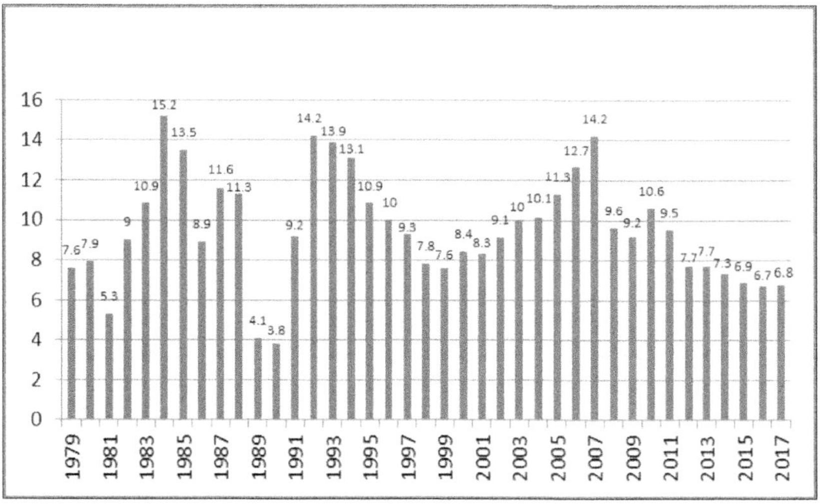

Source: IMF, and Chinese National Bureau of Statistics.

The predictions for the years after 2017 are shown in the following diagram. It appears to be on course for this slight slowing down.

Figure 4. China's Real GDP Growth 2007-2017 and Projections through 2022

(percent)

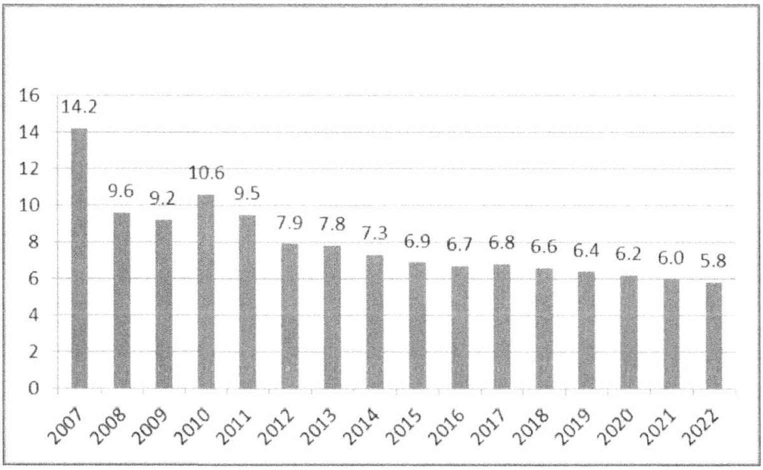

Source: IMF, WEO.

It is worth ending by showing what this means for the average Chinese, who up to 1978 lived in a country still suffering from a century and a half of crises and humiliations and often the direst of poverty. The GDP per capita in 1978 in China, expressed in dollars, was $226 per annum. By 2001 it passed one thousand dollars for the first time – an increase of four-fold in twenty-four years. As the following diagram shows, it had reached nearly four times that amount by 2008, and by 2017 was well over seven thousand dollars. It is predicted to be about £8330 by 2020. As can be seen in the essay below on 'poverty reduction', this has led to the largest reduction of poverty ever known on this planet.

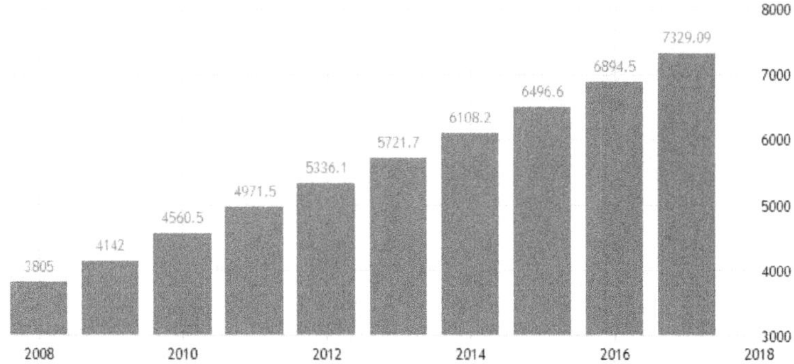

China is not just interesting because of its economic strength. I want to understand it for other reasons of an equally compelling kind. There is something special about China. From its food, architecture and gardens through to its philosophy and poetry, it has the feel of a third kind of civilization. It is neither like the Indo-European civilizations of the West, including India and the Middle East, nor is it identical to the inscrutable civilization of Japan. It is still filled with a certain mysterious otherness.

Not only do the Chinese produce excellent, utilitarian, goods, but we are dealing with a cultured civilization. In poetry, philosophy, music, literature, painting and many other arts, China is a highly artistic civilization. Many of the most beautiful objects in the world have been made in China for the last five thousand years. Chinese things astounded Europeans in the eighteenth century and anyone who has spent any time in China with young Chinese will be aware of this high tradition. Despite the terrible destruction wreaked by the Cultural Revolution, it has survived.

China contains about a fifth of humankind. Chinese civilisation has the longest continuous history on earth, stretching back at least five thousand years. Many of the important technologies in the world were developed first in China and were then transferred to the West. These included the three which the philosopher Francis Bacon singled out as the basis of the modern world, the magnetic compass, the printing press and gunpowder.

*

There are added reasons for making this attempt to gain a basic understanding of China. One is that, as it becomes one of the two dominant powers on earth, there is a grave danger of political confrontation and a mutually damaging 'clash of civilizations'. Such a danger will be greater if China and the West cannot understand each other's history and culture. A small misunderstanding could lead to another World War. It is urgent that we in the West understand China (and people in China understand us).

Secondly, the rise of China alters all our lives in the West, just as America did in the twentieth century. Many aspects of our daily living, our education, food, music, literature, social classes, gender relations, science and technology, will be, and are already, being altered by China. We can try to fight against this but it is happening. Even if we try to reject it in Britain or America, it is happening rapidly in much of Africa and South America, let alone Pakistan or Burma.

So, in order to see what the world is becoming around us, how 'The Other' is shaping and influencing 'Us', we need to understand more about the tsunami that is approaching.

If we fail to understand China, we may be terrified, angry and jealous. If we do come to understand the force and weight of those thousands of years of civilisation, we may still be apprehensive. Yet, if we can master the Chinese wave we may avoid drowning and instead learn the delights of swimming in a new, multiply influenced, world with so many extraordinary and exhilarating features. We may learn to share it and to wonder at hitherto unexplored experiences.

It appears that now is precisely the time to understand something of what is happening in China. Soon it will be too late to understand the Chinese revolution, for a reason pointed out two centuries ago by the French writer Alexis de Tocqueville in his study of the French Revolution soon after that momentous event.

Tocqueville[1] observed that, once a revolution has happened, its causes becomes invisible. The greater the revolution, the faster and more complete this obliteration. An account of what has happened must be written quickly, for people cannot remember the conditions which prompted the revolution, or how it proceeded. After the event, they live in a changed world and it becomes assumed as the normal.

'It would seem that the time for examination and judgment on it [the French Revolution] has arrived. We are placed to day at that precise point, from which this great subject can be best perceived and judged. We are far enough from the Revolution not to feel violently the passions which disturbed the view of those who made it. On the other hand, we are near enough to be able to enter into and to understand the spirit that produced it. Very soon it will be difficult to do so. For great successful revolutions, by effecting the disappearance of the causes which brought them about, by their very success, become themselves incomprehensible.'

The revolution in China in the last forty years, arguably the greatest that has ever (or will ever) happen on this planet, means that anyone visiting China today will find it very difficult, if not impossible, to see what has happened or why it has done so. Only by living through the changes, and looking carefully at the situation before the immense revolution of the last forty years, can we begin to unravel what has occurred and begin to understand the deep roots of the world we now see in China.

---

[1] Tocqueville, **Ancien**

2. How has China achieved an economic miracle?

Much of my intellectual life has been devoted to trying to understand the 'Great Transformation', the first economic miracle to have occurred since the invention of settled agriculture some ten thousand years ago. This is the move from an agrarian to an industrial world.

The change occurred in Britain between about 1760 and 1840, starting eighty years before any other part of the world. It was completed just as Germany, France and the United States started their transition. It was unprecedented and set the world on a new path.

Enormous as it is, the causes are very difficult to disentangle because they consist of numerous interconnected threads, like a vast woven tapestry. What happened is like the opening of a large combination lock, with ten sequences of numbers, each sequence containing ten numbers. The chance of opening the lock is ten to the power of ten, a huge number. It was against all the odds and yet it happened. I have written six books to try to explain how and why it did so.[2]

When I started to work on Japan in the 1990s I discovered that Japan, between its opening up at the Meiji Restoration in 1868, and forty years later, during which it had industrialized and defeated both China and Russia in wars, was another miracle. It was transformed from a steady-state, antiquated, agricultural civilization into a modern industrial nation.

Although the miracle is arguably less mysterious than the first transformation in Britain, for the technologies were now available, as they had been for Germany and the United States a

[2]Alan Macfarlane - *Origins of English Individualism, Culture of Capitalism, Savage Wars of Peace, Riddle of Modern World, Making of Modern World, Invention of the Modern World.*

few decades before, it was nevertheless, as the first emergence of an Asian civilization, eighty years before the 'Four Little Tigers' of Singapore, Hong Kong, Taiwan and South Korea, extraordinary enough. I made studies to ty to explain how another island, with a somewhat similar political and social system to that in Britain, had achieved this change.[3]

These two cases, though very different from the recent Chinese revolution, do provide some clues for what is undoubtedly the third economic miracle of the last ten thousand years, on a par in its way with that of Britain. It is far more dramatic in size and speed, if not as original as the first case, namely the transformation of China. The previous chapter has shown something of what happened. What caused or allowed it is still a matter of great discussion and dispute. Some suggestion of an answer to this question will condition our views as to the future development of China.

A highly simplified answer to why the economic explosion which is shaking our world has happened could be based on the work of the greatest analyst of the British case, and founding father of economics, Adam Smith.

In a famous early suggestion, Smith wrote that 'Little else is requisite to carry a State to the highest degree of opulence from the lowest barbarism, but peace, easy taxes, and a tolerable administration of justice; all the rest being brought about by the natural course of things.'[4] Within 'peace' was included internal as well as external (war) violence and by 'easy taxes', Smith did not necessarily mean light taxes, but fair (non-arbitrary), well administered and predictable. They should also be beneficial to the general population and not just to pay for an inflated army and bureaucracy.

In his discussion on China, Smith gave one of several analyses of how a natural tendency, 'the natural course of things', largely

---

[3]Alan Macfarlane, *Savage Wars of Peace, Fukuzawa, Japan Looking Glass, Essays on Japan.*

[4]Dugald Stewart, *Collected Works* (1856) , X, 68.

rising from human energy, inventiveness, love of profit, along with the economic benefits of splitting the productive process into smaller specialities (the division of labour), and a division of labour at an international level through free trade, was usually, in fact, brought to a halt. Smith observed that at his time in the middle of the eighteenth century, all the nations of the world, Spain, Italy, France, Germany, the Ottoman Empire, India had hit what Mark Elvin termed 'the high level equilibrium trap'.[5]

None of these nations or civilizations was becoming richer and in most cases their economies were in decline. Only Britain, and the smaller nations of Holland and new England, were still growing. China had hit the ceiling. Smith noted that while it was not declining, like southern Europe, it seemed clear that the China of his time had made little or no advance on the China described by Marco Polo and his contemporaries by the early fourteenth century.

Smith suggested a number of reasons for China's static condition. Among the most important was that it had shut itself off from international trade and contacts and hence become inward-looking, keeping out improved ideas and the shock of competition. [6] It also had a conservative Confucian bureaucracy, who were disinterested and indeed hostile to economic activities. China also suffered from the side-effects of rice agriculture, which discouraged industrial technologies and led to very rapid over-population.[7] China's cities were not the motors of change as they were in the free and independent cities of northern Europe.[8] The autocratic imperial political system and absolutism was another factor halting growth.

In terms of his three pre-conditions for opulence, Smith could also have pointed to the fact that China's legal system was far from 'tolerable', with a non-existent civil law, no protection for property, no separation of law from politics, an arbitrary legal process and

[5]See 'High Equilibrium Traps' in the A-Z below for an expansion of this

brutal penal code. China's taxation system was very weak, with the State unable to raise money except by coercion. Nor was it peaceful, with frequent incursions from warlike nomads, two of whose invasions by the Mongols and Manchus swept away dynasties, killed millions and devastated the economy. Internally there were frequent rebellions, many of them on a huge scale. Furthermore, the monetary system was very inefficient and banking almost non-existent.

The brief period between the end of this imperial system in 1911 and the start of the warlord period and Japanese incursions in the mid-1920s saw some attempts to cure a few of these weaknesses. Yet from the later 1920s through to 1949, China went through a devastating war against Japan and a huge civil war in which millions were killed and the economy ruined.

What the Communist period of 1949-1978 did was to pull China together, to overcome the threat of foreign invasion and internal risings. It unified China politically and gave it back some of its lost pride and sense of identity. Yet economically it was rather disastrous. There was over the whole period a modest rise in national GDP. Yet the terrible famines caused by the over-rapid forced attempt at industrialization of the 'Great Leap Forward' of 1958-1962 and the shattering of trust and of the educational system in the Cultural Revolution of 1966-1976, meant that by 1978 China, from an economic point of view, seemed as far as ever from the economic miracle which had now spread across Europe, America, Japan and now the Four Little Tigers of East Asia.

Then, from 1978, with inspiration from Lee Kuan Yew and the Singapore break-through, and the example of Hong Kong, Deng Xiaoping carefully and gradually turned the massive ship that is China, full of hard-working, entrepreneurial, rational, people in another direction. He opened free economic zones in Shenzhen and other cities and soon Shanghai. He allowed people to buy and sell and have private property.

He encouraged trade, foreign investment and foreign experts. The legal system was reformed along western lines with a proper court structure and the development of civil law and a legal profession. The banking system was set up properly and then stock exchanges. He encouraged education, so that the schools and universities began to expand rapidly.

Other important measures since 1978 have been the huge government spending, and control of the big companies, for example the three energy giants. The relaxation of permanent residence requirements for foreign firms. The 'revolving door' policy whereby government and non-government experts could move between the two sectors and an active policy to attract talent, business and foreign investment from all over the world, are other factors. The improvements of the quality of life of the citizens in health, education and wages were also factors.

China thus benefited from the immensely more effective technologies which had emerged from the scientific revolution of the seventeenth century in the West, not just machines, but in agriculture, communications and the whole context of a machine civilization, including finance and law. The immense power that Smith had seen in the division of labour and trade was added to the effects of 'Moore's Law', whereby the triangle of invention, innovation and mass production, if unimpeded and fuelled by science, can double the power of given technologies exponentially. As originally formulated by Gordon Moore in 1965 every year, and now happening every nine months and within the massive civilization of China.[9]

China avoided the trap which the decomposing Soviet Union fell into under American influence, rushing into raw western capitalism too quickly, which led to disaster there. The powerful guiding and protecting hand of the Communist Party and a command economy made the transition, however enormous, a

[9] For a discussion of how and why Moore's Law works, see Macfarlane, Intelligent Machines.

smooth and evolutionary one, gradually edging out the older and unproductive sectors, providing huge infrastructural underpinning and great incentives to successful sectors.

After the event, the result looks, as it always does, both inevitable and indeed not that difficult. Yet before it happened, and in the light of so many failures in China and elsewhere, it was far from likely. For it required, as the British and Japanese cases show, far more fundamental and deep structural change well beyond the role of technology or even economic changes. As Adam Smith argued for Britain, and later Fukuzawa Yukichi for Japan, it was a reshaping and rebalancing of all parts of the civilization and the separating out of the normally merged spheres of politics, economics, society and ideology. [10]

Mao Tse Tung and the Party had cleared the fields, ploughed them over and destroyed the inhibiting effects of an all-encompassing clan and family system, of gross gender inequality, of Confucian bureaucracy, of landlordism, of backward-looking conservatism.

Like many great purges or levelling in Chinese history, the civilization was cut back to the ground. Yet, as in previous cases, its massive roots, the intelligence, hard work, ambition, collaborative ability and ingenuity of its huge population, held together by a written language and a unified identity given by its many thousands of years of history was ready for its first successful 'Great Leap Forward'. [11]

Now we live in a world where this great civilization is returning to its high position. The possible future, which I discuss in the final chapter, is of course unpredictable. Yet if we and the Chinese come to understand a little better what is the nature of its unique history and nature, and what are the forces which have lain behind both its long periods of stasis, and its brief ones of

[10]See Macfarlane, Adam Smith; Macfarlane, Fukuzawa Yukichi

[11]See 'Change - patterns of' below.

amazing flourishing, previously in the Tang and the Song, and now in the forty years since 1978, there is more chance that the Chinese will continue their advance. They will not just lift, as they have done, over seven hundred million people out of dire poverty in China, but help to promote a more peaceful, harmonious and wealthy world, which is what they are now doing in many parts of Asia and Africa.

The task for the Chinese is complicated, however, by the level of suspicion and misinformation that has traditionally existed about China in the West. This is compounded by the fear of the rise of China, as well as the difficulty for two entirely different world views to understand each other. I will now try to explain the distorting lens through which China has been viewed, why it is so difficult for a westerner to understand it, and then, in the body of the A-Z, what I think are some of its key features understood from a western viewpoint.

3. The largest, oldest and most diverse civilisation

China is not easy to understand, even for the Chinese. It is vast, covering an area larger than western and eastern Europe and parts of Russia combined. It is hugely diverse, stretching from the almost arctic north to the sub-tropical south and cut through by great rivers and numerous mountain ranges.

China is immensely old, the longest continuous civilisation on earth, reaching back to roots over seven thousand years ago. Confucius and his teachings of two and a half thousand years ago are still considered to be almost contemporary.

China is composed of many peoples, with fifty-six recognized ethnic groups, some of them consisting of millions of people and with a total number of over one hundred million. These groups have hugely varied customs and cultures. We may wonder how we can possibly begin to understand something on this scale.

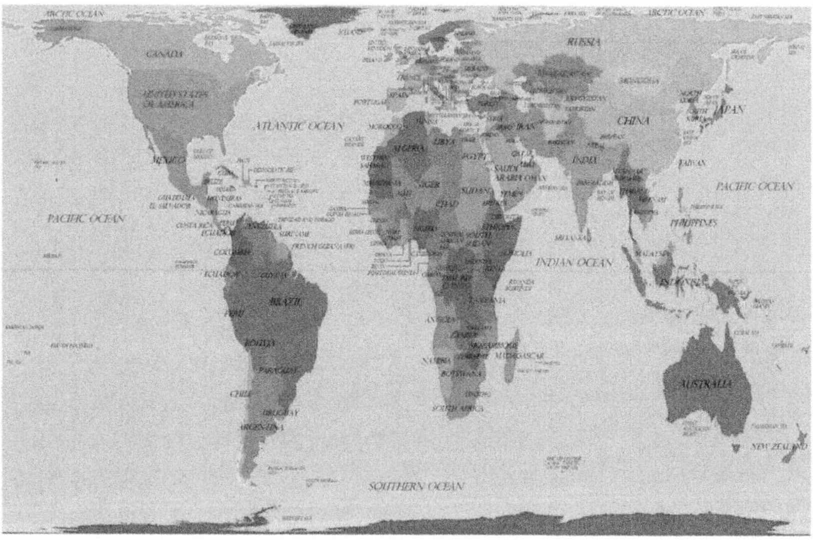

This Peters Projection map shows the relative size of China. It is larger than the United States and if it were superimposed on Europe would cover all of Western Europe, Eastern Europe and western Russia as far as the Ural mountains. This huge size has implications for many aspects of the topics I will be dealing with.

The four-thousand-year dynastic history up to 1911 is shown below. The greatest periods of Chinese culture are thought to be the Tang and Song, though the glories and achievements of other periods are impressive.

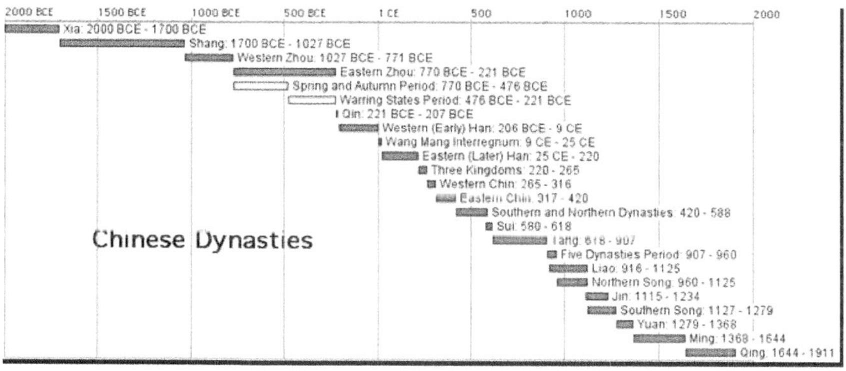

Physical geography and ecology

China covers a vast range of land, from the semi-tropical south to the semi-polar north. Some of the important features of its physical landscapes and ecology are shown below.

Irkutsk
Ulaanbaatar
MONGOLIA
Khabarovsk
Harbin
Changchun
Vladivostok
Ürümqi
Bishkek
KYRGYZSTAN
Shenyang
Baotou
Beijing
NORTH KOREA
Pyongyang
Kashi
Tianjin
Taiyuan
Seoul
SOUTH KOREA
Jinan
Qingdao
Yellow Sea
Lanzhou
CHINA
Zhengzhou
Xi'an
Lahore
Nanjing
Shanghai
Chengdu
Wuhan
Hangzhou
New Delhi
NEPAL
Lhasa
BHUTAN
Chongqing
Changsha
Nanchang
East China Sea
Lucknow
Kathmandu
Thimphu
Kanpur
Guiyang
Kunming
Taipei
BANGLADESH
Dhaka
Guangzhou
Taiwan
Nagpur
Nanning
Hong Kong S.A.R.
Macau S.A.R.
INDIA
BURMA
Hanoi
LAOS
Vientiane
Mumbai (Bombay)
Pune

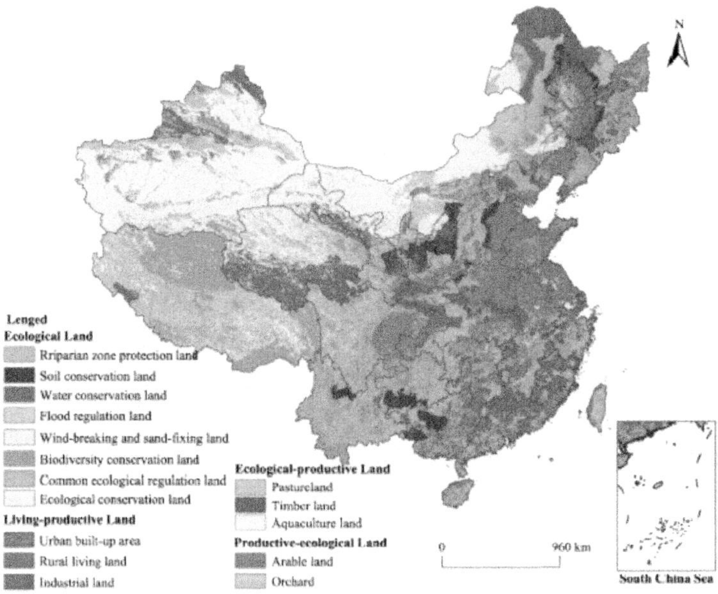
N
Lenged
Ecological Land
Rriparian zone protection land
Soil conservation land
Water conservation land
Flood regulation land
Wind-breaking and sand-fixing land
Biodiversity conservation land
Common ecological regulation land
Ecological conservation land
Living-productive Land
Urban built-up area
Rural living land
Industrial land
Ecological-productive Land
Pastureland
Timber land
Aquaculture land
Productive-ecological Land
Arable land
Orchard
0
960 km
South China Sea

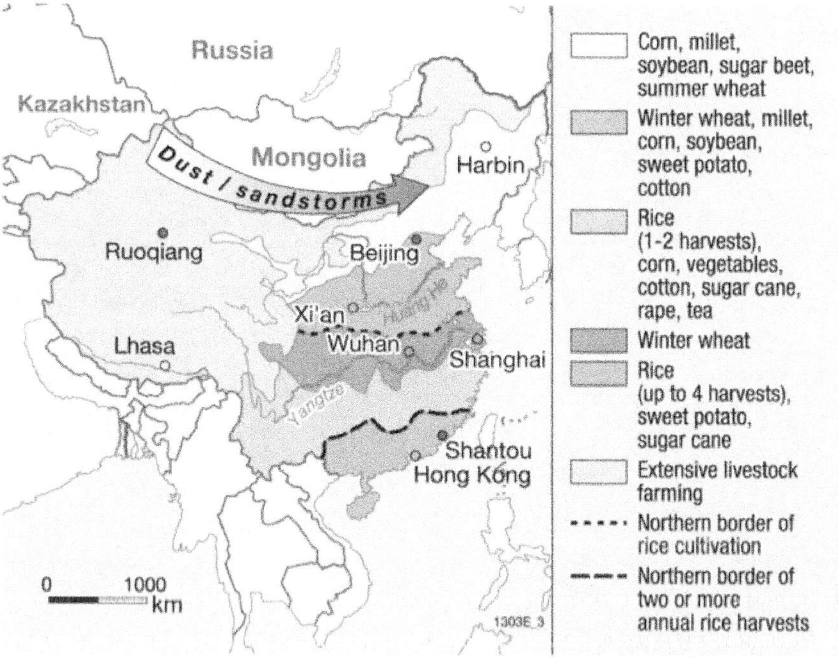

One over-riding impression from the maps of physical geography is of the immensely mountainous landscape of China. The huge Himalayan region extends through much of China, and there are other significant mountain ranges further east. There are really only two large non-mountainous areas, in the east and north-east.

Major cities and rivers

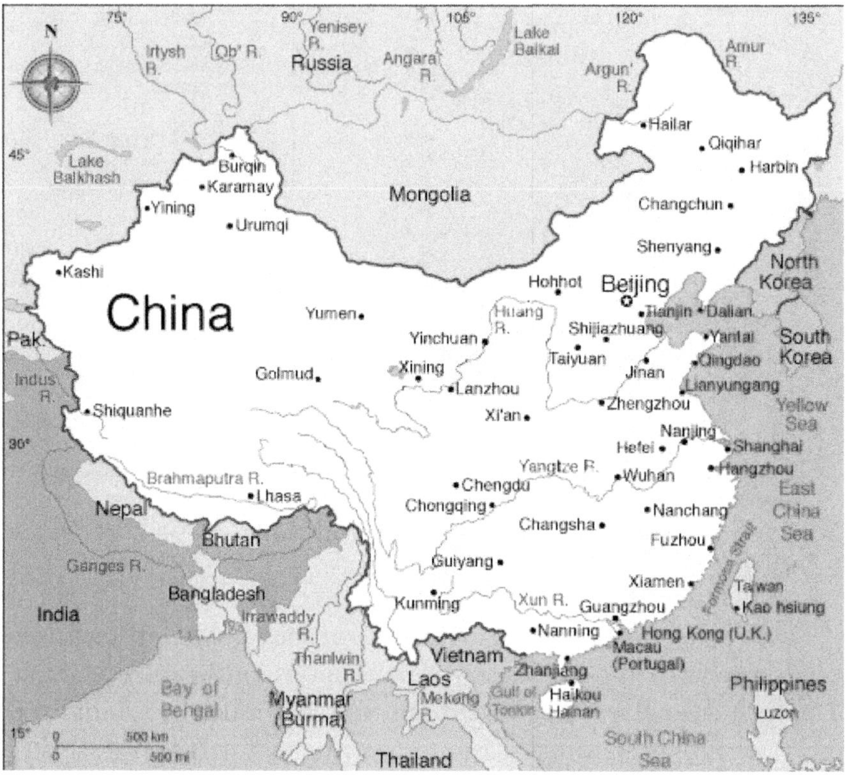

This map shows the three great rivers of China which flow into the China sea in eastern China. To the south is what is called the Xun river, also known as the Pearl River, which flows into the sea at Guangzhou, a city known in the past as Canton. In the middle is the Yangtze, which passes through Nanjing, a number of times capital of China, before entering the sea at Shanghai. In the north is the Huang river, also known as the Yellow River, entering the sea below Beijing. Other great rivers, the Brahmaputra, Irrawaddy and Mekong rivers flow through China for long distances before entering other neighbouring countries.

Major political regions

China is divided into provinces. Each of the larger provinces is the size of a west European country, for example Sichuan and Yunnan are equivalent to France and Spain. The richest four provinces down the east coast, Jiangsu, Zhejiang, Fujian and Guangdong have a combined wealth larger than all the nations of western Europe combined.

Ethno-linguistic divisions

The 'Chinese' are composed of many different peoples. It is also filled with many hundreds of languages and dialects. Something of this diversity can be seen in the following map.

Chinese Linguistic Groups

These maps show very simply that in trying to understand China through time, the scale of the challenge is considerable. We are dealing with an area and population twice the size of western Europe, over a period of continuous history which takes us back more than a thousand years before the origins of Greek civilisation. The diversity of the agriculture and climates is equivalent to moving from Scandinavia to north Africa, and several of the minority groups are larger in numbers than the inhabitants of Greece or Portugal.

It is an immense canvas and the difficulty for westerners to understand China is increased by several other factors.

4. Ignorance and Prejudice

Preface: Seeing China

We look at 'the Other' through a set of distorting mirrors or lenses of which we are unaware. The only way to minimize the effects of these distortions, which we can never eradicate entirely, is to bring them to the surface, to be aware of what they are and what causes them. It is worth examining a few of the traditional, but still powerful, stereotypes of the Chinese.

To give a first rather shocking insight into the later nineteenth century prejudices, here is 'The Mongolian Octopus' by Phil May, a noted British cartoonist, who briefly worked in Australia.

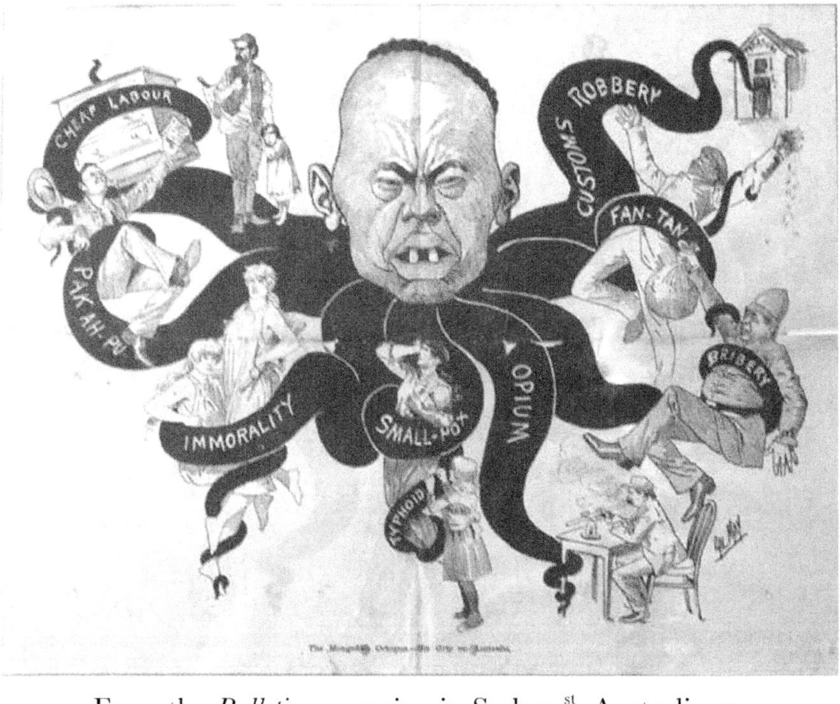

From the *Bulletin* magazine in Sydney[st], Australia on August 21st 1886

The first tentacle: cheap labour

Ever since the West started to encounter China seriously, from the mid-nineteenth century, this has been one of the central sources of tension between East and West.

The British and Americans have come down a path in which, even though living standards and hours of work, particularly on slave plantations or down mines and in factories, seem appalling to us today, were not as extremely depressed, on the whole, as China. The cheapness of labour in China was historically made up of two parts, illustrated in two anti-Chinese cartoons of the period.

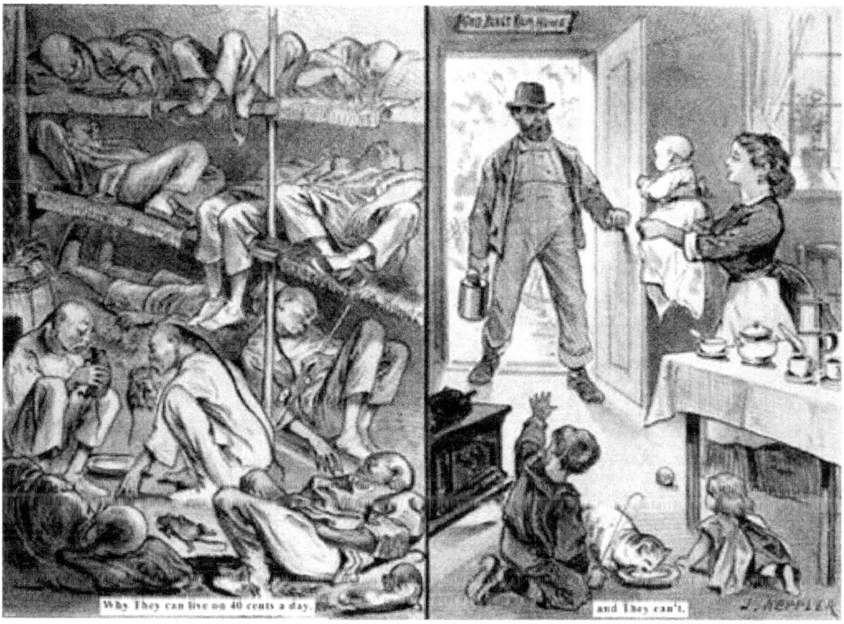

[This and the following cartoons were downloaded from the Internet from searches for stereotypes of the Chinese]

This illustrates the idea that Chinese wants and needs were so few. In the picture this relates to housing, clothing, furniture, having children and pets, and signs of food and drink. There is a half-truth in this in that historically Chinese were used to more crowded and cheaper housing, a very simple diet mostly of grain and vegetables, with little meat and no dairy products.

So the Chinese, whether in China or where they emigrated to, could live on less even than the Irish. Their minimal wages undercut all others. Secondly, they worked incredibly hard, and at many different forms of labour, as shown in the following cartoon.

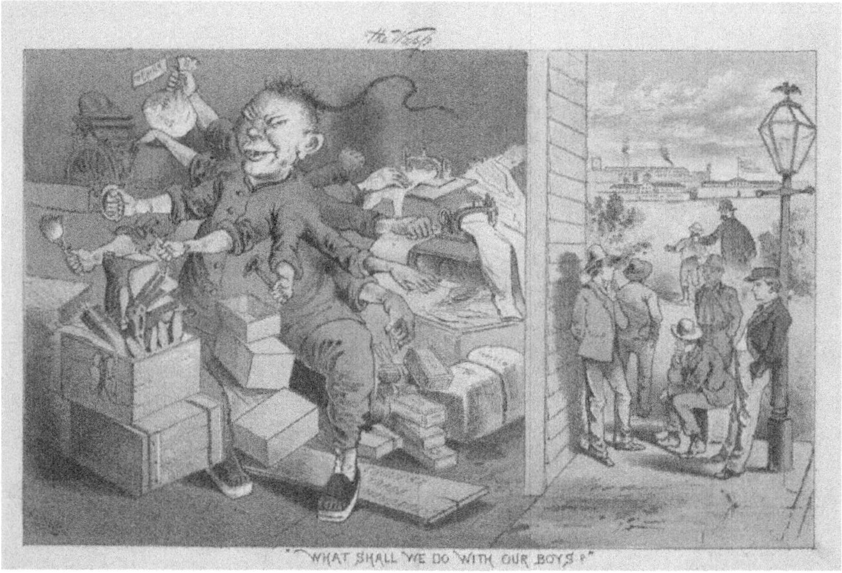

"WHAT SHALL WE DO WITH OUR BOYS?"

There is again truth in this. I calculated when looking at Japan that the average Japanese farmer or labourer in the past worked nearly twice as long as his or her European counterpart, and the same was true of the Chinese. Even today, as I have seen, the children at school and my adult friends in China work extremely hard. Furthermore, they are very talented and able to do many different kinds of work, as is shown in the cartoon. They are practical, rational, dedicated and manually very dexterous.

The combination of these two feature meant that both in the places to which they started to migrate in the later nineteenth, California, Mexico, Australia and elsewhere, and also when they stayed in China and started to make goods for a European market, they could undercut western labour. Without minimum wages and regulations, it was realised that they would soon, especially with potentially huge number involved, put western labour out of work.

This old anxiety continues to this day. It is exacerbated by the speed at which the Chinese have taken to the use of machinery and started to invent new technologies. As part of the advent of globalization, many in the West are threatened by the surge of cheap, well-made, Chinese goods, in the way they were thirty years ago by Japanese competition.

The fact that the West had done exactly the same thing when, with the help of machines, they destroyed huge swathes of production in third world countries, for example the cotton industry in India, is not always remembered.

The competition of Chinese labour is made an even greater threat as we enter an age when, suddenly, many of the old blue and white-collar jobs around the world are being replaced by machines. It is easy to blame the Chinese for 'stealing our jobs', even if much of the theft is actually by machines. There is a deep struggle between two parts of western democratic capitalism. There is a desire to make things as cheaply as possible and hence to use cheap labour whether in India, China or Africa, and another need, to protect one's home population from unemployment and the growing anger the loss of work causes.

China itself faces the same problem. Thirty years ago, the wages in China were incredibly low, so Japan was outsourcing its work to China. Now wages are far higher in China than they were, so Chinese firms are outsourcing their work to poorer countries in Asia and Africa.

The second, fifth and seventh tentacles: gambling and opium

The second tentacle in the cartoon was Pak Ah-Pu, this and the seventh tentacle, Fan-Tan, are names of Chinese games of chance which clearly were thought to ensnare westerners. The British, of course, were also keen gamblers, but on horses, dogs and cards, so they found the Chinese gambling another threatening 'other', especially as it is implied they were drawn into the net of games of chance.

Of course, another one of the huge criticisms, the ultimate hypocrisy, was about opium, a particularly large fifth tentacle above. I examine 'opium', and the Opium Wars in the text but the fact that the British contributed very significantly to the opium addiction of the Chinese in the nineteenth century does not seem to have prevented them from also criticising the Chinese as addicts.

The third tentacle: immorality

The third tentacle is immorality, a synonym for sexual misbehaviour. Christianity and its attendant family systems in Europe are founded on a puritanical attitudes of sex and a bedrock of monogamous marriage. Sex and marriage are supposed to be synonymous. When Europeans encountered nations which see this differently, this simultaneously shocked and titillated them.

The story of hypocrisy and sexism is too well known to have to repeat. It was at its most blatant in the port cities of Japan and China, where westerners both condemned the supposedly lustful and promiscuous natives, while at the same time often frequenting the 'floating worlds' of brothels. They often kept their own concubines. Clearly it was a great source of anxiety, especially in the tension it caused in European monogamy, where many men lived for long periods away from their white wives and families.

What was perhaps most upsetting for many westerners was that the association of sex with sin, central to Pauline Christian teaching, was absent. While the Chinese, as well as the Japanese, are a rather chaste and puritanical people in many respects, they do not see sexual behaviour as one of the major determinants of whether you will go to heaven. Sex is regarded as a natural bodily function, like eating or defecating. Obviously, just like eating and going to the toilet, it needs to be disciplined and controlled. Yet failing in discipline is not a sin, but bad manners, not something God will punish you for, but something others will criticize you about.

The sixth tentacle: bribery

Another source of tension historically, continuing to this day, concerns the way in which a State raises its revenue and the consequences this has on the levels of what, to westerners, seems 'corruption'.

The English from very early on developed a system where taxation was relatively efficient and raised sufficient money to pay those who needed to be paid. Without a standing army, without a large bureaucracy, and in a devolved system where most of the governing was done out of obligation by the gentry class for no pay (in return for their assured wealth) or by unpaid people at the local level, there was no need for a system of 'squeezes'. Those who worked on the numerous state tasks – order, justice, education, local communications, did not have to use their positions to pay themselves.

China falls into the much larger class of countries, for example the Ottoman or Spanish Empires, France in the eighteenth century or Moghul India, where the state farms out the taxes and officials are expected to live off what they can obtain from their local power.

This system, highly criticized by westerners from the

nineteenth century, was known as part of 'the squeeze'. In other words, the powerful would extract or squeeze wealth from those below them to sustain themselves, and those whom they squeezed would squeeze those below them in turn. For example, in China, mandarins acting as judges and giving licences and permits were expected to raise money from these functions, and their officials likewise. It was a ladder of squeezes.

I remember the system being explained to me in relation to India a few years ago, where it was believed to be all-pervasive. A street vendor would be 'squeezed' by the patrolling policeman. The small policeman would pass on part of the squeeze to his superior officer, who would then pass on parts of these little trickles of squeeze to his top officer, who would do the same to a local politician who would do the same to a regional politician and onwards and upwards to suitcases of rupees being left in the Minister's office.

To someone not used to this system, it seems a vast heap of 'corruption', a parallel 'black economy' of power and payments. 'Baksheesh' is the Persian term which was adapted to cover this in India. Nothing of any significance can be done without paying a portion to ease the forward movement of business.

This is one of the forms of corruption which the present Chinese government is trying to deal with, aggravated as it is by the stunning growth of the Chinese economy and the opportunities for 'squeezing' this provides with the vast wealth swilling about.

Westerners have inveighed against squeeze for several centuries, as they did in India, and it gave them the grounds to accuse the Chinese of yet another disagreeable feature, namely widespread corruption. The Chinese, no doubt, could point out that the way in which wealth now buys political power in many countries of the West may be different, but it is equally 'corruption'.

The fourth tentacle: disease

The fourth tentacle is 'small pox, typhoid', the latter attached to a child. This reminds us that another of the background anxieties and confrontations between east and west was over health. This has two major aspects.

Firstly, there were the diseases themselves. The English up to the early nineteenth century had suffered seriously from smallpox, and typhoid was from time to time a serious killer in cities until the middle of the nineteenth century. Yet, on the whole, the British could increasingly feel that the country from which they came was less disease-laden than China. Bubonic plague had disappeared in England after 1665, but continued to sweep over China. Malaria disappeared rapidly from most of England and Scotland from the second half of the eighteenth century. Dysentery declined rapidly, though it had never been very serious in England.

Yet when they reached China, westerners found all these diseases rife, plus others of an eastern kind like schistosomiasis, dengue fever and serious cholera outbreaks, as well as bubonic plague. The Chinese were conceived to be an unhealthy people. Disease lurked and carried away many westerners, especially children, while others contracted syphilis from their Chinese concubines, another sinister danger.

Secondly, westerners could feel that their knowledge of disease and their medical cures based on Greek medicine, Renaissance discoveries and, from the later seventeenth century, the possibility of using microscopes to examine disease vectors, was greater than that of the Chinese. So westerners believed that they had a progressive system of physical medicine, involving operations, leeches and bleeding and sending people to hospitals. All of this was superior to what they considered the semi-magical traditional medicines of China. A Chinese medicine store, with its powdered rhino horn, bear's gall bladder or tiger's tentacles, and drawers of strange roots and herbs, seemed a heap of superstition.

Whatever the relative merits of the two medical traditions, they were clearly miles apart and mutually incomprehensible. Whatever the dangers for westerners in their own countries, they could feel that it was even more dangerous in China. This was another source of friction and of much missionary activity.

The eighth tentacle: customs robbery

Customs robbery, or the wider attitude to trade, is particularly interesting because it is at the forefront of current tensions between certain western countries and China. During the height of their power, the British and then the Americans, proclaimed that all countries should be freely open to British and American goods and services. There might be custom duties, though these should be at a minimum, but basically the doctrine of Adam Smith was anti-protectionist. Trade was believed to be mutually beneficial and no strong barriers should be put up. The 'invisible hand' would regulate the system and natural competition would ensure that the fittest survived.

The Chinese have been great traders for millenia before Adam Smith, but the trade was rather different. It was either through intermediaries along the land and sea silk roads, or in inland China on the huge network of rivers and canals and pack roads of China. As goods within China passed through each territory, they were subject to minor customs, *likin*, or tolls paid to the local power-holders. The Chinese had never allowed foreigners to act directly in the inland trade of China or even along its coasts

When imperial powers demanded open access to Chinese ports and waterways, especially in relation to the selling of opium from India, there was a bitter clash. This continues to this day with America, in particular, demanding the opening up of China, and China insisting on its sovereignty. Now the situation has become even stranger for it is the Chinese, now dominant with their goods, who want free and open trade, and the West, on the defensive, trying to put up the customs barriers.

Other representations

This account hardly scratches the surface of the earlier western prejudices against China. The audacity of the Chinese in standing up against the British desire to import opium freely into China which led to the second Opium War led to calls for vengeance against the dangerous Chinese dragon.

PUNCH, OR THE LONDON CHARIVARI.—December 22, 1860.

WHAT WE OUGHT TO DO IN CHINA.

Forty years later, another well-known image shows how the Boxer rebellion created a further stereotype of the vengeful Chinese, literally armed to the teeth and dangerously trampling over western womanhood.

THE YELLOW TERROR IN ALL HIS GLORY

The western solution

The question, of course, was what to do about this menace. China was apparently crumbling like the Ottoman Turks had done in the West, or the later Moghul Empire in India. In both these cases former great Empires had been undermined, dismembered and destroyed by the West. Perhaps it was time to do the same with China, as the following cartoons around the time of the Boxer revolt of 1900 show.

China was increasingly regarded by western powers as a 'basket case', a cake to be divided up. Nothing was to be learnt from China, but rather it was to be placed under western care and protection. The people might, at times, be nice enough and were certainly hard-working. But the system was a shambles, ripe for western intervention.

Behind this western dismemberment lay economic benefits. China was a vast, rich, egg, nurtured through the centuries and now ready for the West to hatch and make use of. The problem, as shown in the following cartoon, was its size.

(A Troublesome Egg to hatch. J.S. Pughe, 1901)

The solution adopted was to build up 'spheres of influences' where each European nation could develop their interests. By 1910 the move to carve up China was proceeding, though as yet there was not physical occupation but 'spheres of influence' as shown in the following map

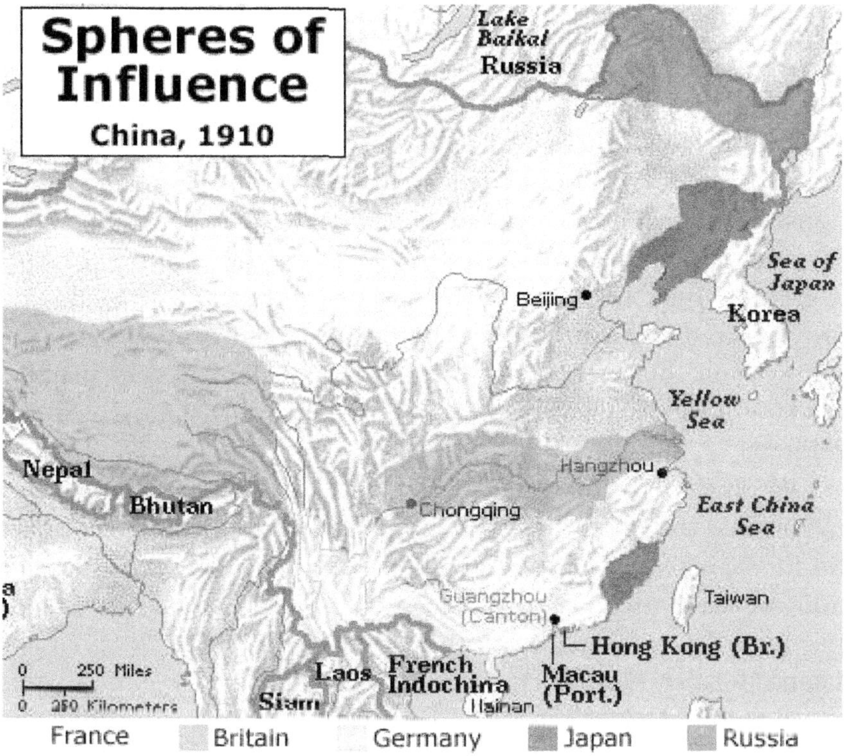

These earlier anxieties and stereotypes of China mainly date from the period between 1820 and 1940. Yet they are only symptomatic of a much larger bundle of mutual misunderstandings which naturally arise when two entirely different civilisations confront each other. It is worth clearing the decks further by briefly outlining further causes of mutual incomprehension between East and West.

5. Misunderstanding

One considerable obstacle in understanding China is that most people in the West, including myself until I started to visit China seriously from 2002, know very little that is true about this great civilisation. What they know is filtered through the press, films, television and now the internet, often biased against China. The consequence is that ignorance is flavoured with prejudice and distorted misinformation. It is difficult to untangle the effects. I can only speak of them in my own case.

The western media usually accepts that China has had considerable material growth, and even concedes that this is largely what has contributed to a fall in the number of the absolutely poor on earth in the last two decades, with well over six hundred million Chinese being lifted out of poverty. Yet admiration for this extraordinary achievement is very usually qualified with warnings that China has destroyed as much as it has created.

We are warned of the vast ecological destruction, symbolized by the largest dam in the world at the bottom of the Three Gorges on the Yangtze, which has covered much of archaeological value and displaced millions of people. The rapid growth of industries, particularly in the Russian and Japanese zones of North East China (former Manchuria), we are told, has created some of the most polluted cities on the planet. It is often asserted that the forests are rapidly being destroyed and water is running out.

We are told of growing inequalities. The rich become rapidly richer, even if the poor also improve their position. The gaps, particularly between the more affluent city dwellers and rural peasants grow dangerously large. Everywhere the old communal values introduced by communism are being undermined by materialism and individualism. The consumer obsessions and competitive striving of the worst forms of raw capitalism are penetrating every area of Chinese life.

Alongside them, it is implied, comes the sleaze which was temporarily suppressed by the communist revolution. The prostitution, drugs and gambling which were once notorious in China is being revived, we are told, mixing in with the worst aspects of international crime. The triads, it is sometimes implied, are infiltrating back.

Sweated labour was always a characteristic of the energy-scarce and industrious Chinese way of life. Now, we are told, the conditions in China's industrial revolution are similar to the appalling sweat-shops of nineteenth century Liverpool or Manchester. Crowds of unprotected immigrants are flooding into the cities. Paid miserably, often injured by machinery, living in virtual slave dormitories, it is they who lie behind the Chinese miracle which has propelled 'Made in China' across the world.

Finally, we are often given a picture of political and religious persecution. China may be becoming a great thriving economy, going through a boom like Japan in the 70s and 80s, but it does not have 'democracy' or 'human rights'. We are told that the Chinese authorities persecute religious minorities as they persecuted Christian missionaries in the eighteenth century.

Political dissenters are kept in detention centres and labour camps without trial. The days of the worst excesses of the cultural revolution may be over, but we are warned that we can see the underlying attitude of the Chinese government in the way it treated its own students in Tiananmen Square in 1989. Individual human rights, we are told, are absent.

Films like 'The Dying Rooms' (1995), made a generation of westerners aware of the grisly consequences of the 'One Child' policy in terms of abortions and abandoned families. Ethnic minorities, and in particular the Tibetans, are oppressed. Minorities such as the Uighurs are put into 're-education' camps which are, in effect, we are told, concentration camps. The press, television and the internet are censored. There is a huge rise in surveillance of the population using new and powerful technologies.

To cap it all, the Chinese are thought to be cruel to animals (especially bears) and eat disgusting things such as dogs, cats and rats. They had a reputation in the past for being dirty and spitting in public. Consequently a predominantly negative picture is often built up.

Quite frankly, as a western consumer of the 'free press', I accepted much of this before I went to China. I tut-tutted, sighing sadly that China seemed to be combining the worst of both worlds, the excesses of capitalism and the repressions of communism.

Some deeper causes for mutual incomprehension

Religion

(From J.G.Wood, *Natural History of Man*, (1868), ii, 187.)

From the very start of the serious encounter with China, with the arrival of the Jesuit missionaries in the later sixteenth century, China was seen through the lens of a monotheistic and exclusive religion. The basic division was between the saved and the damned. However sensitive and sympathetic a number of the missionaries, in particular Matteo Ricci, they were ultimately trying to convert pagans.

The attitude of intolerance, which is always present, was most pronounced during the evangelical period in the nineteenth century. A number of the Christian Missions gained their funds from supporters in the West who were encouraged to believe that the money would go to the conversion of the heathen. The Chinese were idolaters, pagans, damned and deluded. Only through Christ could they be saved.

Such a basic premise, which continues in some forms to this day, was made more powerful by another special feature of China which even differentiated it from India and many other pagan countries.

This was that its people were not just pagans, following some false gods, but seemed to be worse than this. They were atheists. They did not seem to have any God at all and no idea of sin or salvation, of a real heaven and hell. They were without 'religion' as we understand it.

Before you started to shift the Chinese from a false to the Christian God you had to begin right at the beginning, with preparatory work to convince them that they needed a God at all. You had to clear away a confused mixture of Daoism, Buddhism, Confucianism, ancestor and folk beliefs before you could even start to build Christ's church.

The vast population of China were, it seems, outside the religious pale altogether. They were not just outside Christianity. They were not just outside monotheism, not even an Abrahamic faith where you can at least share some common foundations, as with Judaism and Islam. They are outside the whole Indo-

European world which recognizes a separate world inhabited by God or the gods.

Race

A second distorting lens is that of race. The Caucasian white peoples of Europe and America have for hundreds of years had great difficulty in dealing with the problem of race – primarily indicated by the colour of one's skin. Very simply, the lighter the skin (and eyes) the purer you are.

We all know something of the story of this racist legacy in the West, and in particular the horrors it led to in the whole long saga of slavery. It is so all-pervading however, that it is easy to forget its presence.

Racist antagonism fluctuates through time. For example, the British in India up to about 1800 treated the Indians as their equals in many ways and some of them took Indian wives and sent their children to Britain to be educated before taking jobs in the East India Company back in India. All this stopped in the 1790s. A caste-like separation then set in and natives were considered racially inferior, marriages ceased, and this racist superiority complex continued right up to the end of the British time in India in 1947.

The same seems to have been true in relation to China. The early visitors, from Marco Polo, or the Jesuits and up to the end of the eighteenth century did not suggest that a yellow skin made you inferior. Then the same change occurred in relation to China as in India. Expressing itself increasingly through the nineteenth century, it culminated most forcefully in the moral panic about the 'Yellow Peril' towards the end of the nineteenth century, a panic about the strength of China and particularly Japan (which had defeated Russia in 1904-5). It is notable that the peril was 'yellow'.

The whole debate about inferior and superior races was given added, quasi-scientific, status by the social Darwinian theories of the survival of the fittest and the evolution of man. The races were portrayed from lower to higher, along the colour scale, and so the Chinese were higher than Blacks, but of a different caste to 'Whites'.

The changes in racial discrimination and religious intolerance mirrored the shifting power balance of East and West. As long as China was the richest and most powerful nation on earth, that is to about 1820, there is not much sign of extreme prejudice and intolerance. The representations from Marco Polo, until roughly the end of the eighteenth century, vary from the enormously impressed, awe-filled, accounts, to views which still saw China as the greatest of powers, even if it seemed to have slowed in it advance.

Then the balance started to tip and after the humiliation of the Chinese in the First Opium War in 1839, it was soon assumed that the Chinese were racially inferior, religiously pagans to be converted, as well as technologically backward and intellectually retarded. This blended with the rise of evangelical Christianity and evolutionary theories in biology, sociology, anthropology from the middle of the nineteenth century and continued with increasing force until the First World War.

The rise of Japan made it more difficult to continue to believe that yellowness and Buddhist/Shinto/Confucian cultures were innately inferior, until the Japanese 'lost their humanity' in the Second World War. Yet China continued to be weak and divided, undergoing terrible rebellions, famines and attacks from the West and Japan with consequent crippling indemnities until Mao Tse-Tung. Chairman Mao unified the country, but his failed industrial and cultural policies and closed system did not improve China's image abroad. So China was regarded as inferior, retarded, backwards in technology and science as well as morality and colour.

Gender

A LESSON TO JOHN CHINAMAN.

Mr. Punch. "GIVE IT HIM WELL, PAM, WHILE YOU ARE ABOUT IT!"

There was also a great clash on gender relations. The Chinese were in line with almost all civilisations in history, from Egypt and Rome, through Islam and Hinduism and up to the present, in seeing men and women as intrinsically unequal from birth. Men were superior in every respect and women were very often subjected to serious restrictions.

Women were locked away physically, covered over with clothing or, in the Chinese case, with their feet broken and bound in childhood so that they hobbled in pain though life. Women had no independent legal rights and could be beaten or even killed by their fathers or husbands. This was the natural order, it was believed, something that could not be questioned. It was codified in Confucian philosophy, in Roman Law and in the words of the Prophet in the Koran.

The British had for centuries regarded women as equal in the sight of God and equal in law (except in relation to their husbands), with independent property rights which they could maintain even against their husbands and children and parents. They were also free to marry whom they chose. So they found the Chinese situation shocking. Female infanticide and bound feet became matters for huge criticism and it was a strong sign of Chinese inferiority that half the population were so 'oppressed'.

The Chinese, in reverse, were naturally shocked at the freedom and independence of British women. Their provocative clothes and manners made it easy to misinterpret their free actions as sexually encouraging. This could lead to tragic misunderstandings of the kind so delicately analysed in the Indian case in E.M. Forster's *Passage to India.*

Arrogance

Another source of irritation is something which is difficult to grasp, but is very central. This is the sense of personal self-importance of the Chinese and the West. As the West started to expand into Asia and took over large parts of India and South East Asia, it found itself, within China, confronting an ancient and great civilization which, rather than kow-towing to western superiority, demanded, at first, that foreign ambassadors and others should kow-tow to the Emperor and his representatives.

For thousands of years, China had been the 'Middle Kingdom', surrounded by weaker and smaller vassal and tributary states. China had the greatest knowledge base and culture, as well as military and economic power, in Asia. It wished to stress this and keep it that way. Why should they treat these distant barbarians from small and poor countries as their equals?

As the power balance shifted through the nineteenth century, the arrogance, as the Chinese saw it, and the conservatism and delusion as the westerners saw it, grew. It is not easy for two thousand years of supremacy to be overturned, as we are seeing today as the West suddenly realizes that after only two hundred years, it is no longer the undisputed ruler of the world.

Undoubtedly the Chinese were partly deluded and clung on to the notions of self-important supremacy too long, due to their history and pride. And no doubt this was, and, in a different way, is now a cause of irritation. The humiliations of China by the West over the last two hundred years are, amazingly, largely overlooked, but the tension must still be there, ready to surface.

Confrontation and harmony

Another distorting lens lies in a basic difference in the philosophy of life which is expressed outwardly in many features of the West and China – in games, politics, law and elsewhere. This is between a basically adversarial and confrontational western tradition, in its most extreme in the Anglo-sphere (England and the countries it colonised), and a basic premise of harmony and compromise, most obviously expressed in Confucianism, but also Buddhism and Daoism.

If you look at the way in which British lawyers accuse, defend and argue, or the aggressive attitude in the British parliament, you can see they are based on argument and confrontation. The same is found in the tough physical aggression in rugby, football or boxing, the method of teaching through argument and dispute, the directness and often cruelty of British humour, at the traditional pursuits of the English gentleman – hunting, shooting and fishing are all further examples. They all indicate a belligerent, confrontational, aggressive, winners-take-all and losers are losers, attitude.

China was traditionally the opposite. The mandarins did not play rugger, box, hunt or shoot wild game. They did not learn through the Confucian education system by arguing with their teachers or each other. Confucius stressed balance, harmony and mutual respect. It could not be more different.

The result was historically that the westerners, particularly after they gained the upper hand in war, came to think of the Chinese as weak. They were regarded as passive, un-masculine, almost effeminate. Meanwhile the Chinese could still think of their invaders as barbarians, like the Mongols and Manchus who had used violence to overcome them. Westerners were uncouth, boorish and confrontational. They were prepared to damage the precious asset of 'face' or public reputation of others through neglect and rudeness.

The Chinese placed the highest values on intelligence, education, they loved poetry, music, painting and calligraphy. They were the sort of people who in my English schools would have been termed 'swots', 'egg-heads', 'dry-as-dust' scholars. The Chinese saw their tormentors as uncultured, disinterested in the higher things of life. There was plenty of room for continuing misunderstanding and dislike on both sides.

Food

Another area for mutual intolerance was in that most central of cultural markers, especially important in China, namely food. Here the British had for centuries despised their continental neighbours, both because they seemed chiefly to live off vegetables rather than red meat, and because, when they did eat meat, they would eat all sorts of food which the British classified as non-edible, most notoriously the French habit of eating frogs and horses.

When the British encountered the Chinese, they found they were even worse than the French. Not only did the mass of the population live on a thin diet of vegetables, principally rice or millet, with no wholesome bread or meat, or even cheese, but when thy did eat meat they seemed to eat almost everything. In the north they ate horses, donkeys, mules, camels, in the south snakes and rodents, and everywhere cats, dogs and pigs. Even if the animals had died a while ago and were rotting, they were often eaten. It was even confirmed that in times of famine they had been known to become cannibals.

As far as the Chinese were concerned, the British were over-keen on dull, boiled (rather than more interesting fried), foods. They ate too much meat, too little rice and used too little flavouring. Their diet was boring and caused them to smell because of all the meat consumption. In fact westerners were greedy, wasteful, smelly, carnivores, going against Buddhist ethics and engaging in mass slaughter.

Punishments

Another area of difference concerned the law. The British had a tradition of harsh punishments – flogging, mutilation, hanging and deportation. Yet they did not use certain kinds of physical punishments of the kind they encountered in China. There was no boiling slowly in oil, being dragged apart by horses, slow slicing of the body, crucifixion. Nor did the legal system allow (except in very limited cases and periods) the use of torture, which was routinely used in China. So the Chinese legal system shocked and disgusted many westerners, for it seemed to treat humans is if they were just animals, or worse.

The Chinese on their side were appalled, as were the Indians, in a different way, by the western tradition of imprisonment. To lock someone away for years in prison with no human contacts, especially away from their family, was not only a worse fate than death, it was extremely wasteful and expensive. If the prisoner did not labour, who would feed him or her? The Chinese answer for lesser offences was banishment, or the *cangue* (wooden fetters round the neck), which allowed the criminal to be ejected from normal society, but at no cost and allowed the basic contact of a human being with his or her fellows to continue. This was more humane in the Chinese eye.

Property

There was a fundamental opposition between Chinese and British attitudes to property. Private property, the right of an individual to do what he or she liked with goods, lands and business, was enshrined at the heart of British civilisation. Protection against the arbitrary political power of rulers was safeguarded by the system. English law from Magna Carta onwards, and English philosophy, most famously in the work of John Locke, presumed the sanctity of property.

China had never had such a tradition and, through the centuries, might was right. The Emperor, or local power holders, as well as parents and wider clan members, could and did seize the goods and lands of individuals. People were subject to arbitrary power from those who wanted to commandeer them for armies or as labourers to build great walls or canals.

Currently, we see signs of such an attitude continuing in protests by farmers against the seizing of their lands by local government, or the disappearance of rich individuals or companies, only to re-emerge with much of their wealth 'disappeared'. The insecurity caused by weak property rights was again part of accusations by the West, who objected to arbitrary political power.

This was part of a wider difference which can be seen in the fact that the British had developed an immensely complex system of civil law and civil courts to underpin their economic system. This was almost totally absent in China and has really only begun to emerge in China over the last forty years.

Consequently the British thought the Chinese backward and unprotected in their rights and hence demanded that their nationals in China should only be answerable to British law – so-called extra-territoriality, which was also granted to other invading nations. This demand caused much bitterness among the Chinese over the nineteenth and early twentieth centuries.

Gangs and crime

Another of the causes of western scorn for the Chinese, and part of the stereotype was the prevalence of secret associations, and particularly criminal networks, in traditional China. In fact, all peasant societies with periodically weak or over-stretched states have had a proliferation of secret criminal organization. These run much of the black and grey areas of life and are often in alliance with parts of the State. The *mafia* of Italy, the *bratva* of Russia, the *yakuza* of Japan are all well-known examples and to this can obviously be added the famed *triads* of China.

The British came from a small island where the State, for many centuries, had managed to eliminate most organized crime. There were, of course, small groups of highwaymen, smugglers and robbers. Yet there was nothing equivalent to the large criminal networks, often based on family-like ties, on honour and secrecy, with strong rituals of initiation. These run protection rackets and dealt in gambling, prostitution, drugs and smuggling. They are a state within a state. The British were again dismayed and given grounds for feeling both superiority and anxiety.

It may be that part of the contemporary international anxiety that Chinese business organizations, in league with the State, are secretly infiltrating and stealing what is now the most precious commodity, intellectual property in new technologies, partly draws on this kind of suspicion of a criminal world which is very different to the experience of most Anglo-American visitors.

Conservatism and progress

China changes, yet remains the same. To use the metaphor of a tree, it has suffered vast cataclysms, which cut off the trunk above the ground, yet they left the roots unchanged, so that it grows back in much the same shape. Given the vastness, the dangers of disintegration and chaos, the perennial insecurity of starvation and violence, there is a huge emphasis on risk-aversion, which means conservatism in practice.

The new is dangerous. Preserving the ways of the ancestors is the wisest course. China, in its tenacious preservation of language, ancestors, family and philosophy, seemed to be, in the western eyes of the nineteenth and first half of the twentieth century, a very backward-focused civilisation – though such observers would have been amazed at the rapid developments of the last forty years.

The British and American tradition is different. The political and economic situation on the island of Britain has always been more stable. There has been a sufficient legal, social and economic security for people to be more adventurous, to take risks, to experiment. America has also been a much less volatile place.

The Anglo-American system is flexible and, to a considerable extent, forward-looking. America looks to the future. The old is esteemed and preserved where it works in the U.K., yet there is constant evolution. British institutions, whether it is parliament, the law, the economy, the Church, the universities, farming, manufacturing or communications are constantly being revised in small ways. The effect is deep continuity of certain core values, but also people wake to find that, without them noticing, a great deal has changed. The change causes less shock and stress because it is creeping, incremental, evolutionary.

When these two models of change met over the past two centuries, there was mutual criticism. The British objected to the dogged conservatism of the Chinese. Why would they not build railways, factories and mines, import western goods, build a decent communications system including post offices, reform their laws? The Chinese objected to the constant criticisms, pressure to take risks with a system which had worked well enough and was the only known protection against the recurring threats of disaster.

Curiously the situation is somewhat reversed now. Many Chinese are filled with excitement about innovations, new technologies and experiments. It is mainly workers in the older industrial West who feel threatened by this, who desire to retain, or go back to, the older manufacturing and energy technologies, to slow down change, much of it now stemming from China.

Democracy

Another cause of friction appeared early in the meeting of East and West. Montesquieu, a passionate advocate of English liberty, in a critique of contemporary French absolutism in the first half of the eighteenth century, noted that China, like most of continental Europe at that time, was absolutist. There were no checks on the power of the Emperor. All power and authority flowed from him in the highly centralized system. England, he argued, had developed a balance of powers between parliament and the King, with an independent legal system and the separating of religion from politics,

Although many European countries reverted to fascism in the 1930's, for periods of the nineteenth century they had espoused representative democracy. So when people from Europe and America visited China they were highly critical of the apparent continued absolutist rule of the Emperor. After a turbulent break, when the Qing dynasty was removed in 1911, through to 1949, there was hope of something more 'western'. Then China became communist or, in western eyes, absolutist and centralized, which, to a certain extent it is thought to have continued to this day.

It has long been the thrust of the Anglo-American project to encourage 'democracy', their way of government, on all other countries if possible. When such western democracy even in Britain and America was still based on very partial representation - women and blacks largely excluded for most of the period - it was a limited democracy.

China tried to establish a constitutional monarchy in 1906 and had her first open election of the head of the state in 1912 which resulted in General Yuan Shikai being the first elected president of the Republic of China. However, this peaceful approach was replaced during the Soviet Russia-aided 'Northern Expedition' in 1926-1928. After that political power came out of the barrel of the gun instead of the ballot of the hand. The absence of 'democracy' was something to be used as a stick to beat China with, as it continues to this day.

The Chinese, in return, found the confrontational and turbulent model of western democracy a mixed blessing. Many would like a greater balance of power, but many also recognize that in trying to represent and hold together 1.4 billion people, the kind of democracy developed to suit a small island of about five million people in the seventeenth and eighteenth centuries, may have to be seriously adapted.

The argument continues between those who argue for freedom and the 'voice of the people', and those who argue for order, efficiency and cohesion. How it will turn out in the end is obviously impossible to say. 'Democracy with Chinese characteristics' will probably cover it.

Other irritations

There are, of course, many cultural differences which cause friction. There were fundamental differences in attitudes to spitting, to burping, to going to the toilet, all parts of a general attitude towards the pure and the unclean. So the westerners, particularly the more fastidious Dutch and to a certain extent English, started to portray one of the most elegant and self-disciplined civilisations in history as a mass of dirt and disorder.

Added to this were numerous subtle differences which led to misunderstanding and irritation. In parts of the West it was possible to answer direct questions truthfully, even if this might not be particularly to the questioner's liking. The Chinese, like the Indians (and Irish in legend) gained the reputation of being liars, or deceitful, because they answered with what they thought was the best reply, in line with the social relationship, rather than the factual truth

Another source of irritation concerned space. The English

have traditionally valued privacy. They enjoy being alone, or locked safely away in their homes that are their 'castles'. As I discovered when I lived in a China-originated hill society in Nepal, people love to be together. Houses were open, evenings spent huddled with others, crowds were fun, there seemed little idea of private space. We found it very exhausting and I imagine many of the westerners who went to China felt the same. Meanwhile the Chinese were frustrated and hurt by the desire of the westerners to lock themselves away, to be apparently aloof and unfriendly, supercilious and untrusting.

My task

A good deal of the account above is based on the period around 1820-1978. Yet that history shapes us today. The present anxieties about China still use the old stereotypes, if thinly disguised. The Chinese are believed to cheat, lie, deceive, explore any weakness or benevolence which we show. Faced with a resurgence of the new 'Yellow Peril', this time not so much of people pouring into our countries, but indirectly 'stealing our jobs', 'stealing our technologies', 'manipulating the market', 'exploiting cheap labour', 'tricking third world countries into debt bondage through loans', 'violating basic human rights', it is tempting to pick up where we left off.

Almost all of those who promote this largely untrue view have never been to China, or, if they have, have only spent a few weeks in luxury hotels in large cities. So they know very little about the place, have limited understanding of how it works, and are not much interested in its history or culture.

Ignorance and fear, combined with half-concealed political and economic rivalries, are powerful background features. Daily I am shocked by the level of misinformation and bias I see even in supposedly reputable media such as the British Broadcasting Corporation or the better British newspapers and journals.

The only way, as an academic, that I can contribute to

pricking this bubble of prejudice and anxiety, is to explain a little of how China actually works, as I have observed it through extensive travels, conversations, friendships and study of its history and culture through books. The first thing I needed to do was to deepen my understanding of China through visiting it and talking to people and then to repeat this many times, as shown in the following diagram.

The recent growth of China, with our visits there indicated by arrows.

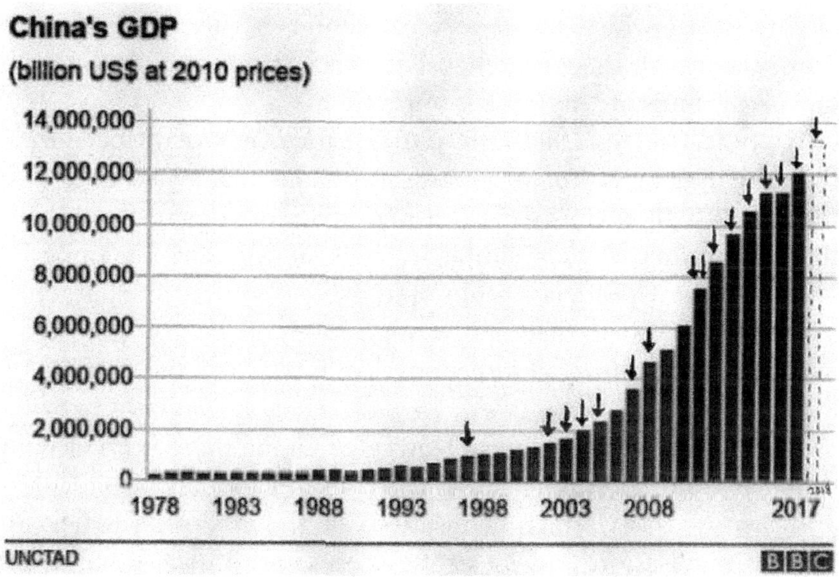

6. Why is China so easy, yet difficult, to understand?

As I tried to digest all we have seen and heard in China, all the experiences of trying to set up mutual understanding through projects in Cambridge, and the extensive reading of the fascinating literature about China, I found a strange problem faced me.

China has been, for me at least, too obvious and too simple. The really difficult cultural cases to solve are not the complex, but the simple ones. The pattern of China was laid down many thousands of years ago. It is like its national tree, the ginkgo, a "living fossil" which has a very elementary structure. If we can grasp this it will be comprehensible, yet it is not easy to find and one of the aims of this book is to reveal it.

I could not see this basic pattern for some years because I thought that in order to cohere and to last over vast ages and territories, China must be a very complex organism. I now find that it is in fact it's very simplicity, both of the unifying Imperial state and the Confucian philosophy which gives it its coherence and power. It is held together by oppositions of the yin/yang kind, and by replications in all directions (like fractals) of the simplest of ideas.

In relation to each central feature of China there is an elegant simplicity and comprehensibility. It is not nearly as contradictory and confused as western civilisations of the recent past. It is an ancient civilisation and its strength and endurance is based on the fact that it has preserved a few, very elementary yet powerful, features. Each of these is easy to explain.

The difficulty comes from the fact that each item in the simple structure that is revealed by learning about China is totally different from what a westerner such as myself is used to. So I am faced by the philosopher David Hume's dilemma. Hume long ago pointed out, 'let an object be presented to a man of never so strong natural reason and abilities; if that object be entirely new to him, he will not be able, by the most accurate examination of its sensible qualities, to discover any of its causes or effects'.[12]

China sets my world upside down, it is topsy-turvy, reversing almost everything that I hold to be self-evident. The basic axioms, the contours or grid of the culture, are absolutely different from my whole upbringing and the western tradition of thought since the Greeks. Let me illustrate this with just one or two of the central features. In each case I will allude to the conclusion of an investigation which is carried out more fully under a number of headings in the body of the text.

Chinese language is renowned for being incredibly simple, the simplest of any civilisation on earth. To me it seems an almost childish system of pictures which was swept away in the rest of the world by alphabetic languages. It could not be simpler in form and structure. Yet it is almost totally incomprehensible to me. I find it incredibly difficult to imagine how I could convey meanings in a language with no tenses, verbs, adjectives and nouns. It is hard to get a grip on it from my background even when I know that it is very simple and can describe its features.

A second feature is how a society is ordered. My own Indo-European world has roughly four 'estates' in the European tradition, the rulers, the clergy and intellectuals, the bourgeois and the peasants. The English case is somewhat different, but basically divides people into functional groups - soldiers, merchants, clerics, teachers, traders, manufacturers, farmers, all held within an embracing three-fold class system (upper, middle, lower).

The Chinese have for several thousand years had a much simpler structure. There are the ruling class the Emperor and his bureaucrats (mandarins) and the rest. There is no fighting, military, knightly class. There is no separate religious order. The vast bulk of the population are a fluid mass of rural and urban workers. It is simple enough, but from my background it is not easy to imagine myself in a world without classes, castes or estates of the realm.

[12] Peter Winch, *The Idea of a Social Science* (1958)

Turning to the traditional system of power, which still persists in other forms to this day, it could not be simpler. All decision-making flows up and down a chain of command from the individual, through the village or small institution, to the town or county, to the province, to the central administration (in the past the Emperor and his close officials, now the Central Party). There is no counter-vailing force, no separate chain of command. It is incredibly simple and holds together this vast empire. Yet from my background, with the contesting forces of the Crown, Church, Aristocracy and Gentry, Business people, Farmers and Yeomen and so on, I find it difficult to imagine such a single-channel system.

Another example concerns my basic concept of myself as an individual. I was brought up to think of myself as my own master. I have innate rights and duties, I can decide for myself how I live and think. The meaning of my own life and salvation lie within me. I should be sensitive and thoughtful towards others, but, ultimately, everything comes down to me.

As I learn about China, I realise that, like the majority of civilisations, it is entirely different. The basic building block of the system is not the individual, but the relation between two individuals. This is clearest in Confucian philosophy, where the stress is on personal relationships: ruler to subject, father to son, husband to wife, elder to younger and friend to friend. So an individual has no meaning except *in relation to* someone else. A single person makes no sense. As in the zen saying, an individual on their own is like the sound of one hand clapping. An individual, or indeed any entity in China, has no separate existence; he or she would be like *yin* without *yang*, night without day, left without right. Everything is relational; meaning lies in the relation, A/B, not in the individual parts A or B.

This is simple enough, but to move myself from an individual-based civilisation into understanding what anthropologists call a 'structural' civilisation of this kind is a huge emotional and mental leap.

Another example among the dozens that will come up in the course of this book is religion. My own world is the heir of a monotheistic, Christian, heritage. Even if I do not believe or attend Church, my life is indirectly soaked in religion. I was brought up to think of 'religion' as a complex bundle of rituals, dogmas, ethics and beliefs about the origins and purpose of life and death. It took me many years to absorb this, but this is 'religion' to me. For a long time, I assumed that every civilisation and society in the world had a religion of this kind, even if the content of the various features was very different.

When I started to study China I discovered that it was all much simpler than this. In this sense (of a bundle), China has no religion at all and indeed no word for 'religion' in the western sense. It has many rituals, but very few dogmas. It is an amalgam of a philosophy (Confucianism), an animistic set of rituals and beliefs (Daoism) and a unique form of Buddhism, Chan or Zen, which is incredibly simple and without any specific features of a religious kind that I would recognise. There is no God, the after-life is vague, there is no explanation of the origins or destination of the world, and the dogmas are absent.

As I will explain below, almost everything we encounter in China follows this contrast between the utmost simplicity and the utmost difficulty for an outsider to grasp. Other examples would be between my own system of family, tracing my descent through both males and females, and the much simpler Chinese method of tracing this just through males. Or between my system which differentiates, since the Renaissance at least, between the eye and the ear, between painting and writing, whereas in China, as in the case of calligraphy, there is no separation.

Or, finally, my system is based on functional interdependence between different institutions - a body with legs, arms, head and stomach, what Durkheim calls organic solidarity. China does not have this, for its system of 'mechanical' solidarity is similar to the simplest hunting-gathering bands in Australia, upon which Durkheim based his contrast.

As I began to appreciate its simple structure, I began to think that China would be very easy to understand. It was based on a very logical, simple, grid and should be easy to read off, in the way that Tocqueville read off America from a few simple paths - equality, individualism, liberty, fraternity. I thought I could do the same with China, and would avoid the nightmare of tracing each path back to its root, which Tocqueville suggested was the difficulty of dealing with England (and as I found, Japan).

Yet while America's principles were comprehensible to Tocqueville, for they were already present in his own background, and indeed the French Revolution had been based on them, none of the principles of China are given to me by my English experience. What I have finally discovered, with surprise and pleasure, is that China is a third case – neither complex (because of its contradictory and tortuous intertwining, like Japan and England), nor simple and symmetrical like America. So, when we know what the simple principles are, will we understand them?

These philosophical difficulties are so important that it is worth re-stating them in a slightly different way. Ludwig Wittgenstein once described the philosophical predicament thus. Humans are like flies, buzzing around inside a glass fly-bottle. We cannot see the narrow way out and are, no doubt, puzzled by the fact that there is an invisible barrier. The duty of the philosopher is to make the barrier visible.

It is a nice image and draws attention to what invisibly surrounds and constrains our minds. This mental glass container is composed of many things, habits of thought and assumptions which we learn from birth. Language is one of the most powerful for it sets limits on what we can think, talk and write about, largely without our being aware of its constraining and empowering influence, as Wittgenstein argued.

If we add to language a host of other concepts which we learn as we grow up, for example distinctions between right and wrong, ideas of time and distance, ideas of value and money, ideas of what human nature is basically like, we can see that we are surrounded by a powerful grid or code of meanings, often assembled into interlocked bundles. These vary greatly between cultures, and change over time. They constrain those who carry them and are usually largely unexamined.

We come across this set of implicit classifications when we try to translate between cultures. For example, a word like 'marriage' has a bundle of meanings which is very different in the array of societies around the world. The same is true of 'religion', as we have seen. The effect is that it is often impossible to translate many of the concepts which we find in English into Chinese or Japanese, and vice versa. The context or frame is different, the resonances are lost, the associations are different, the meaning is 'lost in translation'. This is most extreme with poetry, but affects not just language but many of the things we do in everyday life, from a kiss to a smile.

Of course, each of us tends to think our own cosmology and mental categories are right and normal and those of others are, at best, odd, and at the worst ludicrous and wicked. For a westerner, the set of assumptions that lie behind the classifications attributed by Dr.Franz Kuhn to a Chinese encyclopaedia called the *Heavenly Emporium of Benevolent Knowledge* are strange indeed (a fantasy invented by Borges, and also quoted by Foucault). This divides animals into the following classes:

> '(a) those that belong to the Emperor; (b) embalmed ones; (c) those that are trained; (d) suckling pigs; (e) mermaids; (f) fabulous ones; (g) stray dogs; (h) those that are included in this classification, (i) those that tremble as if they were mad; (j) innumerable ones; (k) those drawn with a very fine camel's-hair brush; (l) et cetera; (m) those that have just broken the flower vase; (n) those that at a distance resemble flies.'

We might think that this invented Chinese example is somewhat exaggerated, but the Japanese numbering system is quite like it. For each class of thing there is a different series of numbers.

The ordinal numbers 'are divided into nearly as many series as there are classes of objects. There is one class for all animals – expect the flying and swimming species, and insects. Another for birds, in which, however, hares and rabbits are included! A third for ships, and junks, and boats; a fourth for liquids drunk with a glass, as water, wine, tea etc.; a fifth for things having length, as trees, pens, sticks, masts, beams, radishes, carrots, fingers, brooms, pipes etc. and so on ad infinitum;' The author stopped there 'in despair, foreseeing that they would fill a volume by themselves'.

[J. Dyer Ball, *Things Chinese*]

These seem odd. Yet I can well imagine that a Chinese scholar who had investigated the Biblical Old Testament, might well find it equally peculiar. It states that there is an invisible God, that He created everything in six days, that He is all powerful and all-loving and yet allowed a serpent to tempt Adam and Eve into destruction. In the New Testament, it narrates how this God allowed his only son to be crucified. And behind it is an ineffable mystery whereby this God is composed of three parts, the Trinity of Father, Son and Holy Ghost. All a very strange and somewhat incomprehensible logic.

The question is whether we have the energy, interest and imagination to suspend our disbelief for long enough to cross the bridge into another cultural system. It is an exciting yet difficult journey. Yet, as Confucius is reputed to have said, every long journey starts with one step. I will start with the letter A and proceed step by step until we reach Z. The reasons for treating aspects of China in this way, come next.

A-Z

Understanding the Chinese A-Z

This book is not arranged in a conventional way, neither chronologically nor into chapters on particular topics – the economy, society, religion or other themes. Instead I have dealt with the main part of the analysis by taking an approach similar to a dictionary or encyclopedia, with headings under the letters A-Z. This has two effects. One is to make the order random, juxtaposing very different topics. The second is to make most of the entries quite short, just a few paragraphs in most cases. The reasons for doing this are as follows.

China (like Japan) is a country where the conventional classification which I was brought up with (sorting things into categories such as religion, art, politics, society, family, economy) does not apply. Many topics, such as calligraphy, Confucianism or martial arts, cross these boundaries. It is unsatisfactory to split the book into compact chapters of the kind I might use for a book on a western nation, though in fact, in a companion volume which partly inspired this one, *Understanding the English A-Z*, I found this approach worked well even with my own culture. The A-Z approach gives me flexibility to treat each topic in its own right and avoid the pitfalls of western classification.

I was partly inspired to make an A-Z by the very informative books on Japan by Basil Hall Chamberlain, *Japanese Things* (1904) and on China by J. Dyer Ball, *Things Chinese* (1903). After I had drafted out my *Understanding the English A -Z* and *Understanding the Chinese A-Z*, I found another, more recent, work, by May-Lee Chai and Winberg Chai, *China A-Z* (2007). A number of topics I have covered in this book are covered there, often at greater length. While there is much useful supplementary material in the Chai and Chai book, our approaches are somewhat different.

China A-Z is partly a guide for travellers to China, so it includes material one would find in something like the 'Lonely Planet' guides. Furthermore, both of the authors, father and daughter, are Chinese, though the daughter lives in America, and neither of them is an anthropologist. Their book, in so far as it is comparative, is a straight contrast between China and America.

The difference between the previous A-Z books and this one is illustrated by the way in which quite a few of the entries in this book start by setting up a simple description of other societies I have worked in, or read about as an anthropologist.

As explained, Chinese concepts are often totally different to anything I had previously encountered, so I approached them by way of comparison with what I already understood from elsewhere. In this book, I try to explore and explain China to myself, and to my readers, by creating a path from the known (my previous experience) to the unknown (for me) China. Or, to change the metaphor, to build small bridges which have one end in the outside world and the other in China. I am trying to preserve some of the excitement and wonder of the process of discovery.

I hope that non-Chinese readers may find that this approach makes it easier to move towards the unfamiliar world of China. In reverse, it may be useful for Chinese readers, for whom this book is also written, to know where I am coming from, to see the framework within which their civilisation is interpreted. Chinese readers can retrace the path, cross back over the bridges I have created, into a world outside China. They can 'see themselves as others see them', to paraphrase the poet Robert Burns.

I have kept the foot-noting, quotations and citations to a minimum. It would obviously be easy to turn each small entry into a chapter, but it seems better to give a swift overview and to allow readers to follow up any topics which interest them, using internet resources which were not available to previous generations.

Each of the many sections here are the beginning of a journey, but are set in a somewhat broader context in the final longer essays.

A

Advanced technologies

When I first visited China in 1996, the level of indigenous technologies was relatively low. The cars were being made under licence by Volkswagen, the electronics by Siemens, the computers were Japanese, the aerospace industry was in foreign hands. The Chinese were, however, learning very quickly, partly by reverse engineering, partly by making agreements with foreign firms to transfer technical knowledge to China as part of a favourable contract.

In this way, advanced technologies flooded into China, but it has only recently become fully apparent what this means. Even when I visited the top science university, Tsinghua, in about 2008, I was told that China would never catch up with American software, and in digital hardware, it would be thirty or forty years before China was on the same level.

Now, although the US has regained its position of having the fastest computer in the world, as of June 2018, China had more computers (206) on the TOP500 list than the United States (124). China's smartphones and laptops are becoming the best in the world. China's 5G communications technology is better than anywhere else and it aims to be the world's leading AI manufacturer within the next six years. The Chinese have built the largest telescope in the world. China's probe has landed on the 'dark' side of the moon, a triumph. China has just announced that it has created heat thousands of times greater than the sun and crossing the threshold for the production of fusion energy. China has just launched plans to build the most powerful brain scanner in the world, costing over one hundred million pounds.

This is causing anxiety in the West. Such anxiety is increased by various pronouncements of an ambitious kind from the Chinese government. The 'Made in China 2025' initiative announced in 2015 aimed to turn China into one of the world's great manufacturing superpowers. A revised version rolled out more detailed plans in telecommunications, railways and electric power, as well as robotics, automation, artificial intelligence in general.

In general, this ambitious plan repeats the pattern which happened when America, copying and sometimes stealing, technologies from Britain and Europe, became the technology giant of the world. Much earlier, the West had taken the great Chinese inventions, printing, gunpowder and the compass and developed them to finally defeat China in bloody wars.

The anxiety felt by Western countries stems from a view that we live in a zero sum, dog eats dog, world rooted in nation-states where if one country improves, it somehow pushes down others. Another view is that we live in a global, highly interconnected, world and that contemporary Chinese developments, just like American developments in the last decades, benefit us all and are, in fact, a product of many countries.

Alphabets

As a western child, I spent many years learning an alphabetic language. Derived from Greece, this form of language changed the world by separating the symbol and the sound from the meaning, making the language totally abstract and symbolic. A, B, C, mean nothing in themselves. Only when they are put together as CAT or DOG did I, as a child, discover that they meant something. Even these words are totally symbolic. TREE neither sounds, smells nor looks like the waving green wonders in my garden. The signified – an oak, ash, maple or whatever – and the signifier TREE are in a purely random and abstract association. This abstraction is a very powerful device, like mathematical symbols, and the power of this form of writing has led the system to be adopted in almost every country in the world in different forms, in Europe, the Middle East, India and almost all of Asia (though with some qualifications in Korea and Japan).

China is extraordinary in having preserved a form of partly pictorial, language which uses a way of writing at least ten thousand years old. Written Chinese is pictographic in its origins, but has evolved into a hybrid of simple and compound pictography, phonic and semantic categorization. Very often each 'letter' or little picture stands for a whole word or idea in a direct relationship. Here are three examples:

人舍木
man house tree

Such an approach makes the language into both a form of writing and of drawing or painting at the same time. Calligraphy, the art of writing, is both painting and writing.

One example which we have in our office is of the words *FAREWELL CAM BRIDGE*, four Chinese characters. The 'bridge' character has been drawn in a way which partly represents a bridge in the bottom right.

The evolution of a few ancient characters through time is shown in the following diagram.

Number	Ornamental motif	Ancient character	Modern character	Meaning
1			巫	shaman
2			米	grain
3			井	water well
4			癸	10th celestial stem
5			羊	sheep

The arduous task of learning upwards of two thousand characters by heart, both for reading and writing, instead of the twenty-six I had to learn, occupies much of the effort of children in China, and even more in Japan where another two syllabaries further complicate the system. While this process is enormously daunting to me, I can see how this unique ancient writing system makes it possible for one and a third billion Chinese to understand each other and unites China in an amazing way. It also has other important and lasting effects.

Language conditions what we can see and what we can express, in other words how we think. The fact that the Chinese have such a radically different writing system, joining together picture-words, has shaped their civilisation in innumerable ways. It is impossible for me really to begin to understand how it leads to a different world view and what it allows and prevents. There are brilliant descriptions of some of the effects in some of the best books on China, including Lin Yutang's *My Country and My People*, and good articles in encyclopoedias.

Below I can only hint at some of the consequences which continue today, even after Chairman Mao drastically simplified the Chinese character-set in the middle of the twentieth century. The consequences will emerge again and again in what I write below. If I were fifty years younger and a better linguist I would try to learn some basic Mandarin. As it is, having learnt an unwritten, tonal, Tibeto-Burman language distantly related to Sinitic languages, while conducting fieldwork in Nepal, I can at least appreciate the feel of a language where the tones are so important and a single 'word' can mean many different things depending on how it is pronounced. If I say the word *tree* in a Yorkshire or Cornish or Cockney accent, it still means tree, though it sounds very different. In China, a word (or pictograph) has many different meanings, and these differences are indicated in the written form by an added small marker, or radical.

Administrative levels

One of the great strengths of England for nearly a thousand years has been an extremely efficient system of devolved government down to the local level. People have a great deal of control over their own lives through a nested system of power which encourages people to become involved (often on a voluntary and unpaid basis) in running their lives. This evolved over time, so I will give just one example which arrived in my post yesterday from a local representative of one of our political parties. This included 'A quick guide to local politics' which explained with reference to my specific village, called Lode and Longmeadow, how this worked from the bottom up.

Lode and Longmeadow Parish Council: Your most local tier of government, responsible for things like maintaining green areas, rights of way and ditches.
East Cambs District Council: Responsible for things like bins, housing and housing benefit, planning, leisure and parks.
Cambridgeshire County Council: Responsible for school, transport, roads, libraries, children's centres and social care etc.
South East Cambridgeshire: Your Member of Parliament (MP) represents you in the House of Commons.

The above structure moves from a unit of about a thousand, to a few thousand and ending up with an MP for about 85,000 people. If MPs were elected from such constituencies in China with its present population, a Chinese House of Commons would have to have nearly sixteen thousand members of parliament!

It is interesting to know how China compares to the system described above for Lode and Cambridge. A friend of mine, Wang Hong, kindly explained the system as it works in her own province of Jiangsu, as follows. (It is interesting that she described from the top down).

> China's current administrative management system is referred to as the quaternary structure: the provincial level administrative region, city level administrative region, county level administrative region, township-level administrative region. China has a total of 34 Provincial Level Administrative Regions, including 23 provinces, 4 municipalities, 5 autonomous regions and 2 special administrative regions.
> Under the province, the nation is generally divided into cities. Under the city, we are further divided into counties, and the county administrative region is then divided into town and township.
> For example, Jiangsu Province has a total of 13 cities, including Nanjing, Suzhou, Wuxi, Yangzhou, Changzhou, Zhenjiang, Lianyungang, Yancheng, Taizhou, Huaian, Xuzhou, Nantong, Suqian. Under those 13 cities there are a total of 96 counties and 1,300 townships.

Ancestors

A Chinese man was once asked by a westerner why he and his countrymen believed so strongly in ancestors. He rightly replied that the question should be put the other way round. Why do Europeans and Americans, and particularly Protestants, not believe in ancestors? We should remember that all the classical civilizations, and most of the world today, from Africa through India to the Far East, believe that a veneration and commemorations of ancestors is an essential duty in life.

Although formal ancestor commemoration, with large ancestor halls with the names of (male) ancestors on the walls and frequent ceremonies to honour them, have declined sharply in modern China, especially since the anti-familistic policies of the Mao era, ancestors continue to be important in relation to graves and burial rituals. They remind us of the vast importance of ancestor beliefs through Chinese history.

Of course, I think of my parents and grandparents and I even have trees planted in my garden which I associate with them. I sprinkle water on the snowdrops and read a poem where half my mother's ashes are buried on her death day. I keep many photographs of them, and feel sad on the death date of my mother and father, though I have already forgotten those of my maternal grandparents who brought me up. I do not pray or talk to any of them, I don't give them gifts, I don't fear that they will do me harm if they are displeased. They are dead and gone, perhaps in Heaven, even if, as I doubt, such a place exists. There is no retained link to them except in memory.

The Chinese, perhaps the most extreme ancestor-focused civilisation in history, live with their ancestors. Francis Hsu, the anthropologist of China, named one, of his books 'Under the Ancestor's Shadow'. Travelling through the great cities in the autumn the streets are lit up with little fires where paper money is being burnt to the ancestors. Their tombs are swept on a certain day and before the Communist period many people kept a tablet in the house with the name of ancestors and even today some keep photographs. Even sophisticated and ultra-modern young Chinese admit they believe that their ancestors are still somewhere near and need respect.

This can be seen as a reflection of the immensely powerful family system of the past, or the huge respect for parents and grandparents which is a central feature of Confucian philosophy. Whatever the reasons, I find it difficult to imagine how it must feel to live under a great-grandfather's shadow, to believe that when something good (or very often unpleasant) happens to you it may be because you have pleased, or angered, a long dead ancestor.

I would not dream of going to an English church, or to the grave of one of my ancestors, and putting up small messages to my ancestors, as young Chinese do in the Shinto and Buddhist shrines, for example for success in exams.

The contrast of an ancestor-less world like mine, with the hints of ancestor-beliefs in Catholicism with its masses for the dead, Purgatory, graveyards with family putting gifts and flowers, is already a surprise to me. Yet the contrast to the ancestor-soaked worlds of most of the earth's inhabitants, and above all the great ancestor-worshiping civilisation of China is even more startling. This again poses the question; how did we lose our ancestors? The answer is complicated, probably a combination of the kinship system and the monotheistic Christian religion.

Animals

I have lived my life in an animal-soaked country. Both domesticated animals – sheep, cows, horses and pigs – and pets, particularly cats and dogs, have abounded. If you had gone into an English village at any time in the last eight hundred years you would have found it filled with all of the above, as well as chickens and ducks. What was there, of course, depended on which part of the country you were in, particularly whether it was arable or pastoral. Yet animals teemed everywhere and even in the cities which, until the end of the nineteenth century, were filled with horses, pigs and chickens. Animals were the backbone of the English economy, they were central to English identity and the English have long been known as pet lovers.

Yet when Isabella Bird visited Japan and China in the later nineteenth century she noticed the absence of animals. In Japan there were none, except for a few chickens. In China there were very few, apart from pigs and ducks. Why is this the case and what are the effects?

The causes are multiple. The dense population of China left little space for animals and human labour was cheaper than keeping large working animals. Growing rice is best done with human labour. You did not need wool for clothing when you had silk and hemp. Very little meat was eaten because of the cost and because Buddhism forbade it. People saw meat as a luxury and the population was lactose-intolerant because no animal milk was drunk. When they needed horses for warfare, the Chinese obtained them, usually in exchange for tea, from the pastoral nomads who bordered China in the central Asian uplands.

You might eat fish, duck and pigs, but that was it – and most were too poor to eat meat other than on special occasions. Even when we visited a remote village near the Great Wall in 1996 villagers spoke of the special delight of the improvements so that they could eat meat once or twice a week.

I find it hard to imagine living in a country with no, or very few horses, sheep or cows. The meadows and pastoral uplands of my childhood would not exist. The roast beef, mutton and lamb would be absent. The sports of fox-hunting or horse racing could not exist. All transport and ploughing would be without the aid of animals. The absence of pets I will deal with elsewhere.

Yet if I had come from much of continental southern Europe for most of the last half century I would have found China less strange, for they were not as animal-abundant as England. Over the centuries, as population increased, much of Europe went in the Chinese direction. Even in the early twentieth century in parts of France the barges were pulled along canals by women, not horses.

Now, as we eat marvellous feasts in Chinese restaurants, perhaps noting with surprise that you have to specially ask for rice, which is considered hardly necessary amidst the plentiful dishes of fish, meat and vegetables, it is difficult to remember this divergent past. Yet it is a divergence which affects everything.

Perhaps something I note elsewhere, the ethic of immense hard work of the Chinese, is related to this. Historically, animals did at least half of the agricultural and transport work, and provided the energy in early industries (mining, milling) in the English past. To the Europeans, the English were proverbially over-fed and lazy. The Chinese had to do the work themselves.

Having lived for several years in a Himalayan village without wheels, windmills, electricity or horses, I have seen the back-breaking work. Yet the people I lived with did have stalled buffaloes, oxen for ploughing, sheep and goats. Without those, the work on the steep mountain rice and maze terraces, the grinding effort of back, legs and arms would have been intolerable.

Although China now has huge animal production and imports, the shadow of a largely animal-absent past is still there and accounts for some of the other patterns we will encounter. Everything from the absence of leather shoes in the past, the field shapes, the diet, the body shape to work patterns are subtly affected by domesticated animals and their presence or absence.

Animal calendar

As I grew up I was taught to date and measure my life in accordance with the Christian calendar. I was born in 1941, first went to boarding-school in 1950, went to University in 1960 and retired in 2009. Each of these was a number of years since the supposed birth of Christ. The years ticked by and there was nothing cyclical about them, no association between the abstract number and my character or destiny.

The only hint of such an association was when I was told that the month of my birth made me a Sagittarian and that astrology meant that I had a certain character because of that. Yet the year of birth had no particular significance.

When I went to work in a China-derived ethnic minority in Nepal, the Gurungs, I immediately encountered, and realized the importance of, the ancient twelve-year animal calendar. This was based on the following:

Everyone knew they were born in one of them and could tell their age by working out a multiple of twelve.

They also knew that if they were born in the year of the rat, they would have a different temperament to the year of the tiger. Because some years are more auspicious than others, it has been noticed that the birth rate goes up and down in relation to this. When your year came around you have a special feeling of excitement in the New Year celebrations.

When special multiples of these arrived, you celebrated in a special way. In Japan, you become an infant again and count your age from zero when you reach sixty. In Nepal, there is a special chaurasi puja at the age of 84 (seven times twelve being very auspicious). In China, also, sixty is a special age.

All this gives life a circularity, the revolving cycles of the years. It encourages a symbolic association between humans and animals, an affinity of character which I have never felt. There is something more powerful than in being associated with a star sign with which I am familiar.

Animal symbols

The English have their animals, important in folklore and in their symbolic system. Parts of this have usefully been laid out in the classic work by Keith Thomas, *Man and the Natural World* (1983). Among the animal spirits were 'were-rabbits'. A 'were' creature was one which could change, usually at night, into a human. The English thought of certain birds or animals as lucky or, like magpies, black cats and ravens, as unlucky

The symbols of the English royal family and English nation are a fabulous beast, the one-horned unicorn, and the mighty lion. You will see them on heraldic devices, appearing in children's stories such as *The Lion, The Witch and the Wardrobe*, and in the architecture of royal foundations. In poetry and plays the English are exhorted to be like the lion – brave and fierce and noble. Yet I have nowhere felt that its importance is more than symbolic.

Nor is another mythical beast, the dragon, of much significance, even though my life by chance was associated with this mythical animal having been sent to the Dragon (preparatory) school (actually named after a Dragon class sailing boat).

Yet anyone who knows anything about China will know how central a dragon is much of Chinese culture. They will have seen dragon festivals, dragon dances on special occasions, boat races, dragons adorning imperial palaces. The dragon is clearly very important and no doubt there is seen to be some unity between the huge, fire-breathing, flying dragon, which features in martial arts films such as 'Flying Dragon, Crouching Tiger', and the Chinese people. In brief, the dragon is the mightiest of creatures, master of rain and water and associated with the Emperor.

Another important animal is the fox. It is reputed to live to a great age. When it reaches fifty it can turn itself into a woman, at a hundred a seductive girl and at a thousand a powerful god with nine tails. Fox spirits have to be appeased with offerings.

A third important animal is the tiger. It is a zodiac animal and represents bravery, though rather surprisingly it is regarded as *yin*, or female, particularly when shown with a dragon, which is *yang*. It is a protective motif and keeps away demons. It is so powerful that many parts of its body were traditionally used for medicine.

In fact, whole books could (and no doubt have been) written on the symbolism of animals in art, literature, Daoism and elsewhere in Chinese life.

What is clear is that, in line with the huge symbolic and associative system of China, people can read a painting, building or piece of literature with thousands of associations and cross-references in their mind, expanding and linking the sound of characters and the meaning of the natural world.

Here I will just select just the animals A-B featured in an article on 'Animal symbolism in Chinese Art' (http://www.chinasage.info/symbols/animals.htm). The rest of the alphabet can be seen there.

Ant 蚂蚁 mă yĭ: hard-working and well-ordered. The second

part of the name (yi) means righteous, denoting its apparent display of Confucian virtue.

AO 鳌 áo (Giant Turtle): featured in creation myths, where the earth (as in Terry Pratchett's 'Discworld' novels) is placed on the back of a giant turtle. They are supposed to eat fire, so are often at the end of roof ridges to keep fire away.

Badger 獾 huān: symbolize happiness because the sound of their name (huan) is the same as 'joyous, happy, pleased'. They usually appear in art with magpies since also this also symbolizes happiness.

Bat 蝠 fú: the character for bat (fu) sounds the same and looks similar to 'good fortune', so a symbol wishing good luck.

Bee 蜜蜂 mì fēng: when combined with a monkey in art, they mean aspiration to high office. Because bees pollinate they represent the male gender and when combined with peony flowers, this shows a young man seeking love.

Bear 熊 xióng: strong and brave and symbolizing the masculine side. A good talisman against robbers.

Butterfly 蝴蝶 hú dié: sometimes a symbol for a quest for love, in particular in association with plum blossom means a quest for blissful love. The most famous is in the story of the Daoist philosopher Zhuangzi, who wondered if he was a butterfly or human dreaming.

Architecture

I come from a country which has certain building materials, a speciaal ecology and a philosophy and aesthetics which has shaped both our ceremonial and domestic architecture and the nature of our towns and cities. With plentiful wood, especially oak, with stone and thatch, with much middle-class wealth, the houses I have lived in, even when recently made, have been substantial and well built. The one I live in now has lasted nearly 400 years – and that is not old in England. It is solid, warm and substantial. Many English houses have cellars and three or four floors. Built of brick, stone and sometimes clunch (mud and reeds), they have provided privacy and good shelter for generations of the English.

When I travel in China and ask to see old houses, I am told that the building materials – in the south mainly bamboo and paper and reed, in the north some stone but little wood – combined with possible earthquakes, and turbulent political events with mass destruction —means that very few private residences of over one hundred years survive. Those that do, in the old parts of Chinese cities I visited only fourteen years ago, have almost all been pulled down. Vast estates of high-rise flats, often more than twenty stories or more, have replaced them. In the countryside also, even in the remote ethnic minority area, there are few old buildings.

Traditional houses in China were without basements and cellars and only one story high. Even the elegant many-chambered houses of the Mandarins and rich merchants, with courtyards and lovely fish and flower-filled gardens, were single-story, as were houses in cities. The architecture was quite uniform and the important thing was to get the correct geomantic alignment, the *feng shui*. It was essential to provide, in richer houses, a place for entertaining and display, and, in smaller houses, especially in the north, a fire-warmed bed (*kang*) and a large *wok* for cooking.

Recently all this has changed. When thinking about why it is that so many million Chinese appear to be happy to live in the apparently soulless, crammed, small flats in the sprawling high-rise cities, I wonder whether their happiness largely derives from this past. Coming from a cold, cluttered, poorly constructed village house into the warm, efficient, well serviced flats must feel rather special.

The architecture of Chinese towns is also intriguing in its influence. In the past, cities were usually designed as fortresses, an administrative centre with a huge wall around it. They were often on a grid-like plan, with a large central square, most famously with Tiananmen square in Beijing. Such squares still exist in many modern cities which are now mega-cities, dozens are much bigger than Manchester, Liverpool, Chicago or Los Angeles.

At present, China has thirteen cities with a population of over ten million, and the three or four which are mega-cities with well over twenty million, are characterized by a residue of the boulevards, squares and regular grids of the past. They are filled with huge shopping malls and the bicycles that thronged them have largely gone, though some are being replaced by electric bikes.

Dotted around them and in the country are traces of a pre-1949 world of religious architecture, with Buddhist and Daoist shrines and temples, often climbing up the mountain sides, with their stupas and pagodas and spires of red and gold and embedded in gardens. These ceremonial centres are thriving now, as they did in the past, from receiving donations from wealthy Chinese who hope to turn their profits into merit. Even since 1996 we have seen a vast proliferation of this ceremonial architecture.

At the centre, is the constantly re-built hub of the whole Chinese universe, the Forbidden City, the Emperor's Palace. The Chinese Emperors, from the first Qin Emperors in 221 B.C., have built their awe-inspiring palaces in numerous capitals – X'ian, Changsha, Nanjing, Hangzhou and Beijing amongst them. And in each they have awed their subjects and expressed the way in which everything – power, family, morality, art, economy government, the winds, waters, heaven and earth – come together in the person of the Emperor in his celestial abode.

I sense that my ideas of urban and rural space, what constitutes a home, what makes a house or temple beautiful is very different from the views of my Chinese friends. I mourn the continuing destruction of the remains of old China and its replacement by pastiches and copies, though I have heard that in the last two or three years the tide is turning against this. Yet I also admire a remarkable architectural tradition and a varied and deeply thought-out way of housing a vast population, which has now morphed into the unimaginably complex mega-cities of China.

Armies

I come from an island which was mainly guarded by its navy. It had no standing army and the inhabitants were prohibited from carrying weapons. Yet it was also a martial people, carrying out its wars all over the world, first in Europe mainly against the French, then all over the world as it expanded its huge empire. It relied heavily on paid troops from mountain regions, first the Scots, later the Gurkhas of Nepal.

With all this there was some respect for the army. It was, at least for the officers, a respectable profession, placed alongside other such as doctors, lawyers, clergymen, academics in the ranking system. I was not ashamed that my grandfather was a Colonel and that my father and two uncles enlisted in the army in the Second World War.

I expected the Chinese army to be something like all this, but have discovered that its whole history and spirit is different in numerous ways. At first, in the thousands of years up to the unification of China in 221 B.C, there were enormous, well-equipped armies. Roman or later European armies would have been dwarfed by the many hundreds of thousands or even millions who took part in a Chinese battle, as in the War of the Three Kingdoms.

Yet increasingly, after the unification, the military profession almost disappeared. Without feudalism, and ruled by an un-armed, civilian, Mandarin bureaucracy, the soldier-gentleman of the West never existed. The population were forbidden to carry weapons and there was no standing army.

Yet China faced redoubtable horsemen warriors on all its western borders and constant uprisings of various kinds. To counter these, China devised a strategy of building huge walls with small numbers of troops to patrol them, and also made use of two other measures.

One was to use mercenaries, often taken form the border minorities to suppress other minorities. The troops particularly came from the Yi or Muslim minority who helped the Chinese expand into south-western China.

The second policy was to follow an early arrangement whereby the peasants were also potential soldiers. Huge numbers could be marshalled, but were not a permanent, costly, and potentially dangerous force, because they lived on the land in normal times. They could be raised if there was a need. This was a people's peasant army and its nature has influenced China ever since.

This absence of a military profession and powerful standing army and reliance on mercenaries partly explains why China has been so vulnerable to invasions by the scattered nomads on its borders. It also explains why it was defeated by the relatively puny, if armed with machine guns, forces of the British in the nineteenth century, or the small number of Japanese who took Manchuria in the early twentieth century. In some ways, it explains the military weakness of this huge Empire.

Yet it also explains the hidden strength of China, for the amazingly brave, well-co-ordinated, and determined citizen armies were able in the Second World War to defeat arguably the best army in the world, the Japanese, who had easily over-run the British in Burma and the Pacific.

The Chinese, faced with far superior weaponry and organization, tenaciously fought on. Their losses were immense, over twenty million people died in the Sino-Japanese War. Yet in the end the Chinese won. This is a lesson for anyone thinking of invading China.

All this explains one further thing which long puzzled me. I was told that until recently, when President Xi stopped the practice, the army was regarded by the Chinese as partly a business. It should pay for itself by engaging in all sorts of commercial activities, including manufacture and trading. Perhaps we have a little of this with the spin-offs from the British army and air force in the defence industry, the second largest in the world. Yet it is more obvious in the Chinese case.

My experience of visiting the earthquake area of Sichuan six weeks after the terrible events that killed more than 70,000 people, also gave me a sense of a citizen's army. The army, though huge (one million six hundred thousand) is usually pretty invisible in China. Yet when there is a crisis the troops can act swiftly and efficiently and seem to be just an extension of the ordinary civil service. All citizens have to do two weeks of training as they become adults, so they know what the army is like, and they do not seem to fear it. The army is not a separate institution, but is a set of ordinary Chinese in uniform and they are generally accepted and sometimes admired as such. The amazing spectacle of the opening of the Beijing Olympics gave a glimpse of their precision in action.

B

Bamboo

Bamboo is a form of grass and has unique properties unlike any other plant. Bamboos have a rhizome or lateral rooting system, like grass, which means that they spread very quickly and securely without the need for animals or the wind to spread seeds. Bamboos are almost indestructible and can tolerate high winds and lashing rain because they bend and give way before force and then return to their original upright position. Their leaves and stems are not attractive food for most animals and insects. Bamboos thrive in a wide variety of climates.

For human beings, particularly in eastern Asia where they thrive best, they have many attractions. Indeed, China (and Japan) are aptly termed Bamboo Civilisations. Bamboo shoots are, at certain stages, edible and much used in cuisine. Bamboo shoots are also viewed as an important medicine. The shavings are used for fevers, convulsions and vomiting; the sap as an anti-convulsive, for children's fevers and epilepsy; the liquid from the sap, for coughs, loss of consciousness; the leaves for fever and blood in the urine and lung inflammation.

Before the invention of paper in China, bamboo strips were used for several thousand years as the main medium for writing on, like papyrus in the West. Such strips have survived in large quantities, being very durable. Bamboos were used for musical instruments, particularly flutes. Bamboos were used for drinking vessels, for items of footwear (bamboo clogs are still used in Japan). Bamboos were used as plates, for boxes and containers and as eating utensils. Bamboo was essential as a building material, for floors, for walls, for beams and for roofs. Nowadays in the most modern cities you will see bamboo scaffolding used instead of metal.

Without bamboo, China's material and intellectual culture

would have developed far less than it has. Symbolically, the immensely tough, bending, fast-spreading bamboo can be seen as a very apt metaphor for this great civilisation. Their grace and beauty matches China's art and is a favourite subject of Chinese paintings.

Bargaining and haggling

As an Englishman, I have grown up in a country of fixed prices. When I go into a shop, or onto the internet, I expect to see or hear of a price. If I want the object I pay the sum specified. There are edges to the system where some bartering occurs. In the housing market it is common to offer a lower amount and hope the seller will come down. In open air markets, including the hugely popular car-boot sales, one can enter into haggling, especially at the end of a day with perishable goods. With second-hand goods, clothes or books, there is more room for haggling. Yet, on the whole, most of the time, there is little point – and it could well cause offence – to make a lower offer than the set price.

As soon as I went to Nepal in my twenties I encountered a world where most prices were negotiable. I found it rather distasteful to offer well below the stated price to an obviously poor and sometimes desperate vendor. I realized I was being taken as stupid and slightly ridiculous in just paying what was asked. If I was accompanied by a local they would either scold me for my stupidity, or offer to do the buying themselves. It was my first shock.

It is a shock that continues in China, where in the past most goods did not have a fixed price. This is a much more flexible system, allowing the laws of supply and demand not only to operate at a general level, but also at a micro-level. Every item's value changes with time and context; the time of day or year, the distance it has been brought, the neighbouring competing buyers and sellers. Then there is the personal relationship, for the transactions were often with friends, neighbours, family and to them there was a different responsibility.

I also discovered, contrary to my embarrassment at bargaining and haggling, that to those brought up in such a system, it was an enjoyable pass-time. Through skill, rhetoric, humour, veiled bribes and threats, each side was engaged in a game where one side could emerge feeling a minor triumph. I noticed this with some of my close Chinese colleagues, who even in England would come back, their eyes sparkling, with stories of how through haggling they had got a real bargain. I saw it less in China since I tend to go to shops which have adopted western practices, including restaurants. Yet because of the embedded nature of China, because of its delight in playing with money and achieving a bargain in a traditionally precarious world, such bargaining and haggling is still widespread.

As for a branch of this, bartering, I suspect that this is also much more widespread in China. Bartering means exchanging one good for another, avoiding the use of money; I give you a pound of potatoes, you give me a pound of rice. Such transactions are in many ways efficient and the stuff of village life throughout history. Today bartering is picking up again in advanced capitalist economies since this avoids the tax man. The barter economy may well grow again. Electronic systems such as WeChat seem ideally suited for sophisticated bartering.

Bartering is rather underplayed in my own life. There were times, for example in the hard days of the post-war austerity, when people, my grandmother included, swopped their eggs for someone else's fruit or even help in the garden. Yet I have spent very little time bartering and I suspect that this is generally true in the U.K. and is another difference from China.

Belt and Road

The 'Belt and Road Initiative' idea is an ambitious project launched by President Xi Jinping in 2013. Rather counter-intuitively, the 'Belt' actually refers to the old land silk roads linking China to south east Asia, India and as far as Europe. The 'Road' refers to the maritime or sea 'silk roads' which linked the eastern sea ports of China to south-east Asia and, at times, as early as the eighth century, as far as the Mediterranean. There are also plans for an 'Ice Silk Road', a cooperative venture with Russia to foster development in the Arctic region.

Investing huge sums of money in this project the Chinese want to build a communications network of roads, railways and ships, and also the digital communications systems which go with this, which will unite Eur-Asia, from eastern China to the U.K and western Europe. The scheme is even more extensive than the ancient silk roads, for it will reach across the Pacific to South America and across the Indian Ocean to Africa.

It is a characteristic of rising and self-confident Chinese Empires in the past, for example the Tang in the eighth century, that they open or re-open links along the silk roads (described elsewhere) for the exchange of goods and movement of peoples and ideas. This plan is another example.

On the plus side, the project is using the huge resources and skills of the Chinese, which have already made China into one huge, integrated, communications network in a period of about thirty years. Among other things, this helps develop Chinese technology and put to work the many thousands who were previously employed within China, thus helping to avoid problems of employment.

The project is also helping many poorer countries to build a good communications infrastructure, essential for raising people out of poverty. Having raised over half a billion people out of poverty within China, one ambitious goal is to do the same for a an even greater number, in partnership, around the world.

On the negative side, its critics think that the project is part of an imperial design by China to control much of the world. It could be aiming to do this through soft power, through making the recipients of aid into debtors, through controlling the important communications that are built into the future. Of course, most of those who criticize China for this have been engaged in much more blatant imperial expansion for the last several centuries, usually backed up by military force. Some fear that the alleged beneficiaries of the project may in fact become the dumping ground for China's excessive outputs at home.

Whatever we think of the scheme, it is important to be aware of what is happening. This is the most ambitious physical infrastructural project in the world. In the decades when America and the west controlled third world development, not much was done to provide a decent infrastructure. Many countries in Africa and Asia still struggle with the legacy of colonial empires. China is trying to lift large parts of the world up to its own level of extraordinary roads, railways, sea and air transport. In doing so it is daily changing our world.

Books

I come from a bookish family. My mother was a great reader and writer, books filled our home and I was familiar with the bookish and library-filled worlds of Oxford and Cambridge universities for most of my life. I have collected books and have a large personal library, dovetailing with my wife's large second-hand book collection.

I love books and assumed that the English with their great poets, novelists, essayists and historians were the most bookish people on earth, even if up to ninety percent of British households have no book other than comics in their house and are currently closing their public libraries at an ever-increasing rate.

Yet when I encountered China I realized what a real bookish civilisation, the greatest in history, looks like. The Chinese tried to preserve the ancient writings from the time of Confucius onwards. Their education system was based almost entirely on reading and copying classical works. The Chinese invented the great medium for books, paper, thousands of years ago. They invented the first printing press some 700 years before Gutenberg in the West. The oldest printed book in the world, the 'Diamond Sutra' in the British Library, is Chinese.

The size and proliferation of Chinese books is staggering. The great compilations of Chinese classics or encyclopoedias of knowledge which in the West ran to a few dozen volumes at the most, was often composed of hundred if not thousands of books. Writers, and especially poets, were among the most respected individuals in China. Almost all the population were literate at the lowest level, including women, for well over the last thousand years, being able to read and write a few characters was essential. The Chinese leaders were not just politicians, but writers and calligraphers like Chairman Mao, or Xi Jinping whose two volumes of speeches and essays have just been published in translation. Books were revered, and paper written on should not just be throwing away but given a decent burial through incineration.

Libraries were also important and continue to be so to today. Sadly they have been deprived of many great works by the ravages of the Mongol and Manchu invasions, civil wars and periodic purges of books by Emperors – a tradition started by the First Emperor who ordered the destruction of all books up to his time in 221 B.C. and copied much later by Chairman Mao who ordered the destruction of much of the surviving classical literature of China.

Yet today books, bookshops and libraries thrive, even as digital media becomes the most favoured way to convey information. So I discovered in the great new city of Shenzhen that they had the biggest book fair in the world and the largest single-floor bookshop, which is also a place for debates, performances and many other events. Shenzhen has a huge public library, crammed with readers who overflow onto the stairs. If they want to borrow books at night, they can present their identity card to a vending machine, call up the books they want, and these are downloaded like a drink or ice cream.

China is the civilisation of the book, all the stranger because both learning to read and write Chinese takes far more effort than doing the same with alphabetic languages

Boxer Rebellion

This title does not refer to the western sport of boxing, or to those squarish underpants that some men wear, but to a strange and tragic event which occurred only a little more than a century ago, the Boxer Rebellion of 1899-1901. I have a particular family interest in this since a distant relative, William Carles, was the British Consul in Tianjin at that time and was present as the western powers assembled the army which they hoped would end the siege of missionaries and others in Beijing.

The movement was an anti-foreign, anti-colonial and anti-Christian uprising started by the 'Militia United in Righteousness', known as Boxers in English because they practiced Chinese martial arts, known in the West as Chinese boxing.

A messianic movement emerged, whose leaders spread the word that those who practised a kind of martial art would become invulnerable to western bullets. Such a belief in invulnerability to guns has been found in similar movements in North America and Melanesia. It usually ends up with the tragic slaughter of the innocents.

The movement started in Shandong province and converged on Beijing. Initially Empress Dowager Cixi supported the Boxers. Diplomats, foreign civilians and soldiers, as well as Chinese Christians were penned into the Legation Quarter in Beijing for nearly two months. An eight-nation alliance of American, Austro-Hungarian, British, French, German, Italian, Japanese and Russian forces lifted the siege.

What happened then is yet another disgrace in the sad book of western aggression. There was a 'carnival' of loot, mass rape and killing. Much of Beijing, along with its beautiful old buildings and wonderful gardens were destroyed and precious objects sold off and sent to the West. After the bestialities of two Opium Wars, the Chinese learnt something of what Western 'civilisation' meant in practice.

On top of this gratuitous barbaric behaviour, the allies forced an almost bankrupt and tottering Qing government to pay a huge amount in reparations. They demanded 450 million taels of silver, approximately $10 billion at 2018 prices and more than the government's revenue over more than four years. This was one of the final tipping points in the collapse of the Qing empire in 1912, from which ensued over 35 years of civil war and chaos, destroying millions of lives.

Bribery

I grew up in an English world where I hardly heard about bribery. At school, university or in my later working years it was not my experience that if I wanted to achieve something – get into a school or university, win a law case, buy some land or a house, get a professional qualification, pursue business – I needed to pay someone for this in a secret way. I was shocked to hear that over much of southern and eastern Europe one had to pay bribes to advance in the educational system. I was shocked to find when I went to India and Nepal that almost everyone had to pay bribes to those above them to keep their jobs or to get any kind if serious permission or permit.

Of course, I knew that the English used other, indirect, ways to achieve their goals – membership of golf clubs or Masonic lodges or old school associations, a box in the opera, a swop of favours. Yet as I examine my own life, and the lives of many generations of my ancestors revealed in their letters and diaries from the seventeenth century, I am struck by how bribery of any kind is generally absent.

China, as we will see in the account of bureaucracy, has had bribery built into the system. The situation is certainly not as bad as in many parts of the world today. Yet the constant anti-corruption campaigns, about which we hear daily, are just one sign of the difficulty.

What strikes me from the English point of view, and was recognized for example by Robert Hart in the nineteenth century is that, rather than attacking the symptoms, locking up corrupt officials etc, the treatments should get at the causes. These concern the gap between what one can earn and what one needs to live on. It also requires attention to the nexus between politics and economics.

It has been observed that the characteristic form of bribery and corruption in America consists of amassing fortunes in business – and then buying your way into political power. In China it is reversed; you get to your political position, often through education, hard work and skills – and once achieved you can recoup the expenses.

All this will continue until it is realised that the solution, whereby the state pays judges, teachers, police and others enough so that they do not have to use their positions to provide for their families, should be adopted.

Of course, it is not as simple as this. The scale of bribery may well increase with rapid economic growth and China is growing exponentially. Yet the legacy of a past governmental system and way of rewarding individuals need to be addressed even more urgently

C

Calligraphy and painting

I was brought up in a western tradition of alphabetic writing and post-Renaissance art which makes an absolute distinction between writing and painting. This was succinctly put by Leonardo da Vinci when he said 'Painting is poetry which is seen and not heard, and poetry is a painting which is heard but not seen.' In other words, in my world, the eye, which sees the world around me, and the ear, which hears the sound of words, are absolutely distinct.

I had assumed until recently, when I began to learn about one of China's greatest contributions to world art, that this was universal. Then I was taught otherwise by leading Chinese calligraphers. Especially I remember an animated display in which a calligrapher danced as he wrote, explaining the poem was also a painting. I have hanging in my office a huge, ten foot, calligraphy which has the two characters for CAM BRIDGE - but they are written in a way which is also a fairly abstract, but recognisable, painting, of a river and a bridge. This can be seen under 'Alphabets' above.

This made me realise how huge the artistic and perceptual divide must be between myself and my Chinese friends. When they read even ordinary Chinese characters, but especially poetry and works written in fine calligraphy, they are receiving powerful stimuli through both the eye and the ear. They receive information, perceive truth and beauty in a different way. They fulfil Keats' great hope – 'Beauty is truth, truth is beauty , that is all ye know on earth and all ye need to know'. Hence Chinese aesthetics and communications have potentials which I cannot experience.

It works the other way around too. Not only is what I would have classified as merely 'writing' also painting, but painting is also writing. This starts to explain something that has long puzzled me, namely the highly stylized, non-naturalistic, nature of great Chinese paintings. I knew that Chinese painters have, since the Song dynasty, been perfectly capable of very accurate painting of people and nature, just like post-Renaissance western artists. I knew that before the discovery of accurate single-point perspective by Brunelleschi in the fifteenth century, the Chinese could paint in very accurate, if moving, perspective, as in the famous painting 'Along the River during the Qingming Festival' painted in the first half of the twelfth century by Zhang Zeduan

Yet instead of doing this kind of naturalistic painting developed in the West from the Renaissance on, the Chinese painted either small studies of birds, flowers, trees or landscapes which were almost all composed of misty mountains, rivers and a few very small figures in the foreground.

For a while I thought that the fact that most highly literate Chinese were deeply myopic, that artists painted from memory rather than on the spot, that their tools were brushes on a scroll laid on the floor, were the factors which pushed them toward their Chinese style, and, once adopted, their patrons did not want anything else. All these may be part of the explanation, but now it seems that an added understanding occurs if we think of the paintings as writing as much as painting. It is taking calligraphy one stage further.

In effect, instead of writing the Chinese character for a mountain, cloud, human, fir tree, they paint the symbolic character for this, which bears a rough resemblance to it, but whose main weight is the fact that the audience will read it as a symbol.

A mountain stands for many things in Chinese thought – power, closeness to heaven, a retreat from the world, a closeness to nature, it is semi-sacred and evokes a romantic devotion as it did for the English Lakeland poets or, later, Welsh poets. In short, we have to realize that paintings are poems, they are not dumb, and that poems are paintings, they are not deaf. Hence the great passion for both art forms in China today, as in the past.

Canals and waterways

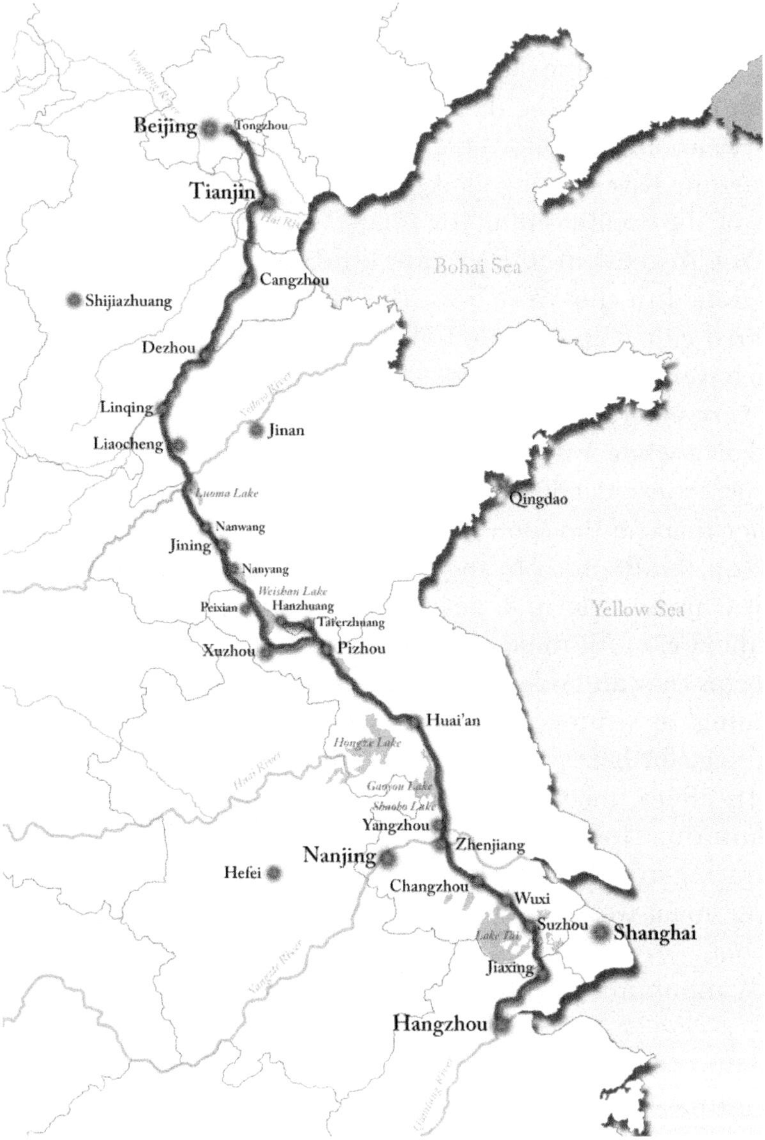

The Grand Canal

Alongside the Great Wall, the Grand Canal is the other wonder of engineering of early China. The oldest parts date back to the fifth century BC but the various sections were connected in the Sui dynasty (581-618 AD). It is over a thousand miles long and has many locks on it. It is often crossed by other rivers, small and large, in complex aqueducts. It is wide enough for boats to travel in both directions at the same time. It was constructed principally to carry gains and other goods from the rich south to the colder but politically powerful north.

In recent years there has been a growing water crisis in the north, especially in the vastly expanded mega-city of Beijing which has more than twenty million legally registered inhabitants, and many others who are not registered. Beijing has been running out of water and I heard dire predictions ten years ago. Now the natural flow of the Canal has been reversed and the canal has been turned into a water-carrying pipeline from the huge rivers of central China to the north.

Of course, the Grand Canal is only one of innumerable waterways in China. Many older Chinese cities feel somewhat like Venice – canals running through the backed-up housing with the famous moon-shaped bridges frequently crossing them. Suzhou city in the south is one of the more famous of these canal cities and on some of the canals there is still a lot of activity, even with night-soil boats still collecting refuse.

The canals of his hometown of Haining were echoed in the river/canal of the Cam when Xu Zhimo the famous Chinese poet spent time there and wrote his most famous poem 'On Saying Goodbye to Cambridge', filled with the sights and sounds of canal life, the water weeds and willows and birds.

Canals were, alongside the rivers, a central part of Chinese economic and social life. The roads were often very difficult to use, being rocky, rutted, crossing innumerable mountain ridges and fast flowing rivers. The waterways took a huge burden off land transport. Yet they also had their own burdens. For while much of the pulling of boats in England was by horses, the effort of moving the millions of ships up and down the waterways of China was mainly done by human labour. Long teams of strong men, called trackers, dragged the boats up the foaming rivers, straining every muscle as they scrambled over the slippery rocks and moved along the high and precarious walkways. Others pulled or punted the boats up the canals and crossed the huge lakes of China.

Finally, canals, rivers and lakes were a source of one of China's main source of protein – fish. Fishing with nets, cormorants, and damming the rivers was a central occupation and no Chinese feast would be complete without a large fish.

Change - patterns of

I have had the good fortunate to live on an island which has evolved through the centuries without any major tragic disruptions, that is invasions or large revolutions. Unlike all Continental European countries, England has not been invaded for nearly one thousand years (apart from, in a minor way, the Scots in 1715). Its language, law, economy, polity, society has not been deeply damaged by another race or nation.

Nor has England gone through any dramatic social or political revolution in the last thousand years. Only the English Civil War of the mid seventeenth century and the temporary replacing of the King by Oliver Cromwell might have been such a change. Yet Cromwell died and the King returned and the event was a half-successful rebellion, modifying things significantly but not overthrowing the previous structures.

For these reasons, I think of my country's history as like the growth of a tree, from its Anglo-Saxon roots and young trunk, becoming ever larger and more complex, but basically never challenged.

When I look at China I find something unfamiliar. China is characterized by periods, sometime as long as three or four centuries, of peace and order and then a cataclysmic eruption.

Lin Yutang has seen a repeated pattern of cycles in Chinese

history which gives us a general shape for the last several thousand years. It is an intriguing suggestion, as follows.

> For the striking fact is that Chinese history can be conveniently divided into cycles of eight hundred years. Each cycle begins with a short-lived and militarily strong dynasty, which unified China after centuries of internal strife. Then follow four or five hundred years of peace, with one change of dynasty, succeeded by successive waves of wars, resulting soon in the removal of the capital from the North to the South. Then came secession and rivalry between North and South with increasing intensity, followed by subjugation under a foreign rule, which ended the cycle. History then repeats itself and with the unification of China again under Chinese rule, there is a new bloom of culture... [13]

Childrearing

In my English infancy, childhood and adolescence, I had experienced and come to assume a certain distancing pattern. From early photographs I can see that I was placed in a separate cot from birth, put in a wooden cage or playpen, encouraged to be as independent as possible. By the age of four or five at the latest, I was an independent person, and at the age of eight I was sent away to boarding school. From then on, though I loved my parents, they were becoming strangers. As I reached my late teens and twenties my parents became friends and equals. The bond was still strong, but only because they had shown so much love and support.

Both my parents and I were aware that I was likely to fall in love, marry, and have children. My first and deepest attachment would be to my wife and children, my parents would be secondary.

One of the shocks I received when I went to Japan was to learn of the *amae* or mother-son complex. This was Freud's

[13] Lin Yutang, *My Country and My People* (Chinese 1998 edn), 28

Oedipal love of son for mother, but on a far more intense scale. It started at birth, for babies were not put in a separate cot or room, but slept until perhaps five or six with their parents. The children were never put on the earth, but carried on their mother's or sibling's backs all the time. They were breast-fed until the next child came along – often until seven or eight. All this made the mother-child, and especially mother-son, the strongest bond in a person's life.

My preliminary observations suggest that China is not as extreme as Japan, but is very different from my experience. Children often sleep in the shared bed, especially if this was the traditional heated *kang*. They were not sent away to school to board, or, if they were, this did not break the bond with their parents.

It is clear that the traditional Confucian family system assumed that the vertical bond – of children with their parents – as in the duration of mourning, or punishments for family violence, made the vertical relationship far more important. The vertical bond with parents was traditionally perhaps twice as strong as the lateral one with a wife or husband. Those born were regarded foremost as grandchildren rather than children. The daughter-in-law could be dismissed by her mother-in-law at her pleasure. Children never separated psychologically from their parents and were not able to treat them as equals, as friends.

The huge dislocations of the attack on the family during the period of Mao's leadership of the Communist party, the one-child policy, the fragmentation of life through migration of the young to the cities, has eroded all this. My young friends are more independent. Yet all of them maintain, or feel they should maintain, a much closer relationship with their parents than I experienced. My young married Chinese female friends invite their mothers or mothers-in-law to live for long periods with them, sometimes to help with babies, sometimes just out of responsibility and for companionship.

Another of my young Chinese friends has a very strong,

if ambivalent, relationship with her mother. She both craves her support and advice and feels deeply attached, but as an emancipated young lady who has tasted the West, she also resents it when her mother tries to take control of her life

In sum, the English, and that includes Americans, are unusual in turning children into equal and potential friends. Normally, and here India and Japan join China, you remain a child to your parents until they die. You never become a fully independent adult to them. And to you they remain your responsibility, your shield and your anchor.

Chopsticks

I was brought up in a civilisation where food was eaten with knife, fork and spoon. I did not know that parts of this arrangement were only about five hundred years old, nor, unless I dimly remembered my childhood in India, did I think about the fact that the majority of the human race did not eat in this way. It seemed natural, if a little awkward. I was taught that the way I ate with these utensils defined my class position – eating peas with a knife, or leaving the utensils in a certain way at the end of the meal would be strong signals.

When I went to do fieldwork in a Himalayan village, my wife and I tried to continue to eat with a knife and fork as a way of clinging to our western identity. All around us, everyone ate with their hands, also an art in itself, in the manner which was far more 'natural' than fork and knife. All over India, Africa and elsewhere, one eats with one's hands, washing them before and after the meal and being careful to use the right hand, avoiding the left hand which is used for toilet purposes.

When I went to Japan in 1990 I encountered the other equally popular form of eating, with chopsticks, which covers another third of mankind. Here I was kindly offered knives and forks in friends' houses and restaurants, but I quickly realised, as I did in

Nepal, that it is only gracious, and much appreciated, if one eats in the native way. If one can master the art, which, like riding a bicycle, cannot be formally taught but becomes an easy habit with practice, then one's hosts will be really happy.

I also discovered that chopsticks were perfect for picking at the special kind of Japanese/Chinese food. In England, I was used to things that needed to be cut up, particularly meat, but also tough vegetables, and puddings and soups need a spoon. In China, the meat is already cut into small pieces before it reaches the table, fried in oil and spices, and, in wealthier settings, served in many dishes. Vegetables are also cut into small bits.

You do not need a knife and indeed, as potentially offensive weapons, they were, my friend Gerry Martin told me from his early trips to Hong Kong in the 1970's, banned. He spent much time trying to find a knife. Only certain butchers were allowed them.

Chopsticks are, in fact, a nice compromise between the hand-eating world, where there is more danger of contamination of food and some feel uncomfortable by the stickiness, and the elaborate fork-knife-spoon western system. There are downsides to chopsticks. Vast stretches of forest have been felled to produce them, though plastic is now starting to replace wood. And there is careful etiquette: the chopsticks for personal use and those for lifting food from the communal bowls are different. Yet there is something graceful and rational about extending one's fingers by means of artificial claws, which is what chopsticks are.

Cities

There is a wonderful book on imagined cities of all kinds in China at the time of Marco Polo by Italo Calvino, *Invisible Cities* (1972). Sadly the truth is not quite as delightful as his fantasy. I discovered this as we started to travel through the vast cities of China, many of them larger or on a par with London or New York. They all seem now to look much the same at first acquaintance – huge boulevards and malls in the centre, numerous roads and ring roads, then mile after mile of enormous, twenty-plus floor, tower blocks. Thousands of these stretch as far as the eye can see as you drive out of Beijing, Tianjin, Shanghai, Chengdu, Guangzhou or elsewhere.

You might think that this uniformity is recent, overlaying the variation in city architecture you find across Europe, from the jumbled, contorted and winding cities of England, through the highly planned baroque cities of parts of France and Spain, to the walled and winding cities of Italy. In fact, learning about the history of cities in East and West, I now see some of the reasons for the basic uniformity in China and the different feel one has in London or Beijing, Florence or Chengdu.

In *The City*, Max Weber distinguished three major forms of city, which reflected their functions. The separate and fully functional city, where entering the city, according to the proverb, made men free, was only to be found in northern Europe and Britain. Here the cities were commercial centres, seats of government, legal entities with their own rules and self-government, perhaps military centres.

In the ordering of society, the bourgeois or city dwellers stood traditionally alongside the nobility/rulers, the church and the peasants as one of the four major estates of the land. They were proud and independent.

The second form was to be found in southern Europe, where the degree of autonomous legal power and self-government was much reduced, though there were periods and places, such as the time of the Italian city states, where cities were total worlds, with walls and self-government.

The third kind of city, Weber suggested, covered the rest of the world, from the Islamic and Indian cities through to China. Here a city was basically a fortified, densely populated area where the government kept troops and it was used for administrative purposes. There might be markets and some manufacture. Yet the city had little autonomy. There was no strong guild or local self-government, no powerful group of ruling burghers administering a special law. They were geographical rather than social and political entities and they had little power against other forces, particularly the Emperor of Khan.

If you had travelled through China over most of the last thousand years you would have found vast cities, for example Hangzhou in the twelfth century was the largest in the world. And they might be fabulously wealthy and some, like the Venice of the East, Suzhou, had areas of great beauty. Yet in terms of power and society they were not separated off. Citizens had no special powers or privileges, the cities had no particular power in relation to the Emperor.

In this way we can think of China as the greatest urban civilisation in history. Both in the past, and increasingly today, as millions pour into the city from the countryside and there are at least four cities with reputed populations of over 25 million, it is a great city civilisation. Yet also we can think of it as hardly a city civilisation at all in the way we know.

This is not to say that Chines cities with their absence of the old community bonds of the countryside are in any way ungoverned or chaotic. It constantly amazes me in my travels through small towns turning into cities, to small cities becoming mega-cities, how orderly they are. How is the vast planning, building and operation of all that transportation, sewage and electricity, done?

It is in its way a miracle – a new London is being created every few months. China's urban population today is 810 million, well over half of the total Chinese population. It has been a huge change from 1978 when only 170 million Chinese lived in cities. It is the largest rapid urbanisation in recorded history. Yet this has been achieved with apparently little disruption. On the whole, the Chinese cities I have visited are clean, efficient and, though thin on parks in most cities, quite comfortable. They may shock a westerner from a low-rise country like England, yet they are undoubtedly extraordinary. Perhaps, after all, Calvino's world can be found again, in the all too visible cities of China, as wondrous, in another way, as his fantasy cities of the past.

Clash or harmony of civilisations

The idea of *The Clash of Civilisations* was popularised by the American international relations expert and sometime architect of America's plan to carpet-bomb Vietnam to drive the peasants into towns, Samuel P. Huntington. His confrontational article of that title, with a question mark at the end, was turned into a book without the question mark and published in 1996. Although it is not openly stated, America's current aggressive-defensive attitude to the world is largely based on Huntington.

Huntington advocated the building of physical walls and visa barriers to prevent immigration, for one of his three main enemies was multi-culturalism. His other two main targets were 'Islam', which he regarded as a single doctrine, and China. In relation to the latter he wrote a chapter to work out whether it was still possible to attack and destroy China before it overtook America. He concluded that it was indeed, even in the 1990's, too late. War with conventional weapons would end in a stalemate and nuclear weapons would blow up both countries.

Instead he recommended indirect attacks, arming China's enemies from without and supporting dissident movements from within. He did not focus, as I recall, on President Trump's preferred method, a trade war, including banning Chinese investment in America.

Huntington's views are, of course, part of an age-old western tendency to see the world as a battle between the godly - Us - and the heathens/pagans and those allied to Satan - Them. It is implicit in much missionary work and in aspects of the European imperial expansion into India, Africa and South America. It sees the world as a meeting place for great conflicting forces, material and ideological. Life is seen as a battle between Good and Evil, Truth and Falsehood, Democracy and Dictatorship, Freedom and Bondage, Capitalism and Communism.

The Chinese vision from the time of Confucius onwards has been different. It recognises that there is inevitably difference, opposition, tension in life between competing peoples and ideas. Yet the task of the individual and the state is to bring these oppositions into alignment. Although it does not draw on the western idea of the dialectic of Thesis, Antithesis and Synthesis, it is like that.

Often put in terms of the idea of the Golden Mean, the choice of a path which treads between extremes, and which tries to combine the best of alternative views, it is the synthesis of conflict. It believes that differences cannot and should not be suppressed, but, as with musical harmony, the different instruments or voices should be brought into alignment.

Interestingly such a view, which stresses mutual respect, tolerance, collaboration and cooperation rather than one side vanquishing and destroying the other, is quite akin to that of the first great theorist of capitalist economics, Adam Smith. As a moral philosopher, he believed that humans are subject to a never-ending tension between self-love, selfishness, Darwinian survival and egotism, and social love, kindness, the desire to love and be loved, mutual collaboration. The trick is to find the Golden Mean between these extremes.

This Golden Mean operates not just at the individual level, but also the level of the State. One should recognize that it is not altruism, but self-love, which drives the butcher or baker to sell his goods, it is self-love, the decision to engage in profitable marketing and haggling and competition which makes for the energy of capitalism.

Yet Smith also realized the vital fact that it is not a zero-sum game. When an individual or State transacts with another, both gain. It is not a war but a constructive and collaborative effort. Good trade benefits everyone. The division of labour, central to growing wealth, necessitates individual and States to lay down some of their narrow short-term desires in pursuit of larger goals

Smith saw that the wealth of Scotland and all of Britain arose out of people working in harmony. He saw the enormous positive effects of trade on Glasgow and the trade could also benefit the peoples with whom the British traded. So it is not a zero-sum-game.

What was true of Smith's age, on the eve of the industrial revolution, with a world population of about three quarters of a billion, with slow and expensive communications, is more true in our globalised and inter-connected world. The unconscionable view that we can go back to a war of all against all, where the most powerful will benefit from crushing its friends and foes, never worked and is clearly irrational nowadays

As in love, when we give we receive, and when we receive we give. The Confucian-Smith vision is the only one which will avoid world disaster. Even Huntington realised it is too late for America to directly crush every rival. In fact, all it has to do is to think of these rivals as its partner and the problems go away.

Clocks

One of the puzzles which faced me as I started to learn about China was why, having been at the forefront of time measurement about eight hundred years ago, China gave up its lead and handed the baton over to Europe.

One part of the story revolves around the great clock built by the polymath Su Song (1020-1101) (mathematician, astronomer, cartographer, horologist, medical doctor, pharmacologist, mineralogist, zoologist, botanist, mechanical and architectural engineer, poet, antiquarian and ambassador). This was a magnificent device, as the picture shows.

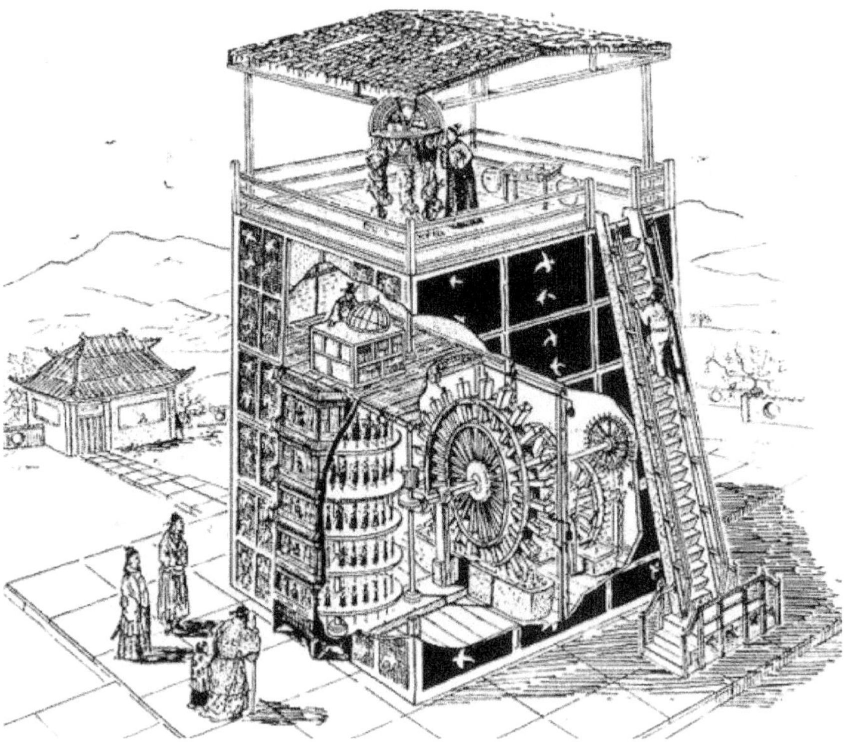

The escapement mechanism of Su's clock tower had been invented by the Buddhist monk Yi Xing and government official Liang Lingzan in 725 AD to operate a water-powered armillary sphere. Su's armillary sphere was the first with a mechanical clock drive. Su's clock tower also featured the oldest known endless power-transmitting chain drive, called the "celestial ladder", as depicted in his horological treatise and 133 different clock jacks to indicate and sound the hours.

In China the clock was dismantled by the invading Jurchen army in 1127 AD and never successfully reinstated. If such a break-through as this clock had been made in the West it would have been widely reproduced, copied and improved over the centuries. Though there the process started later, possibly derived from China, there was rapid progress from the first great clocks down to the elegant and accurate watches which, by the late seventeenth century, were amazing the Chinese when they were brought over by the Jesuits and which fill the museums of the Qing Emperors.

Yet Su Sung's clock was abandoned, the parts lost as described above, even though a manual on how it was made survived. Reasons for this difference are multiple, including the absence of a need for clocks in a basically agrarian civilisation in China, the absence of competing cities and nations, each keen to develop technology, the secrecy surrounding inventions in China, and the cost.

Yet whatever the reasons, it is a revealing story about Chinese knowledge. And it is all the more astonishing when we look at what is happening in China today. There is daily improvement in technologies of all kinds and the whole of China can be seen as one integrated, huge, clockwork machine, even more impressive than Su Sung's clock itself.

Clubs and associations

Clubs and associations are central to all our lives in the West and my experience through boarding schools and then a life in universities has made them particularly central. I knew this also through my study of history and political philosophy, which showed that the voluntary groups which they denote were the core of Anglo-American civilisation and that associational life has been at the heart of England for over half a millenium.

I knew this, but I only realised its full force when I went first to Japan and then to China as a visiting academic. I immediately asked to be shown the university common rooms, the students clubs, the numerous associations. I was told that they hardly existed. They were either absent, or very weak. The great Fukuzawa Yukichi had recognized their importance in the West and introduced a fairly succesful Gentlemen's Club, the Kojunsha, in Tokyo. It was not copied.

I was used to the idea that if you had mutual interests and wanted to share and pursue them, you set up or joined a club, economic, political, religious, sporting or educational, to help you pursue this. Individual citizens are too weak to achieve much on their own, but if they band together then can achieve a lot.

The club or association is set up by private individuals without a government charter for it is not a licensed corporation. You are elected to membership and can be ejected. It has premises, assets such as a library, sports ground or eating place. It makes you feel part of a larger group, but still free. It has a name and bank account, it has rules and officials. It is the backbone of English sport, art, education, politics and economic activity. Its importance is recognised by Francis Hsu when he chose one word to denote China, India and America, and called his book *Kin, caste and club*.

This title also provides one of the reasons why I have found so little associationalism in China, though there is a surprising growth of virtual, semi-autonomous, associationalism on the internet. This is the word 'Kin' in Hsu's title. Chinese philosophy, for example, that of Confucius, envisioned only two actors – the individual master of a family and the State. Confucius would have liked Margaret Thatcher's famous comment – 'There is no such thing as Society'. There is nothing outside the ties of kinship, membership of a geographical unit, usually a village, and the abstract ties to the Emperor. So there is no space for associations.

This appears to be one of the most interesting areas to watch in changing China. Given the experience of associations, of a quasi-religious kind, which have always been suppressed in Chinese history, the Party is wary of organisations which appear to give people an autonomous strength independent of the state. In this they share the view of most civilisations. Up to the end of the nineteenth century throughout Europe all clubs had to be approved by the government. If you wanted to hold a meeting of more than a dozen people in France you needed a police licence.

This continues in Russia and much of the Middle East today. It continues on Chinese campuses where all student clubs have to be licensed by the university and are strictly controlled. It might seem also to be the case in British universities. In Cambridge, a student club which is recognised as a university club, and hence given support and official status, has to be registered. Yet there is nothing against people setting up informal, non-registered clubs.

The question is open as to whether China will be able to embrace associationalism. It was found essential in the West where the family is weak and fragmented, where people are highly mobile and individualistic. Now that China has espoused many of the institutions of the West, where the family is also fragmented, where religious, caste or class do not provide effective groupings, it would seem obvious that Chinese lawyers and politicians should investigate the associational principle. The huge benefit in giving meaning and self-determination to the mass of people's lives could be incorporated into the ancient hierarchical and centralized system of China.

The Chinese have been so innovative and flexible in incorporating most of the apparently incompatible institutions of capitalism, that it could not seem to be beyond their capacity to do the same with civil society.

Colours

The classification and symbolism of colours is diametrically opposed as between China and the western world in which I grew up. I first started to notice this when I heard the anthropologist Edmund Leach talking about how his time in China had shocked him, in particular when he realized that the colours of life and death were reversed. In China, white is the colour of death, whereas black is the colour of death in the West.

One of my own shocks was when I was learning a Chinese-derived Tibeto-Burman language in the Himalayas and became intrigued to find that there were no separate words for blue and green. When I pointed to the sky, the Gurungs said that it was 'pingya'. When I pointed at the grass, they said 'pingya'. I quickly ascertained that this was not some kind of colour blindness. The Gurungs could see the difference perfectly well. Yet their colour classifications did not distinguish the two colours.

My own system has four primary colours, red, yellow, green and blue. It does not count black and white as colours in themselves, but rather as absence of colour. The Chinese recognize black and white as colours, but also have three other primary colours, red, yellow and *qing*, a conflation of the ideas of blue and green. This is interesting from all sorts of angles.

One is that it privileges the red-yellow (gold) end of the spectrum. In China, gold is the imperial colour, in Japan it is red, while in Britain the royal colour is at the blue end of the spectrum, namely purple. The fact that a near-sighted person (myopic) sees the red end of the spectrum much better, and the readers/writers of Chinese characters become short-sighted through eye strain, seem somehow connected to this.

Another aspect is the symbolism of colour. Anthropologists

have done much work on colour associations. Victor Turner, for example, suggested that in his African group the three-fold colour classification, of brown, red and white, was related to the importance of faeces, blood and semen – three bodily substances. Be that as it may, what do the Chinese associate with their colours?

I know that black and white are pivotal in the yin-yang oppositions. Black is night, female, left, nature, emotion. White is day, male, culture, reason and so on. Thus if you include black or white into artistic representations it has numerous associations, as Junichiro Tanizaki showed in the related Japanese system in his book *In Praise of Shadows*.

In China, an early book to mention the symbolism of colours was in the third century BC, the Huai Nan Zi, a book on astronomy and geography. Local folk books from the first century B.C. through to the seventh century AD also give a full description of colours.

The final book in the seventh century was 'The Five Circulation', taken from the *i Ching* idea, which follows the associations in the chart I have under 'Elements' elsewhere, as follows:

Yellow/earth/the only person who could use yellow was the emperor
Blue/east/spring/ young life/energy
Red/south/summer/ happiness/ prosperity
White/autumn/west/ recession/sorrow/death
Black/north/winter/serious/formal/dawn and start of new life.

The Emperor's palace up to two thousand years ago was black/formal/serious; since the first century the ceiling was yellow, the walls were red. Thus the Palace Museum in Beijing has roof bricks of yellow, while the walls and pillars are red. Only the Emperor used yellow roof tiles, while senior officials had green roofs.

All this is part of the five-stage circular system because it moves round the elements: wood-fire-ash-soil-new plants (wood), just as it moves round the colours. In the middle, around which they circle, is the Emperor who can communicate with Tien (heaven), and hence directs the seasons and the elements.

Confrontation and harmony

I was brought up in a very confrontational culture. As a young child I played with toy soldiers, tigers and lions, pretend guns and bows and arrows, competitive games with balls and bats. I learnt that life was a struggle, a battle, an ongoing 'survival of the fittest'. This home life of confrontation became much more pronounced when I went to boarding school. Playground games such as 'conkers' and marbles, school games of football, cricket, hockey and rugger, athletics, swimming, boxing and other sports, all were based on winners and losers. Playful battles taught us to outwit and overcome others, which was also emphasised in our class-work.

Even our conversation was full of teasing and sometimes bullying. And our Christian religion had hymns such as 'Onward Christian Soldiers' and the idea of a constant battle against Evil and Satan. As we began to learn of the history of Britain we heard of endless battles and wars both within and against foreign enemies. We were taught that English law was based on argument and confrontation, as was the political system where the two main parties were constantly arguing and disagreeing and trying to outwit the other.

I came to assume that confrontations, battle, struggle was the basis of life. I learnt that my society was held together not by love, but by competition – Conservatives against Labour, God versus the Devil, Oxford versus Cambridge and many other binary oppositions. We were joined by the differences and the struggle.

It was therefore a shock to go to Japan, where there was an emphasis on harmony and Confucian ethics. Yet Japan also had a contrary streak, the Chrysanthemum, but also the Sword, as in the title of Ruth Benedict's book. There was a fierce warrior tradition and the samurai were an armed military elite. Fighting was also important.

The shock was greater in China. There I have found a vast civilisation whose prime ethical directive is the promotion of mutual respect, peacefulness, bringing contraries into alignment rather than emphasizing them. The population were forbidden to carry arms, there was no armed warrior class, there were few competitive team games.

What held and holds China together is the ordering of life so that all potential conflicts are minimized. Respect and mutual responsibilities, calmness and acceptance, reason and practical solutions are all important.

This is not to say that there is no violence. In China in the past, there has been a fierce criminal code and frequent bloody uprisings, so there is plenty of physical conflict. Likewise, for thousands of years, there has been a battle between the Han of the plains and the ethnic minorities on all the landward borders, as well as the neighbouring states of Vietnam, Thailand, Burma, Russia and Korea.

Yet the ideal is peace and harmony. Life is not seen as a zero sum game where I can only succeed if I put you down. Society is held together by mutual needs and mutual endeavour. A son needs a father, and vice versa. A subject needs an Emperor and vice versa. Bringing ourselves into alignment with each other, and with the spirits and the natural world is the goal.

As I look back on the disastrous and violent history of my western world and the model of continuous struggle that lies behind it, I must say that I find the dream of harmony central to Buddhism, Daoism and Confucianism very attractive. In our incredibly interdependent and integrated world, we cannot afford to go on with our warlike ways. China's inspiration towards something more peaceful is welcome and timely.

Confucius

I am used to the idea that much of my life is shaped by great thinkers who lived two and a half thousand years ago. I know that the sayings and actions of Jesus have altered all aspects of my life, from morality to art. I know that the ideas of Plato and Aristotle, of Homer and Pythagoras, still condition the way I think and act and I know that this is the case with the Buddha or the Prophet Mohamed for their followers.

Yet there several distinctive features of the huge legacy of Confucius which make it essential to understand a little of his thought if we are to understand China today.

One concerns the force of his memory. In daily life, people still constantly refer to the wisdom of Confucius as if he had lived yesterday, even more than, today, the sayings of Jesus or Aristotle are in the West. There are Confucius temples and endless commentaries. Children learn his thoughts at school again, after a period under Mao when he was suppressed. He is like a father to the country, always at people's shoulders, not dead but alive. I realized this when I stood as part of the crowd celebrating Confucius' birthday at his birth place in Shandong Province, or when I visit Confucius temples dotted round China.

The most important feature is the content of his sayings and stories, and those of Mencius and other later interpreters. One is the idea of the Golden Mean, namely that the middle way, the absence of extremes, of fanaticism of any kind, should be pursued. Listen to both sides of an argument and then take the best of both and create a middle track. The effort of China today to try to find a middle way between western, individualist, scientific, capitalism and the ancient traditions of China, combining the best in a new form, is an example of this.

A second key idea, related to the above, is the prime goal of harmony. Harmony does not mean uniformity, absence of difference. It means, as in music, notes which are different in pitch, but do not jar with each other. Hence the harmony of nations does not mean that China has to be the same as America, or the reverse. It means that they are in tune, they strengthen each other by a form of integration through working by the same scale or set or rules.

A third central idea is of innate respect and difference of status. The five important relations of Confucianism are parent-child, husband and wife, elder sibling and junior sibling, elder friend and junior friend and ruler and subject. In each case you are born into the relation and you cannot alter it. In each case it gives the superior immensely more power, though this is combined with the duty of benevolence and protection. So the father can do anything with his children, and likewise the husband and Emperor. This code naturally sticks in the throat of western individualists who believe in the natural equality of humans.

Yet the code, when added to Confucius' joining of the family hierarchy to the State hierarchy in a series of powerful analogies, so your father is your Emperor, your husband is your Emperor, and your Emperor is your father, is immensely powerful.

There was, however, one unresolved tension in what strikes outsider as a recipe for total submission bordering on totalitarianism: if you were confronted by a clash between your allegiance to your father and to the Emperor, the father came first. This mean that if the Emperor ordered you to kill your father, and you felt this unjust, you should not do so.

Conservatism

Throughout my education I was encouraged to take risks, to be ambitious, to try new things, to be creative and inventive. Much of my formal learning put an emphasis on risk and creativity and this increased as I reached sixth form and university. The same strategy, to stand out by doing something unusual, unexpected, counter-intuitive and inventive, was central to the huge part of my life spent in games, play and hobbies of all kinds.

My culture seemed to place a premium on the quirky, the non-conformist, the English eccentric, the surprising element in culture and behaviour. This has continued through my career both in my teaching of students, who are reward for their risk-taking and creativity, and in always feeling free in my own lecturing or writing to do new things, to go against a trend, to throw over old ways if they hampered.

All this made me assume that such a creative, innovative, non-conservative approach was normal. Then I went to Japan and was constantly told that 'the protruding nail is hammered down', that the old ways should not be attacked, that to stand out in any way is dangerous. There were elements of risk-taking and many great writers and reformers such as Fukuzawa Yukichi are another side to this. Yet I began to see another world.

In China, there are huge pressures against risk-taking. Traditional Chinese education for centuries inculcated respect for the old ways, rewarding conformity and obedience to authority. The authority of the ancients, of one's teachers, of one's parents, of the Emperor.

The administrative system in the past made any kind of innovation or departure from custom dangerous. If something went wrong and one had not followed the approved and traditional methods, then a mandarin or other official would be severely punished. I have discussed this frequently with current government employees and they still feel the pressure from above, which they pass on to those below them, not to take risks. The absence of innate human rights or civil or criminal courts which would protect the individual from arbitrary punishment led, over the centuries, to constant wariness and insecurity.

Custom

The first great book on the English legal system was Sir Henry de Bracton's thirteenth century *On the Laws and Customs of England*. We may wonder why both 'law' and 'custom' were needed in the title, for surely law includes custom. In fact, in England, they were separate and equal. Laws were the general rules, often made by Parliament, which applied to all. There might be a law that property goes to one child, but local custom determined whether this should be the first or last born. Law states that there should be support for the poor of a village, but custom suggests how this is done.

Such a system has the great advantage of providing a general, agreed, framework which unites a whole country, alongside a flexibility for different communities to run their own lives, to decide on the many details appropriate to them. Thus the customs of those living in the mountains will be different to those of the plains, of fishermen different from farmers.

Custom tends to apply particularly to culture – to food, dress, housing, language and manners. For example, in Cambridge University, there are university laws relating to disciplines, examinations, enrolment. Yet each College has its own customs of how the meals are arranged, what people wear and the way teaching is done.

I have not come across such a formal distinction in China, though it is bound to exist, for China is a hugely diverse place. So there are national laws set from the centre, but each village or town is bound to have its own traditional ways of doing things. What is different is that in England the customs are a recognized part of the national system and protected by national law, as Bracton's treatise shows, whereas in China the imperial power can override them if it wishes. Custom is thus both enormously important in the huge civilization of China, yet it is unprotected. In many periods in Chinese history, most notably in the Qing imperial period (1644-1912), the customs and rules of the central administration were very different from that of the majority of the population.

In the British case it was a distinction which was also central to the swift development of a huge Empire. In each new place Britain conquered, the laws of England were applied universally. These mainly concerned property and the preservation of peace. They were not concerned with local customs. So, as long as you kept to the laws, it was up to you in Burma, India or Africa what you did in your customary life – your food, religion, family life. Hence there could be uniformity with tolerance. It is a model which China may find interesting as it continues to face its ancient problem of unity with diversity.

D

Disasters

I come from England which, over the centuries, has been mercifully free from 'natural' disasters. It has been largely free of earthquakes, there are no volcanoes or tsunami, there are no swarms of locusts or terrible sand storms. In particular, it has mostly been free of the three 'natural' disasters which, for thousands of years, have killed millions of Chinese. These are the three scourges starting with 'F', namely flood, fire and famine.

Although English rivers still flood to this day, and the sea likewise sometimes surges inland, most recently in 1953 in East Anglia when 307 people were killed, the flooding is usually mild in its effects with a few hundred or a thousand or so homes flooded.

In contrast, the three great rivers of China, especially the northernmost Yellow River, were notorious for their uncontrollable floods. A great deal of Chinese effort was put into trying to mitigate this and over two thousand years ago, the Chinese became the greatest hydraulic engineers in history.

Yet against the sudden melting of the central Asian ice or heavy downpours of rain, there was frequently nothing which people could do to prevent the flooding. The result was that great cities, sometimes with over a million inhabitants, were completely destroyed – sometimes again and again – and vast areas of arable land were inundated with water. Whole civilizations were swept away and the great floods continued, with a relatively recent one in 1931 killing between half a million and three million people. Vulnerability and fear of death and loss of crops was ever-present.

Fire was another ever-present danger. Of course, there have been serious fires in British history, for example the Great Fire of London in 1666. Yet by Asian standards this was a very small fire – some 70,000 homes were destroyed and there were only six verified deaths. Partly because the British building materials incorporated a good deal of stone and slate, partly because the towns were small and spread apart, partly because cooking was often done in stoves and not open fires, and partly because early measures were taken to cordon off fires, the risk from fires seems to have been less acute in Britain. This is reflected in the fact that the British developed effective fire insurance schemes from the end of the seventeenth century onwards.

We can see proof of the absence of recurrent fires in the fact that many central parts of towns and villages throughout England preserve a large numbers of buildings, or parts of buildings, going back to the fifteenth century and earlier.

China and Japan are very different. In the latter, a great Japanese city like Tokyo or Osaka burnt down, section by section, every seven years on average. The same is true of great Chinese cities, for they were basically similar: very crowded, built of highly combustible wood, bamboo and paper, filled with open fires on which people cooked. It is hardly possible to find old streets and builds in China dating back more than a few years. For example, the historic city of Lijiang has been burnt to the ground several times recently, with the most recent fire which destroyed the old centre dating to 2014.

The Japanese invented a device for fire-proofing their storage houses filled with precious possessions. The Chinese, knowing that the prevailing wind was from the north-west, built a slightly separate storage area in that part of their courtyard since it would be less likely to be burnt down if a fire started in the house. What is certain is that there was no insurance system in China which, given the widespread fires, would have been prohibitively expensive.

The third 'F' is 'famine'. It has been calculated that a famine occurred somewhere in China every year over many centuries, though there has been no famine reported in China in the last fifty years. Like India, China is one of the most terribly famine-ravaged countries. The mono-cropping, the instability of the weather, especially drought, the poor communications, the fact that many families were very poor with few reserves, the long distances from the sea (which in England offered alternative emergency food and supplies by boat) as well as the dense population which destroyed much of the forest and over-fished the rivers, were all factors in causing famine.

The results were appalling. For example, the terrible northern famine of 1876-9 led to the deaths of between nine and thirteen million people in a total population of 108 million. In the worst province, Shanxi, five and a half million out of a total fifteen million are thought to have died.

The cause of this devastating famine seems to have been prolonged drought, though the aftershock of general disorder from the Taiping rebellion of ten years earlier also contributed. This recent famine compares with the last famine in the U.K.—the terrible Irish famine of 1851 in which potatoes became diseased, leading to a million deaths out of a total population of a little over eight million.

It is very difficult to imagine the effects that a perennial threat of famine might have. The English, with no national famine since 1315, were so far from this state of affairs, that they were bound to be shocked by what they found in China, even though they saw the terrible realities in India and Ireland.

More generally it is really difficult for me, brought up in a land of relative plenty and economic stability, to imagine how such terrible disasters, recurring time and again through history, would affect me. Obviously, they would cause me to emphasise caution, conservatism, hard work and investing in my family as the only slight protection against disaster. This level of anxiety and threat was a different world to the comparative affluence and security which China has built up over the last forty years. The change must feel like an extraordinary miracle for many Chinese, though one that cannot be taken for granted.

Divination

Whereas the very earliest Western writing systems seem to have been invented for economic purposes, to record exchanges and trade and perhaps tax, the earliest Chinese writing was developed for semi-religious reasons: oracle bones used for divination, the earliest being from about 1200 BC. This reveals the different orientation from which these two ends of the Eurasian continent started.

In my own experience as an English person, divination – namely a system using physical signs to read the future – has always been located at the fringe of my life. My grandmother sometimes looked into the tea cups at the shape of the leaves and taught me how to divine the imminent arrival of a tall, dark, handsome stranger or some impending disaster. Early on, I was taught to read a few of the natural signs in the countryside such as magpies ('One for sorrow, two for joy, three for a girl, four for a boy....'). Numerous popular divination techniques are chronicled in Keith Thomas' *Religion and the Decline of Magic* (1971) and they show that, for centuries, certain signs were understood to be lucky or unlucky. Horoscopes were read and the stars were watched; there was always an element of this in England.

Yet it was only when I encountered China that I discovered a world which I had read about in relation to certain African societies, in which divination is central to life. Since the whole of nature, according to Daoist thought, is filled with elementary forces – the winds and waters and many other spiritual creatures – which determine our lives, it makes sense to find out what is happening and establish any causality. This is not like English water-divining to find a hidden well or spring, but rather aims to find the more abstract and elementary movement of forces.

This process is also called geomancy and has been treated in many anthropological and other accounts. I have supervised a Ph.D. on the importance of *feng shui*, or the proper alignment of buildings, and have begun to realize that a vast hidden force of magical and invisible power surrounds the Chinese. If one is not aware of this, one can be caught unawares.

In Japan with its similar beliefs, I was constantly surprised to see Shinto priests conducting rituals and being consulted at the opening of great new buildings and bridges. I was surprised when I was told by a Chinese friend that the prospective shop she was thinking of renting in Cambridge had unlucky *feng shui* and that the misfortune would have to be reversed by a *feng shui* master before the shop could be taken.

One of the earliest Chinese divination books is the famous *i Ching* of the eleventh century B.C. Before this book, the earliest method was to divine with tortoise shells and buffalo shoulder bones. Then a special grass or reed grass was used as in the *i Ching*. From the Tang dynasty coins were used, though much of the earlier knowledge of how to divine had been partly lost by then and folk ways replaced the ancient knowledge.

One method used at this time was to open a book randomly and a character was then chosen and then the diviner examined the meaning of this. Another method was to get a bunch of different sticks, perhaps bamboos with some characters on them, and put them in a container and to choose one.

I have been told that most Chinese still use divination, even if, as in the case of Mao Tse Tung, who used divination in a temple in Shanxi before he became Party Chairman, they are ardent communists. And of course, for millenia, the rulers have used the stars, astrology, to try to forecast the future and make decisions. For example, in 1975 a professional astrologer pointed out that a comet was dying, which portended Mao's death.

A close friend found divination very popular at university less than twenty years ago. The method used involved a rice winnowing tray made of bamboo, piled with sand. A stick was put in the middle and the tray shaken and the stick would write a character, from which divination was made. The 'wizard' would close their eyes and shake it. She said that normally women were wizards. She enquired from the 'pen ghost' whether she would get an M.A. and later a Ph.D., and it predicted this accurately to her satisfaction. She was also warned through divination of a serious law suit which occurred some years later.

Her father has divined for over twenty big company-managers dealing with real estate, using the *i Ching* to forsee the future, and charging over £1000 a time for his work. The clients will have a question but not tell her father, who will examine one of the 64 characters – and will explain what it means. All of the clients said it was very accurate, though the predictions were necessarily vague "things will get better" etc. Several have been promoted, as predicted, one or two are in jail.

Dominant superpower

China was the world's leading superpower until about 1840. For two thousand years it had been the richest, largest and most sophisticated civilisation on earth. Then, from about 1840 to 1940, Britain and its Empire was number one, though in the second half of this period, Britain's dominance was challenged, first by Germany and then US. From the Second World War to the present, the United States of America has been the world's dominant power. In the first half of this period, US superiority was challenged in the Soviet Union and Japan, but since 1989 and the fall of the Soviet Union, and the crushing of the Japanese challenge, the United States has been confident in its position as the only global superpower.

The situation is now in flux and we may be reverting to a period when changes occur in world supremacy. In terms of purchasing power parity (PPP), that is the amount a nation can purchase calibrated to the cost of living, China surpassed the U.S. a few years ago and is the richest nation on earth. If present trends continue, China will surpass the U.S. in absolute Gross Domestic Product within ten years. China is also likely to surpass the U.S. in technology and science, as well as political influence, within the next generation.

The last two great changes in leadership were masked by the confusion of war. Consequently, they were not so visible and perhaps more gradual. The Opium Wars transfer of power from China to Britain, and the change in status that followed the conclusion of the Second World War from British to American supremacy, were not too conspicuous and partly a bi-product of war. The current transformation is discussed interminably and very visible for all to see.

A dominant superpower is unlikely to make way for its rival, especially if it espouses a zero-sum game philosophy, namely that another's gain is its loss, and if it assumes that the rival superpower is motivated by the same hegemonic desires as its own drive to empire. With such assumptions, the struggle may be perceived as one of life and death. At present, there are many discussion in America about how to crush or 'defeat' China before it overtakes America. This problem of the clash when one dominant power is challenged in its position by another is interestingly discussed in Graham Allison's *Destined for War: can America and China escape Thucydides' Trap?* (2017).

In such a context, China has to tread very carefully. When I first travelled to China, the general sentiment about the future were modest and careful. The tradition was that of Deng Hsiao Ping.

The period between about 2000 and 2016 was one of reasonably amicable relations between America and China. China had fifteen years of very rapid growth, protected by a set of modest statements about how China would never catch up with America. In fact, it had no desire to do so, and played the role of the respectful younger brother or junior partner. The changing economic reality was clouded by the woes of the West – the events of 9/11, the wars in Iraq, Afghanistan, Libya, Syria, the economic crash of 2009. As far as America was concerned, the possible threat from China could wait.

Now, however, as the mists lift and a more outspoken China proclaims its ambitious plans to make a vast 'One Belt One Road' system spreading Chinese influence right across Eurasia and even Africa and South America, the Americans are fearful of what they see is being proposed. Other plans, namely to make China number one in artificial intelligence and advanced technologies by 2025, are perceived as an additional threat. The increasingly strong calls for the recognition of China as sovereign over large swathes of the Pacific in the South China Sea is a third worry. If we combine this concern with many internal problems in the U.S. – social, economic and political – there are many reasons that can help to explain why America is on the warpath.

Personally, I feel that the humble approach forwarded by Deng is the right one. It is what one might call the 'Grandmother's Footsteps' approach. Grandmother, in this English game, is very strong, but a bit deaf and with her mind on other things. She stands at the end of the lawn looking into the distance. The children form in a row and then creep towards her. If she hears a sound, she rapidly turns round and any child she sees moving is sent back to the start line. The art is to move very slowly and creep forward, 'softly softly catchee monkey' as the proverb goes. This would be the approach I would adopt if I were China.

China has to realise that whatever it does in the present situation will be interpreted in the worst possible light, attributing to it the Machiavellian and Imperialist goals which lay behind western imperial expansions from the Portuguese and Dutch onwards. It is advisable to be as humble, modest and openly collaborative as possible. As great Chinese generals have known in the past, this is a long game, and calm and seeming inaction on the surface is often the best policy.

E

Earthquakes and floods

I grew up on a quiet little island which has been spared almost all of the cataclysmic 'natural' events that shatter lives and hopes all over the world. I do not, in my daily life, have to worry about earthquakes and tidal waves, typhoons and hurricanes, volcanic eruptions or massive flooding, or even droughts. Nature is calm and rather predictable. A little bit of snow, or high wind or heavy rain, nowadays tend to throw the English into a mild panic and their communications are disrupted by even relatively minor events.

Going to Nepal brought home the lot of most of humanity. The precipitous slopes of the Himalayas were prone to frequent and devastating earthquakes, the rivers could become raging torrents and would sweep away fields and villages, while hail or drought could easily sweep away a year's food supply. Life suddenly appeared precarious and livelihoods vulnerable.

Japan, if anything, was worse. Rocky and precipitous like Nepal, it also suffered more frequent earthquakes (though a terrible one hit Nepal and the edge of the area in which I work in April 2015). I first experienced the giddying feeling of earthquakes in Japan. While they were very unsettling, we were assured they were just minor tremors. Recently we have watched the terrible tsunami and typhoons which constantly batter Japan. All this, I had concluded, helps explain something of the fatalistic, resigned, unsettled nature of Japanese attitudes and philosophy. Life is transitory, death never far away. The Japanese know that we live in a chaotic and unpredictable world, we can just hold on and hope to survive.

The natural world of China is, to a certain extent, in line with Japan. Periodically, there are terrible earthquakes. We were present just after the Sichuan earthquake and we visited the still-raw devastation of shattered schools and villages some six weeks after the event. The coasts of China are struck by terrible typhoons and hurricanes. China is home to some volcanoes, though their effects are less dramatic in relation to China's size than those in Japan.

There are, however, two natural events which have deeply shaped Chinese history and character and both concern rain: too much or too little. As described elsewhere, China is a river civilisation. Its beating blood is pumped down the great rivers, especially the Yangtze, Yellow River, Pearl River and what becomes the Mekong and Salween rivers. The control of these rivers and of the numerous canals have been one of China's greatest achievements. This manipulation of water ways has led to a hydraulic civilisation which led the world. For example, the state of Qin constructed the great flood control system at Dujiangyan, near Chengdu, which I have visited several times and was impressed to see that it is still working to irrigate about two thousand square km of land in the Sichuan plain. It was initially constructed around 256 BC.

Yet these mighty rivers are still not fully controllable and there are still great floods. In the past it was even worse. We were astounded to learn, for example, in the great city and former capital of China, Nanjing, that there were layer after layers of buried cities, covered with mud over the ages. Vast archaeological treasures await excavation here and elsewhere. The floods, as across India, are also what sustains much of the agriculture. Yet the fear of flooding has always been present in the densely populated river valleys.

The contrary fear, of massive droughts, when the rivers dry up and silt, and the wet rice fields in the south and the maize and millet in the north wither and shrivel, are equally great. There have been great droughts in different parts of the vast expanse of China very often. And because of the monoculture and difficulties of communications, millions can die or suffer terrible malnutrition in such events. Much of China, unlike England or Japan, lies far from the sea, hundreds or thousands of miles away, so the back-up of sea products and the ease of communications along the ocean have not been there as a protection for most Chinese over most of history.

Again, I find it difficult to imagine living in a country where natural disasters are never far away. Perhaps they inure you to suffering and make the man-made disasters of war and violence, or the natural disasters of disease, seem less of a shock. Perhaps they explain again the tenacious, tough, resilient temperament, and the floating philosophy with its world of unpredictable forces which geomancy aims to domesticate. It is certainly something that stretches my imagination and needs to be remembered by people who live in less volatile places and climates.

Eating

'The English eat to live, the Chinese live to eat'. This remark summarizes my experience. I come from a country where cooking and eating seems to be again becoming central, having been less important in my youth. 'The Great Bake Off' and cookery programs fill much of television. Restaurants and gastropubs fill many city centres and villages. My life's experience until recently was rather different.

As a child, through the years of rationing after the Second World War and beyond, eating together was fairly marginal. At school and at home, we ate our food speedily and with appreciation, but although communal meals were part of my school, and later, University, life, the joint meal with friends or family was not central to my socializing. Team and other games and hobbies were where major social interactions took place. A puritan culture looked on modesty, restraint, and simplicity in food as a virtue. Though there were one or two special meals, at Christmas or a wedding, on the whole I would never have placed food at the centre of my civilisation. Cricket, drinking tea, reading, hobbies and clubs were the hub, but not communal food.

This view was challenged by experience in Nepal, where

though the food in a mountain village was simple and repetitive, eating together was clearly central to life. You asked people 'Have you eaten?', rather than 'How are you?'. Long hours were spent eating together, often with extended family and co-villages. Food was central to the elaborate death ceremonies and to weddings.

My experience in Nepal was further challenged by Japan, where the food was often exquisitely prepared, but seemed to be consumed at a great pace and often in silence. There was heavy drinking in the bars after work, but communal, leisurely, eating where deals were done and connections cemented did not seem central.

It did not take me long to realize that food is absolutely central to Chinese culture. You could say that China is food, food is China. Chinese food is, to my taste, delicious, with huge regional variations, wonderfully cooked and spiced and beautifully presented. Yet it is not the quality alone which makes it special.

In a way which I find difficult to pin-point, communal eating seems both highly expressive and instrumental in a way with which I am not familiar. Through food, you express your warm feelings, your respect, your desire for further friendship, and your appreciation of being part of a group. We see this in some British institutions to a lesser degree. Such sentiments are particularly found in peasant societies such as India and China where the family meal, often with a set of kin or neighbours, is the main demonstration of unity.

When my Chinese friends come back from tours of China, they do not show me many photographs of buildings or events, but linger over photograph after photograph of meals. They seem to read the meal in the same way as they read calligraphy, painting, or a piece of opera. It is the mixture of textures, colours, the way it is served, the authenticity and freshness – and the expense – which is carefully scrutinized as an index of what the host or those participating in the meal truly feel. As much as conversation or playing together in my culture, food tells the

Chinese a huge amount about the nature of their relations. It is a kind of dance or play, but with foodstuffs.

Then there is the instrumental side. It took me some time to realize that the communal meal was often the most important time for negotiations to be concluded. Of course, I was aware of the 'business lunch' when a potential partner would take you out to further a publicity deal, job appointment or whatever. Yet in China it is more fundamental.

Very often there is a longish period of sounding out, checking of credentials, mutual investigation, done through intermediary contacts and nowadays supplemented by the internet and online presence. The meeting then consists of formal speeches and perhaps exchange or examination of some papers. Yet at this stage nothing is settled. When the sumptuous meal is well under way, the food and modest alcohol and general atmosphere of happy humans being together, which Durkheim suggested was the origin of religion ('effervescence'), then in a kind of variant of *in vino veritas* (in wine, truth), the deal is somehow ceremonially, almost religiously, clinched. Trust is confirmed, no written contract is added, but the relationship is somehow solemnized.

The fact that the Chinese restaurant is one of China's greatest exports is not just a coincidence. Both the content and form of Chinese communal eating is one of China's greater contributions to human happiness. The atomistic individualism of a MacDonald's or Kentucky Fried Chicken is in great contrast to the hotpot and the circulating foods of China.

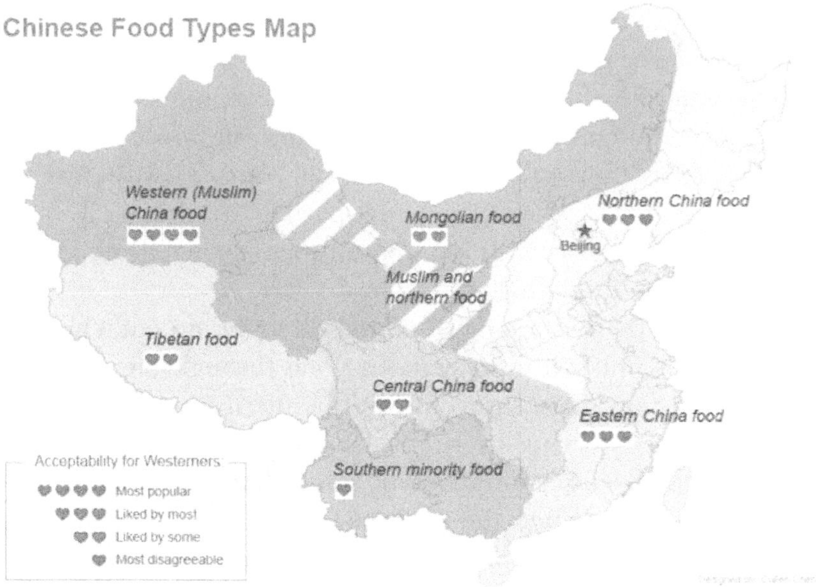

Education

When comparing the spirit of Chinese and British education, there are some profound differences. First, British schools and universities started under the umbrella of Christian religion and are still both visibly and invisibly influenced by this. Chinese education, apart from limited Buddhist education, has been secular. A single God lies behind our western philosophy, and training of religious leaders was a principal role for schools and universities.

Second, Britain was and is a class society and elite education was for the small group of richer and older families, the gentry and aristocracy. This is much changed now, but our famous schools and universities were designed for an elite class. China has never had a class or caste system, though growing affluence is now creating the seeds of such a system. Chinese education was established to select and train efficient bureaucrats to run the country, not to teach a general style and wisdom to a group of ruling families.

Third, the economic system, until very recently, was totally different. Britain for many centuries has been a consumer, market-based, capitalist society, in which trade, manufacture and large landowners and rich capitalist corporations dominated. Britain needed to train people to go out and make money in its cities, capitalist farms, or in the largest Empire the world has known.

China until very recently was a peasant economy, interested in small-scale economic activities and trading, but without an overseas Empire, little banking, few large corporations, and a place in which non-market values and forces predominated. China's education system was not dedicated to the production of entrepreneurs, inventors and shop-keepers. All this is rapidly changing, of course, but the two civilizations started from vastly different points when it came to the goals of education.

Fourth, the intellectual roots of the two systems are totally different. The UK tradition is rooted in the ancient classical world – Greece and Rome – with a strong later mixture of medieval Christianity and Arabic learning. The British tradition is a questioning, dialectical, truth-searching, innovative tradition with an open vision of truth. Understanding comes as a gradual revelation through the Socratic method, through a search for the underlying principles and patterns which are yet to be discovered in the universal laws laid down by a single God. In learning to discover new things through various forms of logic, rhetoric and mathematics, there is not a great emphasis on looking back to a closed and finished revelation of truth in classical texts.

Chinese thought has different roots. There is a strong imperative to look back to the great sages, to remember and respect, to elaborate and critique, but less of an emphasis on probing the future and discovering new things. Indeed, there are no new things under the sun. Respect, conformity, ritual, harmony, preservation are the key concepts. Truth is already known and there are serious dangers present in originality, ingenuity, questioning, argument and confrontation.

Education in the UK comes from roots which suggest that what education should do, from one's first school to the end of University, is give you the tools of thought; the methods, approaches, expertise to solve problems as they come up. A person is apprenticed to an intellectual master and learns the craft.

In China, traditionally, education was like filling up a mental library. There were a finite set of already-discovered things to know, a set of standard texts. Once these were memorized and mastered, there was nothing more to learn – just the practice of virtue, the organization of rituals, the living of an ethical life and the passing on of the tradition.

The traditional Chinese system was suitable for the many centuries when the amount of knowledge about the world changed little and written texts were precarious. Yet, it is the exceptional British version which is now accepted as the norm, a system which seems more appropriate for a world of expanding knowledge which began with the twelfth century Renaissance (or even the Greeks) and has continued, at an increasing pace, ever since. No individual can hold all knowledge in their minds. But they can learn the tools of thought.

Since the thirteenth century, England has basically had a constitutional monarchy with the King under the Law, a powerful set of countervailing forces and a growing tradition of parliamentary government. England had no standing army, a very small permanent bureaucracy and a strong legal system. Power was devolved down through the system and diffused to the localities.

In China, people all looked upwards towards the source of power at the Imperial centre, where there was a powerful bureaucracy and some military force. Each level is carefully articulated with that above – village, district, province, centre, all focusing in the end on the Emperor who was both the ritual and the political head.

Clearly the education in a de-centralized, lightly bureaucratized, system like the UK reflects its social and political structure. For example, there is a great space for self-rule, independence and autonomy. One of the main roles of elite schools has been a training in independence, judgement and self-sufficiency. Learning to rule responsibly is embedded in the 'prefect' or senior boy system in public schools.

The tradition of debates and speeches, of clubs and freedom, which boarding schools developed, encouraged and reflected self-rule and is shown in its extreme form in Oxbridge with its self-governing Colleges and, traditionally, a great deal of University independence. There was hardly any training in bureaucracy in English education until the later part of the nineteenth century.

China is different. There is a mountain of paper, writing is predominant, there are numerous regulations, a written bureaucratic world and the country is ruled through a tiered system of delegation. In China, everything is based on learnt precedents, following the code, automatic obeying of orders and relatively little discretion. In England, one makes the precedents, uses one's trained reason, questions orders if they are not satisfactory. Chinese education was therefore above all about loyalty, respect and conformity – deference to power whether in the shape of parents or the State. This is now changing rapidly. Many of the best Chinese schools I have visited recently are encouraging critical thinking and more out-of-class activities.

Elements

There are five elements in China, Wood, Fire, Earth, Metal and Water. These align with colours, directions, planets, seasons and many other things as in the following diagram. This system of elements and associations is central to Chinese thought, J. Dyer Ball discusses them and says that 'the whole of Chinese philosophy is based' on them and medicines, architecture, agriculture and many other things are dependent on this system.

The system is as follows, according to a table in *Wikipedia*.

Element ♦	Wood ♦	Fire ♦	Earth ♦	Metal ♦	Water ♦
Color	Green/blue	Red	Yellow	White	Black
Direction	east	south	center	west	north
Planet	Jupiter	Mars	Saturn	Venus	Mercury
Heavenly creature	Azure Dragon 青龍	Vermilion Bird 朱雀	Winged Snake 螣蛇	White Tiger 白虎	Black Tortoise 玄武
Heavenly Stems	甲, 乙	丙, 丁	戊, 己	庚, 辛	壬, 癸
Phase	New Yang	Full Yang	Yin/Yang balance	New Yin	Full Yin
Energy	Generative	Expansive	Stabilizing	Contracting	Conserving
Season	Spring	Summer	Change of seasons (Every third month)	Autumn	Winter
Climate	Windy	Hot	Damp	Dry	Cold
Development	Sprouting	Blooming	Ripening	Withering	Dormant
Livestock	dog	sheep/goat	cattle	chicken	pig
Fruit	plum	apricot	jujube	peach	chestnut
Grain	wheat	beans	rice	hemp	millet

Emotional warmth

I come from a famously reserved nation. The English, and within them the most buttoned-up and undemonstrative class within it, the upper middle class, are very keen to hide emotion. In my family, parents and grandparents, uncles and aunts were quite undemonstrative; understatement, the smile and handshake, the stiff upper lip in adversity, all this was what I saw around me. My boarding schools put a high premium on stoical forbearance, on formal relations, on not showing what you felt. Showing emotion was a weakness.

It was therefore a shock and a relief to spend a year in Nepal where we swum in a warm sea of affection and expressed emotion. The children cuddled, adults pressed up against you unself-consciously, you greeted joy and grief with open emotion. You could wear your heart on your sleeve.

My next experience, in Japan, took me back to my English upbringing – magnified. The Japanese never kissed or touched in public. They were ultra-private and reserved. I glimpsed that behind the strong masks they wore to cover all emotion a deeper and intense set of feelings were there, but it was well covered.

I expected in my ignorance that China would be much like Japan, but I was completely wrong. From long years of friendship with young Chinese, through many varied contacts, I have found that the Chinese are like a hugely magnified version of the Gurungs of Nepal. You greet with warmth, shaking hands and perhaps later embracing, both males and females. You do not stiffly shake hands as the British do, or bow like the Japanese, except on very formal occasions with important people. You find that at a dinner, where it is customary to go around drinking with each person present, you talk with great warmth. When you mix in a crowd or stand in a photograph, people press against you, women or men appear to feel no embarrassment at having your arm over their shoulder or round their waist – and usually reciprocate.

Children are like the Gurung children, spontaneous, affectionate, full of smiles and chat. Older friends write you long emails about their inner lives and friends are very open about all their hopes and fears. There seem to be few masks or barriers, even with a stranger from a distant land. You very quickly feel adopted into families, and young people quickly make you feel they are your adopted children – showing great loyalty, putting themselves out for you.

The emotionalism of the Chinese is in some ways a paradox since the Chinese are also highly rational, practical, down-to-earth and strategic and calculating.

The things which I was taught were expressive of emotion – painting, poetry, friendship, eating together in an animated way – are absolutely central to the Chinese, indeed are the core of China. There is nothing that Chinese love better than forming into a group over a meal, laughing and telling stories, reciting some poetry and admiring a beautiful painting or piece of poetry. The Scots half of my personality rejoices in the warmth which I always feel in their presence and I marvel that after the dreadful history of the last two hundred years, much of it caused by my nation, they should treat me with such deep friendship and obvious affection, even giving me the blogosphere nickname 'Meng Yeye' or 'Cutey Grandfather'.

F

Face and honour

I have long believed that there were only two main systems related to human self-image (in the eyes of others). The honour and shame cultures of the Mediterranean region, which also exists to a certain extent in Islamic and Indian civilisation, the Balkans and Russia, are based on a sexual opposition. Men are honourable, that is to say they avenge their wrongs, guard their women from dishonour, stress their masculinity or *machismo*. Women are the potential source of shame, which will damage them and their men if their purity and virtue is threatened in any way.

The above cultural complex is very widespread, but I did not find much of it in English history. In the English past men were not striving for *machismo*, there were few feuds, vendettas or duels. A man was not expected to kill or seriously wound someone who impugned the honour of his close family relatives – mother, daughter, sister or wife. Indeed, he would be imprisoned or executed if he did so.

What was important in England was honourable, that is gentlemanly, behaviour. Keeping your word, kindness and consideration, honesty, trustworthiness, these were the prime virtues which brought esteem. Loss of reputation as a trustworthy person spelt disaster in politics, business and many other professions. The Protestant religion stressed this concept of honour, for God was not pleased if you started to attack others because they threatened your dignity or the purity of your women.

To my surprise, I have now found a third variant in China. This is not really either of the above. As yet I have not fully understood how the concept of 'face' works in China, though I am told that it is ubiquitous and very important. It appears to be partially tied up with self-esteem, adherence to Confucian and

Buddhist values. It also seems to be to do with others' respect for you.

My difficulty in understanding the bundle of meanings, as well as the importance of the concept, can be seen from three short quotations. Arthur Smith starts his book *Chinese Characteristics* (1890) with 'Face', and writes that 'Once rightly apprehended, "face" will be found to be in itself a key to the combination lock of many of the most important characteristics of the Chinese.' He points out that it means that one should not directly accuse anyone of an offence, as they will lose face and deny it, whatever the evidence.

May-Lee Chai and Winberg Chai re-emphasize the importance and the difficulty. They write:

> Face is perhaps the most important concept to understand about Chinese culture and also perhaps the most difficult as it reflects values that are so very different from those in contemporary America... Face is your public persona, your social standing, your pride, your dignity, your scruples. "Saving face" is the act of preserving that appearance of dignity, and it is something that Chinese will go to great lengths to preserve. "Losing face" is the ultimate disgrace... From a practical point of view, visitors to China should always keep in mind that when something goes wrong – at work, at school, on a tour – they should never openly, publicly, and loudly blame their guide or colleague, even if it is entirely that person's fault. (May-Lee Chai and Winberg Chai, *China A to Z* (2014)

When I asked my colleague Qin Yuchen what 'face' means, she wrote as follows:

"面子" (Face) as you mentioned, is tied up with self-esteem. From my understanding, "face" is a neutral word. The word itself has two meanings. The first meaning is "prestige and self-esteem". It is one of the most important virtues in traditional Chinese culture. Gentlemen and ladies always emphasise it.

The second meaning is "surface", the image in the eyes of others. In this case, when you say someone cares too much about his/her "face", it is to say this person is vain and superficial, cares too much about views of others. Compared to the West, Chinese people care more about their self-image in others' eyes. They always live under the pressure of others' judgement. Thus the concept of face becomes ubiquitous.

Elsewhere I analyse how we can only understand China if we realize that everything lies in the relation between things and between people. It is a relational, structural, civilisation. A single hand clapping makes no sound. In this context, 'face' becomes the central mechanism. It is the inter-action, the mirrored image in the other's eyes, that gives life meaning. All, in the end, is about 'face', about how you are seen in the mirror of another. From this follows the disaster if that mirror shows you up badly.

The concept of 'face' helps me to understand the enormous pressure my Chinese friends still feel under from those around them, despite all the recent changes in family and other structures. It also makes me realise how difficult it will be for the Chinese to come to terms with the openly confrontational, often aggressive and rude, culture of the West. The kind of remarks that are made in English schools, law courts, business meetings or parliament, openly critical and putting people down, must be very difficult to comprehend or accept.

There is some overlap between the Chinese concept and the ideas developed in Erving Goffman's work on *The Presentation of the Self in Everyday Life* (1956), where he describes how people put on a mask when they meet others. Goffman further distinguishes the 'Front Stage', where we perform before others, and the 'Back Stage' of our private life. In his book written over half a century before Goffman, Arthur Smith anticipates this and writes 'In order to understand however imperfectly, what is meant by "face," we must take account of the fact that as a race the Chinese have a strongly dramatic instinct. The theatre may almost be said to be the only national amusement...'

Goffman developed his ideas while doing anthropological research in the Shetland Isles off Scotland, where 'face' is more important than it would be in many parts of the U.K. Yet even when we look through Goffman's concepts, we are still far from understanding this Chinese idea. I come from an individualistic culture where, while other's views of us are important, from my infancy I was taught that it was my own self-valuation that was the ultimate test. I was brought up in a Protestant tradition where my relations to God, and when he had withdrawn, to my own conscience, that mattered.

This diametrically different attitude to what constitutes us is well shown in one of the most popular poems in the English language, Rudyard Kipling's 'If'. The last verse shows the inner-directed self-confidence which all my upbringing and education was trying to instill in me. Do not care or worry about what others think of you. Rely on yourself.

If you can talk with crowds and keep your virtue,
Or walk with Kings—nor lose the common touch,
If neither foes nor loving friends can hurt you,
If all men count with you, but none too much;
If you can fill the unforgiving minute
With sixty seconds' worth of distance run,
Yours is the Earth and everything that's in it,
And—which is more—you'll be a Man, my son

Fashion

When we look at English records dating back to the fourteenth century at least, it becomes clear that the English have been great *fashionistas*. Whether you look at male and female clothing and footwear, hats, household furnishings, arts such as painting and music, language and learning, all are rapidly changing generation by generation and often decade by decade. For example, a book written in later sixteenth century England by William Harrison, shows that almost every aspect of the material and artistic life of his countrymen had changed dramatically in the fifty years before he wrote.

This tradition of constant change in fashion picked up speed as the English economy grew and went through a consumption revolution in the eighteenth and nineteenth centuries with the import of ideas and goods from its growing Empire. It changed ever more rapidly as England changed from a basically agricultural and rural to an industrial and urban society in the two generations after about 1780. Such perpetual change is something I have always taken for granted.

As I retrieve the story of my life in the last seventy-five years I see every kind of fashion going through constant change, jazz to pop to rap, skirt lengths going up and down, art and writing and communications constantly changing and huge class and gender changes.

I came to assume that all societies are like this and that basically humans are inventive, that they get restless and bored, people persuade them, through advertising, to change their ways. I assumed that constant and restless change was the norm.

As I read the history of China until about 1949 I encountered something totally different. It was something noticed when thinkers like Montesquieu in the eighteenth century commented that the world of mid-eighteenth century China seemed to have hardly differed from that described half a millenium earlier by Marco Polo. In that period, Europe was transformed, but China seemed almost frozen.

Of course, there were also changes in China. New crops like potatoes and maize came in from the New World. New methods of making pots or carrying out the tea ceremony or of painting were developed. Each dynasty had its distinctive styles and fashions – Song, Ming, Qing were different.

Yet compared to what was happening in the West, it was the conservatism, the persistence, the repetition of rhythms that struck many commentators and visitors. For many centuries, a Chinese grand-child often inhabited an almost identical world to what into which his or her grandfather had been born.

Whether this reflects a deep backwards stressing strand in

Chinese philosophy and language, or a necessary caution in a highly insecure environment, or the absence of a capitalist economy and marketing system which pushes new fashions, is not easy to say. What we can observe is that if you look at the clothing, food, housing, music or painting of the Chinese in 1200 and in 1900 you find remarkably little change.

From this, if one were writing about China in the 1930's at the time of Lin Yutang, one might have predicted that the Chinese are averse to changes of style and fashion, and that they would always be conservative. Yet Lin Yutang's great great nephew whom I met eighty-five years later in the city of Shenzhen lives in a world where things are changing every day and week at an astonishing rate.

China is now filled with fashion and fashion change. In everything from clothes, though music and art, it is bubbling both with desire to import the latest fashion brands from the West and also a great deal of native creativity. Going from Cambridge, where things are constantly changing, but much remains the same, to Chinese cities is like moving from a conservative, staid, calm and repetitive world to something seething and boiling over.

The extraordinary switch from fashion-stability to rapid change needs explanation beyond the obvious opening to capitalism and advertising. It shows an amazing flexibility and curiosity among the Chinese. The Chinese have always been brilliant at imitation and importing of ideas when needed, as have the Japanese, and they are now putting those skills to great use and giving the world new fashions. China is becoming one of the fashion centres of the world.

Fat and thin civilisations

It has been suggested that it is fruitful to make a contrast between what have been termed 'Fat' and 'Thin' civilisations. A 'fat' civilisation is one where most people have enough decent food so that their body weight is acceptable by modern standards. A 'thin' civilisation is one where many people are perpetually malnourished, stunted or thin. The example of the former that I know best is England. Even compared to Scotland to the north, in the past the English for many centuries have been comparatively affluent.

English houses were substantial and reasonably insulated, their furniture relatively well made and comfortable, clothes were, for many, warm in winter and cool in summer. They wore good leather shoes and often hats. They ate reasonably well, with meat, white bread, butter and cheese for many. They drank well with beer, cider and later tea and coffee. They could afford to keep pets, to have holidays, to work on the whole less hours and less exhaustingly than their Scottish or European (apart from Dutch) neighbours. They were a prototype 'fat' civilisation, not just recently, but, with notable exceptions during the industrial revolution, stretching back to the world described in Chaucer's poems or Shakespeare's plays.

The reasons for this rare affluence are multiple. They included a very productive agriculture, a widespread use of non-human power in the form of wind and water mills, domesticated animals, coal and wood. Good sea and river communications and foreign trade added to the wealth. The fact that the population grew very slowly and was relatively light on the land, that people married very late and had few children so that they could accumulate, helped. The power of a large middling sort who formed the backbone of government at all levels ensured a taxation system which did not deprive them of their surpluses. Credit was cheap, the market worked well, it was easy to borrow money, jobs were usually plentiful.

When I read about the history of Chinese civilisation over the centuries I am shocked at the condition of the vast majority of mankind, which China represents, over the last thousand years, only relieved by the burst of wealth across the globe in the last fifty years.

Many travellers to China and commentators from the sixteenth century onwards described a world where the vast majority of the population, in Tawney's metaphor in his book on China in the 1930s, lived always on the edge of drowning in poverty. Their noses were just above the water of hunger and disaster, so that every few years a wave would drown many of them.

The conditions for this vast majority were the opposite of the English – the housing, clothing, furniture, food and drink were often inadequate or worse. There was immense hard work and little sense of security.

The reasons for this also reversed the English situation. There was constant threat of war and violence. The arbitrary taxation system confiscated any visible gains. The land was increasingly overworked and unproductive. There was little to aid human effort, little use of mills and domestic animals. The population built up rapidly with young age at marriage and a desire for heirs, and then was cut back savagely in a crisis.

Of course, there were exceptions. The small scholar class and a few merchants lived reasonably and even opulently and in a leisurely way. Yet they represented less than one in ten thousand of the population. Almost everyone lived the kind of life of hardship and toil I witnessed over the years in a highland Nepalese village, where I calculated that the average wealth of a family was perhaps a tenth of that of those in my study of seventeenth century English villagers.

Yet my Nepalese friends would have been considered fortunate by the majority of Chinese through history. They had ample heating, ate meat and drank milk and had considerable periods of leisure. They lived in relative comfort partly through remittances from abroad. Real thinness I saw in the streets of Calcutta as a boy and can be seen in heart-rending photos and later films of China right up to the massive famines of the late 1950's.

If we are to understand the Chinese we need to remember this difference. Although thinness has not been personally experienced by those Chinese aged under about forty, many of them the well-fed only children in 'one child' families, have heard the stories and talked to their elders. They know about the world from which their civilisation has only just escaped. It would be good to imagine that the huge effort China is currently making, having lifted over half a billion Chinese out of poverty, to do the same in the belt across from Pakistan to Africa, is at least in part motivated by these memories.

Compared to all of this, the experience of the United States, for example, is entirely different. The settler years were difficult and the Great Depression in the early twentieth century led to large misery. Yet in comparison to China, America has always been well padded and in the last eighty years hugely so. It needs a real effort of imagination on the part of western observers to guess what it must be like to come from such a different civilisation.

Festivals

My calendar in the U.K. is punctuated by a number of 'Bank Holidays', devised in the later nineteenth century to give workers a day's rest, and a few calendar festivals reflecting the seasons. In the Spring there is Easter, remembering the resurrection of Jesus. In Autumn there is the Harvest Festival and in late autumn the Guy Fawkes fireworks. Around the winter solstice, there is Christmas which heralds the birth of Jesus. These festivals, particularly Christmas, are starting to be celebrated in China and my young Chinese friends now often send me Christmas and New Year greetings. In return, I send greetings on the two main Chinese annual festivals.

The first of these, and the most important, is the Spring Festival. This celebrates the start of the Chinese New Year, which in 2019 is on 5 February, not the January 1 as it is with us. It is the longest holiday festival, lasting about 23 days. Many activities occur, such as dragon races, fireworks and making dumplings. This allows families to re-unite over the huge distances of China.

For these weeks, hundreds of millions of Chinese travel vast distances, often by train, to spend time with their parents, children and other relatives. This often continues with feasting and meeting dozens of relatives. There are exchanges of gifts, gossip and general networking, often involving discussions of potential marriage arrangements. At the end of this is the Lantern Festival, a festival dating back over two thousand years. Billions of lanterns are lit and many drift off into the sky or down the rivers.

Then, at the mid-autumn solstice (full moon), there is another national holiday, this time lasting a week. Again, if possible, families come together to celebrate, especially through the giving of moon-cakes – rich cakes made with various fillings and with Chinese good-luck characters on the top. To be invited to such celebrations, or to be given a box of moon cakes, is an honour for an outsider. This is also the time for various other activities, including boat racing, parades of dragons and various sports and dancing, and—of course – for fireworks.

There are numerous other festivals, many regional but also national. Among the most important are the following. The Dragon Boat Festival. This falls on the fifth day of the fifth month of the Chinese Lunar calendar. The representative activity is racing Dragon boats, on water and also on land. The Qingming Festival around the first week of April is the time for visiting graves to pay respects to the ancestors. It is also known as the Tomb Sweeping or Cleaning Festival. Many Chinese families take a picnic out to beauty spots to celebrate.

Some Chinese also celebrate the Winter Solstice Festival on December 21st or 22nd, when it is customary to eat dumplings with the family. In the summer is the Summer Solstice celebrating the longest day. Finally, there is the most important of the seven festivals of the lunar calendar, the Hungry Ghost Festival, around

August 15th in the western calendar, July 15th in the Chinese lunar calendar. Bonfires are lit and ancestors are welcomed back and paper money is burnt to placate the dead. This is one of the three festivals, referred to collectively as the 'Three Great Ghost Festivals'.

Looking at all this absorbing activity, several things strike me. It is surprising to find how many festivals there are (for there are also many others), how long some of them last (a week or more in several cases), what huge efforts people make to travel back to their home villages and family to celebrate them. They also revolve almost entirely around the family, both the living and, in several cases, the dead. Only Christmas for the British has something of this family re-union aspect, and the family in the British case is usually the nuclear family of grandparents, children and grandchildren, characteristically from four to a dozen people. In China there may be several dozen.

The festivals, many dating back thousands of years, seem to be relics of an ancient moon-worshipping civilization (for many are tied to the lunar calendar) and an ancestor-venerating society. It is yet another instance of the fact that this earthly world and the world of hidden forces, in this case the moon rather than the winds and waters, are not separated. Ancient calendar events give a rhythm to the life of a people who, until forty years ago, were preponderantly living an almost purely agrarian life.

Another feature is the amazing survival of these ancient elements. Driving through huge new cities, with vast sky-scrapers and modern trains and car-clogged roads, you suddenly see the pavements lit up with little bonfires and people burning paper money, or, at other times, everything festooned with lanterns. Past and present come together. Below a sophisticated urban landscape, there still lies a magical world of ghosts and other invisible forces.

Finger-nail guards, bound feet and manual labour

I was pleased to be given a silver 'finger-nail guard' by my friend Gerry after our first visit to China. This is about four inches long and protects the little finger on one hand, which has a long, uncut, nail of that length within it. It was worn by mandarins and other high officials. Gerry suggested that no society which encouraged its literate class to have such an ostentatious sign that they never went near manual work was likely to have an industrial or even scientific revolution.

Since then, as I have thought about Gerry's remark (Gerry was a successful inventor and industrialist), it has made increasing sense. The British class system in the past was such that work of a physical kind and contact with the natural world was not considered ignoble. Gentlemen could also be farmers or manufacturers or traders. They could use their hands for physical tasks or sports as they liked. The constant improvements in agriculture and manufacture were the result of this practical emphasis. I came to appreciate the deep difference between a finger-nail civilisation and a 'hands-on' civilisation.

The ruling class across the European Continent up to the twentieth-century were similarly of the view that physical labour and contact with nature was demeaning, even impure. The extreme form of this view is in India, where Brahmins are prohibited from all physical labour. To plough, chop wood, look after animals would strip a Brahmin of his ritual purity.

China is caste-like in this respect. Status is gained by success in intellectual exercises through the examination system. Mandarins are not noted, as were their British equivalents, for physical prowess, for sports, rowing, riding and shooting. The British knew that success in their system, where the class structure was fixed but where it was quite possible for the individual to move up (or down), came from money. Only constant striving with body as well as mind could achieve this – hence the boarding schools and their emphasis on physical activities.

In China, another expression of this tendency towards the devaluing of physical work, was not directed to make the hands useless for serious physical work, but rather the feet. And in this case, it was the feet of women. Many civilisations seclude their women, usually by separating them off in some way. Sometimes this is done in a harem, or by keeping them locked within the house, or covering their faces and bodies.

The Chinese mainly used another method, the tradition of breaking the feet of their girls and then binding them tightly to deform them to fit tiny shoes. The system is reputed to have begun in the tenth century, at the end of the Tang dynasty. Millions were subjected to this and lived a life of perpetual pain, hobbling around in their tiny shoes, their 'lotus feet', being erotically attractive, so it was alleged, for men. It debarred women from much productive work and crippled them much more than the finger-nail guards. The system of bound feet was only abolished in the twentieth century.

Flowers and plants

The English pride themselves on their gardens, from small to majestic, and have been at the forefront of the research and breeding of plants. Yet they are not always aware that many of their plants actually derive from China. From the seventeenth century onwards, the trickle turned to a flood from the later eighteenth century. The plant explorers and collectors imported many of what we now take to be native English plants – flowers, fruits (including rhubarb), shrubs and trees from China, as well as from much of east and south-east Asia.

The famous plant collector, E.H. Wilson, referred to China as the "Mother of all Gardens" for it is the origins of more than 30,000 plant species, or one eighth of the world's total. If one were to magic away all Chinese-derived plants from town streets and parks, private gardens and stately homes in the UK, they would suddenly be very empty – with perhaps two thirds of their species gone.

The vast proliferation of wonderful species in China has often struck me in tours to remoter parts of that country. Particularly along the slopes of the jutting spurs of the eastern Himalayas, with its epicentre in the warm and wet provinces of Yunnan and Sichuan, is a flower growers and buyer's paradise.

The Chinese adore flowers, as any acquaintance with their wonderful gardens and their high arts of poetry and paining will show. Flowers and trees are not just plants, but become incorporated in the highly complex symbolic landscape of China. When a Chinese sees an iris it may remind him of spring, a peony symbolizes fame and wealth, a magnolia was once only owned by the Emperor and represents beauty, a lotus is associated with Buddhism and symbolizes purity, a lily is associated with fertility, an orchid with love and beauty, a chrysanthemum with long life, a hibiscus with fame and riches. And, of course, it is not just the flower itself, but its particular colour and how it is arranged or placed in association with other symbols which is meaningful. Many of the flowers are also important in traditional Chinese medicine.

G

Galactic Empire

I was brought up in a civilisation dominated for some hundreds of years by the nation state. My own country, England, has been a nation, that is a place with its own separate laws, language and sense of identity, for over a thousand years, largely because of the sea that surrounds it. The continental nations like France, Italy or Germany only became nations as well as states in the nineteenth century. All of Europe, despites its partial unification into a European Union, is a set of nations who are proud of their distinctive character. They may have overseas Empires, as Britain did all over the world, yet they are basically bounded entitities in distinction to others. France does not feel an inferiority and deference to Germany, even if Germany is more powerful economically, nor Portugal to Spain.

Coming from such a tradition, it is natural for me and other Europeans or Americans to assume that China has been like this. We assume that it is a nation, despite huge variety in language and customs over its vast territories. We assume that it sees itself as a 'nation' opposed to the 'nations' surrounding it. We assume that historically China has been at peace or war with other nations, like Vietnam, Burma, Tibet (when it was separate), Korea and Japan, in the same way as Britain against France or France against Italy.

In fact, our own experience blinds us to a very different concept of what we might call a Galactic Empire, that is to say an Empire based on the idea of a galaxy of powers. At the centre is the sun, by far the most powerful and ancient, the Middle Kingdom between others, not a nation but a hub or focus, spreading out in all directions. The centre of this is the Emperor, whose rays spread out with ever decreasing strength to the limits of China and then into neighbouring states.

The neighbouring states circle round China like the planets. Each keeps its own course and is in essence independent, but all are caught up with the gravitational pull of the sun and all their lives are influenced by it.

Each of them stands like a son to a father, or a younger brother to older brother. They pay respect, send their ambassadors and their tributes periodically to the Chinese capital. They sometimes rebel and then there are wars. On the whole, however, the benefits of trade and protection outweigh a marginal diminution of status. They are not China, but they are part of the 'Sinosphere' or sphere of influence. Thus, much of what we think of as characteristically Japanese, Vietnamese or Korean derived from China. They are part of the 'greater China'.

This different conception of nation and empire lies behind one of the most interesting recent developments in China, the One Belt One Road Initiative. This again conceives of China as the hub of a huge network. It is similar to older models, but now stretches much further, to Africa and South America as well as to the actual bordering countries. It is potentially on a far greater scale thanks to the hugely increased power of modern communications and infrastructural technologies. The sun's rays spread ever further.

Gaokao and education

The *gaokao* is the universal, standardised, educational test taken by all Chinese who hope to go to university. It is both a cause of great satisfaction and also huge anxiety throughout China.

The satisfaction comes from the belief that it is a largely fair, uncorrupted, system which gives everyone the same chance to go to a good university without the chance being distorted by the wealth or social position of the individuals who take it. It is taken at precisely the same time throughout China and it is difficult to cheat. In this way it is a direct descendant of the centuries of imperial examinations, where millions of Chinese through the ages sat in little cubicles and wrote their essays in order to compete to reach the next tier of the system which could, for a tiny minority, lead to the very top level of China.

It is, of course, recognised that if you have the means and connections you can go to a better school and afford better out-of-school tuition. This means that there is some built-in bias, but it is as limited as possible and open bribery of examiners or other forms of cheating are difficult. To achieve this for the vast population of China, which has some two hundred million people in education, and where you are dealing with children in the most remote ethnic minority village on the border to the sophisticated centres of Shanghai or Beijing, is an amazing achievement.

The anxiety that runs with the approval is the realisation of the huge strain it places on young children and their parents. The fairer the system, the less a person can blame their failure to reach their goals on someone else. All the stress is on the individual and school and an obsession with testing and rote learning is known to stifle creativity, criticism and even happiness. Young Chinese are hugely stressed from primary school onwards, aiming at the dreaded *gaokao*, which will determine which rung of the occupational ladder they will be on for the rest of their lives.

Coming from the more relaxed, if less fair, world of 1950s and 1960s Britain, where it mattered less how you did in formal examinations, except in the case of entry to grammar schools, I can see how stressful the system must be. I can also see why many of the more affluent Chinese are trying to avoid this examination, either by opting for the International Baccalaureate stream within some of the best Chinese schools, which opens up western university entrance, or else sending their children away to western schools, at any age from twelve onwards, and certainly around sixth form.

The *gaokao* is, of course, one feature of the extraordinary nature of Chinese civilisation, namely that traditionally almost all social mobility was focused on examination success. China, unlike every other civilisation on earth, made education, the mind, the criteria for promotion. Without class, caste or other permanent ranking systems, all hinged on learning the skills to be an administrator. It was both very narrow and yet rather amazing to find hundreds of millions living in a world where mental ability is so highly valued, above martial prowess, money making or even religious merit.

Gender

The gender revolution during the last century is one of China's most impressive achievements. For at least two thousand years, women had been regarded as inferior to men. This was built into the core of Confucian thought, which emphasised the superiority of men over women, and also baked into the family system based on male descent, male inheritance and arranged marriage.

The inferiority of women reached its extreme during the last millennium when the breaking and binding of women's feet became widespread and when women of the upper class were kept shut away in women's quarters.

Missionaries and reformers from the second half of the nineteenth century tried to elevate women. Women's education at more than the very elementary level was introduced from the 1920's. Yet it was really only under the Communist regime from 1949 that women's position rose rapidly. Mao saw women as equal to men. They had fought alongside men in the civil and other wars, and he brought in reforms which made them effectively equal to men.

This new valuation has largely continued. While women still are noticeably absent from the top levels of the Party and under-represented in administration and business, elsewhere they can be seen as an equal part of the labour force. The one-child policy clearly contributed to their freedom. There is a necessity for women to carry on working and many families have two earners.

Thinking of my friends in China, many of the most

outstanding and respected are women, from millionaires to professionals of all kinds. In the married couples I know well, the wife is clearly equal in all decision-making. In schools and universities, women are doing as well as men.

In other words, in only eighty years there has been a revolution in the relations of the sexes. Men and women are still recognised as different – *yang* and *yin*, and the sex-based division of Chinese civilisation continues to be one of the bases of Chinese thought. Yet the difference is no longer placed in a hierarchy, and the long-recognised fact that the male principle contains a core of the female, and vice versa, as in the *yin-yang* symbol, also softens the opposition.

Ghosts

I have a distant relative, M.R. James, who, among other things, was a famous ghost story writer. His stories take the reader from a familiar, safe, world into an increasingly frightening place where nameless, faceless, creatures rise up as unhappy spirits, left wandering the earth after murders and other tragic deaths. His stories were part of a revival of interest in spirits in England in the later nineteenth century. As conventional religious belief faded, a parallel world of table-tapping, séances with spirit mediums and ghostly encounters increased.

Yet, on the whole, the English have not been great believers in ghosts. Nor have other grisly phantoms such as vampires and werewolves been very important in everyday life. There was belief in witchcraft and there were fairies and elves, yet the walking dead seem to be on the margins.

The importance of ghosts in Chinese history to this day is well known. They appear in plays and operas. They arrive in cemeteries and at special times of the year. They are a salient feature of popular culture. There are five categories of beings – normal people, spirits, ghosts, holy persons and abnormal creatures such as foxes and goblins. It was in the seventh century that an author wrote a long piece on ghosts, though Confucius and others much earlier had mentioned them. Confucius said that if you believed in them, you would see them, otherwise not.

Even now people believe in ghosts. For example, Chairman Mao never decried ghosts. Before the cultural revolution he asked somebody to write a book called 'We are not frightened of ghosts' – anyone who didn't listen to him was a ghost. The book included many 'kits' or recipes to get rid of ghosts – for example taking off your hat and brushing your hair. Those who were arrested and tortured during the cultural revolution were called 'buffalo ghosts' and 'snake fairies'.

Anybody after death can become a ghost, but if you are not frightened of ghosts they cannot harm you. A friend's mother often told her that if she was ill it might be a ghost causing the problem and she would burn money to placate it, though this verges on ancestor beliefs. This friend experienced a ghost when she was six or seven. When one of her mother's colleagues died, she felt a white shadow to be near, saying 'where are you'. Another friend, a university Professor, tells us that he is very frightened of ghosts – he once saw something like a ghost, a man without a head.

A baby who is born in the middle of the day, we are told, won't see a ghost because of the strong sunshine, but those born in the evening may see ghosts. Many children sense ghosts, but by the time they become adults their minds are covered over with information and they no longer see them. This is similar to Japanese belief in *kami* or spirits, often seen by children but less by adults.

Gifts

I was brought up in a culture where gifts were rather limited in their timing and function. Gifts tend to be given at certain special occasions such as birthdays, Christmas and weddings. They are mainly given between family members, particularly an older generation to a younger one. And they are entirely expressive. They demonstrate the affection felt by one family member for another.

Nor is there an expectation of a counter gift. The gift is an object, filled with meaning because of the relationship and occasion, but not containing any 'sprit' or element which required its return. Gifts generate no 'interest' in the financial sense and they are to be avoided in many relationships. It would be thought odd, even verging on bribery, for a person to give gifts to officials, teachers, superiors in a business etc. It would be thought that the 'gift' has strings attached to it – some hope or implication that a return favour is being sought.

I read about gifts in other societies where the gift is thought to have 'spirit' (*hau*) which goes alongside the physical object. This spirit transfers a pressure to the recipient to reciprocate, perhaps with a larger counter-gift, in the future. In this way, gifts can be a form of reciprocal communication, a speaking through things. I was therefore prepared for the large role of gifts in Nepal and later Japan, where the wrapping of gifts and their ornate character has been much noticed.

Yet it is in China that I have encountered a world of gifts which I found quite puzzling at first. In almost every encounter with new Chinese colleagues and students in Cambridge, they come bearing gifts. Often these are expensive. After receiving a painting, a piece of jewellery, calligraphy or a box of tea, my friends tell me that the gift is worth some hundreds, if not thousands, of pounds. I usually have no counter gift to offer except time and warm words. At first, I felt quite anxious. Was there expectation of some future favour I would be expected to offer a reference letter, a word in the right ears, a visa application endorsement?

Over the years I have come to discover that the gifts are largely expressive, not instrumental. They show the respect and happiness of the donor about the meeting. They carry no 'spirit' which demands reciprocity, even less than a gift to the Buddha or Daoist spirit of good fortune.

Of course, there are forms of gift-giving which verge on an attempt to buy influence – the traditional 'red envelopes' given by employees to their boss or to school teachers. These have recently been banned by the Chinese government, a sign of their supposed corrupting influence. Yet, on the whole, the Chinese add gift-giving to food, the warmth of friends, greetings and conversations to create an array of ways of integrating a new-comer into their networks of connections and social groupings.

Ginkgo and durability

The national tree of China is the ginkgo – in fact it is not a tree but a kind of fern and hence has a kind of leaf dissimilar to any of the more modern forms of leaf which we find on trees.

It is a very appropriate symbol of China for several reasons. One is that, appropriate for the longest surviving ancient civilisation on earth, the ginkgo is very old, the only 'tree' which survives from the age of the dinosaurs and before the last great ice age. It is at least fifty million years old as a species and has not changed since it first evolved.

Second, it is immensely hardy. When the Japanese dropped an atom bomb on Hiroshima, the only things to survive near the epicentre of the bomb damage was a pair of ginkgo trees, which survive to this day. This toughness ensured its survival when most other vegetation was frozen to extinction. The Chinese are similarly very tough.

A third feature is that like the Han people, the ginkgo has an amazing ability to propagate itself and expand. Part of the reason for this is that it comes with two different forms of propagation.

It produces a fruit or seed, which is highly valued in traditional medicine to this day, useful against many diseases. If necessary it can also propagate by the more unusual method of dropping roots from its lower branches, which set up clones of the main tree. This double means of propagation is similar to that of another great symbol of China, the golden rain (*koleuteria paniculata*) which both seeds and puts out succours.

The Han have seeded, rooted, and succoured and are now to be found all over the world. They are immensely hard-working, adaptable and work closely together.

The final point takes us back to the strangeness of the ginkgo, (often called the maidenhair tree after the fern which it is). Like the bamboo, it is special and there is nothing else like it on the planet. China is also in a class of its own, and like the ginkgo is the sole surviving member of its species. It carries into our world elements of an ancient world, before the birth of other nations. China is something ancient yet modern, and so too is the ginkgo.

Glass

I knew very little about the history and effects of glass and had thought almost nothing about such a ubiquitous substance until, nearly twenty years ago, I started to work with my friend Gerry Martin on a book on the world history of glass.

As we explored the subject I became more and more aware of what a magical substance glass is, a third state of matter, neither solid nor liquid, translucent, immensely strong, malleable, bending light and potentially increasing the power of man's best sense, sight, many times over.

I began to see that without glass, the European Renaissance could not have happened; as Leonardo da Vinci, for example, noted 'the mirror is the master of painters'. I also began to see how without glass, the scientific revolution could not have happened. For example, the Galilean and Newtonian break-throughs, or the discovery of the vacuum by Robert Boyle, of microbes by van Leuwenhoek, could not have been achieved. Glass made, or at least permitted, the emergence of my modern world.

When I turned to China and Japan, where I had assumed that a similar sort of use of glass would be found, I was amazed to discover that this was not so. While the Chinese knew of glass technology at last two thousand years ago, and made fine coloured blown glass jewellery in the Tang dynasty, the type of glass-making that developed in Venice was not present in China until it was introduced by the missionaries in the late seventeenth century. The Chinese, like the Japanese, more or less forgot glass until they bumped into it again when the westerners arrived with their amazing glass instruments and drinking vessels.

There are many obvious reasons why the Chinese did not bother with glass. They had good substitutes for several of its uses, paper for windows, fine porcelain for drinking from. For these reasons, they did not bother with a process which consumes a huge amount of fuel. Yet its absence is clearly one among several major reasons why China had neither a western-style Renaissance nor a western-style scientific revolution. Without glass, both of these dramatic changes were impossible. Glass was the missing key, even if one cannot argue that if you have the key you will necessarily unlock the door. Glass was a necessary, but certainly not a sufficient, cause of our new world.

Green energy

For many hundreds, if not thousands, of years there has been huge pressure on the natural environment in China. As elsewhere in the world, over time, traditional agriculture tends to cause a destruction of the forests, clean rivers and rich soil upon which the farmers depend. Over-grazing destroyed the pasture land. These are normal tendencies but they have been exacerbated in China by special factors.

One is the longevity of Chinese civilisation. Most civilisations only expanded into their farming lands a few hundred years ago. In China, much of the land has been used for agriculture for over a thousand years. Natural fertility in the soil, prime forest, pure waters have all been used again and again until they are depleted. Second, the population of China has grown in spurts, and particularly in the last half millennium, rising from sixty million in 1550 to over one and a third billion now.

Third, the lashing of Pacific typhoons in the east and the spreading sands of the high plateau deserts in the west has long been destroying agricultural land. If we add to this the fact that much of China consists of rocky hills and mountains, especially in the north, west and south, then we can see what lies behind R. H. Tawney's remark after his visit to China in the 1930's that the Chinese have been enormously economic and careful about everything 'except of forests, which have been plundered, with prodigal recklessness, to the ruin of the soil, and of the labour of human beings...' [i]

Tawney was only half right. The natural resources were not squandered out of carelessness, but for reasons explained elsewhere, especially the 'tragedy of the commons' described under property.

In sum, when Tawney did his survey in the 1930's, China looked to be in a dreadful situation. The *Farmers of Two Thousand Years*, to quote the title of F.H. King's classic on Chinese agriculture, had entered a spiral of ecological destruction.

Yet when we look around now, we find the situation is changing dramatically. I have been to many areas where serious attempts at re-afforestation have been made, and with some success. Even parts of the western deserts are being reclaimed. Currently the forest coverage is stated to be about 23% of China, which we might compare to 10% for England. The pressure on energy resources, traditionally through wood and more recently coal, has also been reduced. China is now one of the leading producers of the technologies needed for green, non-carbon, energy. Vast wind farms, solar energy panels and hydro-electric plants are being deployed. China is leading the world in the conversation about and the production of green energy. China has started to turn the corner and offers the hope that its lead and approach can be followed.

Guanxi

It is essential to know who you can trust. For any kind of activity which requires more than one person, you have to have a basis for successful co-operation and collaboration. This is provided in most societies by a mixture of several institutions. One is the family. You can trust and work with other members of your family because you have long-term assurance of mutual interests, sentiments of closeness, knowledge about the other, and guarantees of good behaviour because of a set of overlapping ties. Your father, brother, nephew or cousin is someone who shares your blood, your ancestors, your social world. Outside the family the world may be a hostile and dangerous place, especially if there is a weak or non-existent system of law to appeal to if you feel you have been wronged. Inside the family there is safety.

The second enforcing institution is neighbourhood. If your life is in a village where people have known each other since childhood, there are pressures against dishonest behaviour. You face common threats with your fellow villages and rely on each other in many activities.

A third possible basis for trust is religion. This is especially strong in a minority religious group which is different, and often persecuted, by the majority. There is a high level of trust between Jews, Quakers and others with a strong religious ethic of mutual trust and harmony guaranteed by God.

In my own English society, these normal mechanisms of trust are weak. The family is small and fragmented and does not have common aims. There is high geographical and social mobility so you are constantly encountering strangers. There is some ethical pressure towards virtue from Christianity, but experience shows that fellow-religionists can be as untrustworthy as anyone.

In this situation, the British developed other avenues of mutual collaboration and ways of punishing those who betrayed trust or failed to live up to their contracts and promises. These included the powerful force of reputation in specialized roles, a trustworthy lawyer, or clergyman or businessman came to be known as such. Then there was a generalised ethic of virtue implanted through the Protestant religion, which warns that lying, cheating and other antisocial behaviour are sins and will be punished in the afterlife.

Above all there was, and is, a very powerful and complex legal system, particularly focusing on regulating economic life and underpinning the necessity for honesty, to the spirit as well as the letter of the law, in the Equity courts, based on the ideas of decency, fairness and honesty.

For many centuries, China could rely on the two main mechanisms of kinship and village cohesion to underpin its social and economic life. Even with these, there developed a system of 'relationships' or 'connections' or *guanxi*, to fill the space, for instance in long-distance trading, where relations of trust with strangers had to be made. This mechanism, which means that you can enter into many kinds of dealing, from marriage arranging to borrowing money or sending goods to distant places and waiting or payment, in the absence of a fair, predictable and strong commercial legal system, has become much more important in the last forty years.

The family is increasingly fragmented. The rates of geographical mobility are high and people often move to huge cities where they have fleeting relations with strangers. So, there is a need for something like the level of impersonal trust found in parts of the West. This cannot be provided by the legal system, which is still in the early phase of its development. Another form of establishing trust widely found in the Anglo-sphere, namely the multitude of clubs and associations, is also weak in China.

The Chinese have built up their *guanxi* mechanisms in ways that articulate much of society and economy. It is easy for a westerner who is unfamiliar with this sort of network to assume that *guanxi* is blatant, or concealed, corruption, and indeed it can become so. It can also be a system of exchanged favours, favouritism, interfering with the supposed open and accountable systems supposedly present in the West. It looks as if people exchange favours in a blatantly underhand way. And indeed this does happen.

Yet the essence of *guanxi* is the establishing of a relationship of mutual trust in an untrustworthy world. It often operates when a third party knows the two parties entering into *guanxi* and can pledge for their dependability. A *guanxi* network is built up over time and each satisfactory transaction strengthens it. It is extremely efficient and it is difficult to conceive of how a huge and diverse civilisation like China could operate without it. It is not a black economy or systematic corruption, but a system of 'friends of friends' similar to that found in Mediterranean Europe.

Gunpowder and fireworks

The philosopher Francis Bacon singled out the invention of gunpowder as one of the turning points in history, one of the great discoveries along with printing and the compass, that differentiated the moderns from the ancients. He did not mention that all of these inventions were imported into Europe from China where they had first been discovered. Nor could he foresee the different trajectory of the uses of gunpowder which tells us a great deal about the differences between East and West.

Gunpowder was discovered in China in the ninth century during the late Tang dynasty, and the knowledge quickly spread across the great Empire. It was adopted and used in shooting projectiles at marauding horsemen, often more for the frightening effect than the actual killing. Yet over the thousand years after its discovery, gunpowder weapons were only slowly developed in China. By the nineteenth century, there was not a great transformation from the situation a thousand years before.

The English who fought in the Opium Wars of the nineteenth century with machine guns and armoured steam ships with huge cannons, the soldiers carrying effective rifles, were amazed at how primitive the Chinese weapons were. The cannons on the walls of forts often turned out to be fake wooden ones, or not to work at all, and the English troops could pick off their enemies while well out of range of the antiquated Chinese muskets.

There are many possible reasons for this divergence. One is that such gunpowder weapons were not very useful against the bow-carrying horse riders of the central steppes. Nor were they very effective against the huge ramparts of the walled cities. They may also have been seen to be a danger to the Empire if they fell into the hands of the mass of the people.

In Japan, after effective gunpowder weapons were introduced by the Portuguese in the early sixteenth century – significant that they came from Europe and that the Japanese had not found a source, as they did for so much, from China – they flourished for about a century. Then the Shoguns totally banned all such weapons, except for a few which they kept in their armoury. They realized their potential danger and the Chinese may have felt the same.

In Europe a world of competing nation-states fought incessantly and so pushed gunpowder technology forwards rapidly. Those who objected to it as inhumane or ungodly such as the Ottoman Turks, lost the final wars. Those like the British who armed their ships with the latest cannons won them.

In China and Japan, the older methods of warfare were preserved and so when the final confrontation of advanced western gunpowder weapons and their ancient armies took place in the middle of the nineteenth century, the West was at a huge advantage, for, among other things, the British weapons could fire much more accurately, rapidly and over longer distances.

It is a lesson China has not forgotten. Ringed by the nuclear missiles and warships of America, China has invested, not as heavily as America, but in a substantial way in the latest weaponry.

If the U.S. launched either a conventional or nuclear war against China, it would not be a repetition of the Opium Wars. There would be no winners, but huge devastation.

Meanwhile, rather than developing ever more sophisticated gunpowder weapons, the Chinese found a better use for the new substance – fireworks. Chinese fireworks are ubiquitous. On all auspicious or special occasion, fire crackers are let off and the firework display at the Beijing Olympics of 2008 was a suitable tribute to their amazing history.

H

Health and health care

Coming from a western tradition of medicine, several things strike me as very different about the situation in China over the centuries, although that difference is rapidly diminishing as western-style medicine and hospitals have moved into China in the last forty years.

One contrast is in the idea of a medical profession. Since the Greeks made rapid advances in medicine, and particularly since Arabic medicine spread and medieval universities developed from the thirteenth century, Europe experienced a dramatic increase in both medical knowledge and training. One of the core subjects of the universities was medicine, and there has been an important profession of doctors in western countries for hundreds of years. Their status was on a social level with lawyers, clergymen and academics. There were set texts and examinations even if, to us, the methods appear crude.

There has been nothing equivalent in China until the last forty years. Medicine was not taught in the ancient academies and played no part in the Confucian-inspired examination system. There were, of course, many practitioners of Chinese traditional medicine, but there was no medical profession as such.

Alongside this, the industrialized treatment of the sick, dating from late medieval, often religious, houses for the sick, through to the growth of hospitals from the seventeenth century, was largely absent in China. The sick were not placed in beds in separate buildings. One consequence was that there was no nursing profession.

Clearly the basic concepts of what disease is, how the body works and the best remedies has been totally different. Although there were some elements of similarity in the medieval western idea of the different 'humours' and treatments for 'hot' and 'cold' ailments, and the use of herbs, there was a gulf.

Basically, since the Greeks, the West considered the body as a machine, whose separate parts might become faulty and should be treated by a physical intervention – the use of strong medicines, bleeding and cutting away damaged tissues.

In China, the body is on a continuum with all of nature. It is looked at as a whole, one interconnected living entity like a tree, where the parts intercommunicate just as the leaves of a tree are connected to its roots, and branches to the trunk. Furthermore, the body is part of much wider forces, so that it may be influenced by the winds, waters, moon and stars.

In this situation, the aim is to bring a suffering part back into alignment or harmony through the use of techniques such as acupuncture. To place a needle in the neck or shoulder may relieve pain in the foot, for example. Through the use of the many herbal and animal cures, among them ginseng, rhubarb, tea and parts of bears, tigers or animal ivory, the body can be restored.

Given this background, by the 1950s, during the Communist period in China, the Party could not draw on any long tradition of western-style knowledge, hospitals, doctors and nurses. Furthermore, the huge population of China, subsistence farmers spread out through innumerable remote village, were not in a position to use expensive doctors and hospitals. So there emerged a typically ingenious and unique Chinese solution, the 'barefoot doctors'. The word barefoot emphasized the humble, poor, amateur nature of the briefly trained people who were sent out to bring simple medicines to vast number in the rural villages. They only carried a few simple remedies, were paid very little, yet could help alleviate much suffering.

This movement was replaced by modern, western-style, medicine after the 1980s, although this existed beside traditional Chinese medical methods. Now China has some of the best hospitals and doctors in the world and, at a very basic level, medicine is free and available to all. Yet the barefoot doctor campaign remains an inspiration for other poor countries in their early phase of rolling out basic health care, as in parts of India or Africa.

It may also be an inspiration for the future. As medicine becomes ever more expensive, especially hospitals, and population grows older, an obvious solution to much of the stress this is causing is to create very localized, semi-amateur-yet-trained, para-medics, working for the local community, who can deal with many smaller ailments.

I practiced such a scheme in a Nepalese village for fifteen years, and realized that a very simple training of a day or so to a local villager, and a store of a dozen basic medicines, could alleviate up to half the causes of daily pain in a place which was far away from hospitals and clinics. The Chinese are also pioneering such an approach with similar methods at the village level, and hence providing inspiration with an alternative approach.

Unlike almost all other countries, despite its huge economic growth, China is year by year spending more of its GDP on health care. From 2003 to 2018, China's total health expenditure increased from 658.41 billion yuan to 5799.83 billion yuan (approx 70 billion to 600 billion pounds), and the proportion of total health expenditure to GDP rose from 4.8% to 6.4%.

High-level equilibrium traps

One of the great puzzles in Chinese history is why the early promise of this civilisation by the thirteenth century never blossomed into the first modern economy and society. By the late Song dynasty, China was an extraordinarily advanced and sophisticated society. Alongside the earlier great inventions of paper, silk, printing, tea, ceramics, gunpowder and the compass, the Song made the first mechanical clock and the first power-driven weaving loom, anticipating the work of Arkright and others in the West by half a millennium. The currency, commerce, urban life, were all hugely developed and China was by far and away the largest and most powerful civilisation on earth.

Yet when Montesquieu and Adam Smith surveyed the world, half a millennium later, China had changed and developed little. It seemed static, or even receding, and they were puzzled at its inertia, especially in comparison to the dynamics of the West.

There are many suggested explanations for the non-development of China, but before considering one of them it is worth pointing out that China was not exceptional in its stasis, but quite normal. Looking from China at Europe, it would have been observed that the same thing had happened over the whole of the southern half of Europe at a slightly later date. If you had looked at Spain, Portugal, Italy, southern France and Germany in about 1600 you would have seen a huge dynamism, creativity and a thriving economy in both agriculture and industrial production. There were lively universities, strong autonomous towns and cities, limited monarchies and governments.

If you had looked at the same area around 1750, as Adam Smith observed, the whole area seemed to be going backwards. The universities were either closed or moribund. The towns and cities had been hugely weakened by absolutist rulers. There had been widespread plague and illness. The agriculture was declining with less use of animals and serious over-population. The terrible Thirty Years War of the seventeenth century had ravaged much of the area and the balance of powers had given way, from Russia to Spain and particularly in France, to autocratic and absolutist rulers. Italian and Spanish science and literature had faded to a shadow, and the Inquisition had gained ever more power. It was a story similar to that of China.

This suggests that a wider solution to the original China-focused problem needs to be found. Both ends of the Eurasian continent seemed to have hit some invisible buffers. Indeed, this is part of Adam Smith's message. There are limits to growth in traditional agrarian economies. Only a certain amount of energy can be converted by animals and plants and growing population. The loss of ecological diversity, forests and water, and degradation of soils starts to make the laws of diminishing marginal returns on further inputs of labour become ever stronger.

What happened in both cases can be described in the term co-invented by Mark Elvin in his *Pattern of the Chinese Past* (1973), which addresses these problems in China, namely 'The High-Level Equilibrium Trap'. Elvin describes how economies tend to grow relatively rapidly to a new peak, and then stop rising at a high-level-equilibrium, and perhaps to decline, rather like the letter S. This is in the nature of economics and is also a consequence of the laws which Smith's successor, the second great western classical economist, Thomas Malthus, described.

Malthus described how resources grow rapidly, but then population grows ever more rapidly, only to meet the inevitable buffers of war, famine and disease. China can certainly be seen as moving along this Malthusian path. Between 1700 and 1830, for example, the population rose from about 100 to 400 million. There was increasing poverty and soil deterioration. It was trapped here, as in other ways.

Seeing this high-level trap, a limit to growth with conventional technologies, as inevitable, makes us aware that the real problem is to explain how one society alone, Britain, managed to escape from this trap along a path of industrial growth based on fossil fuels. It is clearly not just the presence or absence of usable coal resources. China had huge coal reserves, as did Japan, and of course the Ruhr valley of northern France and Germany. This did not allow China, Japan and Germany to escape. Other parts of Europe only joined the British path some two generations after the first industrial revolution. It was not an easy shift.

What is extraordinary and worth commenting on is the current reversal. The dynamic West of earlier centuries, and particularly America, seems to be locked in another high-level equilibrium based on the older technologies of the first and second industrial revolutions – steam and then petro-carbons. The inevitable negative side-effect with global warming threatens to destroy many of the gains. Yet now it is China that looks most likely to provide the break-through into a new path which releases us, for a while, from some of the traps.

China leads the world in the production of solar and other renewable energy technologies. It is pioneering new communications technologies, of both a physical and digital kind, and has the fastest growing computer industry and the most advanced research on artificial intelligence. When one visits, it feels like China is a far more modern and sophisticated society than any other.

Instead of being regarded as a backward, spent, introverted and enervated civilisation, it is now a hope for the future, an alternative to the increasingly threatening and polarised worlds of the West.

Hong Kong

I have visited Hong Kong a number of times and have always been impressed by its bustle, its curious blend of China and Britain and its interesting history. It is far from the place which my distant cousin Robert Swinhoe first arrived at in 1854 and describes in his *Narrative of the North China Campaign of 1860* (1861). Then Hong Kong was just a small set of rocky islands off the coast of China, inhabited by a few fishermen.

The British, however, saw its potential as a toe-hold into China and they obtained it as a colony of the British Empire in 1842 as part of the reparations after the First Opium War. The colony expanded to the Kowloon Peninsula in 1860 after the Second Opium War. This colonisation was extended when Britain obtained a 99-year lease of the New Territories in 1898. The British honoured this agreement and Hong Kong and Kowloon were returned to China in 1997.

Until I looked into its history a little more, I assumed that Hong Kong's growth had been steady and impressive from the start. Yet it appears that even by the 1950s, and after the short Japanese occupation, it was a far from impressive place, run down and with much poverty. Its rise was almost exactly like that of

Japan's, in the 1960s onwards. It became one of the 'four little tigers', an economic miracle alongside the two other Chinese ethnic tigers of Singapore and Taiwan. People tried to find some common denominator to these, talking of 'Confucian capitalism', or British or Japanese influences, but no single explanation seems to fit.

Hong Kong prospered and was noted as an impressive example of western capitalism. The strength of British law and an uncorrupted civil service and administration were praised. Yet it is also notable that the British over their long hold on the island showed no enthusiasm for local democracy, so when Hong Kong was handed over to China it was still run basically by a small administrative bureaucracy, not elected by the people.

Dire predictions were made about what would happen when it was re-absorbed into China. A number of Hong Kong inhabitants used their British passports to move to Canada, the UK and elsewhere out of anxiety at what would happen. Yet the Chinese absorbed Hong Kong in a flexible 'One Country, Two Systems' policy. Hong Kong became a political part of China, but its economy, law and civil service were left largely untouched.

It has thrived within this dual system and although there are periodic movements to gain more independence and to do what the British never did, that is to institute an elective democratic government, on the whole the people I have met in and from Hong Kong seem reasonably satisfied and many of them feel part of China. They are aware that Hong Kong depends on China for many things, much of its trade, its water supply, its electricity and its defence. It is unlikely, even if the Chinese were willing to let it be independent, that it could achieve this.

Its importance for China, having lost and regained Hong Kong, is symbolically very high. It is also a valuable intermediary space where full blown capitalism and communism can mix and mingle. It might even be, if one were cynical, regarded as China's off-shore tax haven, something like the Isle of Man for the British. No doubt many mainland Chinese are investing and building up businesses there in an atmosphere where they feel somewhat more protected from the attention of the central state.

Yet Hong Kong is ever closer to the mainland, with the recently opened high speed rail link which joins Hong Kong to Shenzhen in a twenty-minute journey. Hong Kong is now, in some ways, a suburb of Shenzhen, a city which is already richer and more populous than Hong Kong.

Humour

A great deal can be learnt about a civilisation by looking at what people laugh at. Who jokes with whom, about what, in what form (slapstick, burlesque, irony, satire), all are indicators. What are the subjects for humour and what are the reactions to humour?

My own British culture is one where humour is very important. The English love irony, satire and crazy humour. Much of their greatest literature, from Chaucer onwards, has been filled with humour of one kind or another. When I went to Nepal, I was delighted when I got to the stage where I could make jokes in the Gurung language and people would laugh. I found that my British sense of humour seemed to be well understood and my friends were full of laughter and joking. I am not surprised that I have had a similar experience in China.

There seems to be an overlap between British and Chinese humour. At one end, there are some things which are central to British humour, but which are more or less absent or taboo in China. In particular, it is rude and not funny to embarrass anyone in public in China, to make them 'lose face', to look ridiculous or lose their dignity. This kind of humour is very central to British life through the centuries.

Thus, the kind of humour in the 'Spitting Image' series popular in the UK, which made several leading figures such as the Prime Ministers Margaret Thatcher and John Major look ridiculous, as well as many other well-known figures outside politics, is impossible. None of this would be acceptable in China, hence the furore when a cartoon likening the Chinese President and his Vice President to Winnie the Pooh and Piglet appeared and were quickly banned. Much of the joking and banter in the House of Common would be taboo in China and indeed a great swathe of British humour, from Chaucer, through Shakespeare to Oscar Wilde, would be out of bounds.

Much of family life is also not to be joked about in China. The whole area of marriage, a subject of much English humour, is not one to be included in public joking, and one also has to be very careful when joking about sexual matters.

Then there is a very large area in the centre where China and the UK appear to overlap a lot. My young Chinese friends and other authorities I have consulted constantly speak of how 'Chinese humour is not very different from British humour', which must be true since I have, as mentioned, found it so easy to share my English sense of humour with Chinese audiences and in private conversations. The Chinese have an even greater love of absurdity, I am told, than the British, but both share this amusement. So, the crazy, absurd, kind of humour in 'Monty Python's Flying Circus', or John Cleese or Rowan Atkinson's work goes down well in China.

Both cultures also like 'deadpan' humour where the comedian says very funny things without any facial expression to show it is a joke. Also, both like irony, saying one thing on the surface and meaning the opposite. This is one of the most important of English forms of humour and is much appreciated in China also where it is often combined with a rather bleak, depressed, self-abasement.

There is even a sharing of bad or pointless jokes. These are called 'cold' jokes or non-jokes in China. They are jokes without an ending or punch-line, that are designed to be dumb, sometimes called 'Dad jokes' in America, or, in another variant, 'shaggy-dog' stories (with a feeble ending after a long period of suspense) in the UK. The humour comes from the awfulness of the joke. It is 'cold' in China because, like ghost stories, they send a shiver down the spine instead of a laugh and hence cool you down on a hot day.

Moving to the area where China has its own special forms of humour, we can pick out several things. One is that Chinese jokes depend much more on cross-references to the huge store of Chinese history and literature and hence cannot easily be translated into English. The jokes, like the art, is much more allusive, referential, almost symbolic.

Secondly, the difference between the English language and Mandarin and other dialects makes for a considerable gap. Humour or sarcasm is expressed in English with the help of specific, generally understood, intonations. It is far more complex when you have a tonal language like Chinese. There are thousands of homonyms (two words that are spelled the same and sound the same but have different meanings) and homophones (each of two or more words having the same pronunciation but different meanings, origins or spelling). A lot of Chinese humour, much more than in the English case, is based on puns derived from these features.

These characteristics lie behind one of the best-known forms of Chinese humour, which is in fact more like theatre. This is *Xiangsheng* or cross-talk. This is very fast-paced, filled with puns, and includes song and dance. It is an art form, combining speaking, imitating, teasing and singing, performed by two actors. There are, of course traces of this in Britain – Morecambe and Wyse are a brilliant example of cross-talk. Yet it is less central in general than in China.

Many other questions remain. Did women and men joke as equals in the past, or about the same things? Did Mandarins joke with commoners? Was the Emperor allowed to joke? There remains much to be discovered in this very indicative area of cultural similarity and difference.

I

Industrial revolution

Historians are united in describing the appalling housing, furnishing, public sanitation and medical condition of the working population during the first industrial revolution in Europe. The conditions which Frederick Engels described for the slums in Manchester in the second half of the nineteenth centuries were appalling – but perhaps even worse earlier. Again, though pictures of workers in the industrial hub of South East China show conditions which are far from satisfactory, they seem, on the whole, to be less dreadful than the early Victorian British experience.

Although I have not been to all of China, I have travelled quite extensively in a number of the industrializing cities and my impression is that conditions in China compare favourably with the western experience, even though the pace and scale of development is so much greater. There is much journalistic criticism both by westerners, and even within China, of the pollution of food, water and air. But the cases we read of are not conspicuously worse, and often far less serious than the appalling conditions of the first industrial revolution, which lasted for more than a century.

Finally, if we think of absolute poverty, of the widespread, begging, destitution, semi-starvation and horrors described by Dickens, Mayhew, Booth, Engels and others, or that we see in other industrializing cities in Africa, India or South America today, China is rather impressive.

During seventeen extensive trips through most of the country, urban and rural, I have never seen any starving people, even when travelling through the central area of the great Sichuan earthquake soon after it happened. Even when compared to Japan with its destitutes under the bridges or in some parks in

Japan, China seems impressive. For example, in the six weeks tour in 2013, going through many crowded streets and markets and joining with the throngs on the national holiday, I only remember seeing perhaps half a dozen beggars, all of them suffering from some very serious crippling defect. Young people or women begging, a common sight in most developing societies, were absent. Of course, it may be that beggars would be moved on by the police, or that I would see more if I travelled on country buses and trains or went to the worst part of cities. Yet on the whole, it is very far from India.

Another feature of the industrial revolution in Britain were the very visible and gross discrepancies of wealth. There were huge landowners and industrialists living in vast country houses, and a mass of impoverished urban and rural workers. Of course, there is an emerging class of super-rich in China. Yet even now the affluent do not appear to stand out from the thronging masses of middling people, and the middling are not a comfortable enclave within a mass of people hardly able to feed or clothe themselves or their children.

These are no more than impressions, yet they are perhaps of value to balance a number of mis-representations which often emerge by taking one or two appalling cases and magnifying them – a child left dying in a street or a baby found in an overflow pipe.

I leave others to explain how China is achieving this unprecedented revolution while keeping the side-effects of misery and anger to a reasonable level. A residual communist egalitarian and socialist ideal and the power of a paternalistic government no doubt help. The technologies to make urban growth more tolerable have improved greatly. The Chinese have been tough, resilient and mutually supportive through the far worse tribulations of the dreadful years of the nineteenth century, and through the appalling privations of the Warlord Period, the Great Leap Forward and the Cultural Revolution. What the older Chinese are experiencing now must feel pretty amazing. I remember peasants in north-east China in 1996 telling us of how they could now eat meat regularly and buy furnishings for their houses. They felt a great change was happening. Since then incomes have gone up ten-fold or more through-out China.

Industrious and industrial

I come from a country which, for many centuries, was regarded by other countries in the West as filled with lazy people. The aristocracy and gentry did nothing much except pursue their pleasures. The townsmen, traders and manufacturers lived a relatively easy life shuffling money and employing others. The agriculture was relatively easy, looking after animals or arable agriculture with plentiful animals and mills.

It is all a matter of comparison, of course. A modern farmer or professional would have found the normal work load of many in pre-industrial England exhausting enough. Yet compared to the grinding work of many French, Spanish or Italian peasants, the English seemed fortunate, at least until the industrial revolution period of sweated labour in mines and factories.

I only discovered what the lot of most societies in history has been when I went to work in a Himalayan village as an anthropologist. There were periods of rest, but much of the time was a struggle to extract a living from the steep rocky slopes with few animals or mills. The stress on the back and arms and legs was almost unimaginable to me, especially the gruelling work of wet rice production. An encounter with Japan sharpened the contrast with my own country. Statistics showed that the Japanese worked much longer hours and in more gruelling conditions than any farmers in Europe.

I was therefore prepared, to some extent, for China and its tradition of hard work. Yet this tradition should not be forgotten. For thousands of years, the Chinese have been immensely hard working and ingenious in their work. In their fight against the floods and famines, the marauding landlords and armies, the difficulties of rice cultivation, which is enormously labour intensive, they worked and worked.

This traditional characteristic can be seen in different forms to this day. It can be found in the immensely hard-working children competing for good universities and working twelve or more hours a day. It can be found in the hard-working groups who have built up the wealth of overseas Chinese. It can be seen in the massive physical infrastructure China has erected in the last thirty years. Just to contemplate the amazing roads and railways, the vast cities with enormous high-rise complexes, and to think of how much hard work must have gone into them is humbling.

Traditionally, partly because of this hard and long work and the low standard of living, Chinese wages were very low indeed – far lower than those for comparable work in the West. Hence their competitive advantage and the manufacturing boom of the last thirty years. Now wages are higher and production is moving to Vietnam, Laos, Cambodia, even Nepal and Pakistan, in search of cheaper labour. Yet the prediction that the Chinese economy will sink because of this seems unduly pessimistic. The incredibly hard and dedicated work, the practical application to solving problems, the ability to work efficiently together will continue to make China a major nation in the new and emerging economic world for the foreseeable future.

Intellectual property

Evolutionary advances in thought and technology usually occurs through chance or experiments, where some better way is found to solve a theoretical or practical problem. How to make silk, paper, porcelain, tea – all are early and game-changing examples from China, and each of these was improved over time. The problem is that if the discovery is good, it will be copied by others and the inventor soon loses the advantages of his or her breakthrough. There are two major ways to deal with this problem and they have long divided the East and West.

In China, there was no form of legal system to protect

intellectual property, no patenting or copyright law, until the last two or three decades. The laws are still being developed and are weak. The only way to protect your discovery was through concealing how it worked, through secrecy, through not telling others outside your closest family how one made special pots or clothes.

Such ubiquitous secrecy slows down the rate of improvements and many useful break-throughs died-out with their inventors or the next generation. It goes with an attitude that, if something is publicly known, or can be discovered through the wall of secrecy, there is nothing wrong with copying it. This collides with western attitudes of the last couple of centuries and is leading to bitter disputes over 'property theft'. By western standards, there are indeed grounds to believe that IPR (Intellectual Property Rights), whether in books, ideas or advanced technologies are not properly recognised or followed in China.

The western tradition may go back to the Greeks and is found in Venice and elsewhere in the fifteenth century. Yet modern patent law seems to stem largely from the eighteenth century when the British, with their immensely powerful and complex court and legal system and flexible ideas of the bundle of property, developed sophisticated copyright and patent laws. They set up a patents office and gave the courts increased powers to back up those who felt their rights had been infringed. This development paralleled other parts of the evolving system of multi-layered property.

Intellectual and production rights can remain in the hands of the patent-holder for a period, yet they have to be broadcast and made known through a formal specification of what is new in the invention. So, everyone knows what is involved, but they cannot make or do anything too close to the process specified in the patent. Inventions are both confined to certain individuals, and yet for general use. This is a variation on the central idea in ownership, described elsewhere, where many things are both held by individuals or groups of individuals with specified rights, but also open to the public – like public parks, rights of way, libraries, schools and universities.

China is working on this, since it is in their interest also to reward and protect their increasingly high rates of innovation. As the diagram below shows, China is quickly catching up with the U.S. in the number of patent applications made each year. The diagram below shows the situation in 2016 and China overtook Japan the following year. Yet there is still some way to go in the introduction of this curious western invention, law-based intellectual property.

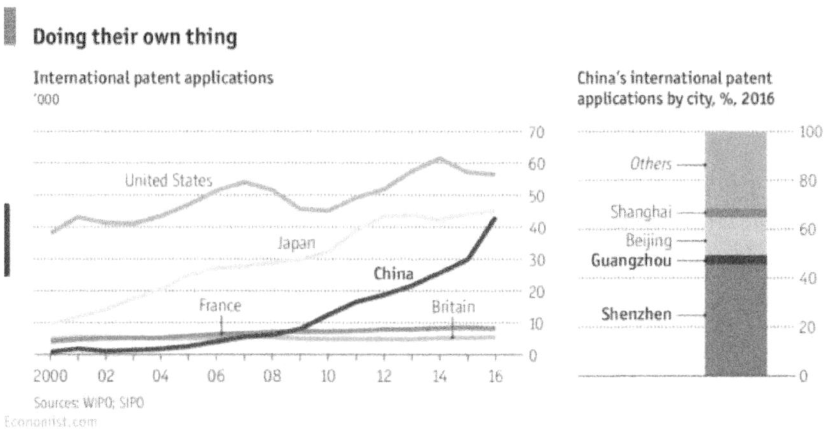

Investment and saving

Coming from a civilisation where money has been widespread and most of the mechanisms of market capitalism in place for over half a millennium, I had never really thought about the problems caused in terms of investment when a previously peasant civilisation tried to move to capitalism. My ancestors for a number of centuries had access to banks, bonds, annuities, a stock exchange, shares in companies, secure ownership of land and housing which brought a good return, trading and business opportunities across the empire. Anyone with some spare cash, some advice and common sense, could invest and get a good return.

I began to sense the alternative situation when I visited Nepal. There were many Gurkha soldiers who had either saved money, or with good pensions, who were returning to the country. The banks offered the lowest of rates. If one invested in a new business that was initially successful, immediately others would imitate it and the market would be swamped. All my friends could do was to build expensive houses and hope for the best.

I have found a similar situation in China. I remember long discussions on the matter with a senior Chinese academic. He was unable to find anything to invest in safely, apart from property, so he was buying flats and houses all over China. The wasteful property speculation in China, where we have seen huge apartment buildings left empty across the country, is one harmful side-effect of this, also caused by the fact that local governments, which own the land, find that one of the few ways they can make money is through speculative building.

Another harmful effect, widely recognised, is that many middle-class Chinese are sending their money abroad into safer and more profitable foreign investment. This is a notorious problem, of course, in all developing countries. Sometimes the reason is to conceal wealth, and in China, where conspicuous savings or wealth has long been pounced on, this is a continuing worry. Property rights were not safeguarded in the way I find in the history of English law and at the centre of John Locke's philosophy of democracy.

The solution is not easy, even though we see the problem. If the Chinese follow that part of the English path that encourages the rising middle class to keep their money at home, to save and invest by giving absolute guaranteed protection, as seems to happen in Japan, that would be a start. At present, however, China is following an alternative path, which is also encouraged by Britain, which is to invest in off-shore havens. Half the tax havens in the world are in British jurisdictions in the Cayman Islands, Isle of Man and so on. They are absorbing huge amounts of money, much of it from illegal activities, and thus reducing the national income of many countries.

Inward and outward looking civilisations

It is worth briefly considering another major distinction between civilisations. This concerns the degree to which they are inward or outward looking in their economic systems. In this respect, we can see that both China and Japan were inward looking and Europe and the Anglosphere were outward looking. What I mean can be seen if we concentrate in particular on the Chinese case.

Although, or perhaps because, China is so vast and diverse, it has always had a problem of understanding and dealing with the non-Chinese 'stranger'. For most members of the Middle Kingdom, through most of history, people from other civilisations were barbarians of whom one might have heard, but with whom one had no contact. This tendency of huge civilisations to be largely ignorant of, and disinterested in, the rest of the world can be seen in the United States today. Surveys have shown that knowledge of the rest of the world, or even the possession of a passport to travel outside the States, is still modest, certainly away from coastal areas.

This inward-looking tendency was exacerbated in the Chinese case by several factors. One was that, from very early on, economic activity – trading, marketing, manufacture – was looked down upon by the elite. Both the Legalists and Confucians, in different ways and for different reasons, placed economic activity by ordinary people at a low level in the social order. Too obviously pursuing money-making in a Mandarin society was demeaning. In the absence of corporate law and in the presence of a powerful government which would seize and tax any conspicuous wealth, large money-making endeavours were difficult to establish. Though there was a vast amount of petty commodity trading in many parts of China, especially on the East coast, large companies for trade and manufacture were conspicuous by their absence through most of Chinese history.

This was combined with the possibilities for a huge internal, small-scale, trade on the immense water-networks within China and the turning away from the possibility of overseas sea trading after the early fifteenth century. When we add in the fact that the two great waves of invaders who established Empires in China, the Mongols and the Manchus, were inland peoples with little experience or interest in maritime or even land trade, we can see the pressures against the development of the patterns we find in western Europe.

The effect was that the overseas trade of China was largely in the hands of people from other civilisations, intermediaries who controlled the exports of silk, porcelain, paper and tea. Along the land silk roads these were early on the Sogdians and the Muslim traders. On the sea silk roads and to Japan they were first the Arab traders and later the Portuguese (from 1515) and other western traders.

All of this became particularly important as the power of the western nations grew. It soon became apparent that the Chinese government did not really know how to handle the outside traders, except in a rather rigid and formal manner. Hence the incomprehension when Lord Macartney brought a trade mission from Britain in 1792, then the tragedy of the Opium Wars, and later misunderstandings. It is not surprising that the Chinese turned to the British expert Sir Robert Hart to organize and oversee their maritime customs system from the middle of the nineteenth century.

Islam

Although official statistics may underestimate the true numbers, it is stated that there are about eleven million Uyghurs, a Turkic minority who are now Muslims, four fifths of whom are in Xinjiang, but with another sizeable group in Hunan. They are also spread across the Stans and Turkey. They were originally Shamanic, then Manichaean, Buddhist and finally became converted to Sunni Islam in the period 934–1212.

The Uyghurs are, in fact, a group of a similar size to the Hui Muslims. The source and formation of Hui Muslims is a very complicated historical process. The first source of the Hui people was the Central Asian tribes, Persians and Arabs, who began to come to the east in the early thirteenth century. Later, they intermarried with the Han people and adopted many Han characteristics. The Hui have often revolted against the Chinese, but also been well absorbed at times, but it is the Uyghurs of Xinjiang who are currently the subject of a concern which it is impossible for me or others from outside China to properly investigate.

The first and most general thing to say is that there has long been friction but, in some ways, it is surprising that it is not worse. The bases of Islam and Han civilisation would appear to be diametrically opposed from their start, oil and water, and mixing would seem impossible.

Islam was founded on conquest and war, so it is often extremely warlike and militant. It is no accident that the Chinese used Islamic troops extensively in their early conquests, for instance in the Ming dynasty, and particularly in the south-west of China. The Chinese leaders clearly trusted these troops enough in fighting rebellions and against minorities and used them as the British did with the Gurkhas and other native troops to widen their empire. Many of those involved in these operations settled down after the conquests and we have come across many Hui (Muslims) in the towns and cities of Sichuan and Yunnan. There are many Muslims, and we filmed some of the last Muslim market streets, with their halal shops, about to be pulled down to build high rise apartments, along with the traditional Chinese hutongs.

There is an impressive Muslim settlement and mosque in the middle of the ancient capital of Xi'an. Here I bought a wonderful cap, which seemed to show the combination of the two worlds. The shape is the traditional Muslim hat, with lines across it, so the structure is Islamic. But the decorations of red and mock jewels are purely Han. In Xiamen, we visited one of the oldest mosques in the world, from the eighth century, and heard of peaceful co-existence since then. The famous admiral Zheng He, who explored as far as Africa, was born as Ma He in a Muslim family.

Islam is, in some ways, the most confident of monotheisms. It is extremely simple in its theology and without a church hierarchy, depending almost entirely on the unquestioning faith of its individual adherents. They are saved by following some simple rules and it is their duty to spread their faith to others, though forced conversion is discouraged. In this system there is only one primary loyalty, to Allah and his prophet. Other Abrahamic monotheisms are to be tolerated, namely Judaism and Christianity. But all others outside this monotheistic fold are infidels, damned to eternal hell and the avowed enemies of Islam. This, of course, includes Buddhist and Hindu civilisations.

Yet it is more complicated than this, for the Islamic rulers of India, particularly Akbar the Mughal Emperor, were extremely tolerant and at times many middle eastern countries were known for their tolerance. It is clear, from the very earliest mosques, which I have visited in eight century Xiamen onwards, that Muslims could well co-exist in China. Indeed, Muslims have contributed a huge amount to Chinese society over the ages, including important roles in administration, science, astronomy, seafaring, martial arts, cuisine, calligraphy and the arts in general. Currently they are also trying to help with the Belt and Road initiative, the nearest reaches of which are going through Islamic nations on the western border of China.

Yet it appears that there is also an element of a 'clash of civilisations' here. As the Han spread west, they absorbed many parts of the old central Asian civilisations on their border. This included large number of Turkic people in Xinjiang who retained their strong ties with central Asia and Turkey. They had a strong sense of identity and often felt this threatened. There have been numerous huge Islamic rebellions. For example, during the Qing dynasty, there were numerous rebellions in the eighteenth century, and then in the nineteenth in the Dungan revolt in Shanxi and neighbouring provinces, (1862-1877) several million died, and in the Panthay rebellion in Yunnan (1856-1873) one million died.

Recently, with the rise of militant Islam and its extreme forms in Al-Qaeda, and recently ISIL, as a result of Wahhabi fundamentalist spread and the bungled western interventions in Iraq, Afghanistan and Syria, these tensions have increased again. A number of the more militant in Xinjiang have proclaimed an independent state, hoping to break away from China. There are rumoured to be a number of jihadis who have returned from Iraq and Syria after the defeat of ISIS there, and others from Afghanistan. Xinjiang is regarded by the government as China's Chechnya, a feared source of rebellion and terrorism. There have been occasional terrorist attacks against civilians in China, though it is difficult to find out much about the identity of the attackers and their motives.

The Qin dynasty government in the past liquidated the much more peaceful Christians because they put God first. The Chinese government is now worried about separatists and extreme religious terrorist activities in Xinjiang. If Xinjiang goes, what about Tibet and Inner Mongolia? They are trying to take measures to diminish extreme religious activity, banning long beards and the *burqa*, monitoring religious services, setting up extensive surveillance and security operations, and placing Communist Party officials as 'family guests' in Muslim homes. Government workers are stationed in each village to eradicate poverty and to reduce religious extremism.

For some in the West this is a cause of much anguish. As in the case of Tibet, when facing a split loyalty, the Chinese are faced with a difficult decision, akin to the old one about how tolerant one should be to intolerance. Yet as Europe faces its own inner demons over the centuries and even today, particularly Jews and Muslims, it can hardly afford to be too self-righteous.

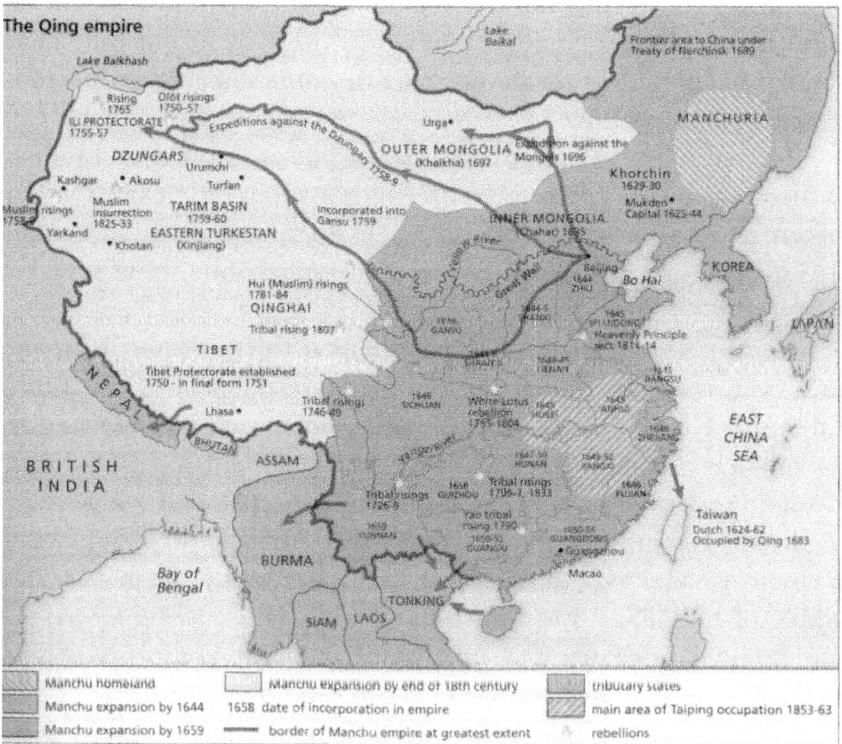

This map from *The Cambridge Illustrated History of China* by Patricia Ebrey (1996), 223, shows very clearly the huge expansion of China under the Qing. It also shows the numerous rebellions, including a number of Muslim uprisings on the western border.

J

Joint responsibility

I am used to a world where I take responsibility for my actions and where I would not expect to be punished for crimes of others. If I was naughty at school or in the home as a child I would be held responsible for my actions and others were not punished alongside me unless they were part of some gang or group that carried out the offence.

This system of individual responsibly is central to English justice and has been so for more than a thousand years. Even a parent is not responsible for a grown child's mistakes, and children are not punished for the faults of their parents, or a wife or husband for their partner's crimes.

From this background I was amazed to find that in Japan, and even more in China, the system of responsibility is entirely different. Chinese law books specify who should be punished if an offence is committed and in what way. Often this means that if one member of a family is found guilty, the whole family, as far as distant cousins and uncles and aunts, suffer as well. Likewise, a single villager will bring down the anger of the judges on the whole of his village. Even the ancestors' shrines may be rooted up and family houses razed to the ground and lands confiscated. This seems very severe and unjust to us.

Yet this also expresses the collective nature of Chinese society. You are not a single individual, separate from others, but part of a larger body, an arm or leg, which implicates others. This applies to the good things of life, for the success of one member of the family or village in the imperial examinations or a business is shared by the whole group. Yet it also applies to bad things, as we have seen.

This has many effects on Chinese ideology to this day. It leads to risk avoidance, for a mis-step can bring severe retribution on your closest family and fellow villages. For this reason you have to be very careful and conformist. It also instils fear in the population and deters them from criminal behaviour in the knowledge of the dire consequence. In a vast country like China, traditionally with few police or soldiers, such a mechanism was essential. The situation is rapidly changing with more individualistic legal codes, but the relics of such a system can still be observed. The shame of one is the shame of all those near to him or her.

Journey to the West

One of the four great novels of China has this title (it is also known as 'Monkey'). It is part of the evidence that the Chinese have long been eager to travel out of China and learn from others. The amazing journeys of some of the early Chinese monks, for example Faxian, who travelled to India and beyond and brought Buddhism materials back to China, is another indication. .

Nevertheless, it is the case that, for long periods, partly because of its vastness and self-sufficiency, China was, in effect, closed up. Even the great voyages to Africa and elsewhere of the Muslim Admiral Zheng He were stopped in 1433. After that, until the early nineteenth century, China treated foreigners, and those travelling from China and returning, with deep suspicion. Such mistrust found justification as imperial nations started to force an entry, as in the mid-nineteenth century Opium Wars.

Nevertheless, there were small trickles of people sent abroad for education. A few were sent by Christian Missions in China in the earlier nineteenth century, and more went abroad, though mainly to Japan, at the end of the nineteenth century. In the brief period of opening up between the establishment of the Republic in 1911 and that later 1920s, when the government collapsed, others went to learn and bring back western culture and ideas. A notable example was the poet Xu Zhimo, who studied at King's College, Cambridge in 1920-1 and tried to import western arts and ideas.

The normal tendency to shut off China occurred again after 1949 and even the Russian influence was shut off in 1958. For twenty-five years, China was largely closed again.

These long periods of closure, preventing Chinese from going abroad and foreigners from settling and exploring anywhere than in one or two eastern ports, undoubtedly slowed down Chinese development. To be too bounded and inward-looking, even with a huge civilization like China, tends to stifle reform and evolutionary change. The fertilizing effects of contrast and of ideas developed in totally different cultures is lost. It is like a rock pool by the sea, which becomes stagnant if it is not refreshed by periodic influxes of the tide.

The contrast of all this is what has happened in the last forty years. Since the 1980s, first in a trickle, then a stream, and now a flood, the number of foreigners who have come to work in China, and, even more so, the number of Chinese, especially young people, going abroad to study, has changed dramatically,

A few brief statistics will show what has happened. Currently, China has more than three times more students studying abroad (nearly three quarters of a million) than any other country, and ten times as many as most of its nearest competitors. In 1998 there were about ten thousand going abroad to study. By 2000 it had reached over 100,000, and by 2015 half a million. Furthermore, the flow of foreign students coming to China is also growing rapidly. In 2003 there were about 75,000, and by 2017 nearly half a million.

At first, those going to universities abroad tended to stay away. Now an increasing number are returning to China, partly because there are more opportunities and an improved standard of living, partly because in certain countries the visa restrictions and employment opportunities have changed so that people cannot stay on after they get their degree.

Foreign ideas, technologies, customs and styles now flood into China, also carried by the ever-increasing number of Chinese, from school parties to older people, who visit Europe and America for holidays. For example, in Cambridge, ten years ago there were one or two thousand, but now there are tens of thousands.

Though China, at times, might like to close itself against global penetration, and sometimes makes it harder to get visas and permissions to work, it is now too late to shut out the outside world, not only because of the media and internet, but also because of the flow of people. A whole generation, especially of the elite, are now foreign-educated and others are attending western-style schools and universities which have been set up by western partners. China and the West are merging through friendships and experience for the first time in history.

K

Kung fu and other martial arts

One of the presiding images of China is of its marital arts, *kung fu*, the Shaolin monks, Bruce Lee martial arts films, or films such as 'Flying Dragon Crouching Dragon'. These have brought to the West the image of the Chinese variants of martial arts. We learn about these arts also from Japan, where they were early taken. In Japan they usually bear the ending 'do' or 'o', as in *ju-do*, *ken-do*, *sum-o*. The ending means 'path' or 'way', as in the *dao* or 'Dao-ism'.

What intrigues me about these arts, apart from the excitement of some of the stories that surround them, is the fact that once again they break down one of the category distinctions which I had taken for granted in my western civilisation.

I had always assumed, until I went to Japan and then China, that, in one category, there were secular games and sports, social events, even if they were often associated at times with political or economic affairs. Another entirely different category were religious rituals like praying, fasting, pilgrimages and going to church. Yet when we look at these 'martial arts' we see that they lie precisely across this distinction, combining elements of both in a way of which we have little experience, though possibly some sports like bull-fighting contain a hint of this.

All the Japanese and Chinese martial arts are clearly sports, contests, often battles of a kind. Yet they are also deeply associated with Daoism (hence the 'dao' ending) and with Chan or Chinese Buddhism or Japanese Zen, the world of monks and monasteries. To participate is a form of ritual, there is a sense of sacredness, of appeal to something beyond this material world, as with the 'way of tea' or *cha-do*, or 'the way of the warrior' or *bushi-do*. You control yourself in the way an ascetic or yogi would do, using breathing exercises, strong self-discipline, ceremonial actions. You use the ideas of absorbing the energy of the *qi* and the strength of your opponent in order to bring victory.

Perhaps the nearest we have had in the west were the knights who went in search of the Holy Grail, or on the crusades. Yet their quasi-spiritual, at times, vocation of war only catches the outer edge of activities which one cannot classify simply as either games, sports, battles or rituals.

L

Landward and seaward

When I arried home from India on a steamship in 1947 as a little boy, I had my first experience of the fact that Britain is an island, surrounded by water. I lived near the south coast and used to collect shrimps and fish on the beach and swim in the sea. From that time onwards, I was never more than fifty miles from the sea wherever I went in England or Scotland. I took it for granted that my country was defended by the navy, that one of my national dishes was fish and chips, that the sea was hugely important in my country's history and culture.

Later I would learn the details. I would discover that the reason England had grown and survived as a democracy was because it was protected by the sea. Just as freedom flourished on the western sea coasts of Europe, in Scandinavia, Holland, the west coast of France, Portugal and into the free cities of the Italian Mediterranean, so liberty and the sea were bound together. I learnt that these areas, and particularly England, spread out across the oceans to found their Empires. I found that one reason for the great break-through in the Renaissance and Scientific Revolution was the ferment of ideas created by seaborne flows of people and new things across the world's oceans.

It was therefore a shock to discover the civilisation of China, which instead of looking to the sea, tended to look westwards towards the vast land expanses of central Eurasia. If we think of China as a huge square then only one of the four sides is bordered by the sea. Even this sea is treacherous, with typhoons and tsunami and for many centuries the marauding Japanese pirates. Nor, with the vast expanses of the Pacific was there a great deal to find there.

It is true that there was trade along the maritime silk road to South East Asia, and that the great Ming voyages of the eunuch admiral Zheng He showed that China could have been a great naval power. Yet the Ming stopped the voyages – they were very costly and gained no practical outcome. They took resources away from the urgent matter of defences against the horsemen barbarians on the western and northern frontiers, who finally broke through and overthrew the Ming Empire.

It is also true that water-borne activities were even greater in China than in Europe. The vast rivers and canal systems made China somewhat like a collection of Mediterranean seas, filled with goods, people and major ports. Yet this again may have diverted attention from the sea and had different effects to ocean contacts.

The hidden benefits of seaward orientation for the development of European civilisations, from the Phoenicians and Greeks up to the Dutch and English, were missing for the most part in China. Another benefit they missed was the protection against famine which the resources of the sea, including the seaweed used as fertiliser on the fields and the ability to transport goods cheaply to famine-stricken areas.

As we try to understand the inner essence of China we have to think of it as a huge interconnected land Empire, drawn along the silk roads to the west. It was in marked contrast to the Mediterranean and Atlantic empires of Europe, which gave us a different world.

Law and justice

In China,the extraordinary integration of the system achieved through joining the power of the family and the bureaucracy meant that it was unnecessary to have more than a minimal legal system, and that system has a number of significant differences from legal systems in the West.

The codes built on each other, but for simplicity let us take the Great Ming Code (Da Ming Lü), promulgated at the start of the Ming dynasty, that is about the middle of the fourteenth century

It had many overlaps with the earlier codes of the Tang from six hundred years earlier, and those of the Qing, four hundred years later.

Several things are particularly striking. One is that almost the whole code is concerned with criminal law, that is the relations between the State (Emperor) and his people. It is a penal law code. There is nothing on civil law, cases to be tried in imperial courts between imperial subjects.

If we compare the Ming code to the roughly contemporary English work of Henry de Bracton *On the Laws and Customs of England*, a work written about a century before the Ming codes and more than ten times as long, it has an entirely different feel. Only a small part of Bracton is concerned with criminal law and punishments. The majority concerns the process of law, rights and duties, the way to deal with property and wealth.

By the middle of the eighteenth century, when the Qing codes were not much more elaborate than the Ming, it took eight large volumes (over forty times the length of the Ming code) to cover English law in William Blackstone's *Commentaries on the Laws of England*. Ninety percent of this is concerned with civil law and the procedure of the courts.

Secondly, the Ming and other law codes, in their evaluation of the severity of crimes, are based on the social relationship of those involved – particularly family relationships. There are at the start of the Ming code elaborate tables of degrees of mourning relationship, based on patrilineal ties and marriage. Each offence is graded according to superiority and distance of relationship.

Thus, for example, to strike or kill a father or paternal grand-father, is far more serious than to kill or strike a brother or son or maternal grand-father. This embedded, status-based, law in China is completely different from the individualistic law in England where, in Bracton or Blackstone, family relationships are almost totally ignored. The Chinese code has strong resemblances to status-based continental Roman law.

A third feature is the absence of any guidance in the Ming

code on due process. Whereas English law books are filled with regulations about how trials are to be held, what constitutes a legal charge, what is evidence, the rights and duties of judges, lawyers, plaintiffs and defendants, there is no hint of this in the Ming code.

It seems to be assumed that when a person was accused of a serious offence he or she will be summoned and questioned by a single magistrate, who would, if necessary, use torture and threats to arrive at some sort of truth. There is obviously no jury, no presumption of innocence, no idea of intrinsic legal rights. There is not even any mention or indication of lawyers in the courts, again a great difference.

Once found guilty, the punishments in the Ming code were ferocious. For example there are five degrees of beating with a light and heavy stick, five degrees of penal servitude, three degrees of life exile, and two degrees of death (strangulation and decapitation) and banishment. The penal servitude, for example, might involve being imprisoned in a heavy wooden 'cangue' (a wooden 'stocks' which imprisoned the head and hands) for months or years. There were other death penalties also, including 'death by slicing'.

The system appears to consist of a very simple set of punishments to maintain social order, to support the distinctions of family status, and the peace and order of this huge empire. An immensely complicated set of courts and procedures, paralleling those present in medieval to modern England to deal with contesting individuals and their rights and duties, especially in relation to property, as far as is now known, were less developed. We are in a world where people are born into a fixed and unequal position based on birth order, sex, parental status and relation to the Emperor. These status divisions are rigidly maintained by the imperial law codes.

Such a system remained in place over more than fifteen hundred years in China until less than two hundred years ago. Then reforms began to be made at the edges of the system. Yet it was only a hundred years ago with the fall of the Qing, that a new criminal code, based on that of Japan, was introduced. By this, collective responsibility of families in criminal matters was eliminated, corporal punishment and slavery abolished, and the use of torture forbidden. Some further progress had been made by the time of the Sino-Japanese war in 1937, but then for the next forty years, all serious movement towards a rights-based and 'modern' form of law was suspended.

Only after 1978, and with growing speed in only the last twenty years, has the whole legal system of China started to be changed to bring it into line with western practices. This is, in many ways, as large, and impressive an undertaking as the economic reforms, and indeed part of that whole procedure.

I have visited an intermediate level court in China and it now compares reasonably well in its process, care and rules with equivalent courts in the West. Discussing with various lawyers in China it is clear that a huge set of reforms have been introduced and, at least in theory, all litigants are treated as formally equal, and the 'rule of law', including the separation of law and politics, is being proclaimed. A large legal profession is being trained, with judges, barristers, lawyers and solicitors.

Yet the older system of avoiding taking cases to court still persists. Recently we visited a new 'model' village near Chengdu. In the administrative building there was a room labeled 'Police'. When we went in, we found only a large table and some chairs. We were told that if there was a dispute between neighbours or family, a policeman might be called. His aim was to bring in all those in the dispute and to try to get them to agree a solution to the differences through discussion, rather than taking the case to a higher court.

One final historical difference which is very striking to me as a student of English legal history, concerns the nature of the distinction between law and justice.

Educated in England, I have always taken the distinction between law and justice for granted. As a child at school, I learnt quickly that there were school rules; don't run in the corridors, don't talk after lights out, that kind of thing. Yet these formal rules did not apply to most of life, which was covered by customs and ethics. For example, in a game of football there were just a few rules, but many things should or should not be done according to norms of justice or fairness.

Furthermore, it was possible to behave strictly by the letter of the law, yet go against the spirit of the law. This why the cry and appeal to fairness, 'That's not fair', was heard so often in my schools. It was widely believed that there was a thing out there called 'justice' or 'fairness', which everyone would agree on and could be upheld. I did not know at that time, of course, that this was a deep-seated feature of English social and legal history.

In medieval English law and onwards, much of English attention was focused on what was called 'equity', another word for fairness. There were equity courts, presided over by the highest legal official in the land, the Lord Chancellor, which protected the rights of the weak – children, women, the poor – and was especially concerned with cases where there was no legal redress through the ordinary process of law, but 'fairness' demanded justice. For example, if papers had been lost or destroyed, if the agreement was just a verbal one but should be fulfilled, if the offence was not illegal but unjust, then the court could act.

In other words, the English have long believed in justice and had confidence that their legal system will protect them and their freedoms.

When we look at China in the centuries up until the middle of the twentieth century, or indeed most of the rest of the world, there is nothing of this. The legal system was cruel, arbitrary, a tool of the rulers. It had no concept of equity at all and was there basically to enforce some simple rules of law against murder, insubordination and treason and against certain forms of cheating. Much of this has changed in China during the last forty years, when there have been extensive legal reforms and much institution building. Although the 'rule of law' still needs to be improved, as it also needs to be in many western countries, the situation is different from that in earlier China.

For these reasons, it is difficult to apply the word 'justice' to the Chinese situation until the last half century. Justice might be an element of the ethics within a family, but that was all. It could not be expected outside the family and village. Such phrases as 'justice must not only be done, but be seen to be done' would be meaningless. The sign of an English gentleman was that he was just and fair. The sign of a good employer, leader of any kind, trader or merchant, was that he or she was just. Justice was as important as honesty and other major virtues.

This gives a country which has such a concept great flexibility and toughness. People can undertake things in the knowledge that as long as their motives are good and they try to avoid harm, they will be protected by equity, even if things go wrong. The weak were protected from the strong and children and women against the old and against men. It is a marvellous institution, even if what is 'fair' is always a subject for potential dispute.

No doubt the concept of justice is now being introduced into the Chinese legal system. Yet, it is very tricky to do this, as many of the continental systems based on Roman law, which essentially lacks this distinction also, found as they tried to change their legal systems from the nineteenth century.

Love and marriage

Because our family systems have been so different for so long and differences still remain beneath the surface, though they are not often talked about, our attitudes to love and marriage in England and China are still somewhat different.

In China until 1949, on the whole, women had an inferior position. They were seen as subservient to their parents, their brothers and even their sons. For many centuries this led to humiliations and cruelty, such as the breaking and binding of the feet of millions of Chinese women for a number of centuries.

All this has changed very rapidly in a revolution in gender

relations in the last sixty years. Chinese communist ideology put men and women on an equal level, and this has made it much easier for women to achieve their true place in the modern world. Yet it is important to remember the background before this relatively recent change and the way in which it affected marriage.

Until a few generations ago, the family determined almost everything about a person's life and all of one's life was affected by family relations. It was believed essential that the children married the right person. The decision as to who this person would be could not be left entirely to the choice of the individuals to be married. It must be planned, like any other political or economic matter, by the whole family.

It must be arranged carefully with the help of marriage brokers and cemented by elaborate rituals which re-arranged the whole set of relatives. It must be accompanied by the exchange of marriage gifts. Love of a romantic kind was not to be the main criterion in deciding who to marry.

This ideology has been shattered by recent events, including the changes in the family system, higher geographical and social mobility, and the influence of western models. In relation to the last of these, the English and American and increasingly European tradition, in which I grew up was very different.

Although it varied considerably depending on social class, amongst the bulk of the population over many centuries young people in Europe were alone in the world during their teenage years and lost their close ties to their birth family. They looked for some replacement, some person to fill the emotional emptiness. The ideology of love marriage gave them the goal. This was combined with a prohibition on sex before marriage and a relatively late age at marriage.

Romantic love was celebrated in poetry, songs, literature and bore a striking resemblance to the desires for acquiring and enjoying commodities in the market capitalist world.

Some of this has also long been true in China, which has a rich tradition of love poetry and novels. Yet, as in many societies traditionally, love and marriage were different things; you might love your wife after marriage, but for many, especially the wealthier, marriages were largely the result of decisions taken by people other than the young couple.

In some ways the difference is not as great as it might seem. The English married mainly for love, but of course they tended to choose those who were of a similar background and attitude to life.

There was another difference in the two traditional systems. In the English case, once they had 'fallen in love' and made their choice, apparently overwhelmed by an irresistible force, the relationship would be expected to be the most important in the young people's life. It was ultimately stronger than that to parents or even to their own children, who would one day leave home. The central bond was a sideways one with a marriage partner. The relationship was seen as a fusing together of two heads, hearts and bodies; they would become 'married friends' – what is called 'companionate marriage'. The vertical relationship with parents or with children, if it came to a contest, came second.

The vast changes which have occurred recently have affected all Chinese over the last three generations and part of the tension and difficulty for many young Chinese is that grand-parents, parents and the young have been brought up in different systems. Your parents cannot understand their parents early upbringing, and likewise they cannot understand you, or you them.

I have often asked young Chinese audiences whether they will marry for love, or through arrangement, and they universally say for love. The revolution is not over however, for I am told that roughly half the marriages in China are still, to a certain extent, 'arranged'. Yet the change means that parents and children have to balance the older demands of parents and kin that they should have a say in your marriage against the new ideologies.

M

Mah Jong and other games

My first serious encounter with China was probably as a little boy of two or three years old in India. My grandmother had been born in Burma and no doubt had there picked up an interest in the great game of China, *mah jong*. Through my childhood, when I lived in England with my grand-parents, we played *mah jong* regularly.

I still remember the satisfying slabs of ivory tiles in their walls and placed on the beautiful orange lacquer rests. I remember the different coloured dragons, winds, the sets of bamboos circles and Chinese characters.

Little did I know at that time of the ancient Daoist and other philosophies that lay behind the symbols. No doubt much of Chinese symbolism and history could be read off the game of *mah-jong*, which is still widely played across China in small villages and great cities. It was invented in its present form during the Qing dynasty, but probably has roots in much earlier games.

Another famous board game, which I have never tried or even watched is 'Go'. That this is even more difficult to win was recently shown by the fact that the Deep Mind computer has taken longer to become the world champion at Go than at Chess. It interests me also because the philosophy behind it is contrasted to the western equivalent of Chess. In Chess you win by destroying the enemy by direct attacks and killing off pieces. In 'Go', which resembles the famous book by Sun Tzu on *The Art of War*, you win by surrounding and blocking your enemy without necessarily engaging in any direct battle. The aim is to win by skill and without the loss of a single soldier. Much of current Chinese overseas policy seems to follow this model.

Mandarins

The nature of Chinese civilisation is shown clearly by their ideal of what a man should be. This picture, a blend of Confucian, Daoist and Buddhist ethical principles, is to be found in the character of the Mandarin.

One preliminary characterization of such a person is given in an account of the superior man in Confucian thought by Karl Jaspers.

The superior man: All goodness, truth, beauty are combined in the ideal of the superior man (Chun-tzu). Noble both in birth and endowment, he has the manners of a gentleman and the wisdom of a sage.

The superior man is no saint. The saint is born; he is what he is; the superior man becomes what he is through-self-discipline.... He is contrasted with the inferior man. The superior man is concerned with justice, the inferior man with profit. The superior man is quiet and serene, the inferior man is always full of anxiety. The superior man is congenial though never stooping to vulgarity; the inferior man is vulgar without being congenial. The superior man is dignified without arrogance; the inferior man is arrogant without dignity. The superior man is steadfast in distress; the inferior man in distress loses all control of himself. The superior man goes searching in himself; the inferior man goes searching in others. The superior man strives upward; the inferior man strives downward. The superior man is independent. He can endure long misfortune as well as long prosperity, and he lives free from fear. He suffers from his own inability, not from others' failure to understand him. He is slow in words and quick in action. He is careful not to let his words outshine his deeds: first act, then speak accordingly.

The superior man does not waste himself on what is distant, on what is absent. He stands in the here and now, in the real situation. "The superior man's path is like a long journey; you must begin from right here." "The superior man's path begins with the concerns of the common man and woman, but it reaches into the distance, penetrating heaven and earth."[14]

[14] From Karl Jaspers, *The Great Philosophers* (1962), p.58

This captures a good deal of the ideal Mandarin, but can be fleshed out by adding a number of other criteria. Here are some which seem important to me: memory, command of the classics, obedience to authority, patience in adversity, loyalty, filial piety, administrative and linguistic ability, mathematical ability, trustworthiness, incorruptibility, seriousness, ritual ability, decorum, good sense, analytical logic, passivity, peacefulness, harmony, able to control networks of associates, aesthetic and artistic taste.

This is how I see him, but it is worth supplementing it with the view from a young Chinese person today. So here is how my colleague Li Shuo sees him.

A Chinese gentleman should:

1.Make unremitted efforts to improve your personality, morality and learning in order to achieve sagehood in the future
2.Behave according to rites and morality
3.Be flexible in different situations
4.Benevolent and lenient to others; not very aggressive or competitive
5.Accumulate calmness and mellowness through time
6.Code of brotherhood; trustworthy
7.Comply with the hierarchy of generations and respect elder people and old teachings
8.Frugal, to counteract misfortune in the future
9.Aspire for a simple life indifferent to fame and fortune; at the same time, have concern for and a sense of responsibility towards the whole world
10.Not adventurous; always attached to the homeland.

It will be seen that this is a strong reflection of a certain kind of civilisation – deeply influenced by Confucianism, but also by Buddhism, Taoism and legalism. It is centrally about harmony, loyalty and observance of the social rituals.

Mandate of heaven and democracy

I come from the cradle of modern democracy. For over a thousand years, and constantly re-affirmed as in the Magna Carta of 1215 or the opposition to, and beheading of, Charles I in 1649, the King has been the servant of the people. His mandate is from his subjects and if he breaks the contract with them by abuse of power, he can be resisted. He does not rule by Divine Right but by working on behalf of his subjects.

This is totally contrary to the absolutist legitimacy of the European continental monarchies from the sixteenth to nineteenth centuries. In Spain, Italy and France and in parts of Germany and Russia, the ruler was given absolute power as God's representative on earth. There were no rights to rebel or challenge the King, for he was the origin of all law. It was a philosophy which prepared the way for fascism and communism.

The Chinese case falls neither into the British or Continental model. It was unlike the British because, while the Emperor had a responsibility to rule his people well, the Chinese people did not elect parliaments or have an independent judiciary, press and university system to hold him to account. For this reason, the traditional Chinese system can hardly be called a democracy in any sense.

On the other hand, the Emperor was not absolute, for he ruled, like the officials below him, with a certain mandate. He was to protect and nourish his people and if he failed in this task, the mandate would be withdrawn. The signs of the withdrawal were various disasters; droughts and floods, insect plagues, wars and disease, foreign invasions. If he could not protect his people, they could rise against him. Consequently, there were numerous uprisings in Chinese history and this idea made it easier to accept a new imperial dynasty, even if it was composed of foreign barbarians or internal ethnic minorities.

The pragmatism and flexibility of this system is essential to the amazing continuity of China. When power ebbs from current rulers, it is possible to feel morally justified in transferring allegiance. This reminds me of the peculiar nature of Chinese chess. When a piece is taken by the enemy, it does not leave the board, as in western chess, but converts to fighting for the former enemy.

Nowadays the situation is changing fast. The Communist Party holds the Mandate of Heaven. As with previous imperial powers, once the Party was the victor in the struggles against the Kuomintang and the Japanese, the Chinese transferred their loyalty to it. Yet the party knows that if things go catastrophically wrong, or the mass of people become seriously alienated, the Mandate will be withdrawn. In this way, the Party gradually bolsters its legitimacy by lower level democratic reforms and limited autonomy for minorities. The Party is constantly listening to concerns and trying to improve life in order to generate loyalty. It is far from representative democracy, but nor is it an unlimited absolutism. It is very different from Soviet Communism or European fascism. It is once again a unique and interesting alternative.

Mao Tse-tung

I have never encountered anyone quite like Chairman Mao, both for good and evil. First, he does not fit my idea of a great military leader and politician, for I have been given scrolls of his poetry, written in his own calligraphy, and am told they are excellent. It is true that Obama writes good books, as did Winston Churchill, but Mao's reputation is on a larger scale and somehow seems anomalous.

Yet the main puzzle I have is how to assess him. On the one hand, he did a prodigious job for China in many ways. Riven by terrible civil wars and the warlord period, the occupation of the Japanese and the dislocation after a century of undermining by the West, he brought China back together again. He unified it, gave it back its self-confidence and a set of goals, achieved something which puts him in the same league as the first unifier of China, the Qin Emperor, to whom he is often likened.

In doing this he also did many other commendable things. He treated women as equal to men and at a stroke wiped away two thousand years of Chinese patriarchalism. He set up a system of barefoot doctors and the nearest China could achieve to a National Health service in its desolate and impoverished state. He destroyed many of the grosser inequalities of wealth by confiscating landlord and large merchant property and returning it to the people, giving them all a basic stake in the country. He realized that if China was to be strong again, it would have to rapidly embrace industrialism.

At a deeper level, he cleared the decks, attacking the four 'olds', Old Customs, Old Culture, Old Habits and Old Ideas. The campaign to destroy these began in Beijing on August 18, 1966, when Chairman Mao met the Red Guards in Tiananmen Square, and the Guards in the capital began to take to the streets to break the 'four olds'. at the start of the Cultural Revolution. These included things like religion, Confucianism, the old family system including ancestor worship. Thereby, as earlier total conquerors such as Kubla Khan or the Manchu Emperors had done, levelling China back to the base.

Mao was unable to get China to grow much from this levelling or drastic pollarding. Yet, two years after his death, Deng Xiaoping in 1978, by slightly tweaking his message, set China free. Its immense growth and rise from poverty has happened. Without Mao, China might well have totally collapsed into a fragmented and impoverished state after 1949.

This is the sixty (or seventy) percent good which many of my Chinese friends refer to when I ask them. Some of them are old enough to have suffered seriously through the Cultural Revolution and some even to have witnessed the earlier famines. He was, on balance, they say, to be admired. Yet he went on too long and power corrupted. His vision faltered and the system of communism revealed its weakness. In this way, they add, he was also forty (or thirty) percent Bad.

What is the bad part? There are two obvious and appalling things which, when I learnt of their full horror, made it difficult to forgive Mao. One was the famous 'Great Leap Forward' in 1958 to 1962. In an ill thought-through attempt to turn China into one vast industrial plant, Mao and his advisors destroyed Chinese agriculture to such an extent that the greatest famine of recent history occurred. Estimates of the deaths vary between twenty and fifty million people dying of starvation and hundreds of millions more suffering serious malnutrition. The accounts are terrible – cannibalism, the agonies of the slow death, the displacements, the cover-ups. It is unbelievable and was unnecessary.

The second is the Cultural Revolution of 1966 to 1976. Here the fact that communism could only be preserved, it was thought, by a growing attack on 'The Other', traitors in our midst, the 'Rightists', meant that again millions died, and alongside them there was a humiliating mass attack on intellectuals, artists and innovators. The 'strugglings' and trials remind me of the Spanish Inquisition.

Alongside the attack on people was a terrible destruction of China's cultural heritage – the ancient libraries, statues, monasteries were burnt and trampled on, not just in mainland China but also in Inner Mongolia and Tibet. It is a vandalism again reminding me of the destruction of previous Empires – the first Qin Emperor and the Mongol invaders. In a vast way it was similar to the destruction of the great cultural treasures of the imperial palace and the wonderful gardens of Peking by the British and French in 1900 in an act of wanton and horrific revenge.

Mao is certainly great, for good and evil. He still smiles in Tiananmen square. The party he built up still rules China. He is still on the Chinese currency. His thoughts are still taught to all Chinese children. Millions flock to revere him at his birthplace and offer him flowers and prayers.

The surprising reverence people feel was encapsulated in

an incident when we were staying with a Tibetan family in Shangri-La, on the border of China and Tibet. The Tibetans, as mentioned, were sufferers from Mao's period as much as others. Yet when we were taken into the family Buddhist shrine, I was amazed to see in the central place of worship pictures of the Dalai and Panchen Lamas - and also Chairman Mao. I asked my hosts how he could be there after all he had done and they smiled and said that Mao was a reincarnate lama, a Rinpoche, and hence a brother of the Dalai Lama – and we all know that brothers have occasional quarrels, but they remain brothers.

Markets and marketing

I come from a country where, certainly for the last few hundred years, the predominant form of selling of products has been through fixed shops, with windows of goods, counters and shelves. Cambridge has an open-air market with stalls and previously the largest annual fair in Europe, lasting a month on Stourbridge common with stalls of goods from all over the world. Yet small weekly or monthly markets have been less important in Britain than permanent shops.

China, much like India, Mexico or other peasant civilisations, was a market-dominated civilisation. Those with goods, particularly perishable foodstuffs and clothing, would bring their wares to an open space or alongside a road in a village, town or city. Each stall specialised in something and often duplicated neighbouring stalls. The marketers, often women, would try to persuade passers-by to buy from them. Many of the purchases occurred after haggling since there were no set prices.

I have visited a number of such markets and been struck by the lively atmosphere, entertainment as well as buying, and the tendency to concentrate on perishable goods.

One particular feature of the system in China has been analysed by William Skinner in the 1960s. He showed that the markets varied in form, frequency and size in a tiered and hierarchical way. A big city would have temporary or permanent large markets. Around it would be smaller towns with markets, spread at even distances from the city, like circling planets round their sun, which were less frequent and smaller. Round each of these towns was a similar arrangement of village markets circling the town. It was a random process, but extraordinarily symmetrical and well organised.

The lay-out of Chinese cities, towns and villages to this day, still mirrors to a certain extent this ancient marketing hierarchy. It is a hierarchy one can also find reflected in the arrangement of schools, of medical facilities, of local government and many other parts of Chinese life. This hierarchical structure of smaller to greater is a central feature not only of economics but of all Chinese life and one of the secrets of China's strength and unity.

Memory and forgiveness

The general shape of Chinese civilization becomes clear when we stand far back from it and survey it over a period of five thousand years. For two thirds of its history, there was little in most of the West except illiterate wandering tribesmen. Even in the last third, China was almost continuously the greatest civilization on earth in scale, complexity and wealth. China was brought to its knees like some great stag by the hounds of imperialism, firstly Britain, then more broadly Europe and America, and finally, the most bitter of all, Japan.

China has reason to feel both proud and even angry at how it has been treated. And here again is something I find surprising – the forgiving nature of the Chinese. The Chinese I have met now acknowledge Mao's mistakes, but on the whole understand why he did what he did, and why, and they forgive him and many mourn his passing. Likewise, they know of the arrogance, racism, imperialism and disgusting behaviour of the British, Americans, French and Japanese – the destruction of the wonderful palace gardens north of Beijing, the forced opium addiction, the germ warfare experiments and the massacres. And above all the nasty imperial stereotypes to which they have been subjected – thieving, lazy, smelly, no-good etc. as their foreign predators depended on them to run their businesses for them.

Yet again I have found little resentment or inherited anger. The Chinese tend not to have bitterness, but to be philosophical. Not once in many conversations all over China has anyone ever alluded to the disgraceful behaviour of Britain since the Opium wars. Even with the more recent appalling behaviour of Japan, while there are museums recording the atrocities and many people speak privately about provocative behaviour and visiting shrines of war criminals and the repeated failure of the Japanese to make a formal apology and to accept many of the features of their activity, generally the Chinese normally keep silent on the matter, although on the fiftieth anniversary of the victory over Japan there were many demonstrations and the Nanjing Massacre Memorial Day has become an important national event.

Mills

I come from a mill-filled civilisation. That is to say, machines for turning natural energy, at first water, wind and animals and later coal and oil, into power have been the backbone of the economy. Even by the time of the 1086 Domesday survey, England had an average of more than one water mill in every village and town. Wind mills, invented in England, later supplemented them.

Mills were used in paper-making, cloth production, for grinding grain. Later they were converted to coal and became the hub of the industrial revolution in the great 'mill towns' of Yorkshire and Lancashire, which were central in the burst of production in the nineteenth and first part of the twentieth centuries.

It seems such an obvious thing to use mills extensively that I assumed China would be similar. Yet I soon discovered that mills were little used in traditional China. A few mills were used in the marshes on the coast to help with salt production. Others were used to lift water and a few simple ones to lift a wooden hammer to beat rice. Yet, given the vast country and potentials for mill machinery, it is the relative absence that is surprising.

Of course, it is easy to think of reasons for the difference. Wheat is best ground in a mill, but rice, barley and later maize in China is not much suited to milling. Fulling mills were not needed for making clothes from wool, since sheep were not common in China. Water was raised by very cheap human labour. Indeed, in general, the ubiquity of cheap labour, as well as the political risk of sinking money into an expensive building that can easily be seized or destroyed, undermined the demand for mills.

Two consequences of the absence of large mills in traditional China can be noted. The first is on the work pressure on individuals. If wind, water and animals can be harnessed to help in agricultural and industrial processes, they can provide a huge boost to human productivity and hence alleviate physical labour and give some leisure. This was not developed in China.

Secondly, the English were used to making and using machines of various kinds to help them. The mills pumped mines, pounded cloth and ground grain. The experimenting with mills encouraged constant innovations and improvements in the concept of harnessing nature through artificial means. All this was the necessary background to the gradual 'industrialisation' of England which dates from the thirteenth century. The final outcome in the eighteenth century was the result of discovering how to convert coal effectively into energy – the steam revolution. Yet it was just a final outcome of a centuries-long process.

In China there was no such tradition of the use of machines to replace human labour. This is yet another reason why, despite huge supplies of potential water, wind and coal energy, there was no sign of an industrial revolution until very recently. Even Mao's failed attempt to industrialize in a few years leading to mass starvation may be linked in some way to the difference.

It works well for periods, but its future is never guaranteed and those who preach a return to the greater simplicity and certainty of bundling everything together, the root of the word fascist or fascisti, have an enormous appeal. The countervailing forces are precarious and form right and left the ancient tendencies towards absolutism are constantly there, as Tocqueville famously pointed out in his book on American Democracy.

Minorities

According to the official classification, there are some 55 minorities in China, that is to say non-Han peoples. In fact, there are many more, for many smaller groups, or divided groups, have been amalgamated into larger units. They form one of the most diverse and largest set of minorities in the world.

The minorities can be divided into three major groups (figures in brackets are millions). There are the minorities, mainly forest dwellers, and mainly along the southern and western borders of China, who include the Zhuang (16.9) the Miao (9.4), Yi (8.7), Tujia (8.3), Dong (2.8), Buyi (2.8), Yao (2.7) and others. It took many centuries and often bloody wars to incorporate many of these into the Chinese Empire and they were often driven south and west before the advancing armies.

Having visited many of these groups, it would seem that the relations between the majority Han and these minorities appear to be harmonious and they often live in autonomous provinces such as Guangxi with a great deal of self-rule. They have preferential treatment in education and their own universities, they were given more freedom under the One Child Policy in the past, and much development aid has been focused on them.

During the Mao period, attempts were made to crush parts of their local culture, language, costumes, rituals, but now the diversity is celebrated. Compared to the often-abysmal treatment of almost identical peoples across Burma and India, the Chinese are managing this difficult relationship on the whole with skill and tact, or so it seems to us. Many people we meet are in fact of mixed Han and minority ancestry and they are allowed to choose to be either – and often choose to be minority, which is more advantageous.

A second group are the mainly Buddhist highland peoples to the west and north, the Manchu (10.3), Tibetans (6.2), Mongol (5.9), Kazakh (1.4). The Mongols and Manchus and Tibetans as well as the nature of Chinese (Chan) Buddhism are described elsewhere. The third group are the Muslim minorities. These are described elsewhere under 'Islam' and consist of two groups, one ethnically Chinese and the other of Turkic origin.

The distribution of some of the minorities in China are shown in this map from the 1991 *Cambridge Encyclopedia of China*. Among other things, this shows the wide distribution of the Muslim Hui group.

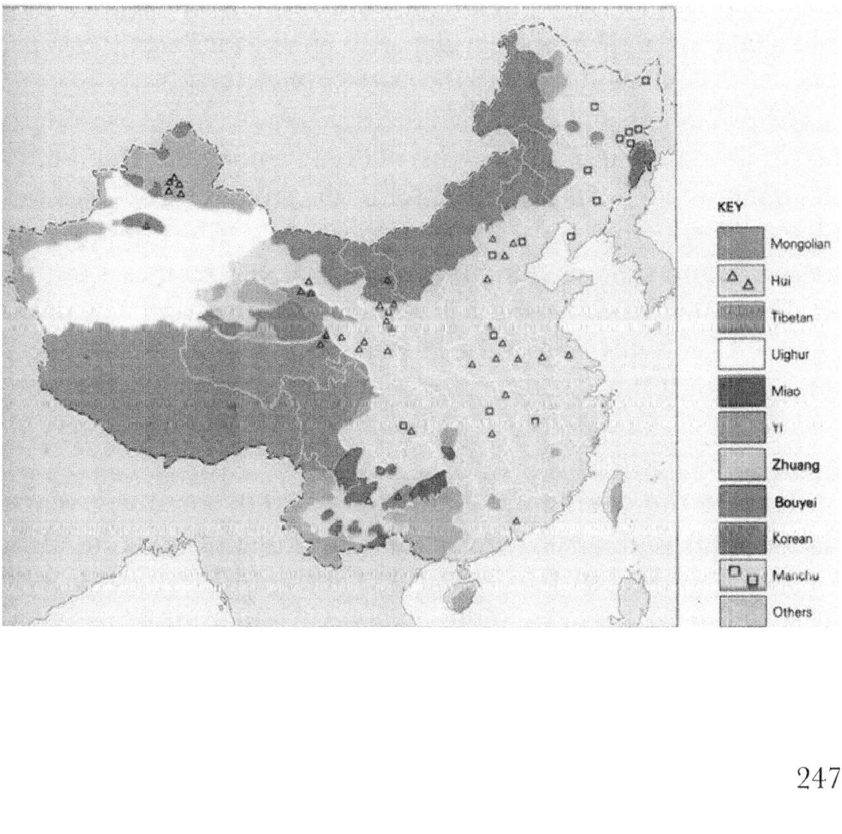

Missions and missionaries

Although there were Nestorian Christians and other Christians in China from the seventh century, the first systematic missionizing efforts started, mainly with Jesuits, from the sixteenth century, including the famous Matteo Ricci (1552-1610). Ricci's linguistic skills, flexibility, admiration for China and talents impressed the Chinese and for a couple of generations the missionaries were warmly received.

They brought up-to date science and technology to China, especially astronomy, and were not seen as a threat. Yet, as they became successful in converting large numbers of Chinese and it looked as if China might switch to Christianity, the Emperors became troubled and ordered the total destruction of all missions and missionary work. Many thousands of Chinese and westerners were tortured and killed in the most brutal way. Exactly the same had happened a century before in Japan, where similar fears that Christians owed their first allegiance to an outside ruler, the Pope, was felt to be intolerable, and they were massacred.

Christian missions continued to arrive however, and as western power increased, they were active not only among the Han but in the minority areas such as the Lisu in the west. The missionaries now concentrated on useful works such as the founding of hospitals and schools, for they found that the Chinese, on the whole, seemed singularly disinterested in Christian salvation. Despite huge sums being raised for mission work, there were very few converts. Only when eccentric forms of Christian belief were fostered, for example by the Taiping rebels, did Christianity in some form appeal widely.

During the communist period from 1949 for thirty years, the missions were again unwelcome. Since the opening in 1978, Christianity has spread again in China and there are now reckoned to be around seventy million Christians in the country, the majority Protestant and it is estimated that it may have more church goers by 2030 than America. Although some of the Christian churches were shut down from time to time, others were allowed and we even found one where the pastor, living at some distance from his church, was paid by the Chinese government to travel to his congregation. Again, the Catholic cathedral in Beijing, closed on our earlier visits, was open in 2018 and selling Church goods and performing services. Perhaps this was linked to the agreement between the Chinese and the Vatican, the latter accepting the principal that the Chinese would have a veto on the appointment of bishops.

Behind the uneasy relation between the Chinese and the Christian missions lies the deep conflict between a system where all political power and allegiance is funnelled upwards to the Emperor, or now to the party, and especially Catholic forms of Christianity, where allegiance to the spiritual head of the Church is very powerful. This gives Protestant missions an advantage, since that branch of Christianity separates religion from politics very firmly. Yet the Protestants tended to attract the Chinese much less because their puritanical and anti-ritualistic and dogma-based variant of Christianity was less exciting than the more magical, mystical and ritualistic Catholic variant.

The following diagram, suggesting that there are now more Christians than formal members of the Communist Party in China, was a surprise to me when I found it recently, though the figures are disputed. For example, the White Paper on 'China's Policy and Practice of Guaranteeing Freedom of Religious Belief' in 2018 put the number at about thirty-eight million Protestants and six million Catholics.

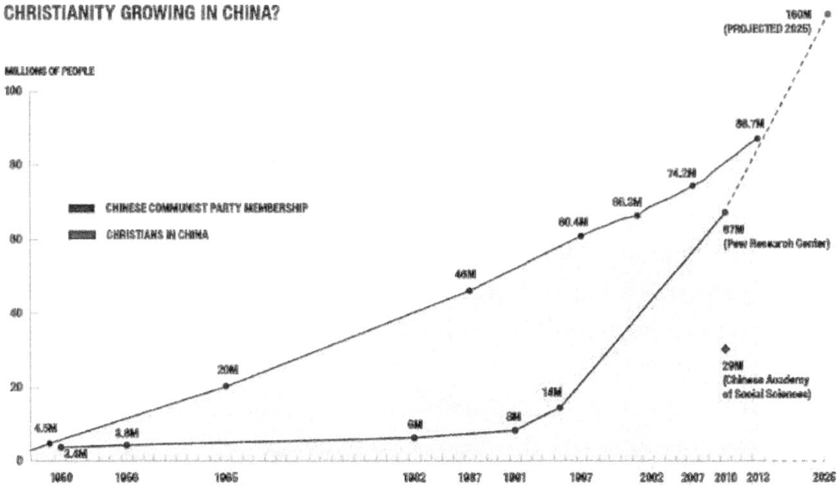

Source: *Religion in China*, Chinese Academy of Social Sciences, Pew Research Center, Fenggang Yang, *People's Daily*, Chinatoday.com, Xinhua News Agency, *Bloomberg*, Charles Neuhauser, *China: A Country Study (1987)* Credits: Eleanor Albert, Julia Ro

COUNCIL on FOREIGN RELATIONS

Modernity

Very few people really have much idea of what modernity means. If you ask even well-educated and intelligent students or their teachers, what do you mean when you say that society A is 'modern' and society B is 'pre-modern' or 'modernizing', they will tend to mistake the symptoms for the causes. They will point to things like living in cities, or having cars and mobile phones, or schools and universities, to electricity and television, to high social and geographical mobility. Societies where people live in the countryside and work in agriculture, and don't have the technologies mentioned above are pre-modern, places which have these features are modern.

This is, of course part of the meaning, but it is quite superficial and means that somewhere like urban parts of North Kora are 'modern', while some rural parts of the United States are pre-modern or 'modernizing'.

Over the years I have developed a different definition of modernity which is both simple and takes the discussion away from superficial technology. It rests on the observation that we can regard human beings as being principally driven by four overwhelming passions or interests. One is the desire for power, control over other people, the need to dominate, the endless competition for superiority. This we often term politics, but it is 'politics' in the widest sense, not just the restricted political life of ballot boxes and political parties, but the politics of all fields of human life, of the family, art and religion.

A second drive is towards wealth, that is to say the need for food, shelter, clothing and other material resources for our bodies. This is often termed economics, but again the 'wealth' we seek is much wider than the restricted field of stock exchanges or formal economics. We seek wealth along many dimensions, leisure, conspicuous consumption and display, cultural capital, to name a few.

The third drive is towards human warmth or recognition, towards love and protection, towards meaningful relations with other humans, whether through the family or other groupings and relations such as friendship. This we call social and is dealt with by the social sciences.

The final area consists of the broad area of ideas and beliefs, including everything from science and education and cosmologies, to religion and ritual. The innate curiosity and the mixture of hopes and fears of a species primarily notable for its large brain and inquisitiveness, makes this a particularly powerful drive, often overcoming all others.

We tend to think in these terms, to conceive of Power/Politics, Wealth/Economy, Relationships/Society, Ideas/Religion and think of them as analytically separate and, in my own English context, separated. This separation is what makes us modern. Yet when I started to survey the societies of the world, as I begun to teach anthropology, I quickly realised how unusual my separated world is, both historically and cross-comparatively.

In very simple terms, I found that for ninety percent of the history of humans, in what were called hunter-gatherer and then tribal societies, there were no separations. The individual lived in groups which were simultaneously based on the pursuit of power, wealth, social worth and ideological unity. The group was all-encompassing.

Only about ten thousand years ago, and this is what we mean by 'civilisations', a change came about when the first separation was made into two, rather than four, parts. On one side the society and economy were placed, peasant worlds where the economy was still 'embedded' within the family and where no distinction could be made between the drive for wealth and human warmth. On the other side were power and ideology, where the emergence of priests, teachers and formal belief systems, often based on writing, became prevalent. The union of power and belief divided the civilisations into the political-religious ruling group, and the largely powerless mass of the people, illiterate and under the control of the militarily and ideologically powerful.

This state of affairs, peasant civilisations with a powerful ruling elite of the combined rulers and priests, continued in most of the world until very recently. Across Europe it was the basic system until late into the nineteenth century. In most of Asia it continued until the later twentieth century.

This is a transition or intermediary phase, neither entirely modern, nor non-modern. We can thus think of *ancien regime* Europe, or Qing China, as two examples of pre-modern, half separated.

The English world in which I grew up is the anomaly, for it is clear that for at least eight hundred years it has separated the four spheres very considerably. The economy was autonomous and based on the capitalist laws of the market and disembedded from the family. There was no peasantry in the formal sense of that word. There was a tension and separation of the Church and State, made final and explicit after the Protestant Reformation, but present much earlier with the tension between the powers in Britain and the Papal allegiances of the Church. And there was no rigid division between a literate, all powerful ruling elite, and a mass of illiterate country folk. England, one might say, has always been 'modern', despite having a pre-industrial economy, and a pre-electoral democratic power system.

If we use this definition and apply it to recent Chinese history, we can see that China has moved along the continuum from pre to modern in many respects, but is still far from being fully modern. The signs of modernity and separation which have long existed in China were momentarily halted during the dominance of the communist party from 1949 to 1978. Communism was based on Marx's vision that we should return to the extreme form of pre-modernity. We should destroy all the budding separations of the State, the market, private property and return to the simple state of what Marx imagined the original, hunter-gatherer, society was like when there were no instituted spheres of activity, for everything was communal. It is the absolute antithesis of modernity even if, as Lenin, and others, pointed out, it needed electricity and industrial production to give it power.

When Deng liberalised the system in 1978 with the first tentative experiments at having a separate market economy, later with private property and private companies, China moved to a quasi-modern structure. Yet it has not yet taken the second step, which is to separate politics from ideology. The Party controls the world of belief and religion with a 'Bureau of religious control', it controls all education, it regulates all communications media. It still keeps the strong link of power and belief which lies behind most of European history of the last thousand years, let alone the Roman Empire, namely that the rulers and those in charge of ritual and education, the clergy or *literati*, are joined. The Pope and the Emperor or King were united. Those who offended the religious powers, for example, were hunted down by the Inquisition and then handed over to the State power, which imprisoned, tortured and executed them as was deemed appropriate.

The present situation of China is thus quite normal and almost universal. It does not really need explaining. What is anomalous and unusual is modernity, the temporary and ever-fragile and challenged, separated, world that emerged in Britain and parts of north western Europe, especially Holland, and then spread to America. That it is fragile and constantly threatened was shown when open, separated, societies collapsed in a few years across all of Europe in the 1930s, with Hitler and Mussolini, following the earlier move to Communist rule in Russia.

Now we see in the onslaught of the current American President on the supposedly separate Law and Media, two of the principal checks on power, an effort to turn America into a new kind of dictatorship or imperial system. Some see this as a 'modern' state regressing to a 'pre-modern' amalgamating of previously discrete parts of the political system. Such a threat seemed inconceivable even three years ago. It leads to the curious situation where we may find that the main bulwark against the descent into fascist dictatorships is no longer the U.S., but China, where, despite the huge power of the Party, the general tendency is towards a more liberal and balanced situation, even if there are temporary set-backs.

The final point to make is that modernity is a work in progress, an ideal, an 'as-if' system. The inevitable overlap and tensions between power, wealthy, society and ideology, which in their more extreme forms we often label 'corruption', are always present. In practice we cannot, as humans, separate our heads and hearts, body and spirits, desire for dominion from a desire for love. We are intrinsically non-modern. Yet we construct the artifice of modernity as the best method to provide individual freedom and happiness.

Money and cities

One consequence of the elevation of the Confucian ideal was the downplaying, not only of war, but also of commerce and money. The Chinese have always been excellent businessmen and traders, highly interested in profit, money and marketing. They have had huge and busy cities and amazingly widespread and connected waterways. Yet the Confucian and Legalist ordering placed the making of money through trade and manufacture below the more honourable toil of peasants in the fields.

In China people were as eager to make money as anywhere and there were occasionally some large trading firms from the nineteenth century onwards (for example in Shanxi and the Yellow River delta). Yet the Mandarin attitude to money-making was somewhat dismissive. A combination of political uncertainties, the division of family wealth between all the children, and, later, foreign competition, meant that there was truth in the old Chinese saying that 'No rich (Chinese) family can remain rich for more than three generations'.

No large, independent estate or order, which is often termed the 'bourgeoisie', emerged until recently. It was difficult to pass on large economic gains to the next generation. Hence few huge family firms emerged, unlike in Japan, India or the West. The great cities had no independence in law and were just seats for the administration, so the town traders remained very vulnerable to government power.

Mongols and Manchus

As explained under 'Minorities', the second large block of minority peoples the Han Chinese had to deal with are those on the north and west, the Mongolians and Manchus. They are, of course, ethnically more or less identical to the Han, a mongoloid people, but because of their habitat and way of life they developed very different social structures, political systems and cultures.

In the early centuries of the Christian era, the Han empire was harassed by steppe peoples from the west, the powerful Huns, but after the Huns had conquered parts of Europe, their place was taken by other nomadic horsemen, the Mongols. The Mongols suddenly coalesced and became a mighty force under Genghis Khan and started to make raids into western China in 1205 and 1207. Previously they had been more or less held at bay, but they then swept across China under Kublai Khan in the middle of the thirteenth century. They razed the cities to the ground, destroyed all signs of settled civilisation and reached as far as south China. Kublai Khan even launched unsuccessful invasions of Japan in 1274 and 1281.

In the process they are estimated to have killed between a third and half of the Chinese population. They became absorbed into the Chinese system however, and between 1260 and 1368 the Yuan dynasty ruled China and historians have more recently found some creative and useful aspects of their rule. They were finally overthrown by the Ming. Nowadays the Mongols are mainly located within Inner Mongolia (within China) with a population of about 25 million, and Outer Mongolia (in Russia), population about 3 million. They are mainly Tibetan-Buddhists and constitute an autonomous region of pastoral farmers.

A similar pattern emerged when the Manchus, further to the east along the northern Chinese frontier, broke through the Ming defences and sacked Beijing and destroyed and killed many Han. Again, they set up a dynasty, the Qing, which ruled from 1644-1912. Part of the later weakness of China arose from the fact that the rulers, including great Emperors like Qianlong and Kangxi were from a conquering minority. Being a minority, they had to rule through fear and an extensive system of surveillance and suppression. Yet they were also in the early period highly successful in their wars and conquered areas which almost doubled the size of the Chinese empire.

Mountains and rocks

Having worked for many years in the Nepal Himalayas before I went to China I should not have been surprised by two aspects of mountains there. Nevertheless, I did not expect them.

The first is how very mountainous China is. From my little reading, and pictures I had seen before I went there, I imagined China as a great flat plain, covered with wet rice fields, ponds and great rivers. Perhaps there were also some gentle slopes with tea growing on them, and some forests, but basically it was flat. Almost immediately I discovered that the rice-growing only applied to the southern half, and that other grains were grown to the north. And I learned that well over half of China is mountainous.

Particularly along its western border, China's lands are part of the Himalayan chain, and above that, of the great uplands of central Asia. Other areas also, such as the famous perpendicular peaks of Guilin, or the mountains of the north, make it basically not unlike my experiences in the Himalaya.

The other surprise was the attitude to mountains. I was aware that in Tibet, in particular, some outstanding mountains were considered to be sacred, the abode of the gods, the site of pilgrimages. What I had not realized was that dotted across China were many sacred mountains. A number of them are covered with shrines and temples, for example outside cities such as Chengdu or Qingdao. Others are pilgrimage sites.

Mountains are regarded as half-way between earth and heaven (Tien), the abode of spirits. They are also the traditional home of danger, of bandits and rebels, as well as the refuge of the ethnic minorities who have been pushed up onto their ridges, or fled there to escape the taxation and other harassment of the state.

Mountains and large rocks have much symbolic importance in China. The first classical literature reference to the importance of mountains was in the 'Poetry Classics' in the sixth century B.C. There was one chapter on 'the High Mountain' in Henan Province. It was the story of a Princess which showed that the mountain connected the earth to the sky and that a great mountain would protect a family.

Sima Qian, the great historian of the second century B.C., wrote a chapter on how China, as a nation, is defined by five great mountains. They are the landmarks of Chinese territory, lying on the west, south, north, east and centre. The most important was in the east, near Confucius' birthplace, Mount Tai mountain. Confucius mentions climbing to the top of the mountain where he could feel that the whole country was very small. This is taken to mean that if the Emperor goes to high mountains and looks round, all the land is in his control.

So the unifier of China, the first Qin Emperor, also went to Mount Tai and held a ceremony at the bottom and the top, symbolizing that he was henceforth in command of the whole of China. Since then the first Emperor of each dynasty has gone to do a ceremony at Mount Tai mount and other important people go there to get protection and a blessing.

In the Tang dynasty, in the 'Dragon Classic', which is about *feng shui,* the Dragon symbol means a mountain. For good *feng shui*, every house should have a mountain behind it to give it strength. The Dragon or mountain symbolizes resources – forest, land, water, plants and animals.

To this day, if one has an important patron one talks about 'somebody is my mountain' or 'Relying on the mountain'. The concept is still influential and expressed widely. For example, the Palace Museum and People's Hall in Beijing have huge pictures of mountains in their main rooms, as does the Chinese Embassy. The many paintings of mountains and water symbolize that the government is very powerful and in charge of the country. In the U.K., government buildings or College dining halls have pictures of important people. In China it is mountains and water that are important, for the Chinese respect abstract power and not so much individual heroes.

Mountains also have an important aesthetic value. 'Fake

mountains', that is the rocks or stones in gardens, or even beside small bonsai plants, should be very beautiful, looking like a pretty lady – very romantic, with a sensuous S shape – or in the shape of a lucky animal like a lion or tiger. Wealthy people designed gardens with 'fake mountains' to express their loyalty to the Emperor who often visited the gardens of rich subjects.

The early beliefs in Holy mountains in Buddhism were perfectly in line with Chinese ideas and this helped the acceptance of Buddhism. There were four Holy Mountains for Buddhists in China, each with an important Buddha in a temple on them. The most important was the Wisdom Buddha on Wutai mountain in Shanxi. This is known as the Wen Shu Shish-Li or Manjushiri Bodhisattva. Every Qing Emperor started their rule by worshipping there and Mao Tse-tung, before he became Chairman, went to this mountain to obtain divine good luck.

During the Qing period and even up to the time of Chairman Mao, the important Buddhist leaders such as the Dalai and Panchen lamas regarded the leader of China as the Wen Shu Bodhisattva. When Chairman Mao was recognized as such in the early 1950s he was dissatisfied since this was just one of the several incarnations and he thought, as the sun, he should be recognized as the Buddha, the Shakyamuni himself. This was one of the reasons for subsequent tension and the troubles in Tibet.

N

Nightmares

China was unified through massive wars and conquests by the Qin Emperor in 221 BC. Since then, given its colossal size, it is not surprising that it has often fallen apart again, with huge and bloody consequences. Its great problem reminds me of my own difficulty with modern technology – I now have so many gadgets that at any time one of them is always breaking down. China's great fear is of social disorder. For centuries the rulers have feared the small spark which, if it catches, can destroy thousands if not millions of lives.

China is so vast and held together by such tenuous force that, as with the famines which historically were present in almost every year in some part of the Empire, there is almost always disaffection and potential rebellion. If this is not suppressed immediately, a small movement can lead to mass eruptions somewhere in this vast realm.

This has been a pattern throughout Chinese history, but let me just confine myself to the period of the Qing Empire from 1644 to 1911. The map at the start of the chapter on China shows some of the major uprisings, partly caused by the expansion of Manchu imperial power, either in the territories of the west, or in creating extra authority over the minorities and the Han population.

In the huge western half of China there were frequent tribal uprisings. Among those noted on the map are the Olot (1750-57), Li (1765), Tarim (1759-60), Hui in Qinghai (1781-84) and Muslim (1825-37). These uprisings and the huge expeditions mounted by the Qing to suppress them and other risings (including the Mongols) need to be understood as the background to current policy. The anxiety of the government in the Mongolian, Muslim and Tibetan provinces, which comprise almost half of Chinese territory, are still there. At any point, it is believed, people could form into a mass secessionist movement which would split off much of the Chinese Empire. Encouragement of such movements by foreign powers adds to the fear.

In the south, centre and east of China, which the Manchus had conquered from the Ming, there are two other major forms of challenge. One is the constant threat, highest in the eighteenth century, of unrest in the vast tribal groups who periodically felt crushed or ignored by Qing rule. Amongst these are the tribal risings in Guangxi in 1790 and risings among the Miao (for instance in 1795-1806 and 1854) and other groups in the southern provinces, including Yunnan, in the eighteenth century.

These rebellions were often put down by a tactic familiar to the British in their Empire, namely the use of one ethnic group to defeat another. For example, the Tujia were used as troops against the Miao and others, just as Uighurs had been used by the Ming to suppress risings in Yunnan much earlier. Nowadays this kind of tribal threat has greatly diminished and the ethnic minorities have autonomous provinces. Yet the war of the Han majority against the large indigenous non-Han is a strong theme in much of Chinese history.

The second type of threat is particularly fascinating and portentous for our times. It is a form of upheaval which is rather unfamiliar to modern Westerners, but bears strong resemblance to the Messianic movements of the mediaeval West. We are also becoming familiar with it in the radical Islamic movements, such as the attempt to form a new form of society in the Caliphate promised by ISIS.

Such Messianic (expecting the coming of the Messiah or Holy One who will end the world) movements are characterized by the sudden emergence of a group driven by fanatical religious zeal. Their message gives confidence to thousands and sometimes millions of people who feel that the end of the world as it is presently constructed is at hand. Often a charismatic figure, sometimes in the person of a Christian Messiah, arises. He (and so far it is always a he) tells his followers that they are indestructible and can turn the world upside down.

They proclaim that the high will be made low and the poor made high. All the present inequalities and sufferings will be wiped away in the new reign of equality and love. Some believe that the French Revolution had elements of this, just as in the same way the Communist Revolution in Russia, and, more recently, Chairman Mao and Pol Pot with their later Communist revolutions.

Three of the most famous of many movements are the following. There is the White Lotus (Buddhist) rebellion of 1796 to 1804, based on a secret White Lotus religious society dating back many hundreds of years. The largest was the vast Taiping rebellion of 1850to 1864 and later the Boxer Rebellion of 1899-1901. The normal pattern was that, beginning with small incidents, gossip and rumours flew rapidly across the country and a core of religious radicals spread their message. Many anti-government interests and a charismatic leader came together. The scale of these eruptions is awesome looked at from the West.

The last White Lotus rebellion lasted nearly ten years and hundreds of thousands died. In the Taiping or 'Heavenly Kingdom of Peace' insurrection, it is reckoned that between twenty and thirty million soldiers and civilians died – roughly equivalent to the deaths in the fighting of the two World Wars combined. Many hundreds of thousands died in the Boxer and the intervention of foreign troops, while ending the rebellion more quickly, led to huge destruction and directly into the fall of the Qing Empire.

Those who believe that the Communist Revolution was yet another such Messianic movement, which succeeded because it occurred at a time of massive disarray in China after the warlord period and the Sino-Japanese war, would point to its costs in human lives. If we add together the deaths in conflict with the after-effects of the attempt to create the perfect kingdom on earth, namely the famines of the Great Leap Forward and the deaths and destruction in the Cultural Revolution, this movement was in some ways the most costly of all.

This is the background we need to understand with China. It is a landscape where everything looks peaceful, orderly and cohesive, but suddenly a small flame is dropped, and within days, millions of acres of woodland and the creatures that live in it are destroyed. In the West, where the nearest we have to this is the rise of communist and fascist movements, we need to understand this background if we are to comprehend the apparently heavy-handed, even paranoid (to westerners), surveillance and crushing of apparently trivial dissent in China today.

The Chinese know their history and they are particularly wary of apparently innocent, small, spiritual and intellectual movements of dissent. This is why they regard the ritualistic cult of the Falun Gong with such concern and why they appear to their friends in the West to be overly concerned by the threats posed by the Dalai Lama or by some Muslim groups.

The Chinese have been burnt before and when even well-meaning activists, lawyers or academics call for 'freedom' and 'democracy' in more than a subdued way, the menacing specter of China's bloody uprisings enters the minds of the rulers. Without understanding this, the reaction to the protesters who were calling for the downfall of the Communist Party in Tiananmen Square, as well as less dramatic challenges to the State, are difficult to understand. China is so vast that, as the Emperors through the ages discovered, it is either strongly bound together, or can fall to pieces with terrible consequences.

Nobility

When I was a little boy, one of the highlights of my school years was taking part as a nobleman in Gilbert and Sullivan's opera *Iolanthe*. I strutted onto the stage in my mock ermine and coronet and sung of the greatness of the House of Lords and my noble blood.

It was only much later at Oxford University that I discovered that the British have never had a true, blood-based, nobility. They have had a class system with an aristocracy at the top, but these are people who, through money or services, have earnt their way into the top tier. They are constantly replenished by rich businessmen and successful professionals, and their line usually does not last more than a few generations. They have no special legal status which differentiates them from others. They are just of a high social status, respected but without any particular power beyond their wealth. I learnt that true nobility, with a caste-like differences of blood separating nobles from commoners, was found over much of Europe, in France, Spain, Italy, but not in England.

When I came to study China, I naturally looked to see if it fell on the side of English aristocracy or of continental nobility. I searched for this estate which in one form or another we find across all of the Indo-European world and even with *daimyo* in Japan and was amazed to find no such thing in China. China appears to be the one great civilisation which does not have a landed ruling class. There is nothing equivalent to nobility or aristocracy. The rulers under the Emperor were the Mandarin elites. There is no ancient and hugely powerful landed class lasting over the centuries, the descendants of feudal barons and earls. This has had a huge influence on Chinese development, making its bureaucratic political system very different from every other civilisation and giving it a special two-level social ranking system which is also unique.

I wondered how recently the nobility had disappeared and

was again surprised to find no such class in China for over two thousand years. A key moment in that disappearance was in the unification of the Chinese empire under the first Qin Emperor in 221 BC. The Emperor gave power to his appointed administrators, raised to a high level educationally, and started to destroy the vestiges of an earlier feudal order of the more normal type. China has never gone back on this and to this day has no hereditary upper class. There were large landlords, largely destroyed by the Communists, but they were nothing like the earlier western nobility or aristocracy. This is a profound difference.

O

Opera

On one of our first visits to China we went into a small 'hutong' house in Beijing where an elderly man proceeded to sing, with great gusto, excerpts from Peking opera. From that time, and after visiting a performance of Peking opera, I assumed that this was the only major opera form in China. Although I tried hard, I could not warm to this form of opera. Without understanding its conventions or symbolism, it seemed to be bombastic, the singing strident and generally overblown.

It was ten years later that on a visit to the ancient and beautiful canal city of Suzhou in the south that I discovered that there are many forms of Chinese opera. The one we saw beside a little lake and then in a splendid opera hall, and later in other cities and in Cambridge, is called *kun-cu*. It was formalized in about the fourteenth century in southern China, although it has absorbed stands and elements of far more ancient melodies and plots within it.

The most famous writer for this opera was Tang Xianzu, known as the Shakespeare of China, not just for his skills, but because he reputedly died in the same year, 1616. His 'Peony Pavilion', written in 1598 – a story of love, dreams, gardens and ghosts – is magical and some of his other dramas resemble comedy interludes in Shakespeare.

This form of opera I find entrancing, magical, deeply moving. The music is ethereal, the singing and movement very graceful, the costumes and make-up dazzling. The operas feel as if they are a beautiful Chinese painting come to life. The themes of love and loss are eternal. As a listed UNESCO cultural heritage item, it deserves to be placed alongside the great preserved art forms of the world. Consequently, we have set up a project to document this opera with objects from around the world, which can be seen at https://www.kunopera.org.

Opium

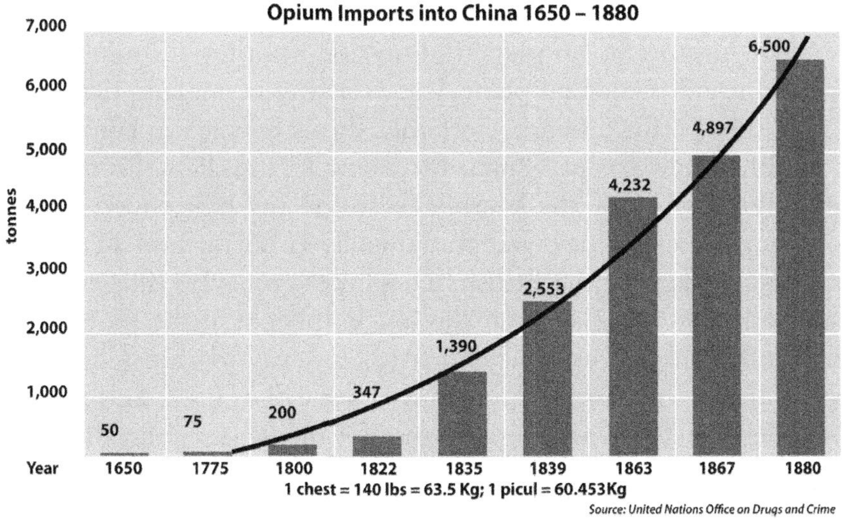

I had a rather simple, and entirely negative, view of the influence of opium on Chinese civilisation until recently. I had heard that one of the causes of the supposed debilitated state of many Chinese in the nineteenth and early twentieth century was opium addiction. Pictures of opium dens and hollow-eyed and crippled individuals were one stereotype of China, where the substance was sapping the energy, wasting the money and using precious land to grow the poppies.

The harm was compounded by western exploiters who, as explained under 'Opium Wars', had used the pretext of resistance to the outside opium trade as justifications for attacking China twice in the middle of the nineteenth century and imposing huge fines because the Chinese resisted, and forcing open treaty ports and grabbing Hong Kong.

All the above has some truth, but as I read further I discovered that there is another story as well. Opium, when not taken in excess, can be considered alongside other smoking, for example of tobacco, as a form of relaxant and stimulation. Perhaps if China had been stronger, we would be now talking of 'the tobacco wars', with attempts to force the British to smoke more, or less, of that addictive substance.

Or opium can be placed alongside another stimulant and relaxant and medicinal plant, tea, as a way of making tired and cold limbs perform better. Certainly, this is how it was commonly used in many parts of China. For example, travellers through the mountain tribes of the south-west found the hills covered with opium poppies, as they were traditionally in Burma and Thailand, nothing to do with the British. They were grown by villagers who smoked opium in the same way as the people in the mountains of south America chew coca leaves as a way to gain relief and stimulus for their work. The plant is not evil in itself, and indeed is widely used in a range of important medicines today, but it is the addiction and surrender to opium that is the danger. Opium can be seen alongside tea, ginseng, artemesia and other plants as one of the great Chinese discoveries – but also, like tea, one of the roots of its recent troubles.

Opium wars

The background to opium is explained above. Here I will very briefly sketch in an episode which, before I researched the history of tea and began to study China, I knew nothing about.

From the 1720's, the British became addicted to Chinese tea and consumed ever greater quantities. Until about 1790, they could pay for this quite easily with silver, which the Chinese wanted. After the partial blocking of the south American silver mines, after American independence and the wars with France, silver became difficult to obtain and the ever-increasing demand for tea put Britain into a highly negative trading position. How were the British to pay for the tea, since the Chinese did not want any other British goods and were even suffering from a surfeit of silver?

The British discovered the demand for opium and

simultaneously their hold in India increased. They found that parts of India, for example Bengal, were excellent for growing highly desirable opium for the Chinese market. That this destroyed much of the agricultural land of parts of India was considered a necessary cost, and that it was known to be feeding a potentially dangerous addiction an acceptable cost. A three-way trade emerged.

The British managed the opium production in India but could cover up the trade by using non-government private traders to ship the product to China, thus making huge profits for individual companies who brought the opium in principally through Canton and southern ports. The profits from the opium was used to buy tea cheaply, and there was even a profit. Some silver started to go back with the East India company ships that helped bring the tea to Britain and made that company wealthy. The tea, when sold in Britain, raised the money which was then sent to India to produce and buy further opium.

The Chinese twice tried to put a stop to this increasingly undermining trade which was, indeed, turning many into addicts. The two Opium wars of 1839-42 and 1856-1860 ensued. The superior ships and guns, including machine guns in the second war, led the British to crush the Chinese into two humiliating surrenders. The results were disastrous for China. After the First Opium War, China was forced to open five ports to the British, cede Hong Kong to them, and pay an indemnity of £21 million, roughly equivalent to $700 million in today's prices. This was a huge amount, more than equivalent to the Gross National Product of Britain at the time, paid from a country already impoverished and with a poor taxation system.

After the Second Opium War, ten more ports had to be opened to the British and other concessions were later made to the U.S. and France. Foreigners were for the first time allowed to travel all over China and foreign vessels could go up as far as they liked along the Yangtze and the Kowloon peninsula near Hong Kong was ceded to the British. Another indemnity of four million

Chinese taels of silver to the British and two million to the French was forced on the Chinese, of the same order of magnitude as the first. This came on top of the devastations of the Taiping rebellion of 1850-1864 when at least twenty million people died.

I have heard some charitable Chinese argue that the Opium Wars were a blessing in disguise because they forced China to open itself and this brought in some benefits. This may have some truth to it. But it was at a terrible cost, and it is difficult to know whether the gradual opening which was already happening would not have blossomed without this external bludgeoning.

Overseas Chinese

The Chinese are deeply attached to their soil and their country but for some centuries they have also been driven by poverty and natural disasters and the desire for a better life to go and settle abroad. They helped to populate and energise the economies of many South East Asian countries, including Burma, Malaya and Singapore. They were the principal labour force which built the early American and Canadian railroads and dug the South American mines. More recently they have brought immense sums of money, hard work and talent to the western seaboard of America, from Vancouver down to San Francisco. They crowd the universities of Europe and America and are living and investing in many western cities.

At first the Chinese migrated, particularly from the eastern cities in Fujian and nearby in the Pearl River delta, as unskilled labourers. Quite quickly, their skills, hard-work and strong cohesive bonds with other Chinese, and great skill with money, meant that they became extremely successful. Occasionally this success led, as is the case of another successful minority, the Jews, to their destruction, in Mexico and elsewhere. Yet they were extremely resilient and moved up the skills chain from Chinese laundries, restaurants and manual labour, to running huge international businesses and successful careers in academia, banking and the technology sector.

There are over fifty million overseas Chinese. Most of these live in Southeast Asia, constituting the majority in Singapore and significant minorities in Thailand, Malaysia, Indonesia, the Philippines and Vietnam. There are growing numbers in almost all the countries of the world and, as a tiny example, in Cambridge I have seen the number of Chinese, both living and visiting, rise exponentially in the last twelve years. In certain areas of the city, more than half of those one meets are Chinese. From observation, many of the Chinese who settle abroad continue to feel a strong loyalty to China. They often return if they can, send money to their relatives and feel a strong identity as Chinese.

Many parts of the world consequently have a Chinese flavour and their absence of caste, their friendliness, their willingness to marry out of their Chinese group, and their linguistic abilities and hard work means, that, on the whole, the overseas Chinese are one of the most successful of the diasporas. This is shown, for example, in the fact that their children often top the educational league tables in whichever country they live. The rapid increase in young Chinese going abroad, dealt with under 'Journey to the West', is another aspect of this.

P

Paper

It is easy to forget that one of the most important communications revolutions in history, the discovery of an effective medium on which to store complex information, which bridged the era from before the birth of Christ until the digital revolution of the 1950s, was the Chinese invention of paper.

The early history and spread of paper-making in China dates back to the Eastern Han period (25-220 CE). During the eighth century, Chinese papermaking spread to the Islamic world and by the eleventh century it was brought to Europe. Paper has to be reasonably easy to make, yet very strong and light. The Chinese discovered that a plant that grows well in China, the paper mulberry, could be processed into paper. I have seen traditional paper making in both Japan and China (it must have spread to Japan from China), and it involves an impressive process of beating, washing, skimming and laying out the intertwined fibers and then storing the sheets. It takes some care, but once the methods are mastered, can produce considerable amounts of paper product. The western paper making, using cloth and much later wood, requires much more energy.

Chinese paper came to be used in many ways. It was not just suitable for calligraphy and for Chinese art, but also for furnishings. There was little or no glass, so paper was used for windows in order to let in light but keep the cold out. It was used for sliding screens which could be used to reshape a living space. In Japan, paper was used as the first toilet paper in the world. It was said to be effective, when made moist and laid over the mouth of a sleeping person, as a disposable murder weapon. In short, China had this marvellous medium about a thousand years before western Europe.

Physical infrastructure

One of the outwardly most extraordinary achievements of China in the last forty years has been in the development of a physical infrastructure linking this vast country. In the 1933 Handbook for China by Carl Crow, we find that China had hardly any railways.

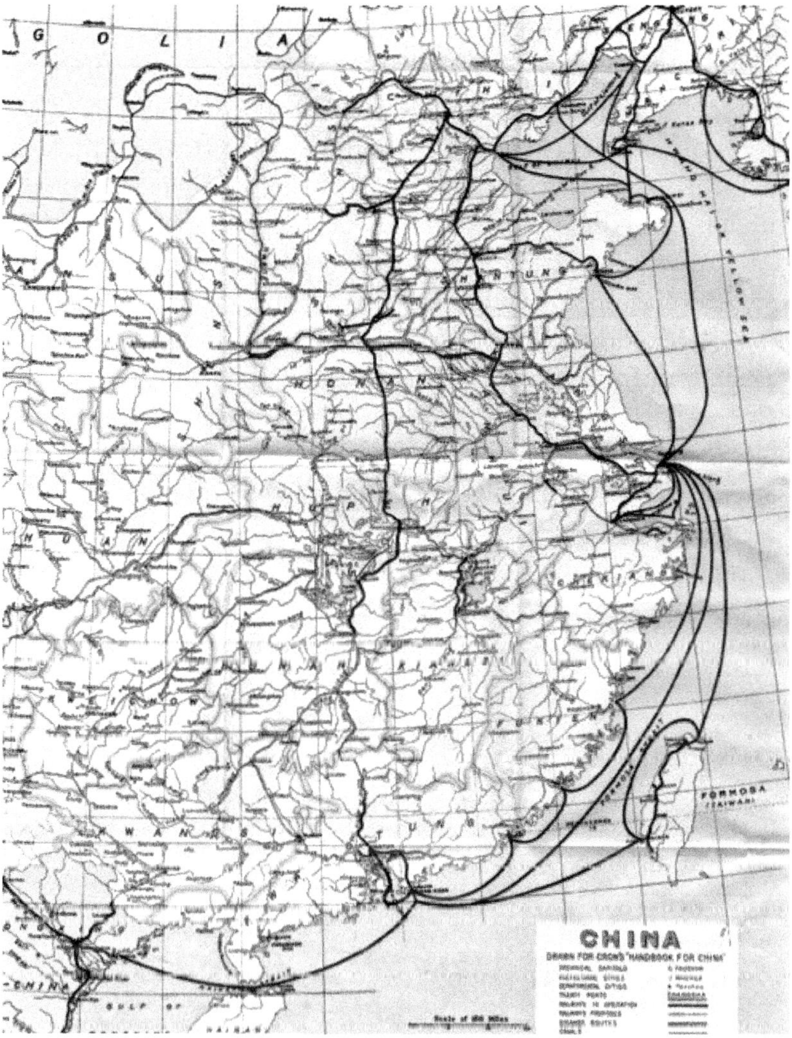

Even by 1978, communications over this huge area, larger than Western and Eastern Europe combined, were still poor. There were few railways, though the railway network had gone up three-fold since the map above and many areas had only dirt roads. The ports were inadequate and there were few commercial airports and those that existed rather primitive.

Now, as you travel up the six-lane highways through remote provinces, cleaving through the Himalayas by way of immense tunnels and over long bridges, you are awe struck. Or as you slide at over 250 kilometres per hour on the bullet trains across thousands of miles you are amazed. Or as you land at elegant airports on excellent flights cross China, or as you see the largest container ports in the world along the eastern seaboard at Shanghai and Ningpo, you can only be deeply impressed. Never in history, to my knowledge, has such a vast infrastructural network been built over such vast and rugged terrain in such a short time. It makes the communications in my home in the U.K. seem old-fashioned and minute, and even those in the States or the most advanced parts of Europe are nothing like what we find now in China. The roads now can be seen criss-crossing China, and they are complemented by railways, as in the following map.

I have been to the remotest of villages on excellent roads. I have recently been from Hong Kong to Shenzhen on a high-speed train through tunnels, cutting the journey time from two hours to twenty minutes. South of us was the longest road bridge in the world, from Hong Kong to Macau, over 55 kilometres (roughly one and a half times the distance between England and France), which had just been opened.

Of course, there are still many problems. One of the worst is the appalling car and lorry congestion in cities. Here, we can see how rising affluence has led to millions of huge cars cramming the ever-expanding road networks. There is vast pollution and people suffer long delays. Hopefully, having sorted out bigger problems across China, the Chinese will address the solution to this too – and soon. Chinese interests and advances in electric and autonomous vehicles may be part of the solution.

Poetry and poets

I have loved poetry since I first started to read it from about the age of eight. Later I tried to write poetry, and became enraptured, particularly by the English poets of the seventeenth century-milton, Herbert, Donne and the Romantics, particularly Wordsworth, Coleridge, Keats and Shelley. And, of course, there is Shakespeare whose plays I studied for ten years.

I came to believe that poetry was the greatest gift of the British to world literature (perhaps alongside novels) and that my country was perhaps the most distinguished and poetry-loving one in the world.

Since visiting and learning about China, I have had to revise my views and learn some humility. China has historically had many times as many people as Britain, and its recorded history of poetry-writing is more than three times as long. Yet even this does not fully account for the extraordinary creativity and volume of Chinese poetry.

For example, I could perhaps name fifty British poets, and

know where perhaps ten of them were born or spent much of their lives. There are maps of Chinese poets which show their home-towns.[15] It is an extraordinary spread, with 2,625 Tang poets, 2,377 Song poets, 3,005 Ming poets and 2,079 Qing poets. The idea of knowing the whereabouts of over 10,000 poets over the last 1500 years is beyond my comprehension.

Poetry is part of people's lives today. Many Chinese, particularly of the older generation, know a great deal about the ancient poets and can recite their poems. I remember realizing the difference in another parallel case when three of my young Japanese friends, aged from six to twelve, were playing card games in which they had to collect sets of famous Japanese men and women poets of a thousand years before, about many of whom they knew a good deal.

Britain has half a dozen major art forms, music, architecture, painting, poetry and other literature. China only has three which are the jewels in its crown, calligraphy as the most important, then poetry and painting.

It is not easy for me to understand how Chinese poetry works, or how you achieve rhyming with pictorial or other single-idea characters. It is clearly very different from my experience. Yet, watching the rapt faces of Chinese when they listen to a recitation of poetry, even at dinners where, for the first time in my life (with Chinese guests) instead of after-dinner speeches there are poetry recitals, I see how much poetry means to the Chinese – more so than to my British collegeagues and friends.

Nor can I easily understand the rather different central theme and position of the poet in the two traditions. The difference is well described by one of the great translators of Chinese poetry into English, Arthur Waley. He writes as follows.[16]

---

[15]The maps are in Edward R. Tufte, *Envisioning Information* (1990), re-drawn from Chen Cheng-Siang, *An Historical and Cultural Atlas of China* (Tokyo, 1981).

[16]Arthur Waley (translator), *One Hundred and Seventy Chinese Poems* (1918), 4, 5

Turning from thought to emotion, the most conspicuous feature of European poetry is its pre-occupation with love. This is apparent not only in actual "love-poems," but in all poetry where the personality of the writer is in any way obtruded. The poet tends to exhibit himself in a *romantic* light; in fact, to recommend himself as a lover.

The Chinese poet has a tendency different but analogous. He recommends himself not as a lover, but as a friend. He poses as a person of infinite leisure (which is what we should most like our friends to possess) and free from worldly ambitions (which constitute the greatest bars to friendship).

He would have us think of him as a boon companion, a great drinker of wine, who will not disgrace a social gathering by quitting it sober.

Another difference is that 'It would not be an exaggeration to say that half the poems in the Chinese language are poems of parting or separation.'

Poetry is an ideal art form for China. As explained elsewhere, China is a symbolic, 'structural' in the French sense, civilisation. Every word, painting or flower points to other things. It is multi-level, mixing the here and now with eternity, the past and present, the human and supernatural powers. Prose or even painting cannot quite capture all of this and music, except opera, is restricted to non-verbal symbols.

Poetry's great strength is that it is multi-level, where the rhythm, rhyme and imagery can evoke deep emotions and appeal at different levels to the reader. So it is a multiplex system of symbols of a very powerful kind. This is clearly why it appealed to me as a child, and appeals to over a billion Chinese, all of whom learn key poems at school. It is a central occupation of the elite. Chairman Mao was a noted poet (as well as calligrapher), and only one of the later politicians and administrators who considered poetry as one essential ingredient part of their role. The Mandarin class were trained in poetry in their education and were partly defined by their poetic ability.

In contrast, it is not easy to imagine President Donald Trump or Prime Minister Margaret Thatcher spending much time writing poetry, or being invited to read their poems at poetry festivals. In China, even today, top administrators, businessmen and politicians in China often practice the art. It is indeed a wondrous civilization.

Politeness and etiquette

Before I went to China, I believe that I had an image of the Chinese as being a somewhat boorish and aggressive set of people. I expected people to push ahead in queues, to talk past you or in loud voices over you, to spit in the streets, not to observe proper body distances, not to say please and thank you.

During my seventeen visits to China, travelling the length and breadth of the country for over a year of my life, I have been very pleasantly relieved of these misconceptions. It is true that the Chinese do not always queue in an orderly way. It is true that the road etiquette, with a free-for-all and cars cutting in dangerously, is pretty rough in crowded cities. I have occasionally seen people spit in the street, though seldom, but I can't remember any occasion when we have suffered, or even witnessed, real anger and rudeness.

Like the Japanese, I found that the Chinese are a polite and considerate people. They say thank you (*xie xie*) and acknowledge kindness or gifts with a smile and warmth. They show careful attention to each other and to us, and constantly show signs of anticipating our every need, often before we are aware of them.

Of course, in an old and ceremonial society such as China, there is a great deal of formal behaviour – some bowing, gestures in temples, gift-giving in an ornate way. The tea and eating etiquettes, for example, are quite elaborate at times. The polite and friendly Chinese habits are shown, for example, in the delightful custom of rising to one's feet at meals and circulating around all the guests, talking and toasting each one in turn. On the whole, the Chinese behave politely and in an egalitarian way, treating women, children and especially the old with consideration and courtesy. A Chinese crowd – and one finds oneself in many – feels calm, orderly and considerate.

I may have the advantage of being an elderly person and a high prestige visitor, so have the pleasure of witnessing the best side of the Chinese character. Yet I have also watched Chinese inter-acting with one another, and have found a refreshing absence of shouting, bullying, apparent arrogance or selfishness. It may be the Confucian focus on harmonious personal relations, or other factors, but, on the whole, it is an extremely easy place to feel comfortable in, even as an outsider.

Population patterns

I come from a country which, for more than half a millenium, has had a rather unusual population pattern, though its peculiarity tends to be covered over nowadays by the fact that the system has recently spread over most of the world. In this balanced way, the number of births roughly equals that of the number of deaths so that the population grows slowly, if at all. This system has now been seen in most of the rest of the world, with the marked exception of certain more extreme forms of religious groups, whether Christian, Jewish or Islamic.

Given the well-known fact that unimpeded fertility combined with an early age at marriage can easily produce an average of ten or more children per woman, and deaths in normal times are much lower than this, it is obvious that, to achieve a balance, one or both of two systems must be employed.

The English method, used for many centuries until the later nineteenth, was to limit the number of years in which women were able to have children. Two techniques were used. The number of women who married is reduced by a custom whereby about a quarter or more of English women never married. Secondly, the age at first marriage was very high, often at about twenty-five or later. This cuts off about ten years of potential child-bearing and with the reduction of the number of women ever marrying means that the fertility rate, given the medium mortality at that time, was only roughly at replacement levels.

The result of this technique is that the English population grew very slowly in the period from the Black Death in 1350 to the start of the industrial revolution in around 1750, when suddenly the population started to grow rapidly because of the need to fill new jobs. In these four hundred years, the economy grew in size four or five times while the population only doubled.

This balanced pattern is historically unusual, though, as mentioned, after the introduction of contraception and huge economic changes, it has now spread to much of the world. The much more normal pattern is the one which China experienced through the centuries.

In this normal 'crisis' pattern, there was huge pressure to have as many children as possible. Children expanded the work force, helped provide for old age, protected you against political threats and continued the ancestral line. They were a pure good, and in order to obtain as many of them as possible, all those physically capable of marriage, should do so, and as young as possible, in particular women in their mid or late teens. Consequently, when there is no abnormally high mortality, the population could, as Thomas Malthus predicted, double in each generation. Despite frequent famines and wars, the Chinese population grew in the period between 1700 and 1830 from about 100 to 400 million.

The nature of a Malthusian or 'crisis' economic pattern, with waves of growth and sudden collapses, is shown in the following diagram and offers a powerful backdrop to much of Chinese history.

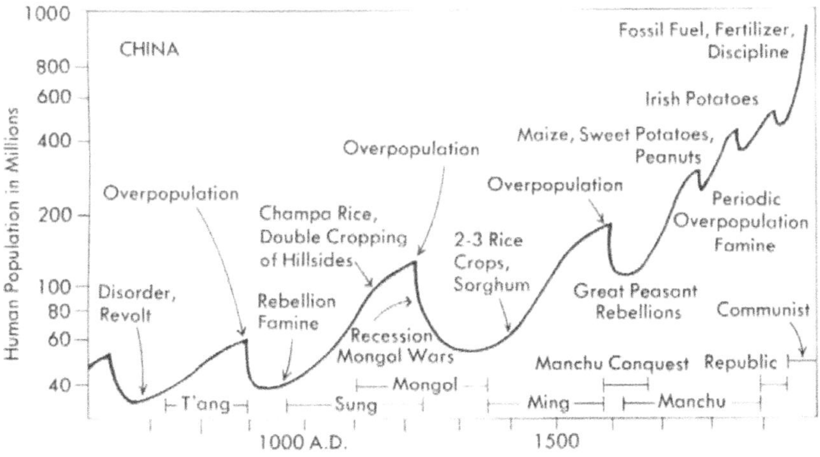

The over-all Chinese population growth, when smoothed out, with the huge expansion in the Qin period and then again in the twentieth century, is shown in the following diagram.

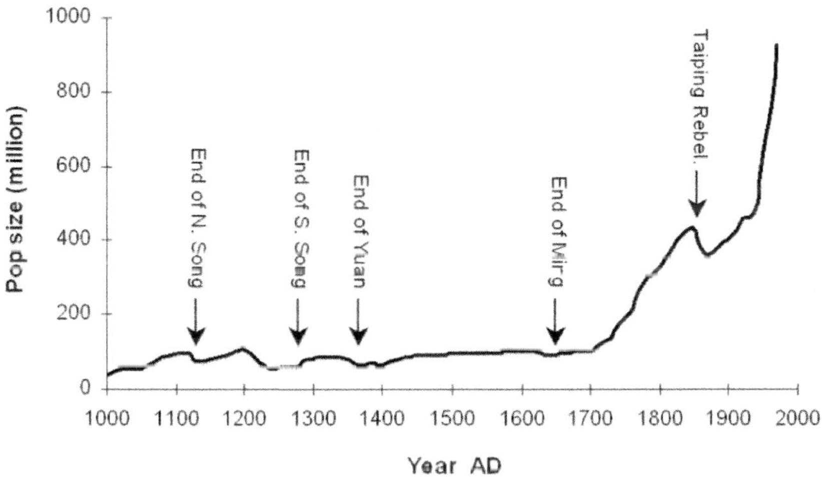

The cost of this system is that it puts a huge strain on the environment and economy, and on the bodies of women. It is difficult to save, for resources have to be put into extra children. The land becomes saturated with humans, leading to more disease and a poverty which will provide little buffer against the periodic food shortages caused by bad weather.

The fascinating later history of this system occurs in the twentieth century. Chairman Mao had long been a bitter critic of Malthus, as had Karl Marx, declaring Malthus to be a hard-hearted capitalist pessimist. Yet shortly after his death, his successor Deng Xiaoping introduced the 'One Child' policy. It lasted from 1979 to 2015, though the name is misleading because about half of all parents in China were allowed to have a second child. It was an extraordinary success in that fertility rates were further reduced. One estimate is that China's fertility restrictions probably averted over 500 million births between 1970 and 2015, with the portion caused by one-child restrictions totalling about 400 million. If this is correct, it is estimated that the current population of China of a little over 1.4 billion would have been something like 1.8 billion if there had no such policy.

There have, of course, been numerous criticisms of what, to the West, looks like a very brutal and draconian measure. There are human rights issues, stories of forced abortions, worry about the damaging effects on the psychology of the 'Little Emperors' or single children without brothers and sisters. And some have even questioned whether the transition to much smaller families using such a method was necessary. They suggest that the fertility transition found around the world from the 1970s onwards would have occurred in China in any case and accounts for some or a good deal of what has happened. This seems to be partially borne out by the following diagram.

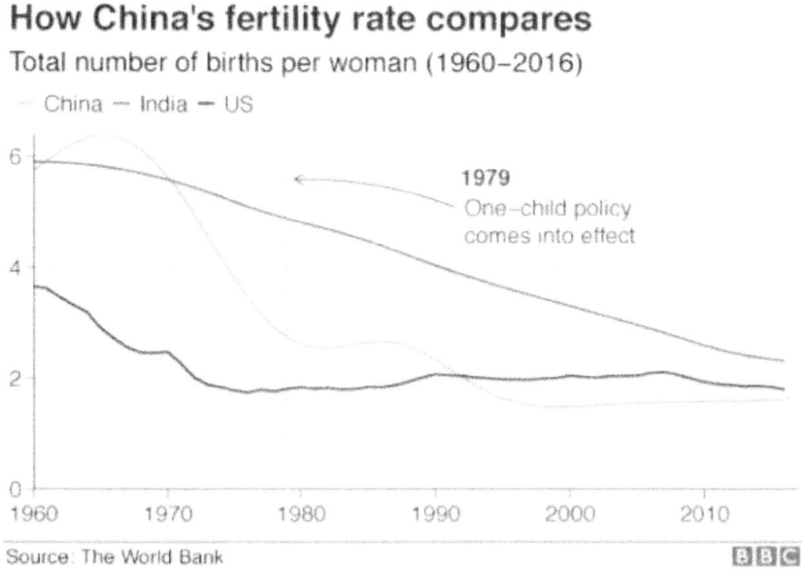

The Chinese have achieved the largest sudden drop in fertility in history, and now that the new pattern has been established, they can take their foot off the brakes. Two children per family is now being relaxed into more than two, yet the birth rate has not surged. It is an amazing story.

One final point to make concerns the ageing of the Chinese population. Like Japan, eastern Europe and other areas, China's population is both ageing and likely to decline in the future. The decline is suggested in the following:

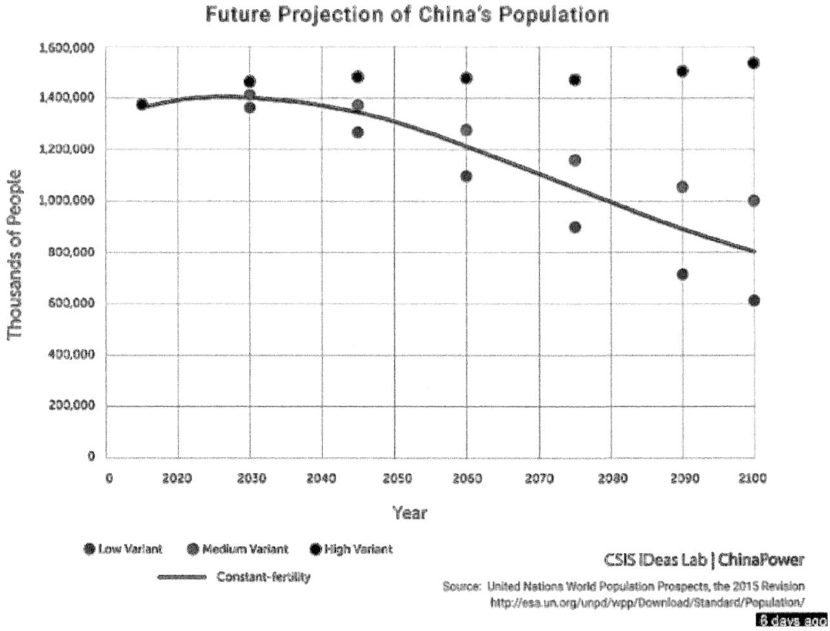

The conventional wisdom among demographers and economists is that such change pose a danger. Yet with modern technologies and the ability of people to work into their seventies or later, old assumptions are out of date. We no longer live in the world of human muscle. An eighty-year old with modern technology will soon be able to do what ten forty-year-olds could do. We have too many people, not too few.

Porcelain

When we think of the great inventions of China – compass, printing, silk, gunpowder – we have to add porcelain, which has had a huge effect on the development and nature of China over the centuries.

Proto-porcelain dates back over three thousand years in China, but glazed ceramics only developed into modern porcelain in the Eastern Han dynasty (206BC-220AD), which China defines as high-fired ware.

By around the seventh century AD, the requirements of whiteness and translucency had been achieved. At that time porcelain of this complete kind was being exported to the Islamic world. In the Song period (960-1279) the craft reached an extraordinary level, which many consider its most beautiful. The manufacture became highly organized and the climbing kilns (dragon kilns) of the period could fire as many as 100,000 pieces in a single firing by the end of the Song.

By the Ming dynasty (1368-1644), porcelain was being exported to Europe, including the highly prized blue and white Ming porcelain which I remember, in later copies, intriguing me with their willow patterns as a child. By 1517, the Portuguese were shipping Ming porcelain directly by sea, supplementing the large trade along the Silk Road. The centre of production, particularly for the most esteemed imperial pieces, was Jingdezhen in southern China.

There was a huge trade. It is reported that the Dutch East India Company, between 1602 and 1682, carried between thirty and thirty-five million pieces of Chinese and Japanese export porcelain and the other great trading companies also carried large amounts.

After the replacement of the Ming dynasty in 1644 there was a lull, but from the later seventeenth century the Chinese porcelain industry flourished again. Some westerners amassed huge collections. From the later eighteenth century, however, when the Europeans learnt the secret of how to make porcelain and when the industrial-style potteries were set up, among them being Wedgewood in England, the Chinese exports started to decline.

Not only did porcelain contribute to a craze for *chinoiserie* in the West and create huge activity in China, it altered many other aspects of life. The nature of drinking tea, for example, altered with the Song, Ming and Qing as new forms of porcelain were made. The presence of the wonderful translucent vessels may have been one of the reasons why China lost an earlier interest in decorative glass.

In the West, glass became an essential part of the Scientific Revolution. In China, glass was not of interest in the form developed in Italy and the Netherlands. So the great divides of the West, with the Renaissance and Scientific Revolution, so dependent on glass, did not occur. One reason for this was the presence of porcelain, cheaper to manufacture (with less fuel) and easier to decorate with symbolic patterns – and wonderful for drinking tea.

Poverty reduction

Even in the 1960s and 1970s, the world was still prone to the kind of famine that had afflicted it over the centuries. There were terrible famines in China, Bangladesh and Ethiopia amongst other places. As well as outright deaths, there were high levels of malnutrition and physical hardship for the millions in Africa, India, China and South America. There seemed little hope of a really deep change as late as the end of the 1980s.

Then, in the last thirty years, hundreds of millions have been lifted above the poverty line so that now the world is far less unequal and filled with misery. What has happened?

Parts of the change, in India or parts of Africa, has been the result of rapid economic growth and technological development. In India, a large prosperous middle class of some hundreds of millions has emerged and the cities are booming. In Africa, particularly since China started to invest heavily in infrastructure and trade, things are widely improving.

Yet by far the most important change has been in China. It has been recognised that between 1980 and the present, around 700 million Chinese have been lifted above the poverty line. This is not an accident, but the result of explicit policy. Whatever our feelings about communism, it is theoretically based on equality and on the hope of a decent life for all. When the Chinese economy started to boom from the 1980s, the government pursued an unambiguous policy of spreading the gains to the poorer, mainly western and rural communities and away from the booming eastern seaboard. This is what 'trickle down' was meant to do in capitalism but it is not automatically achieved. The following diagram, though it is not clear what exactly it is measuring, does show an extraordinary reduction in poverty.

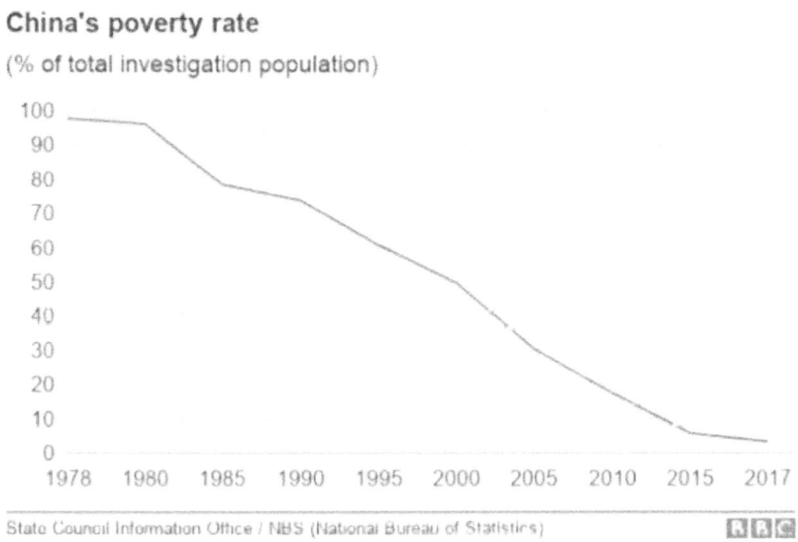

In the home of capitalism – the U.S. – huge wealth coincides with serious poverty and there is little evidence that the government is interested in doing much about the situation. The response has been widespread misery, combined with high crime rates. The answer is to lock millions of (mainly black, male) Americans into prisons In 1980, there were less than half a million in prison; now there are over two and a half million. The incarceration rate in America is currently about 655 per 100,000 population; for China it is 118 per 100,000.

China, meanwhile, is hoping that by making all its population wealthier, including in the remote regions of Tibet, Xinjian and Inner Mongolia, it will earn the gratitude and some loyalty from potentially disaffected groups. We shall see in the next few years whether this policy works.

Printing

Another great invention of the Chinese was printing. Ink rubbings on paper or cloth from texts on stone tablets in China date to the Han dynasty (206 BC - 220 CE). Woodblock printing on paper started in the eighth century during the Tang dynasty, and then metal movable type was pioneered in Korea by the thirteenth century. The Diamond Sutra of 868 AD in the British Library is the oldest extant printed book. The essence of printing is to make a 'machine' which avoids the need to laboriously hand copy or write documents for mass circulation.

Because of the complexity of the thousands of Chinese characters, early Chinese printing was not based, as it was in the West later, on movable individual characters set on wooden trays. Rather, in order to be multiplied, a book or document was engraved on a wooden block, page by page, and then brushed with ink and pressed on a sheet of paper.

I have seen an old-style printing press of this kind in China, watching as the engravers chisel away to make the characters. The block is then inked and pressed onto a sheet of paper, a person collates the sheets, and others sow them into a book. It is a factory for manufacturing information and the process lies behind the vast libraries of books which the Chinese periodically produced, only to be burnt and destroyed in the next great convulsion.

Given this early invention, more than half a millenium before Gutenberg, it is a puzzle to me as to why printing in China seems to have had, relatively, so little effect. In the West, printing is credited with helping cause the Renaissance, the Protestant Reformation, the rise of nation states and vernacular languages, the rise of science, the expansion of Europe overseas and even the rise of market capitalism.

None of these effects are found in China, showing once again that technological changes, in themselves, explain little. A technology can change the world only in certain circumstances of a much wider kind, which is also shown by the other great Chinese inventions such as gunpowder and the compass.

Professions and professionals

The absence of a developed legal profession is only part of a wider absence of most of the professional groups we find in the West. We have seen that there was, over the last two thousand years, no warrior aristocracy, there were few professional lawyers, and hardly any large businessmen and industrialists. Other professional groups were also absent or weakly developed. For example, while there were teachers at the innumerable schools, and there were flourishing academies of a kind, the development of an independent third level university sector did not occur until the end of the nineteenth century. So there was no academic profession of the western kind.

Another numerous profession, the main pillar of education and literacy in the Indo European and Anglosphere regions, the religious orders, were weak. There were from time to time monastic movements with the introduction of Buddhism, but these were hemmed in in the eighth to tenth centuries and never flourished independently again. The Taoists did not have full-time priests, although there were many hermits who retreated to remote woods and mountains to meditate. The Confucians produced scholars but not a priesthood.

Summarizing all of this, China presents a powerful but simple profile. Unlike the fourfold structures of India, Japan and the West, China only had two tiers, the tiny ruling group, the civil servant and mandarins, and the huge majority of small workmen, merchants and the vast peasantry. There was only one ladder of preferment, through education up into the bureaucracy.

Public and private

In most societies, all kinds of property are either held by particular individuals, or by a family group, or they are held by everyone, completely in common. In other words, an animal or field is owned by a particular person or family, while a river, mountain or sea by anyone who has access to it. This leads to the so-called 'tragedy of the commons', where rivers and oceans are over-fished and forests destroyed since their use is indiscriminate.

Such a binary distinction of entirely private or entirely public is enshrined in Roman Law and has historically also been the case in China. It has been behind much of the world's environmental destruction and pollution.

The English legal system has devoted huge attention to the question of property: over two thirds of the law codes and judicial cases are concerned with property rights. In this, England has developed a unique third category of property, which is neither private nor public. These are assets which are not entirely private for they do not belong exclusively to any single individual or family. Yet they are also not public, for only certain people, under certain conditions, have access to them. I have personal experience of this as a member of a Cambridge College.

As one of the Fellows or members of the governing body of the College, I can use the resources – walk on the grass, attend carol services, store wine in the cellars, use the library, use a room. These resources are not available to others outside the group of Fellows. Yet my use of the resources is constrained and controlled in many ways.

This idea of 'the commons', but not in the 'tragedy of the commons' sense, is shown in the common rights in an English village in the past. Certain villagers, holding particular houses, could put a limited number of animals onto the 'common' lands at specified periods, catch fish of above a certain length in certain seasons, cut branches of a certain length from particular trees. It was all carefully regulated.

These 'commons' are now to be found in many aspects of English life – in parks, footpaths and libraries, for example. The system is one which is highly flexible and gives individuals an incentive to improve public amenities.

It is a distinction which China may develop. At present, the tradition of 'public' in the English sense is largely absent from China. Hence China is mostly without a network of rights of way, public parks, clubs and associations, public service in charities and local government. It will be interesting to see if, and how fast, China adopts this alien but invaluable concept, particularly if it finds some accomodation with a communist understanding of mutual responsibility.

Q

Qin Emperor

China was unified, after five hundred years of warring states, by the Qin Emperor, Qin Shi Huang (formerly Zhao Zheng) in 221 B.C. The Qin state conquered all the others and, since then, despite falling apart from time to time and foreign invasions, China has remained essentially as the Qin Emperor left it.

Alexis de Tocqueville suggested that if we want a sure way to understand a civilisation, we should look at 'the point of origin'. The seed contains the tree, the spring, the river, the blueprint the building. The point of origin gives us a strong understanding of all that subsequently happens. The Qin Emperor and the new plans he inaugurated are China's 'point of origin'.

The Emperor destroyed the old feudal system of China, where warring lords had torn the country apart. He replaced the pattern of delegated power to hereditary nobility and feudalism with a new system whereby China was divided into thirty-five commanderies (*qun*). Each was governed by three governors, one who administered in civil affairs, another in military matters, and a third to report directly to the Emperor. Interestingly, now omitting the third – military – governor, the current system in China in the provinces and universities still reflects this, with an officer (governor, vice chancellor), who is accompanied by the Communist Party Secretary who reports to the government. As with the Qin, this ensures that the peripheries are always working in accordance with the centre.

In other words, the Qin changed China from a traditional feudal civilisation into the first, and still the only, centralised bureaucratic empire in the world. Here power was not in the hands of powerful families, but vested in trained administrators. This system continues to this day and is clearly visible in the way in which the communist party is organised and power is distributed through China.

The Qin Emperor made many other important changes. He standardised the weights, measures and coinage. He made a uniform system of road and water communications. He built large parts of the Great Wall of China. His ambition in terms of unifying and extending communications and defences reminds us of the current Chinese 'One Belt One Road', and the China Seas activities.

Tragically, a desire to start the world in his reign ('year zero') and to get rid of the 'olds' (as they were called by the Communists much later, including Confucianism) meant that the Emperor gave the order to systematically destroy the past. All books that could be found were burnt in a move oddly anticipating the Cultural Revolution of the 1960s.

The Qin Emperor died in 210 BC. He longed for immortality and his amazing grave mounds, including the part which has so far been excavated and revealed the terracotta armies that guarded him, were to ensure that eternal presence. Perhaps, if he returned, he would realize that while the graves are starting to be excavated, and he may have physically died, China today has many echoes of his extraordinary vision, for good and bad.

R

Rapid change

Looking back on my life since I arrived back in England in April 1947 from India, I am amazed at how the country has changed. When I arrived shortly after the Second World War had concluded, Britain still held the largest Empire in world history, yet within a few months it started to collapse with Indian Independence. There was still wartime rationing and few people had cars or telephones. There was no widespread television and no mass travel by plane. The roads were thin and windy with no motorways.

Within a few years, the National Health Service was in operation and medicine and dentistry were vastly improved. New schooling systems were rolled out and in the 1960s new universities were opened and many more students attended. In the 1950s, a new popular culture was born, with rock and pop, jazz, folk music spreading widely through the new electronic media of extended-play records and television. There was a re-alignment of age relations with a revolt of the young and a change in sex and gender relations, with the decriminalising of homosexuality and the rise of contraception and the feminist movement.

The period from the mid-fifties to the mid-seventies seemed to be one of revolutionary change around me. The pace slowed down for twenty years and then the internet age began. The last fifteen years, with the rise of mass computing, the smart phone and social media has once again revolutionised our lives.

I feel as if I have lived through a series of massive transformations: industrial, technological, communications, medical, social and cultural. When I look at photographs of myself and the world I lived in some seventy years ago, I seem to be living in another world.

Yet all this is relatively small compared to the pace and depth of the huge changes China has undergone in the same period. The old China was shattered by the Communist period. The basic foundations of China – the family, village and local religion – were all wiped away and two thousand years of Chinese civilisation apparently erased. It was far more thorough than even the French or Russian revolutions and a change of a kind which I have never experienced first-hand. The Chinese somehow survived this attack on all of their established ways, having their foundations taken away and replaced by socialism.

To survive this massive change would have tested the strength of any civilisation but after the death of Mao and the opening up of China since 1978, the country has gone through as great a change again. In forty years, China has gone through an industrial revolution which took England over a hundred years to pass through. It has gone through an urban revolution, the migration of vast numbers from the countryside to the massive cities with a complete transformation in their ways of life. China has gone through many social revolutions – in education, family structures and law. It has gone through such a profound communications revolution that China now has the most advanced internet and mobile technologies in the world. China has built huge cities, roads, railways, airports and factories in a couple of dozen years.

The strains this has put on people are unimaginable and unprecedented and I find it amazing that, on my travels, I have found so few signs of disruption or dislocation. The numerous people I have encountered have seemed resilient, adjusted, calm and dedicated. It is a nation largely at peace with itself and facing the future with hope. I do not know of any other peoples, except perhaps the Japanese, who could have done as well in the face of the extremely rapid and total changes.

Rare earths

'Rare' can have several meanings in English. It can mean very special and it can mean unusual, either rarely found or very difficult to process. Under the first meaning, China has a special resource in a very special kind of soil. This is the loess soil, brought down by the great rivers and deposited over many tens of thousands of years in the Yangtze river delta and the deltas of the Yellow and Pearl rivers, and periodically replenished in great floods. This soil is marvellously rich and, early on, the area became the rice bowl of China. On its foundation, these areas developed their ancient civilisations and, more recently, became the richest part of China. Three provinces in this area – Jiangsu, Zhejiang and Guandong (and Shanghai) – have a combined GDP which is twice that of Russia.

A second form of rare or special earth is clay, and here again with kaolin – the necessary ingredient for Chinese porcelain and which is found in only a few places outside China – the Chinese were extremely fortunate.

The other kind of rare earth is that which carries the technical name of 'rare earth', namely the 17 rare earth elements, including cerium, dysprosium, erbium, europium, gadolinium alongside twelve more. These earths are essential for modern computers, cell phones, MRI scanners, satellites, solar panels, nuclear reactors and much else. They are 'rare' not necessarily because they are not found widely, but because they are very difficult to process. As a result, currently ninety per cent of the world production of rare earths is in China. Alternatives to them could probably be found outside China, as they were in 2010 when China tried to block their export to Japan, but at the moment they are almost all produced in China. Their presence and production in China gives it another advantage as it develops its high-tech projects.

Reinvention of traditions

Much of Chinese history and culture was destroyed in the turmoils of the twentieth century. Numerous old buildings, monasteries, documents and much precious art were obliterated. This makes it very urgent for the Chinese to 're-invent' their lost cultural traditions. How is this best to be done?

One part of an approach may be through examining the concept of the 're-invention of tradition' which anthropologists use. In order to make radical changes appear natural, societies look to their past and find in it proto-types, earlier traditions which they 're-invent'. They do not invent from nothing, but bring bits of the past into a contemporary context. There must be something there already to make the 're-invention' credible.

China is currently engaged in this process. It looks at its history and traditions and tries to see what there is in earlier Chinese culture, particularly Confucianism, which can be re-asserted in the current context. China is also looking at its other traditions – Daoism, Neo-Confucianism and Buddhism. The Chinese are studying the qin, calligraphy, martial arts and archery, setting up Confucius centres, and establishing museums and archives. All of this activity, and a host of books on the 'New Confucianism' are signs of an awareness that, whatever can be saved from the destruction of Chinese civilization which occurred in the nineteenth and twentieth centuries, should be re-examined.

The success of China in restoring its psychological health is of importance to us all. This is not only because the happiness of a fifth of the world's population is directly involved, but also a happy China can contribute so much to all our lives.

Responsibility

From childhood I was taught that I was part of society, not just a member of a family. Indeed, as the years progressed, the balance of my responsibility shifted increasingly to the wider society. I spent most of my life away from home at school and built up the habit of treating strangers with respect and, if possible, kindness. I should help old ladies cross the streets, give up my seat in bus or train to women and the elderly, trust those I met and be courteous and polite to all. If I saw ways in which I could improve society in any way, by picking up litter, by giving to charity, by engaging in local committees (a school board, parish council or neighbourhood watch) I should contribute as much as I could.

In other words, my world was one where I knew that I benefited from the effort and consideration of others, the kindness of strangers, and I should join in this effort. I was constantly admonished to 'cast my bread upon the waters', that is to give freely without any particular goal in mind, in the belief that, if everyone did this, we would all benefit. If I let cars into a queue on a busy road off a difficult side road, others in the future would do the same for me. If I picked up some rubbish and kept the front of my house tidy, others would do the same. My goal was to play a part in relation to all of those in my country, and indeed the world, and this was just as important, if not more so, than my obligation to my close family.

I had assumed that this was a universal ethic, but when I went to India and later China, I found that it is exceptional. Even in southern Europe, I saw signs of what has been called 'amoral familism', that is the belief that morality and obligations are largely limited to the private family. One could see it in the dumping of rubbish in public spaces, in inconsiderate driving behaviour, and in the absence of civility to strangers.

China has for many centuries been based on the clan or family as the unit of moral duty. Apart from friends and the Emperor, all the Confucian relations of responsibility are within the family.

There are still signs of this in selfish driving, in the absence of public service with no obvious reward, in the attitude to the environment. Yet I have detected signs of the growth of civic responsibility where it was largely absent before – from such small things as the decline of smoking, spitting and litter in the streets to the growth of philanthropy and numerous charitable organisations in China.

Rice

It is important to remember that, as part of the map in the introduction shows us above, the older part of China, before the western extensions under the Qing, was roughly split in half, with rice cultivation in the southern part and hard grains such as wheat, millet and, later, maize in the north. So what I say here applies to the bulk of the population, for the south is much more densely settled, but only a part of China's huge land area.

In the rice areas, the crop has had an enormous influence. It was originally domesticated about eight thousand years ago, with competing claims, particularly from India and China as to its first use. It is ideally suited for the rich soils along the great rivers of China, with monsoon rains and warm temperature, though it also grows well in terraced cultivation up on the mountain-sides in the south and south-west.

Rice is a miracle plant. Above all it is hugely productive, feeding more than half the world's population and producing more nutrition than any of the hard grains per hectare. When it is grown in its wet form in flooded fields, it does not require any extra fertilisation. It is so fast growing that in the southern belt of China it is possible to get up to four crops a year, and it is standard further north to get two crops a year. It is this which led Furnivall to describe Burma, once a rice bowl of Asia, as a 'factory without chimneys'. Being largely dependent on the human body for its cultivation, especially in the planting, weeding and harvesting, it can absorb extra labour very effectively.

Particularly after the eighth century Tang dynasty, and the opening up of much of the south, the economic gravity of China shifted to the south – which also fed the north with huge rice shipments along the Grand Canal.

We can very starkly compare the effects of soft grains, particularly rice, but also lentils, with the hard grains, particularly wheat, barley rice and maize. The soft grains do not need animals either to work them or to produce manure. The hard grains need large resources of livestock as we find in Europe and America. The soft grains use huge human labour inputs and as was noticed from Montesquieu onwards, this led to unimaginably dense populations and rapid population growth.

The soft grains encourage peasant owners living on tiny plots. There are few economies of scale or possibilities of building up large estates. The hard grains encourage larger units of ownership, the manors and extensive farms of Europe are one example. The soft grains use human muscle and put no emphasis on supplementary power, whether from animals or machinery such as large mills. The western grains, as in England, led to rapid technological development and the supplementing of human labour by horses, cows and sheep and water and wind mills. The West moved towards an industrial civilization, China moved towards an industrious civilisation.

As Adam Smith and others suggested, and has been picked up by recent writers such as Clifford Geertz with his idea of 'agricultural involution' in Java, rice leads into a trap of over-population and ever-more-divided tiny holdings with incredible amounts of human labour applied to them. Hard grains lead towards the increasing use of non-human energy, a more class-based and unequal society, and, by chance, the break out from agricultural dependence through an industrial revolution.

S

Scholars

The respect for scholars and scholarship varies in degree very considerably from civilisation to civilisation. When I look at how scholars have been regarded through English history, and now throughout the Anglo-sphere, I note that while being a scholar is a worthy enough profession, it is nothing special. Crabbed academics are often the butt of humour and criticism, regarded as 'egg-heads', living in an 'ivory tower'.

'Bald heads forgetful of their sins,
Old, learned, respectable bald heads
All shuffle there; all cough in ink;
All wear the carpet with their shoes;
All think what other people think;

As Yeats put it in his poem 'The Scholars'[1]

The scholars may be listened to within their speciality, but very few have much authority more generally. They are socially on a level with other professions, a university professor is no more to be esteemed than a middle-ranking military officer, a minor judge, a successful business man, a vicar, a member of parliament, and these days, probably below a successful football player or pop star.

In Continental European countries their position appears to be higher. Their books are sometimes phenomenal best-sellers. Their pronouncements are sought well outside their specialty. They delight in the role of 'public intellectuals', becoming as famous as entertainers or sportsmen.

I had looked with envy at the esteem for my French equivalents, but now when I look at the history of scholars through two thousand years of Chinese civilization, my continental friends seem far below the respect for scholarship there. Because of the switch from feudalism to bureaucratic rule, where bureaucrats gained their positions by competitive examinations based on scholarship and which served as the basis of success, scholars ruled the country, alongside the Emperor and his court. Scholars were hugely powerful and, even at the lower levels, were highly respected. Calligraphy, poetry, history, were enormously esteemed and scholars and scholarship played a central role in China.

In good times, this brought them power and some riches, with little competition from any other profession. In bad times, for example during the reign of the second Qin Emperor, or during the purges of the Cultural Revolution, they suffered hugely as the bastions of former knowledge. Perhaps I have been lucky not to be too exposed and have been spared both the highs and the lows.

Self-respect

One side effect of more than one hundred and fifty years of imperialist, racist, aggression from Europe, swiftly followed by Japan, and most recently by western capitalism, is that it has made many Chinese surrender their *amour propre* (self-respect). They have been seduced, bamboozled, or bullied into believing in some kind of Utopian western system against which China is a failure – backward and inferior.

We often find intelligent friends from China belittling or criticizing their own society and its history in a fierce way, while extolling and idolizing some fantasy vision of the West. I came across something similar on a much smaller scale when I first went to Nepal, where villagers would criticize their own backwardness and speak longingly of western civilization. Then there was at least some justification, for the place was technologically very primitive.

China is not technologically backward, at least in the cities, or far behind the West. The provision of education, medicine and excellent electronic infrastructure puts it in many ways on a level with the West and in some respects, noticeably ahead. But the self-flagellation is not so much about the difference in material culture, but rather more directed to cultural, social and political activities.

Many Chinese think that the West is composed of dignified gentlemen, rationality, elegance and taste, freedom and democracy, and that China lacks all of these. There is a double misapprehension here. The picture of the West is beyond rose-tinted; it is rosy all over. And the gloom about China appears to ignore the extraordinary progress the Chinese have made against immense odds over the last thirty years.

I recently visited an old Hakka township. It was a national holiday and the place was so crowded that it was at times difficult to walk down the streets – tens of thousands of people packed into a very small space, of all ages and backgrounds. But there was never a hint of violence or bad temper. People were happy, relaxed, just enjoying the moment with their children. There were no scuffles, arguments, no drink or drunkenness. There were no guns, no obvious policing, all was self-controlled and relaxed. A young Chinese friend had to be reminded again and again to take her mobile phone out of her back pocket, which she said was perfectly safe. Multiply this over a hundred thousand times and that is a good deal of China today.

The undermining of the Chinese 'soul' or core is tragic and one manifestation of what has happened so often and all around the world in the last two hundred years. The missionaries came and proclaimed that the locals were heathens, damned, unreclaimed, only to be saved through abandoning their own culture and following a totally unfamiliar monotheism. Then the Europeans and Americans came with superior military power and proclaimed that the Chinese – whom they had poisoned with opium – were lazy, incompetent and pathetically peaceful, and could only be saved by buying western technologies. Then came the Japanese who did the same. Finally, the same happened with education, arts and sciences where China is derided as second-rate. And there is capitalism, sowing the seed of competition and greed, of materialism and scarcity. And now a new crusade is added, the spreading of human rights and 'demo-crazy', which belittles all China's achievements in the field of legal and political reform.

The Chinese often cringe (at least inwardly) and show considerable respect for what they think of as their western mentors. They are constantly chasing a rainbow, the so-called 'Chinese dream'.

Instead, the Chinese should take some modest pleasure and well-earned pride from what they have already achieved – a miracle. They should admire what is good in the West, but also be aware of its many defects. They should be more realistic and less genuflecting.

There is the danger of moving to the other extreme – of chauvinism, of overbearing nationalism, of arrogance in power and empire. I do not fear this too much of the Chinese. They are civilized, still Confucian-influenced, where most people have an ethic not dissimilar to the ideal of the English gentleman – humility, modesty, self-deprecation, awareness of others.

The phase of lacking self-confidence may well go quite soon. The large numbers travelling to foreign countries and returning should give a more realistic impression of 'the other'. And continuing economic and technological development will add to this. I suspect the Chinese will always be uneasy about being No. 1. But they will, hopefully, with dignity and modesty, resume the mantle of the Middle Kingdom, the single most powerful and creative civilization on earth. In achieving this, all of us will be impacted and involved.

Science and civilisation

The great scholar of Chinese science and civilisation, Joseph Needham, spent the later part of his life documenting, in a series of massive volumes, the sophistication and precocity of

Chinese technology. By the fourteenth century the Chinese had invented most of the great technologies in the world – mechanical clocks, mechanical weaving, gunpowder, the compass, printing, porcelain, silk weaving, tea cultivation, complex irrigation systems, huge boats with internal air devices to keep boats afloat, and an extraordinary educational system based on merit.

If anywhere was likely to break through into an industrial, scientific, kind of world, an observer looking back to the time when Marco Polo in the thirteenth century visited the largest city in the world, Hangzhou, might have predicted that it would be China.

Yet not only did China not develop in this way, hitting what Mark Elvin has called the 'high-level equilibrium trap', but it became weaker, at least relatively, so that by the nineteenth century the richest and most ancient civilisation in the world was humiliated by Britain. This is particularly astonishing in that even until the middle of the nineteenth century, the majority of the world's wealth was in China.

The story is encapsulated in one of Joseph Needham's diagrams.[17]

Needham – science and civilization

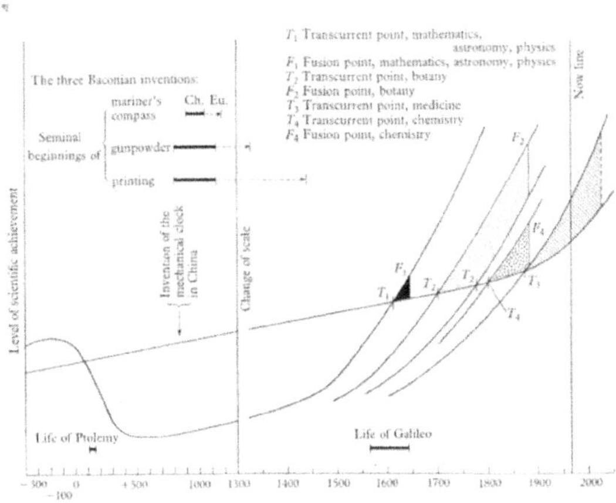

Fig. 99. Schematic diagram to show the roles of Europe and China in the development of oecumenical science.

[17] Joseph Needham, The Grand Titration (1969), figure 99.

The question Needham posed is why the West had a full scientific revolution, that is to say developed a method of investigating accurately the laws of nature, while this did not happen in China.

Several things can be said in a preliminary way about this problem. First, though some revisionist writers from the 1980s have tried to ignore or undermine Needham's findings, they have not succeeded in doing so. The problem remains. A second general point is that a roughly similar pattern is observable in Islamic civilisations. There the technological. achievements were not as great as in China, but the level of Arabic knowledge in a number of fields, astronomy, medicine, mathematics, for example, was higher than in China. It looked by around 1100 that the breakthrough into sustained science would happen in Islam – but it did not.

This second case suggests that the Needham question needs to be reversed. In other words, the puzzle is not the non development in China and Islam, for this is normal, but the puzzle is to explain the extraordinary departure to a new world of knowledge around the sixteenth century in the West.

If we reverse the question in this way we can observe certain things about the western case which were missing in both China and Islam. One was the growth of powerful, independent, universities, where scholars joined together over the generations to discover new things. The early Chinese and Islamic academies were not universities in the western sense and mostly faded away or were suppressed, though there are one or two exceptions, such as the Yuelu Academy in Hunan province in China, which still exists, though it was taken over by Confucian scholars.

A second is the political configuration of Europe. Science often challenges the orthodoxy and scientists tend to be harassed or destroyed. In China and Islam, both uniform and homogenous in many respects, had powerful rulers whose sway extended across vast areas.There were few pockets for new knowledge to emerge safely. Europe, split into many small warring kingdoms, was suitable for dissidence and challenging thought. For example, when early science in Spain and Italy was suppressed by the Catholic church, thinkers fled to the Protestant areas of Holland, Scandinavia and Britain.

A third factor, which Needham himself stressed,is the difference of religion. Islam tends to be conservative, since all knowledge is already revealed in the sayings of the founder and his immediate descendants. Confucius was also suspicious of new knowledge and his followers constantly refer back to the original vision. Christianity is an unfolding and progressive revelation, pointing to the future and the Second Coming of Christ.

Another aspect of this is that Christianity holds that God created a universe underpinned by immutable laws. These were fixed at the creation of the world and they can be discovered by man. Indeed, it is the duty of humans to discover what they are and to spread that knowledge. This is in total contrast to the geomantic and fluctuating cosmology of China.

Chinese Buddhism emphasized that there was no separation of the mental and physical world and the latter was an illusion or mind-created. There are no permanent and deeper laws but floating and ever-changing constellations. The development of science, based on hidden, yet discoverable and, once discovered, immutable and predictable laws, is impossible in such a mental and moral environment.

This cosmology is made even more unstable by Daoism with its magical forces that create endless special and unrepeated events as winds, waters and the stars shift in their alignment. It would have been difficult for the first western scientists to make their break-through if they had already been in the uncertain world of quantum mechanics.

Another feature of western science was that working systematically to discover deeper truths, and to apply these to the solution of practical problems, was an honourable pursuit. The practitioners were prepared to do physical experiments with their own hands. People as high in status as Robert Boyle, Earl of

Cork, or Lord Townsend, one of the inventors of new agricultural practices, let alone numerous clergymen and university teachers, were happy to be engaged in 'science'. In contrast, in China, the Mandarin and small educated elite shunned all physical work and practical experiment, which was demeaning and took them from the purely literary and conservative repetitions of their Confucian training.

Another centrally important component of the western scientific revolution was the development of high-quality experiments using glass instruments. In our book on *The Glass Bathyscaphe* (2002), Gerry Martin and I showed that 16/20 of the twenty major scientific discoveries in the last two thousand years required the use of glass instruments at some point in their discovery. Astronomy, chemistry, medicine and many other disciplines could not have moved to successful science without glass.

The fact that China (and Islam) failed to develop their glass industries after early beginnings into anything equivalent to the pure glass of Italy and the Netherlands not only lay behind the absence of the accurate and precise art of the Renaissance, but also the Scientific Revolution. Glass technologies are a necessary, if not sufficient, cause of science, as are other things such as the vast increases in knowledge which challenged old assumptions caused by the overseas voyages from Europe from the later fifteenth century.

Finally, Needham's suggests that 'capitalism' in the West was an essential factor in western dynamics. Islam had great trading networks, but banking and sophisticated economic institutions and industrial manufacture were weak. China had a huge inland trade and a vast array of petty manufacturing industries. Yet money-making was always regarded as demeaning by the *literati* and the market never flourished with large organizations like the Fuggers or later the Rothschilds or other Jewish or non-conformist groups. The competition and seeking for better processes, the endless striving for better, new, knowledge to defeat competition, and the organizations to mass produce artefacts cheaply when a breakthrough occurred were far less developed in China than in the West.

Sex

In the English world in which I grew up, sex was strongly connected to religion. The Christian church disapproved of sex; celibacy was the highest ideal and bodily lusts were part of the fallen nature of man, symbolized in the awareness of nakedness and expulsion from the Garden of Eden. To give way to sexual urges was a sin and brought God's anger. The body was seen as potentially unclean and sexual relations outside marriage were strictly forbidden. Consequently, much of my life from adolescence onwards constituted a battle against what were called 'unclean lusts'.

With this long association of sin and sex, the change in morality over the last three generations in the West is pretty amazing. The change to a situation of widespread sexual relations in the teen-age years, from dating to full sex, a proliferation of sexual images in the media, the frankness about sex, all is a huge change since I was a boy. And it now sets off the West from China in a different way.

Traditionally in China, without a monotheistic religion, there was no strong correlation between salvation, sin and sex. There should be bodily control and there were often strong social pressures against sexual contacts but it was not tied up with morality, unlike in the West. There was more frankness, less obsession with the sexualized body, less anxiety about sex.

Yet, perhaps counter-intuitively, this means that young people in China seem to be less sexualized than their western counterparts. Dating is still banned in many Chinese schools and the age of first sexual relations is several years higher in China than in the U.K. or America. Watching television and looking at magazines, or just observing the normal clothes of young Chinese and the way boys and girls behave with each other, gives an impression of far less emphasis on sexuality. It may even suggest that, historically, the Chinese have been quite prudish about sexual matters. This may change, but this is how it is now.

Shamanism

Another aspect of the interpenetration of magic and the supernatural into everyday Chinese life is the presence of shamanism. I first encountered a shamanic society in the mountains of Nepal. There I found among the Gurungs, who had migrated down from northern and then through western China, a classic form of shamanism. Priests with special costumes drummed on one-sided drums, using an ancient language for various spells and chants, dancing and sometimes going into trance when they communicated with their spirits.

When I went to Japan, I was amazed to find, after twelve years of not seeing it, that the Japanese not only had a similar form of shamanism, but that the elements of shamanism –that is the fusion of the human and natural world so that rocks, waterfalls, trees and echoes have a force within them – was universal in Japan. The clapping of hands in Shinto shrines is to call these forces, *kami*, down to the shrine.

Perhaps I should not have been surprised to learn over time that this is the same in China. This is not just to note that many of the minority peoples have shamans, for example the *dongba* of the Naxi, or the shamans I have seen dancing with their one-sided drums in films of the aftermath of the Sichuan earthquake. It is much more than this, as in Japan.

Daoism is almost identical to Shinto and works on the basis of a nature infused by invisible forces, which can be approached through the Shinto rituals. While the West seems to have lost all traces of shamanism many centuries ago, though there may be traces of it in early modern Italy or Spain, China and Japan are still shamanic. This is not just in the minorities with acting shamans, but in the deeper cultural feeling of the presence of invisible powers in nature which can be controlled by specialists.

When I discussed the matter in detail with a retired University Professor friend, he said that when he was young, the 'Daoists' did shamanic rituals, to get rid of evil at a death. They were not professional Daoists but were villagers with secret knowledge. When one of his close relatives died, a master with four students attended the death ceremony. One student was reading sutras but they were not Buddhist or Daoist, but used knowledge handed down from ancestors. Another student used drums, a small, round, one-sided drum, and another student used cymbals. The ritual lasted five or six hours. It was to get rid of evil, the drum helping the ghost go to the after-world, the cymbals to inform relatives how to go to heaven.

Another relative died last year and he had to stay awake for the whole night. There was an 'ancestor master', in a costume which was neither Buddhist nor Daoist, who read from a scroll which was not used in Buddhist or Daoist rituals.

Though shamanism is particularly strong among the ethnic minorities, the Han Chinese invite 'Buddhist' monks, in fact not real monks, to perform at death ceremonies. They circle around the coffin, the children wear white clothes and follow them. There is weird and incomprehensible singing, writing and chants in a local language he does not understand.

If they are rich Han, they will probably go to a temple for an orthodox funeral ritual. If poorer villagers, they may use 'false monks', one of which is found in every ten or so villages. These 'monks' sacrifice a cock on top of a coffin and take the blood to the graveyard, burying it with the coffin. My informant thought that this kind of shamanic ritual was to be found everywhere in China, though its actual form would be very different in each local culture. He heard the voice of a dead person coming out of the mouth of one of these shamans and sometimes they use identical body language to the deceased. They also are believed sometimes to go into trance.

One interesting footnote to this is that my informant comes from the middle province of Hunan, which is also where the famous international musician and composer of 'The Ghost Opera' and other works, Tan Dun, comes from. Tan often remarks that early experiences with shamanism in his childhood turned him into a composer.

In sum, there are numerous streams that still flow into the concealed lake of Chinese shamanism. Daoism has strong shamanic roots, the minorities are often shamanic and the Manchu (Qing) Emperors were shamanic – building a shamanic centre in Beijing, for example, when they first conquered it in 1644.

Shenzhen

Shenzhen is a magical city; each time we have visited it and heard about its history and progress, I have sensed that a new world is being built here which will shape all our futures. It is immensely important for the history and present position of China – almost half the patent applications for new inventions for the whole of China currently come from Shenzhen. This justifies singling out this one city for treatment, though, of course, it would be interesting to do the same for a number of other great cities with a rich history and influence.

In the 1980s, Shenzhen was a little fishing village of about thirty thousand people opposite Hong Kong. It was designated as the first Free Economic Zone by Deng Xiaoping in 1992 and started to attract immigrants from all over China. It is now officially a city of twelve and a half million, with perhaps another five million unregistered.

Shenzhen is very wealthy; its taxable revenue is well above Taiwan or Hong Kong. It is being designed and planned as a new city and is extremely efficient, filled with trees and parks, libraries and bookshops. The Shenzhen book fair is the largest in the world and the city has the largest single floor bookshop in the world.

Shenzhen is already on a par with much of Silicon valley, and we are told that within a few years, it will be ahead of anywhere in the world in terms of Artificial Intelligence and renewable energy products. Shenzhen manufactures the best green energy cars and other machinery and is experimenting in new institutes of education and new developments in legal regulations.

When you think of what has effectively been achieved in about twenty years, it is truly amazing. At first, Shenzhen benefited from government support, but we are told that this is not so important now. The Shenzhen phenomenon comes from an intersection of a huge influx of energetic and skilled young people, the absence of an overbearing bureaucracy, a good transport and legal structure, and its location in the golden area which includes Hong Kong and Guangzhou. The richest provinces of China – Guandong, Zhejiang and Jiangsu – surround it. The economic strength of this region alone is already larger than places like the UK or France, and will quite soon overtake Japan.

What I find intriguing about Shenzhen is that it gives us a glance of the future. It is hyper-efficient, filled with the latest electronic devices. Yet it is also, as mentioned, a city filled with parks, libraries, bookshops, galleries, tea-houses and things of the mind. As we move towards a world where the majority of production is done by artificially intelligent devices, Shenzhen will be a pioneer. We can imagine how things may develop. The cities of the UK and much of Europe, and even America, seem old-fashioned and still living in the twentieth century. Shenzhen is a twenty-first century city and one senses something unprecedented here, the realisation of what might be the third industrial revolution, succeeding those of the age of coal and the telegraph, and then the age of oil and the early years of the internet.

Some idea of the growth in personal wealth in the transformation from fishing village to huge city is shown by the following diagram, which only takes the story to 2015.

Shenzhen: Real GDP per capita, 2005 dollars
$32,000
$16,000
$8,000
$4,000
$2,000
$1,000
$500
1975
1980
1985
1990
1995
2000
2005
2010
2015

Shock of the future

Each time I visit China, it seems to have changed greatly since my last visit. This is not just in material ways, with new trains, planes, roads and cities, but equally with the less tangible ways in which people lead their lives. This is something that the Chinese themselves find extraordinary. Those who have advised me on what I should write about in this book often ask me to note elements of this electronic revolution.

The background to the glimpse of the future which China provides for western visitors consists of several features. In my home city of Cambridge in particular, and over the whole U.K, it is difficult to change swiftly. 'If it works, why fix it' is a widespread philosophy. Although mobile phones, electric cars and science parks are accepted, the new technologies face much more resistance than in China. The poor and technologically backward China of even twenty years ago, has leapt into the internet age far faster and more creatively than many older countries for it has no 'path dependency'. In other words it is not stuck in certain grooves of the kind we find in Europe, and even, it seems, America.

Secondly, the command economy of China, described under 'Hydraulic civilization', means that if there is a new idea which needs national infrastructure, then it is rolled out rapidly. Even around 2005, we were amazed to see the electric pylons snaking out into the most remote parts of China and broadband connections and mobile phone coverage spread very rapidly over vast areas with government support.

Thirdly, the Chinese themselves are very flexible, rational, people, not swayed by religious taboos or emotions, and famed for their hard work, entrepreneurial and money-handling abilities, and their ability to copy and surpass others in technologies. They are keen on profit, competitive and highly adaptable. The succession of self-made billionaires in recent years, often from humble beginnings, remind us of the early years of American innovation a century ago, people like Li Ka Shing, Jack Ma and the founders of Baidu and Ten Cent.

Another possible factor is the Chinese written language which it could be argued is ideally adapted for the internet age. It is universally understood in China and extremely efficient in conveying information swiftly. When subtitling some of my films, or in the translations of my books, I see how a long sentence can be reduced to two or three characters and read, because of the shapes, very swiftly. For an age where visual images now dominate on television and mobiles, the pictographic language of China is very analogous and perhaps helpful.

Finally, the huge scale of China, where an innovation or idea can reach millions, or a new product find a huge market, must have a large effect. United by the same written language and political system, 1.4 billion people are a huge gift to manufacturers and inventors. When I give an interview on British radio or television I might expect an audience of one or two million at the most. Recent interviews I have done for CCTV and Chinese national papers have reached audiences, I am told, of over 200 million.

The kinds of break-through technology in which China now leads the world take various forms. One centres around Jack Ma and his business Ali Baba. These consist not only of the vast on-line shopping emporium similar to Amazon, but cashless stores, on-line medical treatment, and payment systems dispensing with the use of cards and cash such as Ali-pay. With Ten-cent and WeChat, none of the young Chinese I meet in China carry any cash, or even a credit card. Everything can be done on the phone, and immediately.

There is no need to arrange transport in advance with the equivalents of Uber, or hotels, or trains and plains, or restaurants, or even bicycles. All are almost instantly available. When I feel unwell at a meal, or need an extra jersey or a book, a friend makes a call and whatever I need arrives within an hour or so.

A huge amount of education is now done online and I am consequently experimenting with turning some of my work into educational animations. A great deal of information is available through the Chinese 'Google', Baidu, even though some material is obviously blocked or filtered. A huge amount of personal information can be uploaded with very efficient equivalents of Youtube, Twitter and Instagram, such as Youku and WeChat, and many apps such as Dou Yin.

In other words, the implications of the intersection of the internet and artificial intelligence, which even here in the slower West we can see daily transforming the lives of our children, is magnified greatly in China.

For me, perhaps, the most striking recent example is WeChat. Three years ago, around 2016, I was unaware of it, even though it had been launched in 2011 and by that year had 889 million active monthly users. Now most people, even including myself a little when in China, use it all the time. What it has done is to take all the separate western platform such as messenger services, skype, online banking, online shopping, uploading of films and texts, and many other new uses which are not yet developed here, and put them into one application. It is incredible fast, capacious and efficient. It is far more powerful than anything I have heard of in the West.

So it is not surprising that the next generation (5G) of computing finds a Chinese firm, Huawei, ahead of the competition in its power and design, and hence is causing considerable anxiety around the world. 5G is already being rolled out over China and will increase the Chinese lead in a new generation technologies.

Of course, as discussed under 'surveillance', there are downsides to all this. Yet their development cannot be ignored. I feel like Tocqueville when he first went to America in 1831 and realised that he was in an entirely different civilisation to 'old Europe'. He was in a land where the slowing hand of ancient history did not apply. Just as America is often described as having been 'born modern', so China in the last twenty years has been born ultra-modern. We glimpse a world which is not yet present in most of the world.

Silk and Silk Roads

It is no accident that the greatest communications system in history, on both land and sea, should be called the silk roads. Although China had several hugely desired commodities which are traded over thousands of miles, tea and porcelain being others, silk was pre-eminent in the early days.

It has been suggested that the earliest examples of silk have been found in graves which date back 8,500 years. There are many examples of silk in Chinese tombs and in books on sericulture from about three thousand years ago. Although the Chinese tried to keep the production method a secret, the knowledge of how to make silk reached Korea, with aid from China, around 200 BC, and India by AD 140. By the medieval period, Italy was the most important producer of silk in the West, most of it being done in the Calabrian region.

Before I went to China in 1996, I had heard of the Silk Road, but apart from the vague notion that there had been a road across from China to Europe, carrying traders and ideas from East to West, I knew nothing of it. Now, with the best-selling *The Silk Roads* (2015) by Peter Frankopan, there is no longer any excuse for such a vague picture.

There turn out to be many 'silk roads'. To start with, there were two sets of 'roads', the land roads (called 'the Belt' in the new scheme) and the sea 'roads'. The first silk roads are believed to have started around 130 B.C. under the Han dynasty, and later divided into two main groups. One set went directly West from China, by various different routes, across central Asia to modern Turkey, Arabia and India, as can be seen in the following map.

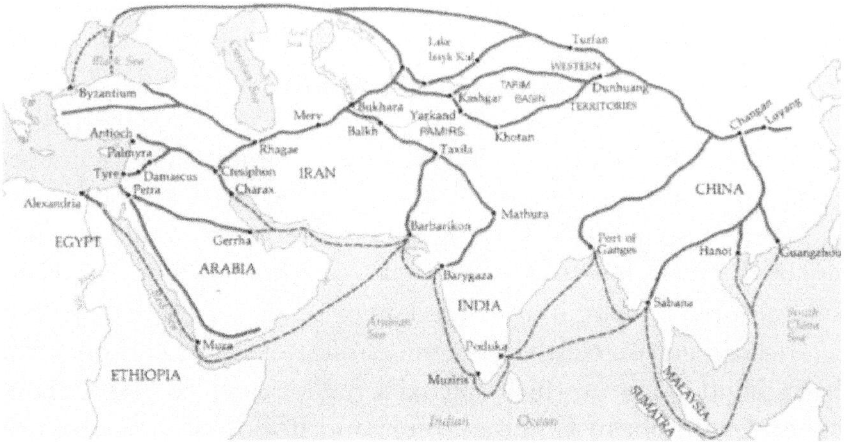

These were the silk roads of which I was vaguely aware, carrying silk and other goods, though often closed by nomadic tribesmen.

Then there was another set of roads going down through Burma and South East Asia, with many ancillary smaller roads, often called the 'tea horse roads', carrying tea to Tibet and the south.

Another set of routes were the maritime silk roads, mainly originating in Canton and by way of Vietnam. These took goods to islands in the Pacific and then onwards through the Sumatra straits to India, the Arabian Gulf and Red Sea. Thus, as early as the eighth century, there were strong links between China and the Mediterranean by land and sea.

Like many things in modern China, the blueprint is very ancient. The current 'One Belt One Road' initiative mirrors sets of roads which existed over two thousand years ago.

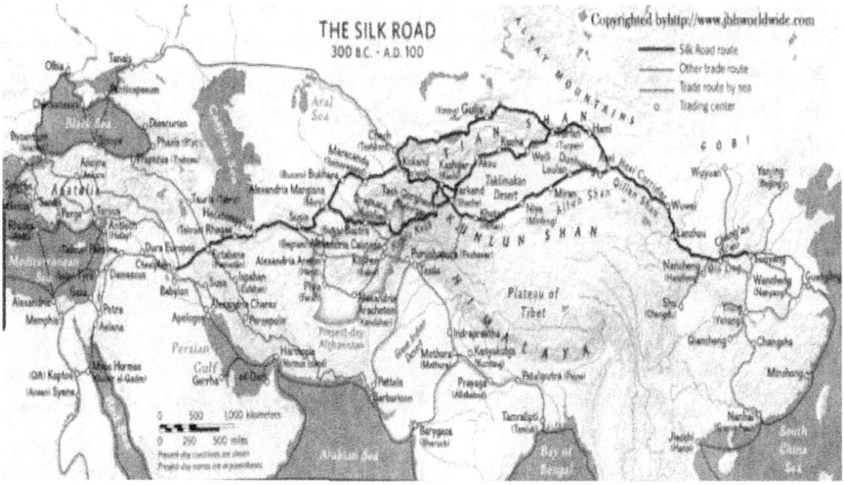

Only through my visits to China over the years have I gradually appreciated the beauty and wonder of Chinese silk. Through good connections to one of the centres of silk making in Jiangsu provinces, and particularly the old capital of Nanjing (Nanking), I am now the proud owner of several wonderful silk ties, with the brilliant reds and yellows of the emperor. They rather outshine the subdued ties of Cambridge University which I used to wear. My wife also has many beautiful silk scarfs, generous gifts from our Chinese friends. Silk and Chinese civilisation are entwined. Silk, with its strength, elegance, beauty, warmth and coolness, seems to be an apt symbol for China.

Sin and guilt

I grew up and live in a western, Christian-shaped civilisation which instils strong feelings of sin and guilt. My Christian teaching emphasised 'original sin': that I was born as a flawed and sinful baby whose sin had to be partially removed by baptism. Humankind had fallen, been driven from the Garden of Eden because of the sins of Adam and Eve. Only through Christ's blood could we be cleansed. This idea has been with me ever since. Every time I lied or felt pride or lust, I was expected to feel deep guilt because I had sinned. This was so even if no-one except God knew of my thoughts.

One of my great delights when I went to the Himalayas to work with tribal peoples, and later to Japan and China, was to realise that others thought differently. I found whole civilisations which had no concept of sin in my sense. They did not believe in 'original sin', or that the body was at war with the mind and spirit.

Of course, if you did something wrong in these civilisations and were found out you might feel shame and loss of face in relation to others. But you had not betrayed God and would not be condemned to eternal fire and damnation unless you repented and threw yourself on God's mercy. Sex, for example, was a social matter, not surrounded by dangerous, potentially defiling, connotations, a cause for guilt.

Of course, the peoples of China are well aware of morality and immorality. They condemn lying, killing, greed and most of the things we proclaim as sins. Yet the moral codes are not, on the whole, entangled with supernatural forces. Daoism and Chan Buddhism do not have the western sense of sin and guilt within them. Instead, an individual should avoid immorality because it will lead them from the Path (Dao) and make it more difficult to escape from the wheel of life to the final extinction of *nirvana.*

Sino-Japanese relations

The relations between China and Japan have been both richly productive and hugely painful. It is not an easy subject for an outsider who greatly admires both Japan and China to discuss. It feels like intruding on the squabbles of cousins, or even brothers. But here are a few brief observations.

In terms of actual relations, there have been various phases. Much of Japanese culture was shaped by China during the Tang dynasty, when a number of basic features of Japan were imported from China. These include the Chinese architecture and planning of the ancient cities of Kyoto and Nara, Chinese music (the court music of Tang China is now preserved as gagaku in Japan), the early governmental systems of Heian China, various sects of Buddhism, Confucian philosophy and a number of crafts and technologies such as ceramics and tea production. After the failed attempts to invade under Kublai Khan, there was another wave of peaceful imports of Zen, powdered tea and Confucian philosophy. From then on, Japan was the younger brother, sending embassies and gifts to its much more powerful older brother, China.

All this changed when Japan rapidly industrialised along the western model in the 1880s. The Japanese observed that European countries attacked and annexed other countries to form empires. Japan had no overseas empire, so Korea and China were obvious places in which to copy the Europeans. Japan decided to do the same with a China weakened by western incursions and the terrible Taiping rebellion. In 1894-5, during a brief war, Japan humiliated China and seized parts of the north, Manchuria, further weakening the Qing empire.

Even then, many young Chinese intellectuals went to Japan to learn about modernity. Yet as China fell into deeper troubles, Japan increased its ambitions. In an extraordinary move, at the end of the First World War, the victorious European powers gave to Japan the large Chinese province of Shandong, the birthplace of Confucius. China had been an ally of the victors, but they disregarded this allegiance. This led to a bitter uprising, the May 4th Movement in China, but it also gave Japan another foothold in China. On the basis of a spurious incident, Japan started to move forward from Manchuria in 1927 and from then to 1945 was constantly at war with China, turning this into a full-scale invasion in 1937.

Japan justified all this as part of its 'civilising mission', the equivalent of the 'white man's burden', proclaiming the setting up of a 'Greater East Asia Co-Prosperity Zone' as a counterpart to western colonial empires. When China resisted, Japan scolded it and invaded it for behaving like an unruly younger brother. The atrocities of the rape of Nanking, comfort women, bombing with chemical and biological weapons, the experimental camps for such weapons in which the Chinese were the subjects, are well known. Over twenty million Chinese died in the long Sino-Japanese war.

Since 1945, and especially in the last thirty years as China has grown richer and more powerful than Japan, relations have again been tense, with America providing a shield and an incitement to Japan. Much of the misunderstanding comes from the fact that while culturally, as we have seen, Japan and China are very alike, at the level of the family, politics and economy, as well as general ideology, they are miles apart. They are as different from each other as are the U.K. and Europe. A small space of sea separates different civilisations in both cases.

Only if and when both partners come to understand their deeper differences, covered over by superficial similarities, but also their common interests in our inter-connected world, will the tension evaporate. There are signs of this already, and signs that Japan is returning to its traditional position of younger brother to the great civilisation on the mainland.

Social media and digital communication

The social media, and the wider digital communications revolution, has really only taken off in the last twenty years, with much of the surge occurring in the last ten years with the spread of smart phones – mini-computers in the form of a phone. This is changing everything. I have found that in a remote Himalayan village, on average the population have two phones per person and the streets and rooms of Cambridge are full of people tweeting, flickering, facebooking and instagramming.

What surprised me about all this in China is how, coming from a technologically low situation some twenty-five years ago, China now feels like the centre and most advanced part of this revolution. Even in the last three years it has leapt ahead, particularly with powerful and cheap smart phones, excellent broadband coverage to the most remote regions, now moving from 4G to 5G, and with amazing social networking apps such as WeChat.

WeChat is a hybrid of all the separated apps of the West. It is like Skype, offering video in real time, it is a money-transferring and paying system, in effect a bank, so that my Chinese friends no longer carry cash. It is a wonderful messaging and emailing system with large free data stores. I have been amazed to find that when travelling around China, an Uber-like taxi meets us as we want it, medicine for a cold turns up magically in the middle of a meal an hour after I mention I don't feel well. All the goods of the Alibaba emporiums are almost instantly available, anywhere, and all journeys are made easy through the mapping system.

Of course, these social media developments pose both great problems, and also opportunities, for the government. The government cannot control the constant communications and instant sharing of embarrassments or outrages. On the other hand, they can trace almost everyone all the time through their phones, and access to all amenities such as travel will soon be monitored through facial recognition software delivered by smartphones. While these exciting digital technologies give China the possibility of a new kind of virtual civil society – joining netizens together into interest groups and action-sets beyond the structures of government – they also place every individual only one click away from those who wish to monitor them.

Socialism with Chinese characteristics

This is a well-known phrase in Chinese intellectual discussions about the nature of socialism and communism within China. It refers to something which is part of an even broader pattern and which I find extraordinary when discussing China. This is the fact that being so huge, ancient and tightly integrated, China was able to absorb and then re-shape hugely different systems and make them distinctively chinese. We can see something on a smaller scale with islands such as Japan and Britain, but the shocks there were usually less vast (though the Germanic invasions wiped out the Roman civilization in Britain) and, being an island, usually made all the difference.

China as a continental empire was invaded again and again, either by entirely different kinds of political and social system, for example in the Mongol and Manchu invasions, or by entirely different philosophies invented in far-off lands, for example Buddhism from India, and recently communism and capitalism from the West.

Yet each time we find that, after an initial period when the new peoples or ideas seem to spread in their pure form, the new political system or ideology became re-shaped by China into something really different. Thus, over the centuries, Chinese, Chan, Buddhism became basically totally different from even its roots or its later development in Tibet. Or the Mongols and Manchus themselves became, in effect, largely Chinese.

The case of communism or socialism fits into this pattern. When the western system derived from Marx in England and Lenin in Russia swept across China, after some years of struggle led by Mao Tse-tung and his armies, text-book communism was attempted, though it immediately had to be adapted to a rural rather than urban civilization. The basic dogmas, the abolition of private property, of classes and class structure, of the State and its apparatus, as well as the old bonds of family and religion, were introduced. For a short while, from 1949 to 1956 there was apparent unity and the Soviets were the model and western capitalism the enemy. The rift with the Soviet Union and breakdown of political relations, much of it about different interpretations of basic Marxist-Leninist ideology and its application in the Cold War, began in 1956 and lasted to 1966 and the relationship was never strongly re-established.

From the very first, the context of communism in a huge peasant civilisation where the communes basically replaced the village communities gave it a different flavour from western communism. Yet it was similar in its immediate effects. Both experiments, in the Soviet Union and China, as now in North Korea, led to the collapse of the economy and there were massive famines. And in both the Soviet and Chinese experiment the abolition of the State did not abolish the need for the centre to exercise absolute power to hold together a civilization no longer united by religion, family or class structures. This had to be done through iron discipline and ultimately by fear and denunciation as in the Chinese Cultural Revolution or Stalin's purges.

Yet as always happens in China, the huge weight of Chinese civilization began to pull communism in a uniquely different direction at the end of Mao's period and under Deng Xiaoping. In effect Deng lightened the orthodoxy, allowing back private property, reforming the judicial and political system so that it was now recognizably a state bureaucracy, encouraging economic growth through free enterprise zones and other reforms.

The result is now a situation where I find it difficult to decide what China is. Is it a capitalist country with a strong socialist legacy and single-party State, a sort of Scandinavia with single-party rule? Or is it still socialist in its aspirations, but aware that without the market and western technologies it cannot compete with the West, aware that the enormous entrepreneurial energy and disciplined labour of the Chinese over the centuries can be best harnessed through a mixed solution? In 'socialism with Chinese characteristics', we have a fusion which is totally different from that in the Soviet period or now in North Korea and offers a credible and working alternative to western individualistic capitalism.

Soil

One of the best-known books by the greatest Chinese anthropologist, Fei Hsiao Tong, is called *From the Soil* (1947). Fei rightly centred his interpretation of the soul of China on the umbilical link between the Chinese and the soil, and particularly the family farm in the peasant village. He knew that this is a feature of all great peasant civilisations, including India, Mexico and Mediterranean Europe, namely that people who work on the land over the generations are very deeply attached to a particular piece of land. Even in southern Ireland, passing the farm down through the generations in the same family—or 'keeping the name on the land'—is an important value.

For many centuries, the vast majority of the Chinese population lived in villages on plots of land held by families, often for many generations. Every rock, furrow, tree and stream was known intimately, for you were born there, married there and died there. And all the landscape was alive with forces and spirits, filled with the graves of one's ancestors. The soil and the peasant were one.

The system is now under huge strain in China. Although still preserved in name in the *hukou* system, which registers every Chinese person at his/her place of birth and guarantees them a tiny piece of land there for life, the tie to the land has been largely severed. Although the vast numbers moving to cities still have to register their original *hukou* when they arrive and may find it very difficult to move this registration, there are plans to abolish the system, except in certain large cities such as Beijing and Shanghai, as a way of preventing too much in-migration.

As we travel through the vast areas of high apartment blocks in great cities, it is difficult to imagine that only three-quarters of a century ago Fei could think of China as being centred on the soil. Beyond a tiny window box or tree-lined street, where is the soil now for the majority of the Chinese population?

South China Sea

The South China Sea is a vast tract of the Pacific, some 3.5 million square kilometres. In comparison, the Mediterranean is only about 2.5 million square kilometres.

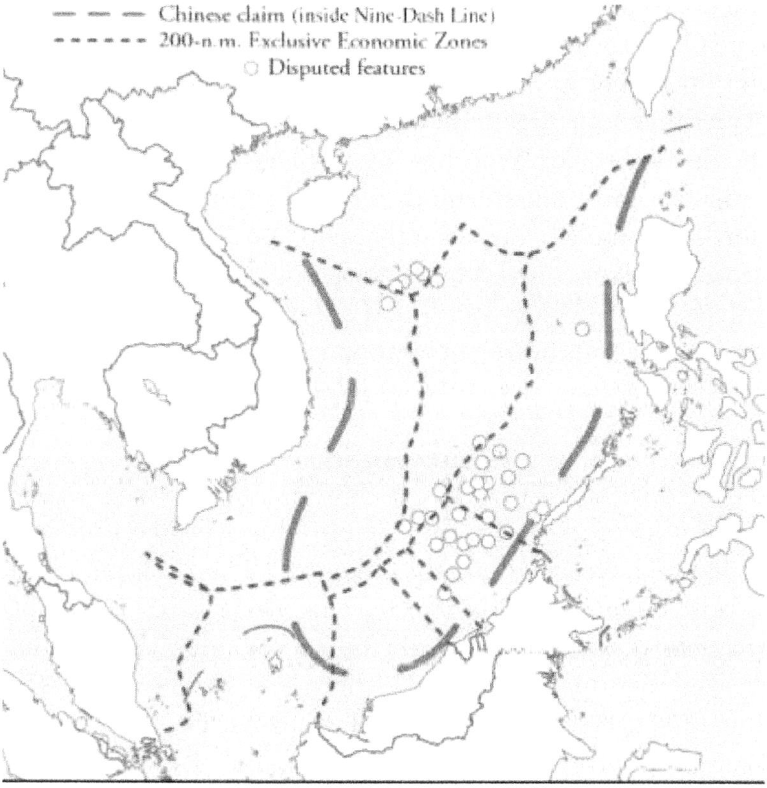

This stretch of ocean is of very considerable strategic importance, and is also believed to have beneath its waves a great deal of mineral wealth, oil reserves and other precious commodities. Its importance is such, and so hotly contested, that some believe that disputes there, with clashes, probably between the U.S. and China, may be the spark that ignites the next world war. For these reasons, it is important to understand a little about its history and the claims by all parties.

In this short space, I can only make a few points. One is that until the twentieth century, this was an area where marauding pirates, especially from Japan, often attacked ships and coastal villages. It was also very difficult to navigate because of frequent storms and hurricanes. The South China Seas were economically only of interest for fishing. In so far as it was owned by anyone at all, there were a few early maps which showed the major islands in it as Chinese but during the long Sino-Japanese conflicts, the islands, including Taiwan, were taken over by the Japanese.

The other source of tension lies in two concepts of ownership of the open sea. The West has long believed that the property of the adjacent land mass extends only a certain number of miles, the furthest usually being, as in the map above, 200 nautical miles. Chinese claims of sovereignty treat the sea as affected by the disputed islands which are dotted across it, most of which have Chinese names and were once tributaries of China.

Surveillance

I come from a civilisation where secret police and serious surveillance have been largely unknown. The dystopian picture of a police state in George Orwell's *1984*, with Big Brother constantly monitoring people is, as yet, and thankfully, an unrealized nightmare. Of course, there have been periods of spies and intelligence-gathering, particularly when England converted to Protestantism in the sixteenth century and the Catholic threat was very real, culminating in the attempt by Guy Fawkes to blow up the Houses of Parliament. Yet, for most of British history, you could speak and write without too much fear of being watched and reported on.

Certainly, throughout my many years as a teacher in Cambridge, I have never felt under surveillance in any way. Now, with the ubiquitous CCTV cameras and the tracking of mobile devices, we do begin to feel that the government may be watching us. Yet, on the whole, the United Kingdom is still a society where you would not suspect that people will inform on you or that you will suddenly be accused of thought crimes or deviance.

England in this respect was very fortunate, even within Europe. The Catholic Inquisition, as well as State spies, were very active over much of continental Europe for the many centuries from the thirteenth to nineteenth, and this continued in a heightened form in the Soviet Union and in the fascist era.

Where does China stand? The first thing to note is that China was always largely governed through the control of information. It was, and is, a vast territory where, at any moment, a separatist movement or peasant revolt or millenarian cult can recruit millions against the Emperor or Party. Traditionally, there was a weak standing army, very few administrators lightly spread out, and enemies on the borders keen to ferment trouble. In such a situation, how can an Empire such as this last for two millenia? The answer is through inculcating fear and keeping records on the mass of the population through a huge network of informers.

This has probably been a phenomenon going back thousands of years, but it is best documented during the Qing period from the 1650's to 1900. The added threat was that the rulers were Manchu, while the vast bulk of the population were Han, so there were constant reasons for disturbance and rebellion, as well as suspicion.

As a consequence, the Emperors, verging on the paranoid in our eyes, maintained a vast and complex network of spies, gathering information on any dangerous-looking activity or writing. All hints of disturbance were reported to the central authorities – who took decisive and forceful action to squash potential trouble.

Surveillance changed in nature, but not in intensity, during the Communist rule under Chairman Mao. People were encouraged to report on each other's behaviour and at extreme periods, in particular the height of the Cultural Revolution of 1968-71, students had to report on their teachers, children on their parents, friends on each other, which led to horrific beatings, shamings and deaths.

Since the opening up of China in 1978, there have been two trends. The obvious levels of surveillance have become lower and there has been some liberalization, albeit with periodic crack-downs. Yet the tools of surveillance have become ever more powerful, with CCTV, facial and finger-print recognition and vast databases filled with internet activities and personal records.

Every person knows they are being monitored and that this is part of the continued attempt to keep everyone in mild fear and anxiety. There are people in every organisation, for instance in universities and school classes, who are asked to report suspect behaviour or remarks. Attempts are made to maintain a great digital wall to keep out information which is felt would lead to incorrect thoughts. Anything criticising the party placed on social media is speedily blocked.

There are quite independent journalists and papers such as the *Southern Daily* who criticise, and I have never found myself censored in what I say in my numerous lectures or in books. For these reasons, it is important not to overstress the similarities with the earlier periods of imperial data gathering and suppression of dissidence.

It is also important to remember that absolute freedom is impossible. In the West there is strict censorship of many things, including for example, criticism of Jews and Muslims, of gays and the mentally handicapped, or the showing of unsuitable images of children or many forms of sexuality. There are well-funded secret police organizations in America and in the U.K., as there are everywhere.

Yet the Chinese situation, as outlined above, is at the extreme end of surveillance. Nowadays, it combines considerable efficiency and powerful new technologies with the continuing features of traditional China, namely a fear of the general population. It has not been forgotten that a tiny spark, some 'Chinese whispers', can quickly become a raging fire, potentially leading to the death of millions, as in earlier times. A relatively small central government keeps disaster at bay, as it always has, by trying to locate these sparks and by crushing them before they take hold.

The problem is particularly acute in the semi-autonomous regions along China's vast border – in Xinjiang and Inner Mongolia. The balance between freedom of action and expression is extraordinarily difficult to maintain and the old policy of severe counter-measures based on secret information-gathering still seems to be the best one for those who run this vast Empire. The only way out of the vicious circle is through building up trust in the people, who are now far more educated, wealthy and sophisticated than before, and who have a greater stake in China's success and peace.

There are also recent developments in harnessing new technologies to monitor and reward or sanction the population which are well-developed in China, but may be rolled out across the world, which we should watch with care.

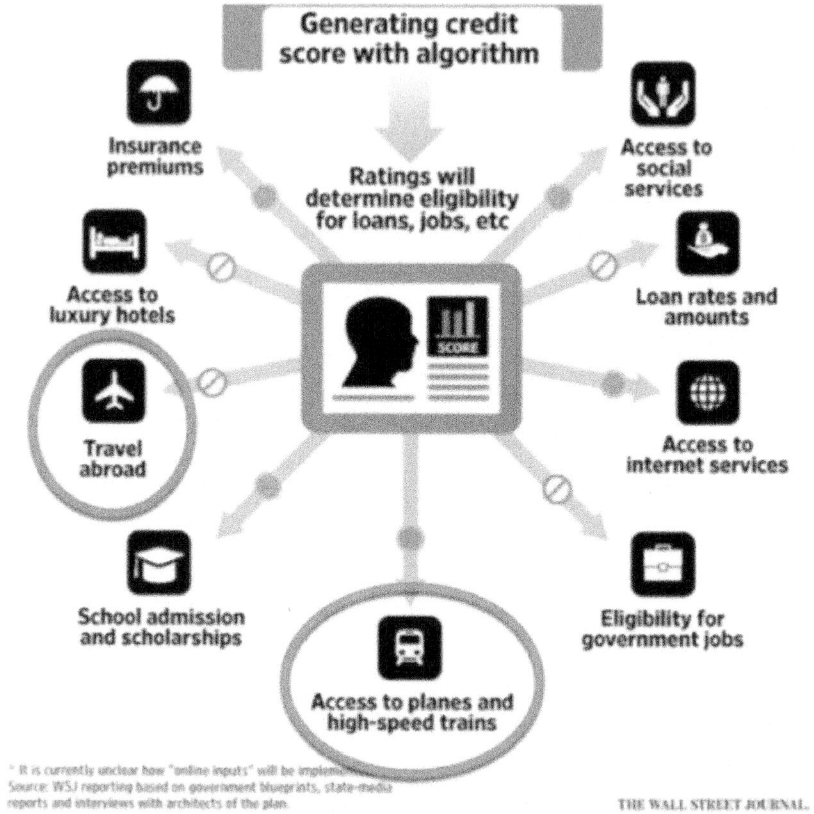
Generating credit score with algorithm
Ratings will determine eligibility for loans, jobs, etc
SCORE
Insurance premiums
Access to luxury hotels
Travel abroad
School admission and scholarships
Access to planes and high-speed trains
Eligibility for government jobs
Access to internet services
Loan rates and amounts
Access to social services
* It is currently unclear how "online inputs" will be
Source: WSJ reporting based on government blueprints, state-media reports and interviews with architects of the plan.
THE WALL STREET JOURNAL.

T

Taiwan

While I have never been to Taiwan, I feel some kind of bond with it because my first cousin (four generations ago), Robert Swinhoe, was the first modern westerner to describe the island and catalogue many of its birds and other creatures. He was the first consul there to conceive the idea of the international Taiwanese tea industry which soon became very important. Swinhoe described how the island had in earlier centuries been visited by Dutch and Spanish colonists who opened it to mass Han immigration. The island was annexed in 1683 by the Qing dynasty and was thus an integral part of China, though it was separated by about one hundred miles of very rough sea. The Qing ceded Taiwan to the Japanese in 1895 after the Sino-Japan War.

Taiwan remained under Japanese control until the Second World War and it was sufficiently separate for it to be the place to which the defeated nationalist leader, Chiang Kai-shek, fled with his Kuomintang government in 1949 to escape from the Communists. When he did, he carried much of the remaining cultural treasure of China with him, which had been looted from museums and collections on the mainland. Taiwan preserves part of an old China that has been lost on the mainland, and it also does so because the simplifications to the language by the Communists were not adopted in Taiwan. Ancient, complex, Chinese characters are found in Taiwan, as they are in Hong Kong.

Taiwan became one of the 'four little tigers' in the 1980's, along with Singapore and Hong Kong, giving a glimpse of what a Chinese-dominated society could become under the right circumstances. Now it is a flash point. The U.S. supplies it with weapons and sometimes suggests it strive for fuller independence and promise to defend it if it is invaded. Nevertheless, the Taiwanese know that mainland China is its major trading partner, accounting for about a quarter of its trade. They also know that the Chinese could over-run or destroy the island very quickly. They also know that several individual Chinese cities like Shenzhen or Shanghai are roughly as sophisticated and rich as the whole of Taiwan. They know that China would never surrender the island to independence, not least because it could cause a chain reaction among other marginal parts of China.

Tibet

When I first went to Nepal in 1968, I vividly remember meeting a group of Tibetan refugees, cold, hungry, children with noses streaming, but singing their plaintive songs high up on the Himalayan mountainside. Further parties of Tibetans would come through the village, begging and selling off their family heirlooms. We visited the Tibetan refugee camp in Pokhara. We also saw mysterious pack trains moving up towards Tibet which I was told were Khampas, tribesmen supplied with weapons and food and encouraged by the Americans to disrupt the Chinese takeover of Tibet. So, like most in the West who are frequently exhorted to protest against the occupation of Tibet by the Chinese, I felt angry and frustrated by what appeared to be naked imperialism.

I have now travelled to the borders of Tibet within China, to fabled Shangri-La and stayed with Tibetans and visited their monastery there, and met many other Tibetans in China and those studying the country in Sichuan university. I have read more about the subject and I realise that while there is much to criticise in the occasionally heavy-handed approach to Tibet in recent years, it is not as black and white as I had thought.

To start with, the history is not as straightforward as those who state that China invaded a sovereign and independent country in 1949 and drove out the Dalai Lama. It is true that during the fragmentation of China after the end of the Qing Empire in 1912,

Tibet was to all intents and purposes independent until 1950. Yet if we look at the intricate history of the relationships between China and Tibet over the centuries, it is more complicated than that.

There have been dynasties when Tibet was more or less independent, for example the Ming, and other dynasties, particularly the Qing, when Tibet was clearly very much under Chinese control. Just to take one example, Fra Francesco di Billi, in his 1730 in his *Brief Account of the Kingdom of Tibet*, wrote that 'In ancient times, when the Grand Lama was both the spiritual and temporal ruler in Tibet, the Emperor of China always gave him supreme authority over it, but when the Emperor gained possession of Tibet, in 1720, he reserved the chief power to himself.' For long periods, Tibet was regarded as a tributary state of China, integrated through Buddhism, and effectively both protected and controlled by China in its foreign relations.

Qing maps, such as the following, clearly show Tibet as a part of China.

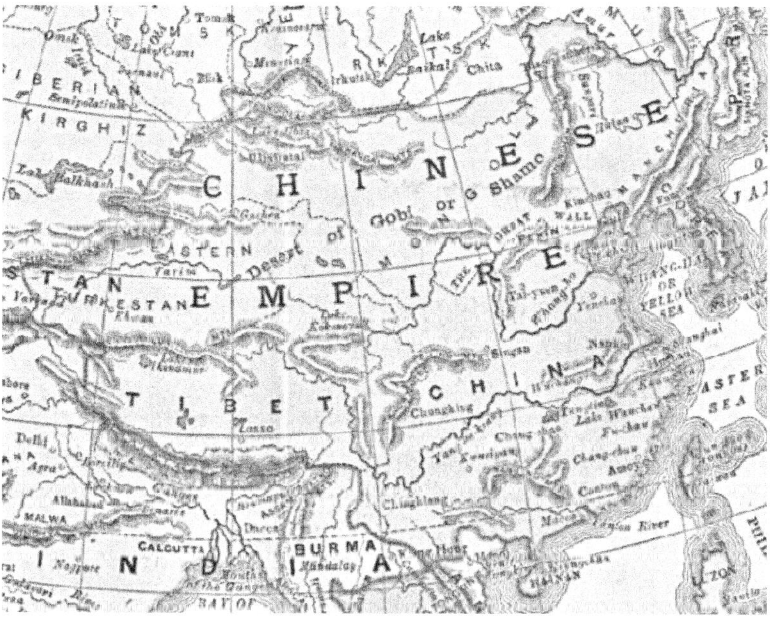

Other maps show other things, and they as well as a useful summary of the opposing arguments can be seen at: https://en.wikipedia.org/wiki/Tibetan_sovereignty_debate

It really depends, as so often is the case, which point of time you take as to whether Tibet is a part of China or not. Certainly, its place as part of China has been recognized. The European Union Leader, José Manuel Barroso, stated that the European Union recognised Tibet as an integral part of China. In 2014, President Barack Obama stated that 'We recognise Tibet as part of the People's Republic of China.'

The consequences of more recent Chinese rule in Tibet is also complex. The Chinese liberated many virtual slaves in 1949, for Tibet was a very old-fashioned feudal society divided between the rich monasteries, and an impoverished general population. In the last thirty years, the Chinese have poured in a huge amount of economic aid and built first-class communications and so the standard of living of most Tibetans has risen very fast. Millions, as elsewhere in China, have been lifted out of poverty. The Chinese government claim that they exempt Tibet from all taxation and provide up to ninety per cent of all government expenditure. During the last twenty years, the economy has been growing at over ten per cent per year.

It is a complex matter, and things are not always what they seem. For example, I was very surprised to learn that in the 1950s, when angry mobs of liberated serfs and eager young communists attacked the monasteries and would have burnt them all down, or at least looted them and driven out the monks, it was the Red Army which defended them against the frenzied mobs and saved many of them.

That the situation is complex is shown by the fact that the Dalai Lama and his representatives have acknowledged that Tibet is part of China, but have asked for a large measure of autonomy for language, culture and religion, including the return of the Dalai Lama himself as leader, rather than the China-appointed Panchen lama.

It has long puzzled me that the Chinese have not worked with the middle way suggestions of the Dalai Lama. They could allow him back, allow Tibetan to be taught in schools and Tibetan culture to be properly protected, and in return Tibet would be a peaceful part of China and not a constant stick which outsiders use to beat China with.

I can only assume that the policy is driven by the fear, elsewhere discussed, of any kind of religion or ideology, whether Christian, Muslim or Tibetan Buddhism (where the Dalai Lama is to a certain extend a God or political figure), where people's loyalty is divided or even primarily to a figure more powerful than the head of China, in the past the Emperor, now the Party.

The solution to this, which helped the British rule the huge civilisation of India and other parts of their empire with minimal force, seems applicable to Tibet. As long as people pay their taxes, obey the general laws, keep the peace, and acknowledge the ultimate sovereignty of the King, Queen or Party, they can continue to pursue their own religion, language and culture. This was the view of the great Muslim Moghul Emperor Akbar when he successfully integrated Islam and Hinduism, and it seems a general recipe which needs to be applied in our complex and overlapping world. Many peoples want autonomy in their culture, but realise they are part of a larger political and economic unit.

Tai Qi

During our many visits to China we have often seen people, usually older folk and in the evenings, out in the parks doing *Tai Qi*. They engage in slow, elaborate, movements of the whole body, circling their arms and balancing their bodies. I assumed it was some sort of semi-martial art or form of exercise like yoga.

It was only very recently, when I went for my first formal lesson, that the philosophy and aims behind Tai Qi were explained. I learnt that the idea was to act as a kind of lightning conductor or radio receiver, using movements to bring down and then infuse the body with the hidden energy or spirit or 'Qi' that surrounds us in the universe. So powerful was this technique that one could feel the heating of the hands and an experienced practitioner could even ignite paper cups without touching them.

Learning this reinforces my realisation of what a different world the Chinese and I inhabit. When I was a child, I believed in fairies and ghosts and a world which was infused with magical forces. Nature and spirits co-existed. Yet, as I grew up, the spirits fled, I learnt that I lived in a purely natural world which obeyed the laws of physics, chemistry and biology. There were no invisible forces that I could summon up with a prayer or magic.

When I went to Nepal, and later Japan with its pervasive magic of which *kami* or semi-spirits were one part, I re-discovered the magical universe of my childhood, but I did not expect to find it in such a seemingly rational civilisation as China, where I would have expected any residual magic to have been swept away by the Communist party.

Yet here I was, standing with my circling hands, trying to roll round the invisible energy and channel it down into my body. I was back in my childhood days when a moment's concentration could turn me into King Arthur or Robin Hood, where I believed I could fly and swim for hours underwater.

Once again this demonstrates that humans can live in parallel belief systems. The Chinese are now highly educated in the sciences and lead a very rational, practical, life. Yet they find no difficulty in believing in powerful forces which cannot be detected or measured by science. In the same way, they fully accept western science-based medicine but also believe fully in acupuncture and various alternative herbal medicines which again cannot be scientifically verified. It is an intriguing world.

Taxation

It was suggested some centuries ago by the founder of modern economics, Adam Smith, that one of the three essential conditions for sustained economic growth, alongside peace and a good legal system, was what he called 'easy taxes'. Many assume that what Smith meant by 'easy' was light taxes, low taxes. This is a misunderstanding. Smith knew perfectly well that the taxation rate in Great Britain at that time was higher than anywhere else in Europe, with the possible exception of Holland. The amount raised per head in England was at least four times that which the French crown could extract from its subjects. So 'easy' does not refer to the amount paid.

What he meant was that the taxes should be acceptable to those who paid them. They were accepted because of certain features. One is that those who paid the taxes would have a voice in how much was to be paid, on what, and for what purpose. English taxes were voted for by Parliament which represented the major tax-paying classes, and Parliament often amended or refused taxes it felt unwarranted.

Secondly, the taxes should be on certain easily taxed and reasonable things, on trade, on certain consumable items, on inheritances, but not on land and housing. Thirdly, the taxes should be predictable – there should be no sudden and unexpected taxes. Fourthly, they should be raised by local people and not by tax farmers (people who were given the right to raise taxes in return for paying some of what is raised to the government) or corrupt government officials. Fifthly, and most importantly, it should be clear that the money raised by taxes, whether at the village, town, country or national level, should be used for useful purposes. They should be raised for helping the poor, for bridges and churches, for keeping a navy and occasionally an army. They should not be used for an inflated bureaucracy, idle courtiers or for the nobility.

Because taxation was well organised and generally fulfilled all these conditions, the English Crown was able to raise substantial sums and local government was also reasonably funded. People paid their taxes and tax avoidance was difficult. The positive situation remains to this day. The rich pay more than the poor, people are trusted to fill in their own, relatively simple, tax forms and to declare their wealth honestly.

China falls within the majority of pre-modern societies where taxes were anything but 'easy'. The Emperor found it very difficult to raise any substantial sums by taxation and it was only from the 1860s, for example, that Robert Hart and other British officials made the customs duties and taxes into a serious, uncorrupt, revenue-raising, operation in China. Over the centuries, the results of the weak taxation system are the root of much of China's problems in the past and last into the present.

One feature was that the Emperor had to employ a kind of tax-farming strategy. He did not have the money to pay his servants, the Mandarins, the imperial bureaucrats at the centre, or even the army. Instead, they were expected to raise the money for their own salaries and expenses. They were given powers – the trying of court cases, the issuing of permits, the regulation of economic activities, which could be used to raise their own living expenses. This obviously led to constant abuses and corruption but was built into the system. The Mandarins and others were unaccountable, they acted indirectly and secretly.

The system of using your official job in order to raise extra income on the side continues to this day. Many government employees in all fields are not paid enough to live on and educate their children, especially in cities. For this reason, they have to have second or third jobs or find ingenious ways to use their official position, say as a teacher or doctor, to earn the extra amount needed to live reasonably well. This generates the continual threat of 'corruption' against which the government is constantly battling.

A second method the imperial authorities had to use in their desperate search for funds was the plundering of the successful and obviously wealthy. A city, business or farming family that became successful and rich over the years became the object of attention and would suddenly find itself stripped of its wealth on some trumped-up pretext. This happens to this day and a number of billionaires and successful businesses have suddenly been put under pressure to contributed substantial sums to the government. Many approve of this levelling process which often targets obscenely wealthy individuals and diverts their wealth to useful causes. Yet it is also damaging since it leads to a general atmosphere of distrust, insecurity and a tendency to smuggle money out of the country to safety, to the avoidance of risk and innovation, and to being careful not to attract attention. It also slows down capital accumulation by successful entrepreneurs and keeps levelling things down to a humdrum level.

In the past, the absence of a good taxation system weakened the Chinese Empire and made it choose a path of force and violence for its projects and defence. It led to the leasing out of taxation powers to a lower level of individuals who were not answerable to the Emperor and had to use all opportunities to make themselves rich.

Things have improved considerably and the extraordinary infrastructural spending of the last thirty years and now the One Belt One Road initiative indicate that large amounts are flowing into government coffers. Yet even here there are structural weaknesses. The main asset that local governments usually have is land, which they either own or occupy, and then sell off to developers on a 70-year lease. This has led to over-building and a form of building inflation where many of the properties have never been occupied. Adjustments are still needed in order to raise taxes in an orderly and fair way.

Tea

Tea (*cha*), the leaf of the *camellia sinensis* steeped in hot water, is the most consumed substance on earth (by humans), after air and water. Tea has changed the destiny of the world, helping to enable large events such as the industrial revolution, and smaller triggering ones, such as the Boston Tea Party which led into American Independence.

Tea has altered the social world, through the rise of women's status, new fashions, the tea ceremony. It has changed religion – Buddhism and tea in the far east are deeply entwined, as are nonconformity and tea in Britain. It has influenced art and manufacturing (porcelain for example) in powerful and lasting ways. Tea led to the success of the East India Company and hence the conquest of India. And tea has done this because it is cheap, light, durable, easy to grow and enormously attractive as a drink because of its invigorating (caffeine) and medical (flavinoids, polyphenols) benefits.

Tea was first domesticated, it is said, in the Bulong mountains on the border of China and Burma, and we have visited slopes there with many tea trees of over a thousand years old, and we have been close to one which is over three thousand years old in Yunnan. As the son of an Assamese tea planter, I am surprised to find that what surrounded me as a child is so old and so important.

Tea has been one of the principal causes of China's success. Tea spread widely across the population of China about 1200 years ago during the Tang dynasty. The success of that and subsequent dynasties, particularly in the south of China, the richest area, owes much to tea. Tea helped prevent the spread of water-borne diseases and may have reduced the spread, or even eliminated, malaria. It gave people the energy to undertake the immense toil of intense rice cultivation, as it did in Japan. Later, tea was the main trade item from China to the western peoples of Tibet and Mongolia, and to the south and east along the tea-horse roads to Burma and India.

For a while, tea made China rich in its trade with the West and particularly with Britain. Today again, it is a major source of foreign currency earning. It has been credited with developing the special form of Buddhism known as Chan or Zen, and influenced the art and architecture of China and Japan. It has been suggested that the general calm of the Chinese population, using a natural non-alcoholic drink, is related to tea. Tea has thus been a great blessing for millions of Chinese over the centuries.

Yet it has also been, in an unintended way, a cause of some of China's worst disasters. Some believe that it was the export of Chinese brick tea to the Mongols and later the Manchus which fuelled their civilisations and helped them to successfully invade China. In this reading, the Chinese gave their enemies their vital food-drink, without which the upland peoples could hardly have survived.

Then, during the nineteenth century, as described under 'Opium Wars', tea, the British desire for tea without means of payment, led into the tragedies of two wars, increased opium addiction, and the weakening of the Qing Empire. That Empire was further weakened from the 1880's when the British developed an alternative source of tea in Assam, and later Ceylon, starting this by using Chinese labour and plants. Some stark figure tells the story succinctly:

The Customs Annual Reports for Amoy [Xiamen], in 1896 reported as follows: 'The annual value of the trade has fallen from Hk Taels 2,000,000 a quarter of a century ago to less than Hk.[Hankow] Taels 100,000 to-day, and the cultivator, whose plantation formerly supplied him with a comfortable income, is now compelled to plant rows of sweet potatoes between the tea-bushes to keep body and soul together.'

Dyer Ball writing four or five years later commented that 'Tea has now disappeared from Amoy. There were no shipments to London direct from Hankow in 1900, for the first time on record.' This collapse of the tea exports ruined countless peasant households and diminished the already low tax revenues of the

Qing.

Without tea, China would be a very different place today, if it existed at all. And our visits to China – sampling the delights of black, white, green red, oolong and pu'er tea all over the country – would also have been deprived of one of the greatest pleasures.

Tea ceremonies

Some people joke that tea is the religion of the British. It is indeed true that tea is both a central part of British identity and on some occasions, the taking of tea has an almost ceremonial and sacred feeling about it. Yet it is when you go to Japan and China that you encounter the extraordinary 'way of tea', or *cha-do*, which turns this plant into something very special.

Again, I first encountered this in Japan when I attended ceremonies in ancient tea houses, walking down the special path through a mossy garden, crouching to enter, leaving all mundane items like phones, watches and shoes outside. Then there are the intricate tea preparations with the whisked powder tea, the crawling forward to receive it and careful conversation, the feeling of something special being present amidst the flowers and scrolls. We were so impressed with all of this that we built a Japanese-style teahouse in our garden.

I had assumed that the Japanese, as they often do, had taken the far simpler current form of tea ceremony which had originated in China and elaborated on it, requiring a training of years and often lasting an hour or more. Nowadays in China you will be served tea everywhere, but seldom is it more than a matter of a careful cleaning of the tea bowls and gracious serving.

Recently, however, I read about and participated in re-enactments of Tang and Song tea ceremonies. The Tang process is exactly like the elaborate Japanese ceremony with powdered tea. I realise that the Japanese have preserved an ancient form, as they have also done with court music, a Tang tradition which has died out or been replaced in China. In China, the tea ceremony evolved through the Song ceremony which is simpler and more like the present one.

Yet whatever the ceremony, it is evident that tea and its ceremonies of drinking have profoundly shaped many aspects of Chinese life, from ceramics to Buddhism, as explained elsewhere.

Team games

Much of my childhood and adolescence, both in boarding schools and at home, was spent playing team games; both formal ones like football, rugger and hockey, and informal ones with my friends. I now realise that this was to teach us many of life's lessons – how to work as a team, how to survive defeats, how to enjoy the pleasure of shared endeavour. I also often point out that many of the world's team games were either invented or formalised in Britain.

When I visit Chinese schools, even the best in the country, I am surprised at how little emphasis is placed on team games. There is some running, daily physical exercise drills, ping-pong, and perhaps swimming, but there is little space, and even less time, for all the team games I played through my childhood.

I had thought that this was because China had never known such games, the only competitive games and sports being archery, fencing or marital arts where two or more individual compete as single players against others, but not in a team.

Recently, however, I have seen reconstructions of older periods on television which, if accurate, suggest that during the Tang dynasty, for example, there was a form of football (though it was much more individualistic than English football), and a form of polo, again quite individualistic. So the idea of team games was present, but not greatly developed.

Nowadays, however, the Chinese football teams are a national embarrassment. I suspect that very soon large efforts will be made to improve school games and people may realise that, in our interconnected world, the ability to play with others in a team is a vital part of any education.

Temples and shrines

I come from a Christian country where the residues of that religion, the cathedrals and churches, have been preserved extremely well, thanks to the good fortune of long eras of peace and relative prosperity. From the magnificent cathedrals, to numerous ancient parish churches in almost every village, England is filled with religious buildings, and now with mosques and Hindu and Buddhist temples too.

I should not have been surprised when I went to Japan to find numerous temples and shrines. Yet they did surprise me, as they do in China, for several reasons. One was that I was often told that the temple was also a shrine, a Daoist one within a Buddhist one, or the other way around. My monotheistic background could not imagine a mosque within a Christian church, for example.

A second surprise was that everyone I spoke to, people who had often just been to such a shrine to make small offerings and say prayers, were adamant that these places had nothing to do with God. They were places where you contacted some numinous power, but no God resided there and the power was not in any way human-like. It was like going to a public phone box to make a call. These places are set apart, sacred in a way, but not like my churches.

In China there were further surprises. There are many Confucian temples as well, yet Confucius is not a God, just a philosopher, and one largely uninterested in religion. Yet he is worshipped. And on our last trip, we visited Chairman Mao's birthplace in Hunan province. Millions come to worship Mao with gifts, flowers, prostrations and prayers as if he is a God.

Another surprise is that there are so many shrines and temples. I had been led to believe that they were destroyed in the cultural revolution, that communism – and China is still communist – thought of religion as the 'opium of the people', delusional, and to be suppressed. Yet there are not just Christian churches but innumerable Buddhist monasteries and temples and Shinto shrines. It is intriguing to see many millions now flocking to these monasteries and temples, in many cases combining this with membership of the Party.

Terracotta army

We get very excited in the U.K. when someone discovers a hoard of Roman coins or Anglo-Saxon jewellery. Elsewhere in Europe there are still major finds, but they are dwarfed in scale and importance by what we have observed in China.

I remember in 1996 my shock at first encountering the long ranks of warriors, fashioned in terracotta clay, each with a lifelike and different face, thousands of them in pits which were still being excavated. They were buried to protect the first Qin Emperor in 210-209 B.C. and were only discovered in 1974. They are only part of much larger excavations which are yet to be made.

I was equally astounded when we visited an early stage in the excavations near Chengdu where they discovered, largely in 1986, a major Bronze Age civilisation called Sanxingdui, dated at between the twelfth and eleventh centuries B.C. The figures, two of which are below, bear no resemblance to other Chinese civilisations and seem more akin to Easter Island statues.

In 2018 we went to Changsha, the capital of Hunan province, and were shown an amazing reconstruction of the goods and grave of a high-ranking lady, the wife of Marquis Li Cang at the Mawangdui site near Changsha, excavated in 1972-1974 and dating back to about 180 B.C. Because of the care with which she was buried, she is probably the oldest, fully-preserved, human torso in the world, complete with hair and skin. She died over two thousand years ago and was buried with a wealth of books, clothes, medicines and other goods.

All these finds date back to the last half century or so. They are being added to daily. For example, there is a current project on the Liangzhu culture – the last Neolithic jade culture –in the Yangtze River Delta which reached its prime some four to five thousand years ago, around the same time as the Egyptian pyramids, and then suddenly disappeared. It had an advanced agricultural system, including irrigation, paddy rice cultivation and aquaculture. Houses were built on stilts and there was even a walled city. The civilisation suddenly disappeared about 4,200 years ago.

The immense excitement of Chinese archaeology arises from an intersection of the grandeur and antiquity of China, where many civilisations rose and fell over the last four thousand years, added to the fact that archaeology as a science only dates back about one hundred years in China. During half of that period it was not possible to do much because of wars and political upheavals. Only now are the riches being uncovered, though sadly this is too late for many of them. The flooding of the Yangtze valley in the Three Gorges Dam covered more than 1,300 archaeological sites, and though as much as possible was moved, untold future discoveries were covered over.

The Great Divergence

This refers to the title of a book published in 2000 by Kenneth Pomeranz. Pomeranz argued that Europe and China were on a similar economic level and on a similar trajectory until about the first decades of the nineteenth century. Then Europe became industrial and much wealthier and China remained as before. The main causes of the divergence were that Europe had ample coal supplies and that it profited from large overseas colonial possessions.

The thesis is bold and part of a wider set of books written in the 1990s as it became obvious that China was again becoming a world-level economy. The conclusion was drawn from this re-emergence that the whole idea, held by comparative thinkers from Montesquieu to Max Weber, that there was something special about the West, that it was at a deep level different from China and had achieved something unprecedented by a 'European Miracle', is wrong.

The argument was a refreshing undermining of the often patronizing and Euro-centric vision of many western comparative thinkers. It argued that the view taken by some of them, for example Karl Marx, that China is stuck in a static 'Asiatic mode of production' or 'Oriental despotism' is mistaken.

There are, however, many weaknesses in what is sometimes call 'the California School'. I will just list a few of these as it would take a book to discuss all the counter-arguments which have now been accumulating since Pomeranz published his book.

The suggested causes for the divergence are mistaken. China had very large coal reserves, not only in the north east, but even in the heartland, the south east, which Pomeranz concentrates on. Coal alone, anyway, as the late development of coal-rich northern Germany and eastern France shows, in itself will achieve nothing. China also had a large overseas trade along the maritime and land silk roads and with neighbouring 'tributary' states. It also had a huge 'empire' of a kind along its recently acquired western border absorbed by the Qing, including Tibet and Xinjiang, as well as in Taiwan and Manchuria. Furthermore, as the case of Spain shows, having a rich overseas colonial empire does not necessarily lead to any kind of break-through.

Furthermore, Pomeranz distorts the comparison by choosing on the Chinese side just the richest one per cent of the land mass of China, the Yangtze delta and comparing it to the whole of Europe, including the much poorer areas. If he had made the comparison between China and England or Holland, the result would have been very different. He also tends to deal with a static cross-section in the late eighteenth century, thus ignoring the centuries-long build-up of wealth in countries like England since the middle ages and the stationary nature of China since the Song.

Above all, by ignoring everything apart from input-output rice production figures and other economic measures (which have been disputed by specialists) he conceals the immense differences in the context of economic development. There is no serious discussion of the political or legal systems – for example taxation, property laws and the level of protection for economic activity.

There is no serious discussion of the class system and wealth differentiation or of family structures and work patterns. There is no discussion of the role of science or advances in new technologies. For example, Pomeranz pays no attention to Joseph Needham's many volumes which show how different China and the West were in their development of reliable knowledge about natural laws and in practical technologies. There is no discussion of culture, of religion or of ideology. To write a whole book with scarcely a mention of Christianity and how it differs from Buddhism, Confucianism and Daoism is unlikely to have much impact on Max Weber's famous work.

The book thus contains some interesting half-truths and a reminder that China was the greatest economy in the world until about 1820, in terms of total GDP. It also reminds us that we now know that there is nothing which intrinsically prevents China from becoming the largest economy again and that the West having first made the break-through, China, like Japan a century earlier, can do the same. Yet the story is infinitely more complex than that told in *The Great Divergence* and similar books.

Toilets

I was brought up in a country which invented the flush toilet or W.C. and modern sewage systems. I was taught to regard my bodily evacuations as disgusting, pure dirt. Later I discovered as a historian that 'night soil' (the euphemism for faeces) was occasionally used by gardeners for vegetables and, around a few western cities such as London and Antwerp, where it abounded, was carried off as manure. On the whole, however, with plentiful animal manure, my civilisation did not value night soil.

Even when I went to work in a Nepalese village, there was no use of night soil and, in general, throughout India it is considered highly polluting ritually and disgusting as well. Only in the Kathmandu valley, to this day, is it used for the crops in certain villages.

Yet, when I worked on Japanese history I discovered that the re-cycling of human waste, captured in ingenious ways and left in jars to let the harmful germs die, was universal. One person living in a room in Osaka paid rent, two people, generating more night soil, paid no rent, three people were paid by the landlord. Without night soil the Japanese could not have fed themselves.

When I started to work in China I found a similar situation. Sometimes the conversion into something useful was even more direct. I have been to villages where the latrine is placed above the pig-sty and the excrement is soon absorbed into pork. In turn, the pigs evacuate into the fish ponds and the fish recycle their waste. Elsewhere I have seen small toilets placed in the fields alongside busy roads in the hope that travellers will use them.

One upshot of this is that while I regard all things to do with urination and defecation with distaste verging on disgust, a private and embarrassing matter, my Chinese friends are far more relaxed. Such bodily functions are, in essence, no different from other where we ingest (eat and drink) or evacuate (sex or sweat). It is all part of life and nothing to become neurotic about.

Torture

I come from a country where the law is unique in the world in forbidding torture. From the medieval law codes up to the present, torture, both physical and mental, have not been a part of the legal process. Unlike traditional, continental, Roman, law over the centuries, or Chinese law, where a confession had to be extracted, usually with torture, before an individual could be punished, there was no requirement for an individual to admit guilt under English law. You can go to the scaffold or prison protesting your innocence. That is your right.

Of course, England – and now the U.S. – with its secret 'dark' rendition centres and camps like Guantanamo Bay, do not always live up to their ideals and we currently have an American President who supports torture. Yet, on the whole, with the exception of treason trials during part of the sixteenth century, English law has banned torture. It is believed to undermine law because people will confess to anything if pressed hard enough.

China is part of the vast majority of civilisations where torture was for many hundreds of years an accepted part of the legal process. Not only is it necessary to have a confession, but it makes the job of the magistrates, who had very few police assistants, much easier. It also fitted the idea of group responsibility. A suspect would be tortured to find out his or her accomplices, who would be tortured in turn until hundreds were implicated. This was the method of the Christian Inquisition for three centuries in the West.

I have no way of knowing if torture is still used, as some allege, in the current Chinese system. Certainly, it was used in the cultural revolution when many thousands were subjected to humiliations and beatings in order to force them to confess and implicate others. And I have heard stories of people disappearing suddenly and re-appearing with stories of beatings, sleep deprivation, long periods of solitary confinement.

If such allegations are to become something of the past, then China will clearly have to follow the British path of instituting *habeas corpus* (no detention without a formal charge, in court, with the accused represented by a lawyer), and complete transparency in criminal cases. As suggested elsewhere, this will have to be combined with the use of a jury system, the only effective protection for individuals against state power. China may go down this path, finally moving away from an entirely different system of law which it used for thousands of years.

Traditional Chinese medicine

Before I went to China, I knew nothing about Chinese traditional medicine. I suppose I would have known that, like India with its alternative *Ayurvedic* tradition, China and Japan had their indigenous medical systems. How they worked, whether they were effective, what their main constituents were, however, were not subjects I knew anything about.

Now it is different. Alongside my bottles and boxes of western medicines and my visits to the doctor, I now have a selection of traditional Chinese remedies. I first learnt of their efficacy when I trapped my hand in a slammed car door in China. The inevitable pain and swelling completely vanished a few minutes after applying Chinese medicine. Since then, I have avoided many bruises and swellings by applying this.

Then, when I and others had serious muscle pains, we applied what we were told, were dog-skin patches, though I later learnt this was just their name, and the pains evaporated miraculously When I suffer serious colds, they often vanish after drinking Chinese medicine.

Based on entirely different concepts of the body and how it

works, leading to the arts of acupuncture and massage as well as herbal medicines, China has developed one of the great medical systems of the world. Through the usual methods of discovery, that is random variation and selective retention of what works, over thousands of years of mini-experiments over a vast land mass, the Chinese have identified many important techniques and medicines, many of them plant-based.

Until recently it was difficult to test them and see how they worked. But now, as we do the tests, we find that they are indeed amazing. For example, *artemesia* (dog wood) is the basis for the modern generation of anti-malarials and its propagation won China a Nobel prize recently. Tea, *camellia sinensis*, is now known to be one of the world's greatest medicines, curing or alleviating many diseases and, among other things, destroying the bacteria of typhoid, cholera and dysentery. Ginseng is also clearly highly effective.

The West has developed a powerful parallel system of medicine, but there can be no doubt that, as elsewhere, we should unite the best of East and West to lower pain and suffering across the planet. Chinese medicines, especially tea and *artemesia*, rank among the world's greatest medical discoveries. That the biochemical structure of these two plants is almost identical is more than a coincidence.

Triads

It was not until I became an anthropologist and taught courses on the mafia, *yakuza* (Japan) and triads (China) that I realised how different my native England was in relation to organised crime. The penetration of law and state power on the little island of Britain, the weakness of the extended family, and the open acceptance of dissidence and criticism of the state, combined with other factors to mean that the above forms of criminal violence are largely absent in British history. There have always been criminal gangs, and they remain to this day, but they are on a far smaller scale than the mafia and are much less of a threat and presence than they were in Japan or China.

The Japanese version, the *yakuza*, is a guild (*za*) which controls gambling, prostitution, mass entertainment, money-laundering and other activities which lie on the edge, semi-legal as it were. I have found myself outside a *yakuza* recruitment offices which was openly advertising, and the police have been known to arrange parking for the *yakuza* and to provide annual protection and work closely with them. They are a valuable intermediary into the semi-legal.

The Chinese triads are much more like the mafia than the *yakuza*, for they constitute highly secretive and totally illegal organisation, held together by *omerta* or honour, with sacred codes, language and signs. They revolved around the family, '*cosa nostra*', or family-like bonds and were especially to be found in the city ports like Shanghai, where huge levels of 'black' activities related to narcotics, prostitution and gambling were located. They help to create a stereotype of China dating back to the gangster movies of the middle of the twentieth century.

No doubt some triads still operate, but they are a pale shadow of their earlier existence. I have never encountered any mention or discussion or allusion to them on my various trips to China, and it looks as if the eradication of the triads was another positive achievement of the Communist regime. Secret organisations, however, are endemic in states which try to contain discussion, criticism, alternative visions too strictly and there is always a danger they will return.

U

Universities and academies

I had long assumed that if we put on one side the early Greek academies of the time of Plato and Aristotle, and early Buddhist quasi-universities such as Nalanda in Bihar, India, which was a seat of learning from the fifth century BC up to the 12th century AD, then the oldest true surviving universities in the world started roughly with Bologna (1088) and Oxford (1096). These early western universities were followed by Paris, Cambridge and others. I thought that only in the last few hundred years had the institution spread, first to the United States in the seventeenth century and then around the world. The current Chinese universities, dating from 1893 with Wuhan, 1898 with Peking university or 1911 with Tsinghua, are not much more than 100 years old.

Recently I had a chance to visit arguably the oldest continuous university or quasi-university in the world, the Yuelu Academy in Changsa. It was founded in 978 AD as a Buddhist study centre, but within a few years became a Confucian Academy.

Walking round it I was surprised to find how similar the physical structure and functions are to an Oxford or Cambridge College. There is a church, the Confucian temple, there is a library, there are a dormitory and dining space, there are also teaching rooms and lecture halls, quadrangles and a large garden to relax in. The function is to teach, in the case of the academy, mainly philosophy, history, literature and the Confucian classics, whereas in the medieval western universities, the subjects would have been mathematics, medicine, history, law, classics and theology.

Discovering this one surviving ancient academy, I learnt that it was one of the four most famous early academies, which later flourished in the Song dynasty (eleventh to thirteenth centuries), hosting many famous scholars and Buddhist reformers. These four were a handful of the more than 10,000 such academies which existed then. It was only in the very last years of the Qing dynasty, the late nineteenth and early twentieth centuries, that the academies were forced to change into training colleges.

This raises the question of why the very early academy movement in China, which predated the western universities by several hundred years, never blossomed into the kind of western universities now being built all over China.

One of the theories is that, as happened increasingly over continental Europe from the seventeenth century, the academies were largely dependent on imperial power. If they showed independence or any signs of free thought, they would be closed or punished. Add to this the periodic destructions by foreign invasion and civil war, when the academies were destroyed physically and their members killed or dispersed, and we can understand the situation better.

If Oxford and Cambridge had been razed to the ground three or four times, their libraries burnt, their teacher killed, one wonders how much of them would have been left by the early twentieth century. The peaceful and lawful environment of England, and the high degree of independence of the universities from royal power, are powerful differences.

Another obvious factor is the purpose of the academy and university. The Chinese academy soon became linked to the Chinese imperial education system, which was designed to train people for bureaucratic rule. The academies were one level of this system. Their function was to train administrators, hence the concentration on the arts and humanities relevant to governing – philosophy, literature, poetry, Confucian classics.

The academies were not established to teach people generic skills, to educate their critical faculties, to encourage people to question or discover new things, to learn the arts of persuasion or collaborative working. They were a training in memory, discrimination and ethics.

The English equivalents from the start were there to train people who might go into a number of professions. They might be lawyers, clergymen, business men, army officers, estate owners, doctors, or teachers. The university was to provide a set of generic tools for any of these. It did so by a mixture of lectures and directed reading. The students were apprenticed to one or more teachers who would assign them readings and then discuss their findings. The modern Oxford and Cambridge supervision system, where two or three students meet weekly with a teacher, is the outcome of this.

The teaching was dialectical or confrontational. The students and teachers would put forward arguments and try to resist and defeat the other, as in a game of tennis. Teaching was a game, a preparation for the confrontational battle of adult life as a lawyer, politician or trader.

Thus, the content taught in the English university was arguably less important than the form. The content could alter rapidly as new knowledge circulated. It could absorb the knowledge-shattering effects of the Renaissance, Reformation, Scientific Revolution, new technologies, new encounters all over the world as the British Empire expanded. It was dynamic, flexible and adaptable.

This contrasts with the Chinese academies, where the purpose was restricted, the content largely consisted of ancient truths, and where the student were taught respect, obedience, deference to authority and the past.

This means that in the nine hundred years after its founding, the Yuelu Academy and others like it would be unlikely to grow larger or become more relevant than they were when they were founded. The western universities, on the other hand, were constantly expanding, innovating and finding new roles and incorporating elements of the society around them.

Printing revolutionised the English universities, but hardly altered the Confucian academies. The divergence grew ever greater, so that modern Chinese universities owe little directly to the early academics, but are largely modelled on western universities.

Urbanisation

Anyone who has recently travelled through China will be amazed by the development of the cities. Small towns a few years ago are now large cities; small cities are now great cities. Just to take one example, the city of Qingdao has gone from less than one million to over ten million in this century. The number of cities of more than ten million in China, with some of them over twenty million, is very considerable. Basically, within one generation China has gone through the urban revolution which it took England some three generations to achieve – from a rural to an urban civilization.

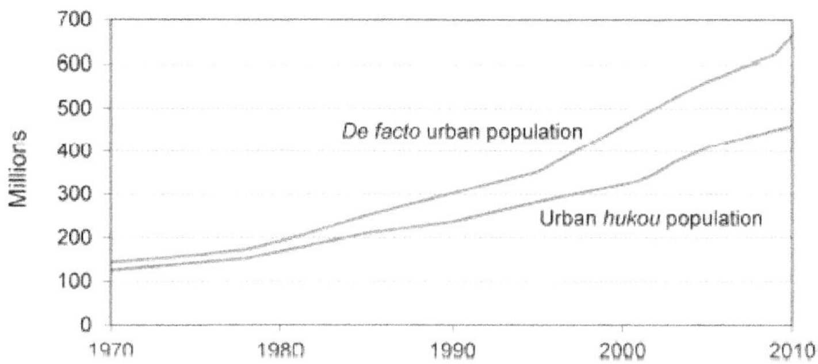

Fig. 2. Growth in *de facto* urban population and urban *hukou* population in China, 1970–2010.

In 1970, roughly one in six Chinese lived in cities. The urban population overtook the rural population in China in 2012. The city population now is greater than the total Chinese population in 1960. The way this is creating huge megacities, and the consequent effect on infrastructure, is shown in the following diagram.

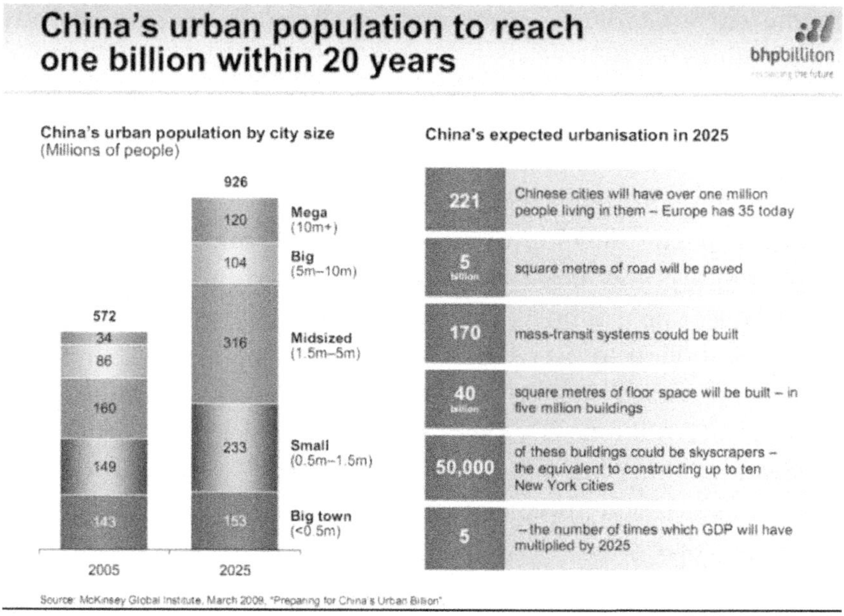

This is a shift unparalleled in the world – nowhere else have so many cities of this size been created so swiftly. It is clearly having vast effects in so many ways – on pollution, on the use of resources, on social relations. It is an urban revolution which is daily changing all of our lives.

When America urbanized in the later nineteenth and early twentieth centuries, a number of sociologists speculated about the consequences of a change from living in settled agricultural communities, where a person was born and brought up and worked on the land, to living in huge cities.

One theme of this work concerned what is called 'urbanism as a way of life'. It was suggested that living in a small community of people one knew well would give people multiple-level connections – relatives, neighbours, friends for life would live nearby. Much of life was oral and was expressed through rituals and co-operative activities of various kinds.

When people move into cities, particularly in the kind of work-related migration which is a central feature of Chinese urban growth, they are cut off from their relatives and childhood friends. They are alone, a fragmented workforce often living in fairly confined conditions, in the vast high-rise buildings which are a feature of Chinese cities. They are lonely strangers amidst strangers, living an entirely different kind of rhythm of life in every way from their parents and grandparents.

There is a new stress on time, privacy, constant hard work with few rests. The landscape is artificial and long-term human contacts are reduced. It would seem to be a recipe for alienation, for the famous *anomie* or rootlessness predicted by sociologists.

What exactly is happening as a result of this great shift to megalopolis is difficult to discern. Yet we know that the Chinese world is now a largely urban one with urban rather than rural values. Village China is now Urban China, as is also happening in India, South America and Africa. And it is happening so very fast – far faster than the slow growth of cities over many generations that has been characteristic of most of human history.

Given all this, what I find amazing is how well the transition seems to be managed. On the whole, cities all over China – Beijing, Qingdao, Shenzhen, Tianjin, Nanjing, Kunming, Chengdu, Hangzhou, Suzhou, Shanghai for example – that we have visited on our various visits seem to be coping, despite their dispiriting (to us) high-rise buildings. There is gridlock in the traffic and bad air pollution. Yet there are also many trees, parks, people old and young playing and doing *Tai Chi* and even often dancing on warm summer nights.

People say they like the new amenities and the high-rise buildings, and there is a notable absence of dirt, disorder or police. It is easy to feel in one of these cities that they have been there for a generation – but on enquiry or looking at photographs it is mostly a creation of the last twenty years. The Chinese world we first encountered in 1996 is unrecognizable today.

Most Chinese are now being educated and growing up in an urban world, far from the kind of civilization which was present even in the period of the New China (1949-78) let alone during the two thousand years of a great agrarian civilization. Everything is changed by this, as much as by the other massive shifts which surround people, but which we do not often think about.

One final point to note is one of the attempts by the Chinese government to control this huge change, which has led to a good deal of criticism. This is the Chinese *hukou* (household registration) system which was introduced in 1958 (though earlier versions go back in China for thousands of years, from where it spread to Korea, Japan and Vietnam) as a classification of the population both by place of residence and in order to allocate certain socioeconomic benefits.

The classification, managed by local authorities, is based on socio-economic eligibility (agriculture/non-agriculture) and residential location (living in urban/rural areas). Since economic reforms in 1979, millions have been allowed to leave for work in the cities, and it is estimated that by 2014 something like 274 million Chinese from rural areas, one third of the total workforce, were working in cities.

Up to now, although they could live in cities, those without a *hukou* in the place where they worked, were generally denied access to social entitlements, such as pensions, medical services and basic education for their children. They had to use their income for this. Recently, however, the government has been considering scrapping the application of the *hukou* system across most of China, though it may be retained in an attempt to control the population in one or two mega-cities such as Beijing.

V

Vast and integrated

I wrote this entry in a moderate-sized city of which I had hardly heard until we visited it, Changsha in Hunan province. It is a city of about eight million inhabitants, twice as large as any city in the UK except London, with a three-thousand year history and in a province the size and population of the UK. Its economy, even though it is not one of the richer provinces, is equivalent to a small East European nation. If we multiply this fifty times or more, we get some idea of China's massive size.

If I ask my Chinese friends whether it is far to another city, they will say not very far, by which they mean the distance from London to Rome. Air communications and bullet trains have made these journeys relatively easy, but it is not easy to imagine travelling two or three thousand miles to trade or fight in the past. The roads were terrible, the country is very mountainous with fierce rivers. Reading the accounts of travellers up the Yangtze or across the Silk Road, or the extraordinary Long March of the Communists in the 1930s, gives a sense of the distances and difficulties. It is really very difficult for any of us to comprehend this vast size and variation. Coming from the tiny and highly homogenous island of Britain, it is particularly difficult.

I have only gradually become aware of the scale by criss-crossing the country, from Liaoning on the edge of Korea on the north to the borders of Burma on the south-west, from Shanxi in the north to Guangzhou in the south-east. We have been to the remotest areas and the largest cities on earth, and each is different and special.

After the experience of European national conflicts, the endless wars since the collapse of the Roman Empire through to the European Union, it is a source of amazement that since the unification of China in 221 B.C., the country has mainly stayed together, and indeed constantly expanded and absorbed huge new swathes.

I would have thought that given all that it possesses, the Chinese might be relaxed about letting those on the margins who want to be independent gain this. Who cares about Tibet when you have an economy hundreds of times that of Tibet? Or Taiwan or Hong Kong now no longer crucial to the Chinese economy. Why not let them all go?

Yet perhaps it is the very size and diversity which leads to an intransigence which surprises me, particularly as my homeland, England, calmly allows a fifth of its people and a third of its territory – Scotland – to vote for independence.

If you have a vast area such as China, there is always a risk of secession, bits can fall off the edge. Yet the Chinese fear that if one part successfully leaves, it will provide an inspiration and model for others. If Hong Kong goes, why not the Uighur area of Xingjian, Inner Mongolia or Tibet? These areas combined would reduce China's land area, if not its economy, by about half. And after that, perhaps the remoter provinces with large minority population in the south – Guizhou, Guangxi, parts of Yunan and Sichuan, might also get ideas. It is a nightmare and something the Chinese cannot easily accept.

The Chinese think of themselves, even with their huge diversity, as composed of one group. They may be Manchu, Miao, Yi, and Dong, as well as Han, but their imagined and actual walls create the community of 'China'. China is seen as a living soul, pulsing through the millenia, a great nation and people who are not prepared to lose face, or to contemplate what are conceived of as organs integral to the Chinese body to be dismembered. To cut off Hong Kong or Taiwan is to lose an eye or ear, particularly bitter in that both of them were seized after defeats by foreign powers in the nineteenth century.

Taiwan and Hong Kong were sheep that had gone astray and the rejoicing at their return makes contemplating another loss especially bitter. The fact that the Chinese believe in the mission of making their people happier and wealthier, similar to the 'civilising' mission of the British with their Empire, also makes any rejection and calls for independence an even more serious loss of face.

Violence and war

Up to the unification of China in 221 B.C., China was filled with warring armies and bloody wars. After the abolition of the landed aristocracy, the militarization may have decreased a little, but there were numerous later wars, including those of the Three Kingdoms (220-280 A.D.), involving huge armies. The Tang and then the Northern and Southern Song again saw a decline in internal warfare, but the threat from the Mongols made China a warlike place. Yet after the Mongol invasion, the clans and warriors were again weakened during the Ming dynasty.

The Manchu (Qing) dynasty from the middle of the seventeenth century was aggressive, expanding over a vast area to the west of China and incorporating it, and putting down minority rebellions, partly caused by its policy of taking over the administration of hitherto largely autonomous areas. Then in the nineteenth century China was subject to frequent attacks (including the Opium Wars) and vast civil wars, including the Taiping and Boxer rebellion. The twentieth century was one of terrible wars. For example, perhaps twenty million Chinese died as a result of the Sino-Japanese War from 1937 to 1945.

Yet, despite all this, one can say that while warfare was endemic, China was, compared to much smaller but highly divided Europe after the fall of Rome, relatively less riven by internal wars. There was no equivalent to the small states of Europe, with their later strong nationalism. Furthermore, while the Emperor had large numbers of armed troops, much of the defence of the country and local policing was done by peasant families who were settled in dangerous areas. In return for holding land they could be mobilized when there were invasions or civil disturbances.

It is all a matter of scale and degree. China, like all great civilisations, was originally founded on violence. Yet it is far from the extreme in this respect. Certainly in the period since the Second World War, if we compare China to the United States, the involvement in overseas wars is far less extreme in China. Although involved in Korea and Vietnam, there is nothing equivalent to the bombing of Vietnam, Cambodia and Laos, or the wars in Afghanistan, Iraq, or even the blockade of Cuba. 'Regime change' is an American, not a Chinese, speciality. The current expenditure of the United States on its military is much greater than that in China. America's spending in 2015 was 3% of its GDP, China's 1.2%. With $1821 per capita in America and $95 in China, the total of American spending is nearly four times the amount of that in China.

One effect of all this is that the methods of war, the weapons and tactics, reached a high level, but did not develop as fast as they did in the warlike West. So that while the navies and armies of China were roughly on an equivalent level to those of western Europe in 1500, three centuries later the British could humble this mighty Empire in the two Opium Wars with far more advanced weaponry and training, with France, Germany, Russia and then Japan following.

W

Wall(s) of China

For many, the enduring image of China is of the Great Wall, stretching across the mountainous region of northern China, with its small turrets and towers. In fact, what we see today is just part of the thousands of years of wall building from the start around the seventh century B.C., especially famous being the wall built in 220-206 BC by the first Qin Emperor of China. Much of the remaining wall is from the Ming dynasty.

A map and diagram gives an impression of the many walls, which stretch nearly four thousand miles (further than the distance from London to Jerusalem, as the crow flies), of which the main wall spans about 1500 miles.

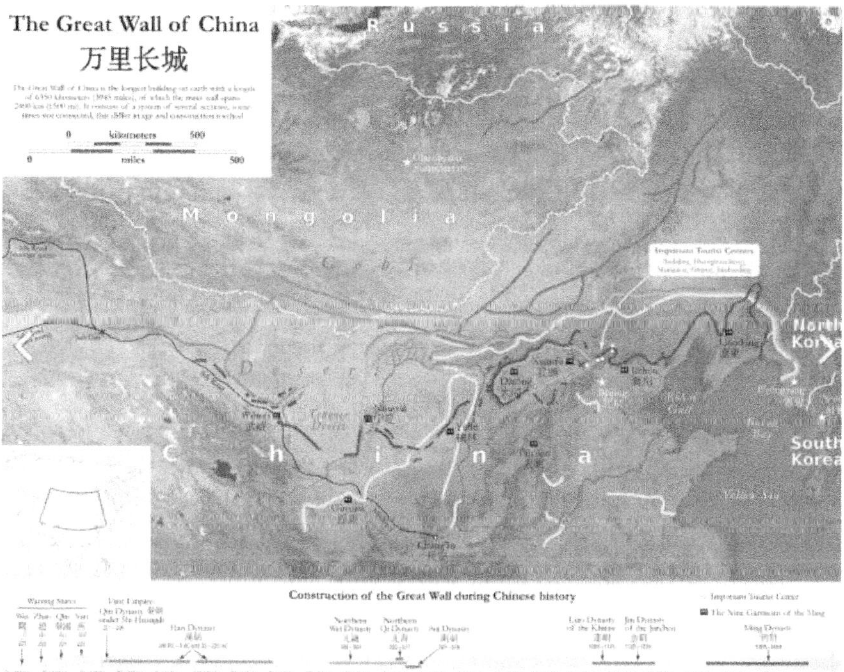

The more than twenty walls that have been built over the millenia had the main purpose of keeping out the nomadic tribesmen on the borders. Walls were not built against the forest-dwelling minorities to the south who posed less of a threat.

The walls tell us a great deal about China. They tell us of its great wealth and coercive power – and cruelty. Millions died, and millions more were enslaved to build the walls. The control over workers to make these extraordinary monuments continues to this day in the construction – as extraordinary in its way as the ancient walls – of the communications infrastructure of China. The massive roads, bridges, tunnels high-speed railways, airports, electric pylons marching across the hilltops of China, are awe-inspiring. They have almost all been constructed in the last thirty years.

A six-lane highway, equivalent to a road from London to Jerusalem in length, passing through the spurs of the Himalayas from Beijing to Kunming, and soon onwards to India, can be constructed in a few years to immaculate standards. Road bridges of hundreds of miles in length, with the longest such bridge in the world just opened from Hong Kong to Macau, are being opened. An amazing grid of electricity, radio and internet links has been set up. Then there are the huge dams across the rivers, including the largest in the world (the Yangtze Three Gorges Dam). Again, the wealth, control and organisation to do all is beyond my imagination.

The walls also show China's defensive, guarded, posture. China was the Middle Kingdom, with all that it needed, but surrounded by barbarians. China has veered from periods of outward expansion to periods of closing up. The walls were a signs of closure against marauders. The alternative – opening-up – is again evident in recent history.

The Qing tried to keep out foreign influences, then for a brief interlude after the Republic was inaugurated in 1912, there was a welcoming of the outside, then it closed up again, most notably from 1949 to 1978. The opening up by Deng from 1978 in terms of economy has been a huge success, and in the last few years has turned to an outward thrust in the 'One Belt One Road' initiative of President Xi.

No longer are there walls and no longer are the extraordinary infrastructure projects confined to China, but are now spreading along roads, railways and shipping lanes across all of Eurasia and as far as Africa and South America.

A future visitor to our planet, who had seen the Great Wall of China from outer space, where it is one of the few visible signs that are man-made, would find that the great wall has now been moved to encompass the whole world. We have all become Chinese in some way or other as its culture, cuisine, visitors and communications spread across all continents.

Water management and hydraulic civilization

Historians and anthropologists have suggested a theory to explain why certain civilizations which have grown up around great rivers and irrigation agriculture, hydraulic civilizations, as they call them, have a set of features which are shaped by this background. Oft-cited examples are Mesopotamia, Egypt, and certain ancient civilizations in India. China, with its central need to control and use for cultivation its three great rivers, the Pearl, Yangtze and Yellow, as well as many smaller ones such as that which became the Mekong, is an obvious case.

Sophisticated water controls started to transform China from the earliest civilizations along the Yellow River, whose tremendous floods could cause havoc. A notable example was the water control and irrigation system at Dujiangyan, near Chengdu in Sichuan Province. It was originally constructed by Li Bing for the state of Qin in 256 B.C., and uses the water of the Min River, the longest tributary of the Yangtze, to irrigate much of the large Sichuan plain, the size of a small European country. It is still used to irrigate over 5,300 square kilometres of land in this region. The modern equivalents are the massive dams being constructed all over China, the most famous being the Three Gorges Dam.

In order to carry out massive hydraulic works, not only with the rivers, but also the vast network of canals and even greater set of smaller channels and irrigation ditches to carry water across the rice fields, it is necessary to have a highly developed, usually centralised, administrative and political structure. There has to be a power which can mobilize huge numbers of labourers, often working without pay and to protect others downstream rather than themselves.

It is therefore no coincidence that the Pharos in Egypt or the Chinese Emperors were the pivot of a highly centralized and authoritarian political system. They performed one of the main functions of the State according to Adam Smith, which is to construct and regulate large infrastructural projects which are beyond the powers of individuals, villages or even provinces. The Chinese state did this, and the model of the great irrigation projects was found in other massive infrastructural projects in the past, most notably in the great walls of China and the Grand Canal.

It is not difficult to imagine that this is a path which has recently led to incredible cross-province and cross-Chinese projects. The extraordinary roads from north to south and as far as Lhasa are one example. The railways, particularly the network of high speed trains, are another, as well as the gleaming airports and very rapid growth of air travel. The development of super telescopes, super computers, super scanners which cost vast fortunes and are built by large teams is a third example. The speed and efficiency with which cities like Shenzhen, Qingdao, Chengdu and Chonqing grow in a decade from a few million to well over ten or even twenty million inhabitants, is part of the same massive construction idea.

All of these are pushed through for 'the general good', often over-riding particular interests to bring what are perceived to be national benefits. This is an idea implicit in hydraulic civilizations. The pyramids of Egypt have been re-born in other forms in what has happened in the last forty years in China. The Belt and Road initiative can be seen as a plan to turn the whole of Eur-Asia into a modern integrated system which descends from the ancient hydraulic civilization pattern.

Westernization

For most of the last four thousand years, while China has absorbed some ideas from outside along the silk roads, it has been largely self-sufficient. China contained all it needed and was the most advanced civilisation. This began to change when the Jesuits started to bring some first fruits of the scientific revolution to China in the later seventeenth century. Yet, for another century and a half, China was still the richest and most powerful nation on earth and often haughtily rejected most of western knowledge and attempts by western missions, such as that from Britain led by George McCartney in 1793, to pressure them into trade.

After the defeats in the two Opium Wars and the disasters of the Taiping uprising, the situation changed and there was a growing recognition that China must learn from the West or be colonized like India. The same was happening in Japan which, after the Meiji Restoration of 1868, imported many ideas and technologies from the West.

In Japan, the importation led to a miraculous transformation into an industrial society in one generation. China showed a considerable interest and used western experts such as Robert Hart to modernize its customs, bought western machinery and weapons, and translated many western books, for example the educational series published by W. and R. Chambers of Edinburgh. Yet progress in China's vast empire was far slower than in Japan. Although attempts were made, first through Japan, and then from America and England, to bring in new ideas starting in the 1890's and through to the 1920's, the situation on the outbreak of war with Japan in 1937 was not greatly changed except in pockets in certain cities.

There was an inevitable lull as China tried to exclude most western ideas, except certain technologies coming from Russia, between 1949 and 1977. Then, since 1978, China has eagerly absorbed many western ideas and technologies. I have been amazed at how quickly many western institutions have been successfully absorbed so that China now looks more 'western' and advanced, in many ways, than the west itself.

Yet, there is still a huge debate and interest in how far China can absorb western idea, for example democracy, private property, civil society, the western legal system, an open philosophy, individualism, without destroying the essence of Chinese civilisation. It is a question long ago discussed by the Chinese philosopher Liang Chi Chao, who could not see how the oil and water of these civilisations could come into harmony. It is the big question facing us all, and it is also being asked in the reverse, namely how far can we become Chinese without losing our western heritage.

Witches

Belief in witches and witchcraft is very widespread. A witch is thought to be an apparently ordinary human being who has some inner, concealed, power of a mystical kind which allows them to do extraordinary things like flying at night, conversing with the Devil, turning into an animal, and hurting other humans and animals at a distance. Belief in witchcraft was widespread in Europe between the fifteenth and eighteenth centuries. Many thousands of supposed witches, particularly women, were rounded up, often tortured and then executed, for this offence. Finally, from the eighteenth century, it was decided that it was all a delusion, witchcraft did not exist. Other forms of witchcraft are still found in much of Africa, India and even parts of southern Europe.

I encountered witchcraft beliefs in a village in the Himalayas and some of my best friends were reputed witches. The beliefs declined somewhat as the witch doctors moved away, but the beliefs are still there and to be found among my Gurung friends from highland Nepal who now live in London or Hong Kong.

I was expecting to find witch beliefs in Japan and China. Certainly, in our travels we found similar witchcraft beliefs in the ethnic minority groups in China, particularly in the south west. Among the Dai people as well as the Naxi and the Lisu, we encountered witch doctors and witch beliefs. We also learnt that two thousand years ago, in the Han dynasty, there were beliefs in the Emperor's court that certain people were doing magic against others. And even in the late Qing there were some sorcery beliefs, that is to say the idea that you could engage in certain outward actions, like sticking pins in the representations of others, to do them harm.

Yet, for the great majority of the Chinese Han peoples over most of history, witchcraft beliefs were almost entirely absent. There is no specific word for 'witch' or 'witchcraft' in Japanese or Chinese (*wushi* really means shaman or protector against evil. There has never been a belief in a secret organisation of people who hold devilish rituals, eating children, having sexual orgies, destroying their neighbours animals and killing people.

In extensive conversations and observations across the main parts of China, I have found no interest in witchcraft, though many Chinese children love the Harry Potter depiction of magic and often ask me whether English villages are filled with wizards, and witchcraft paraphernalia is being introduced alongside other western consumer goods.

It is complicated to explain this absence. The European version of witchcraft was clearly closely linked with the Christian Church, the beliefs in the Devil, the Inquisition, the use of torture and a deeper strain of Manichaean thought which sees the world as ruled by the Devil. This is not the case in Africa and India or my Nepalese village, yet there was and still is a belief in witchcraft. We shall need to search for deeper causes, which must lie in the very origins of Chinese philosophy and the ideas of *yin* and *yang*, bodily essences, and the nature of mystical powers.

X

Xanadu

A wonderful poem by Samuel Taylor Coleridge first fired my vision of China when I was a boy of about ten.

In Xanadu did Kubla Khan
A stately pleasure-dome decree:
Where Alph, the sacred river, ran
Through caverns measureless to man
Down to a sunless sea.
So twice five miles of fertile ground
With walls and towers were girdled round;
And there were gardens bright with sinuous rills,
Where blossomed many an incense-bearing tree;
And here were forests ancient as the hills,
Enfolding sunny spots of greenery.

For many years, the vision seemed unlikely to lead to a real encounter with Xanadu until, in 1996, we visited the site of the supposed palace and gardens at Chengde. On a frosty day, we seemed to see the sparkling palace in the magical trees and walked round through a few reconstructed buildings. Then, when we visited the Forbidden Palace and many amazing Chinese gardens, particularly in the southern cities, or travelled on the West Lake in Hangzhou, we caught further glimpses of that vanished beauty.

The poem, with its presaging of war and total destruction of the dream palace is an accurate evocation of China. Again and again, mighty palaces and gardens have been built, quite extraordinary and beyond almost anything in the West. Again and again, a terrible eruption, rebellions, Mongol invasions and most recently the British/French destructions of the Second Opium War and Boxer and then the Japanese in the 1937-1945 war, have laid it all to dust.

China also evokes Percy Bysshe Shelley's famous poems 'Ozymandias', which could equally be set in China.

> I met a traveller from an antique land,
> Who said – "Two vast and trunkless legs of stone
> Stand in the desert. . . . Near them, on the sand,
> Half sunk a shattered visage lies, whose frown,
> And wrinkled lip, and sneer of cold command,
> Tell that its sculptor well those passions read
> Which yet survive, stamped on these lifeless things,
> The hand that mocked them, and the heart that fed;
> And on the pedestal, these words appear:
> My name is Ozymandias, King of Kings;
> Look on my Works, ye Mighty, and despair!
> Nothing beside remains. Round the decay
> Of that colossal Wreck, boundless and bare
> The lone and level sands stretch far away."

China is a long poem of past, and perhaps future, greatness.

Y

Yangtze

I spent my first five years in India, occasionally visiting great rivers like the Brahmaputra or Ganges, or the rivers rushing down from the Himalayas. For the next twenty-five years, I only experienced small Yorkshire and Scottish rivers, and mostly explored the gentle rivers of the south, the haunts of Ratty and Mole and Alice. Again, there were Himalayan rivers in Nepal, but it was only when I went to China that I became fully aware of the extraordinary power and size of rivers.

These Chinese rivers could flood out millions, bury whole cities and civilisations, or fertilize whole provinces and carry immense flows of goods. I saw the great rivers flowing into the Sichuan plain, being divided and distributed by ingenious dams and channels made over two thousand years ago. I saw the Yellow and Pearl rivers where Chinese civilisation began. Yet it is the mighty Yangtze which has most impressed me.

The Yangtze is nearly four thousand miles long, the longest river in Asia and third longest in the world. It is the longest river to flow within one country and drains one fifth of China; its discharge of water is the sixth largest in the world. It flows down from the high Tibetan plateau to disgorge at Shanghai in one of the richest areas in the world. It cuts through several mountain ranges and is most impressive when it drops thousands of feet down through the three long gorges below Chongqing to Yichang and the plains around Wuchan.

I went up the Yangtze in 2003 as the final stages of the dam were being put in place and the final forty metres were being flooded. Later, in 2007, we went down the river from Chonqing, when the dam was finished, and saw some of the villages that had been cut off and watched the boats clearing the debris accumulating on the surface.

It was awe-inspiring being lifted up many hundreds of feet in huge locks, watching the amazing cliffs reeling by, with small traces of the high and dangerous walkways along which the 'trackers' heaved up the boats against the rushing current. We saw some of the ancient towns which featured in the *Romance of the Three Kingdoms* gradually being submerged.

In 2005 we went up the higher reaches of the Yangtze towards its source with a film crew in a project to re-enact the remarkable travels of Isabella Bird in 1897, described in her *The Yangtze Gorge and Beyond* (1899). We saw some of the mysterious old towers, and the point at which Isabella finally thought she had found traces of the Caucasian peoples who had lived there. All these experiences brought home the majesty of Chinese rivers and how they have shaped its history.

Yin and Yang

I grew up without being aware that as a member of British civilisation, I was growing up in a world which is based on binary oppositions, something like the 0 and 1 of digital computers. I was taught that you are a man or a woman, saved or damned, guilty or innocent, brave or cowardly, truthful or lying, Conservative or Labour. Black is black, white is white, heaven is up there, earth down here. This was the basis for a system that is confrontational in its political system, law, economics and religion.

I was also unaware that my civilisation did not see the various oppositions as in any way linked or forming a bundle. In other words, little in my education suggested that male/female is equivalent to day/night, to white/black, to right/left. These were separate matters, though there are occasionally hints of this in the fact that 'sinister' comes from the latin for left. There are elements of these associations in Roman civilisation.

What has impressed me about the basic Daoist idea of *yin* and *yang* has been that it challenges both of these assumptions, and shows that they are not universal. It is also a fascinating conceptual system because it is so old. The underlying philosophy, which is found in the *I Ching* and the earliest writings, goes back well over five thousand years, yet it has survived intact to this day. It is a very ancient cosmology and is unlike any other in the world. Yet, though it is ancient and – like the pictographic language – perfectly preserved, it is strangely modern and up to date.

In terms of binary oppositions, what I did not at first notice about the *yin/yang* symbols is the importance of the element of the other that is contained within each.

Within the female/black *yin*, there is a circle of male/white *yang*, right in its heart or core, and the reverse also. Each characteristic also has its opposite and may be changing into the other. Night contains day, left contains right. Each is constantly giving way and transforming itself into the other. This is, in fact, very close to the instability of modern quantum physics which is based on the same idea, that each element contains its opposite. So yin/yang is a kind of quantum philosophy, but many thousands of years old.

The second aspect it took me time to fully grasp from my entirely different background was the structuralist idea that all oppositions are inter-related. I had read about this in the work of structural anthropologists such as Claude Lévi-Strauss and Edmund Leach, but had never really experienced it until I studied China.

In such a system you have a set of linked oppositions such that:

Yin	*Yang*
Female	Male
Moon	Sun
Winter	Summer
Left	Right
Cool	Hot
Void	Full
Dark	Bright
Soft	Hard
Smooth	Rough
Moist	Dry
Weak	Strong
Still	Moving
Nature	Culture
Yielding	Unyielding

The power of this system is that when you evoke any of these terms in poetry, novels or even conversation, it comes with a bundle of its associations. To talk of night is to talk of all the associations, to talk of women or men is to do the same. Metaphors and parallels abound. This enriches thought immensely, but also makes it difficult to shift attitudes, for a change to the valuation of one of these, for example the male/female relations, has implications for all the others.

Z

Zen – Chan (Chinese) Buddhism

For many years, I had been vaguely aware of Buddhism. My mother had become a Buddhist in her later years and we had spoken of it. I had read some of the classic anthropological accounts of Buddhism, especially in Sri Lanka and Thailand. I had supervised a top Buddhist monk for his degree in Cambridge. In Nepal, I had encountered great Buddhist stupas in Kathmandu and watched lamas doing rituals in a mountain village. In Japan, I had seen the wonderful temples in Kyoto as well as the zen gardens.

All this formed Buddhism into a rather undifferentiated block in my mind. I was aware that there were two branches of Buddhism, *Theravada*, the older form in India and South East Asia, and *Mahayana* in Tibet, China and Japan, but I made little differentiation beyond that. I had gradually become aware that Buddhism was really a philosophy rather than a 'religion' according to my western monotheistic definition.

What I have only recently come to understand through my studies in China is that *Mahayana* itself is split into two. There are the traditional forms, in Tibet and elsewhere, including parts of Japan, but there is also another variety which covers a vast territory, Chan or Chinese Buddhism. This is such a mixed form that in some ways it can be seen as a different philosophy. Let me explain.

Buddhist texts were first brought into China in the second century of the C.E., spreading there by way of South East Asia and Inner Asia. They were brought in by traders and travellers, but also deliberately brought in by a series of Chinese monks like Faxian, who went to study Buddhism in its homelands of Nepal and India and brought back Buddhist scriptures which were translated into Chinese. These writings were not just concerned with ethics and dogma, but also with the practice of Buddhism, particularly Buddhist organization, including monastic organizations.

Buddhism had already split in India by the time the flow to China began. There was the older, conservative, branch of Theravāda and the newer, more flexible, Mahayana. It was Mahayana that principally went to China and this adapted and changed as it encountered other philosophical systems. It adapted to different philosophical ecologies and social conditions. This was its strength, for when it was taken to China, it met several serious obstacles which it had to navigate round.

One problem was the very powerful clan system of Han China, based on descent through males (agnatic kinship), which, when combined with the Confucian respect for parents, meant that the family was the primary loyalty. This meant that the type of monastic system which worked within the more flexible family systems of South East Asia and Tibet (descent through both sexes, cognatic kinship), would not work in China. In the cognatic areas, some or all children could leave home and become full-time monks. In China this was entirely against the grain in a situation where filial respect and duties to work for the family were very powerful. Children in China were bound to their parents and their families. Full-time monastic commitment was much more difficult in such conditions.

The compromise worked out by Chinese Buddhists was an extension of an idea already dividing Mahayana from Theravada Buddhism, namely the idea of a lay, or non-monastic, vocation as a Buddhist. You did not have to be a monk to be Enlightened, and you did not have to make a lifelong vow to live in a monastery. Lay organizations were acceptable and widespread. This has continued within Chinese (and Japanese) Buddhism to this day.

A second adaptation was in relation to the funding of Buddhism. The Indian, Tibetan and South-East Asian tradition of mendicant monks, monks going out to beg for alms or gifts from people outside the monastery, did not fit in China. In the mendicant environment, the giving to the monks was a meritorious act. The gift was transformed by the monks into prayer; the monks took on the burdens of ordinary people in relation to the spiritual life and were paid for this.

Yet this idea of wandering, begging, monks is contrary to Chinese traditions, where there was not meritorious begging. The family was responsible for supporting the old and the sick, or, as I have recently discovered in accounts of Song China, the local officials would set up places for the old and disabled. It was not the custom to give directly to begging strangers, whether lay or religious, whereas such a tradition had been present before the Buddha within Hinduism.

The absence of one of the main sources of revenue for the monks meant that the monasteries needed another major source of funding. The answer, in line with much else in China, was to make the State responsible. The monasteries, and Buddhism more generally, were state-sponsored. So, Buddhism became a State religion, unlike in India where there was nothing like the powerful imperial system which controlled everything.

In good periods, this was a great source of strength. Monastic and other organizations were given lands to work and to rent out and other forms of wealth. Yet it also meant that, as the wealth and power of the Buddhist organizations rapidly grew, they came to be seen as a threat and drain on the State. Most notably this occurred in the almost total suppression of the central parts of Buddhism (but not the village Buddhism centred around the new Chan orders) during the Tang in the ninth century. Buddhism could be reduced to a shadow of itself, as it was periodically through history, most recently in the Cultural Revolution. The formal organization was 'dissolved' and the monks told to fend for themselves.

The crucial period appears to be the Tang. Buddhism flourished and grew very rich and powerful and nearly took over China. Then it was almost destroyed. The earlier forms had been taken to Japan along with Confucianism, but would die away over the next four hundred years until the next wave, the reformed Buddhism of Chan or introspective Buddhism was taken to Japan in the thirteenth century. Thus, there flourished, first in China and then in Japan, a totally distinctive form of Buddhism, as, for example with the Caodong sect of Jiangxi province which has lasted through to the present and which gave rise to the most widespread Japanese sect of Zen, Soto Zen.

This new form of Chan or Zen Buddhism, mixing later with Pure Land Buddhism, takes Buddhism to the extreme where it resembles a religion in its trappings, but which within itself is not a religion. The Buddha is not a God, the world is not real, it is a form of introspective philosophy.

The peculiarity of Chan Buddhism is also related to the way in which, as David Suzuki put it, Chan is a 'natural evolution of Buddhism under Taoist conditions'. Buddhism in China developed from an amalgamation of the earlier Daoist system, as described in *Wikipedia* under 'Chan',

> Buddhism was 'first identified to be a 'barbarian variant of Taoism', and Taoist terminology was used to express Buddhist doctrines. The Buddha was seen as a foreign immortal who had achieved some form of Daoist nondeath. The Buddhists' mindfulness of the breath was regarded as an extension of Daoist breathing exercises. The first Buddhist recruits in China were Taoists.

It is impossible to separate Buddhism and Daoism in China, and into this mix the huge influence of Confucianism also added new colouring. We have a unique world view compounded of three powerful ideologies, recently made more complex by the power of communism in the twentieth century and of a rising Christianity and still-strong Islam.

Reflexions

7. A unique civilisation

One learns a good deal by breaking the jigsaw puzzle of the Chinese into separate pieces, as in the A-Z above. Yet the sum of the parts is more than the individual bits and can remain hidden in such an approach. This is especially the case with the Chinese for it now seems clear to me that China is a *tertium orbis*, a third world, different in its deep structure from anything else I have encountered in my years as a historian and anthropologist.

In this concluding synthesis, I will try to make some tentative guesses about a few aspects of the essential and enduring essence or deep structure of this extraordinary civilisation. For someone who comes from outside China and does not speak or write the language, this has to be tentative. I only include it here because it may help others to pull together some of the features which are outlined in the main part of the text and move to a deeper level of understanding across the social and cultural differences. .

Power

The Bureaucratic Empire

As I studied the later development of this extraordinary integrated civilisation I was mystified as to how and when it had begun. I knew that there were great civilisations for at least three or four thousand years before the Qin Emperor, spreading out from the Yellow River, and culminating in the period of the Warring States from about 475 B.C. to the victory of the Qin in 221 B.C.

This was when Confucius, Mencius and Laotze flourished and laid out their philosophies, but in the context of those warring times their ideas were only marginal. They were encased within a form of political organization which we can term 'feudal' and in that sense similar to that found in mediaeval Japan or the mediaeval West.

In this system, the rulers held their states together by delegating power to noble families, each with their own territories. They passed their family estates to their descendants from generation to generation. The Confucian meritocratic system had no real function here and it's peaceful philosophy of loyalty and harmony was irrelevant.

One of the states, the Qin, centred in western China, began to develop an entirely new system of government in the fourth century BC. This is largely associated with the ideas of the reforming figure of Shang Yang (390-338 BC). He was the Prime Minister of the Duke of Xiao, and one of the founders of what was later termed the Legalist philosophical system, though this is an inaccurate representation of a system based on much more than law and better described as 'methodological uniformity'.

Its implementation destroyed the feudal system of noble families and replaced it with a meritocratic bureaucracy. Henceforth, the top positions in the state were open to all, based on merit rather than blood. This also minimized the role of landowners so that China became a State where there were small and medium peasants and no dominating gentry class.

The effects of this huge change were combined with other profound reforms in taxation, administration and military efficiency (the use of recently developed weaponry, cavalry and better transportation) so that the economic and military power of the Qin kingdom grew. The outcome was that in 221 B.C. the Qin were sufficiently powerful to defeat the other states and the first Emperor of China, as he proclaimed himself, Emperor Chin Shi Huang, unified the Warring States.

In the fifteen years of his reign he set the template for the China we know to this day. He split the country into thirty-six administrative provinces, installed a standardized writing system that would cover the whole Empire (later known as Mandarin and based on the pictographic writing system). He unified the weights, measures and currency. He built many roads and bridges. He enforced Shang Yang's view that no individual in the state, however powerful, should be above the law. He endorsed the Legalist view that the only important people in the state were the top officials and the peasants. Those engaged in other professions, particularly merchants and traders, were inferior and regarded with suspicion – a trait which helps to explain the absence of an effective middle class throughout Chinese history. The suspicion of any power that threatened the ruler was later extended to religious organizations and helps to explain the weakness of Buddhism and other religions in China.

This was the context in which Confucius' vision of a system based on personal relations and on a meritocratic government recruited through written examinations could at last make sense. So China became the first great bureaucratic civilisation, held together by writing, law, officialdom and education, but with basically only two important groups, the civil service and the peasant-warriors.

This first unification only lasted two years, with the death of the Qin Emperor, but the model survived so that within a few years of his death, China was unified again under the great Han state (which gave its name to the Chinese people) which was then to last for over four hundred years.

Under the Han, the Qin revolution was magnified but mellowed as the extreme and ruthless Legalistic philosophy fell out of favour and the message of Confucius and Laotze gained ascendancy. Yet the transformation to an unprecedented new kind of political and intellectual world had been achieved and it is the blueprint which helps us understand China today.

Since the Qin and Han, education, that is the passing on between the generations of basic skills in reading and writing, set within the transmission of ethical codes, has been the heart of Chinese civilisation. The education in itself is different from what has come to be considered 'education' in the West. It was based on learning the classics by heart, absorbing the ethical systems of Confucianism, learning the arts of bureaucratic government – loyalty, memory, discrimination, judgment and fairness. Family status and success in the examination system replaced an older aristocratic system.

So China became the only civilisation on earth which was held together by a largely meritocratic system where potentially anyone could reach the highest levels through mental ability. There was no longer any class of landed nobility, that main pillar of Japan and Indo-European systems.

At a stroke, the arts that were elevated were no longer hunting and fighting, but rather writing, painting, reading, music and thinking. It became the one civilisation which has put the mind and intellect at its core and unified millions of people over thousands of years by way of ideas of the true, the good and the beautiful. The written word became the symbol of unity and the scholar gentleman the highest calling.

When we look at China now we need to remember this 'point of origin', when one civilisation on Earth moved decisively to something entirely new in nature and scale – a bureaucratic, centralised, meritocratic, standardized and unified system able to hold together hundreds of millions of people century after century, whatever the shocks they were subjected to.

This ancient system is, essentially, the one that still largely holds China together today, despite massive recent disruptions. If we want to understand the strengths and weaknesses of China today, we must take into account this ancient but still living legacy. I have met many Chinese officials, including those working in banks, business, academia or schools. They provide hints of the legacy of such a system which was partly destroyed by the Communist period from 1949 to 1976, but in other ways consolidated then. The communist system of the mid-twentieth century has a flavour of a vast bureaucracy, and what exists in China nowadays feels very like this.

The Mandarins, and their successors today, were to be impartial, and hence were moved constantly and away from their home province. They were to be rewarded – not principally by government stipends, but by the profits they could extract from their official position or 'prebends' as they are called. They were all-purpose – in charge of all aspects of life from crime and war, to water control and farming. They were to be accountable to the layer above them, constantly sending reports, watched by spies, their every decision and action carefully monitored.

This layered system of bureaucracy has in many ways served China well, holding together a vast and differentiated people, mostly peacefully, by a relatively small group of trained officials who remind me of the Indian Civil Service in nineteenth century India. It gave all in China the remote chance of moving from the bottom to the top of the social hierarchy through talent in examinations. It produced a sophisticated ruling class, not based on birth or wealth, who loved poetry, gardens, music – elegant and refined and highly educated.

Yet it also had its negative side. The system was inevitably conservative – it was better to go by the old ways, to practice the old and deep precepts one had learnt from the Confucian classics, than to try anything new. It was also conservative because even the smallest decision usually had to be referred upwards through many layers for approval. Hence it could be cumbersome and unadventurous.

It was also venal, that is to say that corruption tended to be built into the system. The bureaucrats were paid far too little to live on, hardly any wages, and hence had to take bribes, favours, and you were subject to huge pressures to help friends and relatives – nepotism. Your followers lived off your connections and by manipulating the system. Mandarins could make serious money, but only through a kind of black economy.

The Imperial System

I was brought up to respect the British Royal Family, but it was a limited feeling. I learnt from a long course in British history that the Crown was under the Law, from the earliest time, through Magna Carta in 1215 and the beheading of Charles I in the seventeenth century. I learnt that the monarchy was limited, the first among equals. I also learnt that the King did not have a Divine Right to rule without check, unlike the French and Spanish monarchs.

It is true that at times the King had some limited magical power, healing certain skin diseases for example, for a hundred years or so. Yet the King was a person, with all the weaknesses of others, just someone who came from a special family and who had been given rights in exchange for responsibilities. The system consisted of many pillars of power – the law, church, army, boroughs, yeomen and middling sort, traders and manufacturers, universities. These pillars went up to the roof and mingled. A symbol of their meeting was the rose in the roof of King's College Chapel in Cambridge. Yet without the pillars, the rose is nothing.

My first encounter with an imperial system was in Japan, but this did not greatly disturb my assumptions about how political power is distributed. For many centuries the Japanese Emperor in his palace was only a symbolic, ritual, head. It was the military leader, the Shoguns, who ruled. The dynasties such as the Tokugawa were named after them. A true imperial system with a single head was only really inaugurated again in the Meiji Restoration in 1868. It only lasted until 1945 and was a palpable failure when it tried to destroy the tension between ceremonial and secular power.

It was in China, as I was taken round the imperial place in Beijing, or read of the imperial dynasties, including the amazing activities of the great Emperors like the Kangxi and Qianlong, and even the last Dowager Empress, that I realised the full might of an imperial system. The Emperor was not just a human being, but a semi-divine ruler sitting on the jade throne, there at the direct command or mandate of heaven. Rousseau's dream of the General Will against whom no-one has any separate rights has come true, for the Emperor is yourself on a higher level, as the General Will is your will, so the Communist Party embodies you.

So instead of many pillars, there is only one – which leads directly from the millions of individual families to the Emperor. The Emperor then used his advisors and representatives, the mandarins, to exercise his authority. He has all power and all authority. His word is law. There is no balancing power, no countervailing force, no independent or semi-independent church, cities, nobility, peasantry. The Emperor is the Sun, there may be small stars but they cannot control the Sun.

This is the theory, though naturally in practice it is more complicated. The Emperor is surrounded by his eunuch advisors, his Generals, his spiritual advisors and his plotting and scheming relatives. He is constantly hemmed in by a thousand plots and pressures. Yet it is all personalized, face to face struggles in the secret chambers. Occasionally it breaks out into huge rebellions which are put down with savagery. Yet usually the politics is kept secret and unchallenged.

One other major constraint is the doctrine of the Mandate of Heaven. How do we know that the Emperor still has heaven's trust? Only by external signs. If life becomes terrible, with floods, famines, invasion, break-down of law and order, clearly Heaven has withdrawn its mandate. In which case a person is justified in switching to the new successful general or invading Khan who has taken over the imperial throne.

This kind of single pillar, uncontested, 'General Will' or 'Will of the People' system, has lasted in China, with interruptions, for over two thousand years since it was set up in 221 B.C by the First Emperor. It is difficult to shake off. One great question in China is how such a system, modified in many ways, yet clearly also continuing with Chairman Mao, fits with the alternative model of democracy which I have experienced through my life.

It is a question which becomes all the more interesting when we live in an age when civilisations like Russia seem to be reverting to their ancient imperial system, and where even America is suddenly realising that its President is totally different in his or her powers from a British, French or German Prime Minister. From an English viewpoint, the American Presidency is currently revealed to be verging on an Imperial position, with the supposed countervailing forces, the elected representatives, the legal system, the press, let along the Church and Civil Society, swept away by Presidential diktat.

It would be ironic indeed if the two great world civilisations swopped systems. If America became a full imperial system, while China gradually adopts some of the checks and balances that are felt to be essential for a modern democracy.

See also under A-Z: Administrative levels, Cities, Education, Law and justice, Mandarins, Mandate of Heaven and democracy, Nightmares, Nobility, Qin Emperor, Taxation, Vast and integrated.

Society

The family, Confucianism and power

I was brought up within quite a small group of close family. The only important individuals to me were my nuclear family of mother and father, my sisters, my grandparents on both sides, and my uncles and aunts. First cousins also might be quite close, but that was it. These were all emotional and protective relations, but the functions of my family were quite limited. After I became an adult, especially after my grandparents died, my cousins, uncles and aunts, all faded away and I was left with my new family of wife, children and grandchildren. It was narrow in range and circumscribed in function.

I was only partially educated by my family. As soon as I went to school at the age of five my teachers and school friends became not only my intellectual, but also, to a considerable extent, my moral and social instructors. My economic links to family members was restricted to my parents and children. I did not work in any family business. I did not expect serious economic aid, for example for education or in a crisis, to extend beyond my close family. I did not know or care much about the political or religious views of my family and would have been shocked if any of my relatives had tried to dictate my views or actions in these matters once I was adult. I chose my own wife, I chose my own job. I helped my mother when she was widowed, but knew that I was of only marginal importance.

In other words, my family and family system does not provide the bedrock, the ultimate organising principle, of my life.

Experience in Nepal showed me the power of the family in the majority of societies, where it is the basis for most of life's work, and this experience prepared me for my encounter with China. Nowadays in China, the wider clan-based family system has been substantially weakened by the policies during the period of Chairman Mao's ascendancy and by recent economic and social changes. Yet the family still remains far more important in China today than anything I had experienced in my own culture.

Parents still feel they have a right and duty morally to educate their children and have a say in their love life and marriages. Children still feel a huge duty to take care of their elderly parents. Wider kin also form an action-set of people who contribute to an individual's success. I soon discovered that my young Chinese friends and students called on aunts, uncles, cousins and others if they needed help of a substantial kind for foreign education or to get a job. They still expect to attend huge re-unions of dozens and sometimes hundreds of relatives at all sorts of family events, including weddings, funerals, Spring and Autumn festivals.

What we see now is a legacy of something far stronger than in the Anglo-sphere, which existed for over two thousand years. The Chinese trace their descent through males, so they can form into named clans. Often these names are widespread Wang, Yan,

Xiao, Li and others contain millions of individuals. The actual clan is restricted to those who can trace their common ancestor back twelve generations. This means hundreds of relatives who you share a bond with. If you adopted someone in the past it had to be from this group. If you married it had to be out of this group to prevent an incestuous mixture of blood.

Often in the past, a whole village was occupied by just a single clan. We have visited such villages with huge halls, honeycombs of rooms where distant and close kin lived together, worshipping the same ancestors, working the family lands together, fighting off other clans, celebrating and suffering together.

These groups were treated as one entity by the State. If a member was successful in the Confucian examinations, the whole group could share the honour. If one member was accused of a serious offence, all the members could be punished, whole village clans were butchered and their houses and lands destroyed. Each little clan group was a mini-kingdom. The oldest relative, quite often a woman, was the ruler and what they said went. They were judges, economic bosses, priests for the whole family.

The intensity of the clan system varied over time and space. Clans were more powerful and extended in the south of China. As noted, they are far less powerful now, unlike earlier days of invasion and disruption. Yet the vast difference between a civilisation ultimately based on ties of birth, blood and marriage – China – and my own English world based on the individual, State and Market, is fundamental.

*

To someone familiar with the history of the small nation-states of the West, the whole Chinese structure is puzzling. How does a system, where a vast country was ruled by a few hundred thousand bureaucrats, without a large instituted police force or army or the support of an instituted middle-class and church, maintain order? And how has it managed to do so for most of two thousand years in what has often been a relatively peaceful and orderly Empire?

The secret seems to lie in another feature which is again simplest to explain in terms of Confucian thought. The heart of Confucian ethics was duty and responsibility between people. It is an ethical order based on the relationship of a pair of people, a dyadic or two-sided link which was replicated along the social and political dimensions.

The essence is the bond between parent and child, particularly the father and the son. This was the fundamental building block. The father's power was almost absolute. He could, in theory, do no wrong to his child and had power of life and death with no appeal. The child owed obedience and loyalty, the father protection and sustenance. The bond could not be broken or challenged. This relationship was then extended outwards in various ways.

One was in a generational direction. All those of a superior generation were owed duty and respect by the young. This obviously applied to the teacher, who was to be deeply revered and obeyed. It also applied between older and younger in the family – an older brother had power over a younger. It applied in relation to sex – women were by birth inferior and every woman owed respect and loyalty to all men.

In effect, this meant that the family became a total world. The child was part of the economic unit, run by the oldest close relative. He or she was part of a ritual unit, for only through the older relatives could the dead ancestors and other invisible powers be accessed. He or she was part of a political unit – the oldest relative stood for the Emperor. He or she was obviously part of a social unit, which arranged his or her education, marriage and contacts.

So China was largely self-administered within the millions of families, both the close family of grandparents, parents and children, but also more widely in the powerful clan system based on tracing one's ancestry through the male line. Such clans were self-governing ritual, economic, political and social units.

Crystallizing the wisdom of previous thinkers, Confucius

had the genius to take this beyond kinship and to integrate it into the general political system by emphasizing the parallel between the relations of obedience and rule within the family and the governing of China. The Emperor was the father who held the system together. The way one behaved to one's father is the way one should behave to the Emperor. So, instead of having to delegate power to feudal, armed, nobles and give them landed estates as payment, the Emperor delegated power to the household heads and supported them if their children challenged them in any way.

When combined with a high esteem for the mass of the peasant producers, and the Confucian educational system which allowed a very bright son to move up to a position of wealth and power through education, this provided a universal lottery which gave all families hope and ambition. Furthermore, this system was policed by the very persons who performed well in the examination system and became the civil servants of the Emperor.

There were contradictions and tensions. The father's power was so great that the son could not approach him closely and did not necessarily feel any affection for him. Another tension was that, while the wife was in the power of her husband, she was also bound strongly to her family of origin and hence there was a concealed war between husband and wife. Another was that there was a potential conflict between loyalty to one's father and to the Emperor.

Another serious tension lay in the question of whether the Emperor could do wrong. Was he to be obeyed whatever he did? Here again there was a well-known resolution. The Emperor's power came from the 'Mandate of Heaven' and that mandate could be withdrawn. Both a cause and a sign of such withdrawal were prolonged catastrophes, famines, wars, diseases which meant one could switch allegiances. Even his loyal followers, the Mandarin bureaucrats, had the duty to oppose the Emperor if they felt there was sufficient evidence to show he had lost the mandate.

Individualism and Collectivism

Looking back on my life, I now see that all of my infancy, childhood and adolescence was designed to make me a self-contained, separate, independent and strong individual. There was a constant process of separating me from my birth-given relations, especially my parents, and launching me out into new constructed relationships with strangers in 'society'. It put me as an individual on a level with all other individuals, with my primary responsibility to myself, a free agent who could decide my own destiny and follow my personal path in my political allegiances, my economic life, in my beliefs and in my social world.

The process began in early infancy when I was put into my separate cot, soon given an individual play-area (playpen) and my personal toys, treated as special and distinct from my sisters. It was re-enforced greatly when I was sent off at eight to my first boarding school, cast among strangers and taught to be self-reliant. It continued through my adolescence as I was given control over my own space, my hobbies, my spending money. Both my school and home life emphasised that I was becoming a member of society and disentangling myself from the strong ties to any family grouping.

All of the essential power to live a successful life were within me. After the final stage of university, which was a temporary sheltered entry into wider society, and the apprenticeship of a doctorate, I married and was, with my wife, a new unit in society.

I took this extreme atomistic individualism for granted and it was only the shock of going to work in a Himalayan mountain village where there were no 'individuals', but only groups composed of people whose primary allegiance was to their family and neighbours, that I realized how odd my upbringing and psychological attitudes were.

In this Himalayan village, mothers were not called by their personal, individual, names but by their relationship, 'mother of x'. Children were not called by their names, but by their birth order - oldest, second, third son or daughter. All the important things in life, from what you owned and what work you did, to your religious life and death rituals, through to political alliances and leisure time, was determined by the group. The group was the basic unit of the community, off which a single individual hung like a leaf. Without the tree, the leaf was nothing.

The shock of the contrast led me to wonder where and when my western individualistic attitudes had emerged, so one of my first books was on this theme and titled *The Origins of English Individualism* (1978). I found that the English were peculiar within Europe, and this peculiarity was not the result of some recent event such as the Protestant Reformation or Industrial Revolution, but was strongly present at least eight hundred years ago in medieval England.

I now had two types of civilisation to think with as models, and when I started to learn about China I immediately realised that it was very similar to my Nepalese village. In every aspect, China was, and still largely is, a group-based civilisation. This does not mean that people go around in small groups and are never alone. What it means is that when a person conceives of themselves, they place the group into which they were born first, and their own individual needs and desires and rights second.

This was more clearly obvious in the two thousand or more years up to 1949, when clans dominated China and no person could conduct their economic, political or religious life without reference to their family. In that period, you had no rights separate from your obligation to your family. For example property was held by the family, not the individual. Your access to spiritual well-being was through your family rituals, especially ancestral ones. The system was underpinned by the ethics of Confucius, which makes the primary relations to parents and siblings the supreme duty of an individual.

The communist party merely replaced the family embeddedness of the individual by embeddedness in the commune, or larger political structure. Again, you were completely bound by others, with little space for individual and personal initiatives.

In the last forty years of market reform and some political liberalisation, seeds of a more individualistic system have been sown. There is private property, people can marry whom they like, they can choose their own career. Yet I sense that behind these appearances of something similar to the individualism I know, the deeper structure is still fundamentally different.

Talking to and observing my Chinese friends, I can see that their every action and thought is modified by an implicit awareness of wider obligations and pressures of groupings, especially their families. They may try to break away, but the systematic separating mechanisms which set me free are not yet there in the socialisation process. So, the attempted escapes are thwarted. China is still ultimately a group-based, as opposed to an individualistic, society.

Social bonds

There is a well-known distinction in sociology between two major ways in which societies are held together. One formulation of this was by Emile Durkheim. He described one set of societies as held together by organic solidarity. That is to say they are like a living or organic being, with a head, body, arms and legs. Each has its function in keeping the body politic going.

The Indo-European world within which I grew up was based on such a functional division of labour. The four great groups, from the Indian caste system in the East to the feudal system of western Europe, were based on four functional divisions. These were the head (the Brahmins and clergy), the arms (the King and nobility and fighters), the legs (the traders, merchants, townsmen, the makers of money) and the great mass of the body, the rural workers or peasants.

I assumed that 'modernity' and a working civilisation depended on such a system of division of labour. In the history of my own country, England, it was modified in that each group was highly stratified within itself – there was no huge lump of 'peasants' for example, and the nobility was replaced by a small, but not blood-based, aristocracy and a very important gentry. Yet, in broad strokes, it roughly conformed. And when I went to Japan I found a modification of the system – there was no clerical group, but the fourth part was made by dividing the bourgeoisie into two separate groups, the merchants and the traders.

At first it looked as if the Chinese, with its placing of the peasants on a higher level than the traders and merchants, contrary to the European ranking, was like the Japanese case. I assumed that China was part of the great organic stratification systems of the world, though again it showed a curious difference to Japan by echoing in some way the Indo-European arrangement of including a class of literati. The scholars in China replaced the samurai/daimyo or warriors of Japan. The rulers were an educated elite, not the sword bearers.

This was strange enough, but as I have deepened my understanding of the Chinese, I have to turn to Durkheim's other type of social organisation, what he calls rather confusingly 'mechanical solidarity'.

This he found in the very simplest of societies, the wandering bands of Australian aborigines upon which he based much of his work on religion and society. Here he found that there was no functional division based on a division of labour. Instead, in these small bands, everybody more or less did everything. Society consists of identical segments, individuals who encapsulated the whole of society within each of them, and could do all the tasks. Each tiny segment was linked to others by one-to-one personal relations. A child was linked through family and parents, grandparents, uncles, cousins, the whole held together by the simplest of one-to-one or dyadic bonds.

Durkheim likened this to an earthworm, which consists of identical segments, placed one-to-one next to each other. As a child who fished for trout with worms, I soon discovered that an earthworm could be cut or broken, and it would then grow into two worms. It had not lost its head or feet; it was infinitely replicable and largely indestructible.

As I looked at the deep structures of the Confucian system in China, which envisaged everything as held together by one-to-one relations extended over the whole Empire, I began to realise that China is the one civilisation based on mechanical solidarity. The child is linked to the father and mother and through them to every person in China, and likewise through a chain of one-to-one links up to the Emperor. It is true mechanical solidarity and where the one-to-one links are not created by nature, they are supplemented by the one-to-one manufactured ties of *guanxi* or connections, as I have described elsewhere.

This means that to understand the Chinese you have to realize that historically, and still largely today, it does not have castes and classes or other functional divisions. The only separation is between the small ruling literati and the rest who are all lumped together. The distinction between say the traders, merchants and peasants in everyday life is not a status difference, and in terms of their roles, people moved back and forth between tasks. Individuals from this mass could move up the educational escalator to one of the floors above, where the educated literati and bureaucracy ruled the country.

Understanding that China falls outside both Indo-Europe and Japan in these models, and, as in the retention of its ancient pictographic script, has retained an ancient social formation of the same class as hunter-gatherers in Australia, suddenly makes it possible to understand several things which before were mysteries.

One was how this vast Empire has held together despite vast jolts over two thousand years. China has been cut and trampled on, yet it is enormously resilient. The enormous power of family and personal links has kept it going. Mongols, Manchus, western and Japanese imperialists could wage war on it and cut off its supposed head, but it was not destroyed.

Secondly, it explains how China has spread. The Han were a

relatively small group along the Yellow River and in central China five thousand years ago. Largely through movement and marriage, they have travelled out and absorbed the people around them, a recent instance being the westward expansion into Tibet, Xinjiang and Mongolia.

The earthworm just grows, adding new segments. There is no limit to its size and getting larger does not, as in most structures, lead to problems of loss of power through growth in scale. It is like Oxford or Cambridge universities, which can add new Colleges of a moderate size and through preserving each unit at a relatively small size of a few hundred students, not lose their special nature.

Structural civilisation

Broadly speaking, we can distinguish two major types of civilisation in history. These can be termed individualistic and structural civilisations. In individualistic civilisations, the prime example being the Anglosphere of Britain, America and the white ex-British Empire, the system is based on single units, individuals, who are linked together in society by 'contractual' ties. By contractual, I mean that the majority of important relations are voluntary, intended, and one-to-one or one-to-many. This is the move which Henry Maine was referring to in his famous statement that 'the movement of the progressive societies is from status to contract'.

'Status' here means the birth-given and unalterable relations of blood, whether of family, caste or unalterable social classes. These status relations dominate the majority of civilisations through history, from tribal through peasant to present civilisations such as India, which are based on caste. The exception was the area of north-western Europe, roughly the area of Protestantism, where associations based on 'contract' emerged.

Structural civilisations are based on birth-given relations and are best approached by the analytic method known in anthropology as structuralism. This is the method which suggests that the ultimate meaning of relations does not lie in A or B, but in the relations of A to B, or A/B. It is like the sound caused by two hands clapping – without the relation, there is silence. You cannot have a man without a woman, black without white, right without left, *yin* without *yang*. These relations are interlinked, so one relation, say left and right, is linked to female and male, night and day and so on.

Being aware of the difference between individualistic and structural civilisations is essential for understanding China. China is undoubtedly a structural civilisation and if I approach it from my individualistic background and apply my inherited framework, I will not be able to understand much of the deeper nature of China. For the Chinese do not conceive of the world as made up of single entities, complete in themselves, linked through artificial, constructed, ties. Rather, the world is already given and fixed in a set of deep relations at birth, parent-child, male-female, ruler-subject, heaven-earth. They are unchangeable and inter-linked in the Confucian order. People are not freely transacting individuals, but parts of a 'chain of being'. They are part of a giant web where each person has rights and responsibilities which cannot be severed.

In order to get inside the Chinese world, an Anglo-Saxon observer has to suspend his or her whole set of unexamined assumptions. Few have been successful in doing this. This perhaps explains why some of the best western accounts of China are made by French scholars such as Marcel Granet. France, which produced the great tradition of structuralist thinkers from Montesquieu and Tocqueville, through Durkheim and De Saussure to Lévi Strauss and Bourdieu, is basically structural, despite an admixture of individualism. It is therefore much easier to empathize, sympathize, make the imaginative leap into an understanding of China for a French thinker than it is for me or my fellow countrymen.

Yet it is also perhaps an advantage to be outside the structuralist orbit, for the shock of 'otherness', which is also a part of discovery, is stronger. I sense, even if I cannot fully understand, how very different China is from everything I am familiar with. This is helpful, for now that there is a strong overlay of western material civilisation it is very easy for an observer to miss the differences. Going to a remote Nepalese village, I expected to find something completely different to that which I was used to in the West. Yet now, if you travel through great Chinese cities, you feel at first that it is very familiar, a world of cars, shops, clothes and western styles. The startling differences which struck earlier travellers are overlaid by globalization.

We need to return to an awareness that China belongs to the world of symbolic meanings and given statuses which anthropologists like Lévi Strauss discussed in south American tribes and others found in New Guinea, or I found in a shamanic hill village in Nepal. China is to me an ancient and preserved configuration as strange as the ancient, preserved, written pictographic language or the ancient, preserved, enchantment of the Daoist-Chan Buddhist world. It is a real, and radical, alternative to my basic assumptions – a challenge, a provocation, but also a delight in preserving a viable alternative against the homogenisation of the world.

Also see under A-Z: Ancestors, Childrearing, Clubs and associations, Emotional warmth, Guanxi, Joint responsibility, Love and marriage.

Thought and belief

The separation of natural and supernatural

One of the best ways to begin to understand China is to use the grand theory devised by two of the greatest social thinkers of the West, Max Weber and Karl Jaspers. This is known as the Axial Age theory. In Jaspers' brilliant formulation as chapter two of *The Origins* and *Goal of History* (1953), Jaspers describes how he had discovered, from his wide research on many of the greatest philosophers in history, that something strange happened simultaneously all over Eur-Asia between about 800 and 300 B.C. From Laotse, Confucius and Mencius in China, through the Buddha and the ancient Hindu scriptures (*Upanishads*) in India, onwards to the Middle East with Zoroaster in Persia and the great Old Testament prophets such as Isaiah and Ezekiel, through to the Greek philosophers of the time of Plato and Aristotle, the whole world shifted on its Axis, like a cart-wheel going around.

Previous to this period, there was no separation between an ideal, divine, supernatural world and this mundane, material, human life. They flowed into each other and the world was filled with enchantment and magic where natural and supernatural co-existed. With the Axial shift, these great thinkers and others suggested that there is a heaven and an earth, a supernatural world which is divided from this world, separate and in tension with it. They set up an ideal world towards which humans should strive and judge themselves. This world is purely natural and no longer just a mixture of invisible and visible forces.

In Jaspers' formulation, China was part of this Axial transformation. He does not comment on Japan, and it was my discovery that Japan was never part of the Axial transformation, being neither pre or post Axial, which gave me the final key to understanding why Japan feels so entirely different from any other major civilisation in the world.

What has long puzzled me is whether Jaspers was right about China. One of the leading exponents of his ideas, S.N. Eisenstadt, has agreed with Jaspers that China is basically part of the Axial world, but with some special Chinese characteristics. Yet Max Weber, the teacher and master of Jaspers, in his *The Religion of China* (1915) places China outside the Axial civilisations. He regards China as a magical, enchanted, world where the major thinkers do not, in fact, fall on the Axial side.

Confucius was not interested in heaven and largely ignored it. Laotse and Daoism obviously believes in a magical world. The *yin-*

yang world of invisible forces is, like Japanese Shinto, non-Axial. Even the Chinese form of Buddhism, the curious Mahayana variant which was totally transformed when it came into China into Chan Buddhism (called Zen when it was taken to Japan) is not Axial. This form of Buddhism eliminates all boundaries between mind and body, spirit and matter, heaven and hell. The fusion in Chan/Zen is not Axial.

We have a rainbow of Axiality. At one extreme, in Protestant north-western Europe and America, we have a scientific, rationalist world where God and heaven are far away on another plane, even if the individual believer has God in his or her heart. This is the extreme case of Axiality and it is the world I was brought up in. I can chart in detail my childhood and education and I find there the systematic elimination of magic and enchantment, paralleled in my case by living in William Wordsworth's Lakeland childhood valley. In Wordsworth's autobiographical *Prelude*, as in much Romantic poetry from Keats to Yeats, we see the battle to preserve enchantment in an extreme Axial civilization. On the whole this is the strongest case, a Newtonian clockwork universe. It is the world to which Weber applies his ideas of disenchantment.

Some enchantment and fusion creeps in with Catholicism and certain variants of Islam. These are worlds tinged with Axiality. We are moving from violet and indigo to blue. Then India is even further tinged, with Hinduism, with a semi-magical religion, a light blue has emerged.

As we move to China we move on to yellow. It is 'Axial-lite'. There are some hints of the separation and tension, yet it is another world to the West and also to India. This partly explains why, to my surprise, when I asked young Chinese where 'The West' began, they said India.

China is its own world, neither Axial, nor non-Axial. We can contrast it with Japan, where we have reached the full red of the Japanese sun symbol, and where we encounter a civilisation which for generation after generation rejected all Axial divisions. Through studying China I understand better how in fact the

Chinese waves of Confucian, Daoist and Buddhist thought which swept over Japan were easier to absorb, for they were already far from fully Axial. They were like a vaccine, a mild variant of the disease which progressively inoculated Japan so that when the final full force of true Axiality in the form of Protestant missionaries and imperial powers of the West arrived, Japan was prepared to absorb and transform their message.

If I am right, then we have to approach China as totally distinctive in its philosophical basis. The distance between the Chinese mixed situation and other civilisations is as great, though more concealed, than the difference between its pictographic language and the alphabets of the West, or between its bureaucratic centralist government and the feudal democracies of the West.

China is a *tertium orbis*, a third kind of world, neither Western Axial nor Japanese non-Axial. With historically a fifth of the world's population and an unbroken history of seven thousand years or more, China is great enough to preserve a set of philosophical foundations which are very different from the rest of the world.

*

This major difference is immensely important, and makes me speculate on why China seems to be neither Axial nor non-Axial. It may be that that when the two great Axial philosophies, Confucian and Buddhist, came into conflict, and Buddhism also has to adapt to a very powerful set of pre existing non-Axial beliefs – Daoism and Ancestor worship – then the effect is different from what we might expect.

Instead of there being a re-enforcement of Axiality, with each philosophy making the other more Axial, in fact they pulled against each other, so that the Axiality of both Confucianism and Buddhism was weakened in the new mix, and further weakened by Daoism, the third leg of the tripod as one Chinese Emperor put it. So China might be described as 'Axial-lite', perhaps a quarter of the way towards Axiality, and further weakened in its Axiality by the strength of the family and kinship system. The fact that Confucianism is, in itself, rather weakly Axial (Confucius was this-worldly, not much interested in Heaven) added to the peculiar situation in China.

As Buddhism evolved within China, it was deprived of some of its tension with another world, and incorporated into the animist world of Daoism. In this extreme form, it poses little threat to the State, it absorbs a good deal of Daoism, and it forms no threat to Confucianism. It is similar in many ways to western Puritanism in being a simple, ascetic, inward-looking, private system, where salvation is by faith rather than works, through inner cleansing and meditation. Yet, in contrast to Christian sects, it does not have God. This difference would have a profound effect on many parts of Chinese development, including the progress of reliable knowledge ('science') in China.

Enchantment

As a child growing up in William Wordsworth's childhood valley of Esthwaite Vale in the English Lake District, I was half conscious of enchantment. Much of Wordsworth's poetry, as that of his companion Romantic poets whom I came to love, Keats, Shelley, Coleridge and later W.B. Yeats, was about the fragility and loss of enchantment.

What this word meant to them and me is analysed in another way by Max Weber when he talks about the 'disenchantment of the world'. It is essentially a kind of pantheism, a feeling, in Wordsworth's words, of the world being more deeply interfused with some kind of invisible power. It is the theme of Keith Thomas' *Religion and the Decline of Magic* and lies behind many of the vivid recreations of childhood enchantment in the tradition of English children's stories from *Alice in Wonderland* through to *Harry Potter*.

I struggled through my adolescence to delay the loss of enchantment and my Oxford university letters and essays which I have analysed show the dramatic battle. Yet in the end I thought that there was no way to retain a deeply interfused and meaningful world where nature was alive, humans and animals inhabit a shared mental and moral world, there was no gap between nature and supernature.

Going to Nepal where I lived among the Gurungs, I entered a world of witches and shamans, where rocks, waterfalls and forests were filled with spirits, where animals could take a human form and humans could enter into animals. All this reminded me of what I had lost. I rejoiced in what I thought were the last vestiges of a 'pre-modern' world which would fade as capitalism, individualism and science played their usual dissolving role. I did encounter hints that this might not be so simple. For example, there were anti-witchcraft rituals in cities in which young Gurungs admitted that, even after western education, they still believed in witchcraft and ghosts. Yet I put this on one side.

The great shock was coming to terms with Japan. It was so rational, scientific, urban and 'modern' on the surface that it seemed the last place to find enchantment. Yet, as I began to see little flickers of something else on the edge of my vision, and talked to my closest friends, I began to realize that behind the Japanese mirror lies an enchanted, magical, world. It was like entering one of the animator Miyazaki's films, a sudden dropping into a parallel reality, as in 'Totoro', 'Howl's Moving Castle', 'Spirited Away' and others.

In a moment, as in English childrens' stories, or Keats' 'Ode to a Nightingale' or Yeats's enchanted poems, I could enter a world just as real as the physical world, filled with meaning and beauty – and terror at times. It also reminded me of M.R. James' ghost stories, starting here, now, safe and rational and then suddenly encountering a parallel world, odd and disturbing.

Japan is clearly an ancient, enchanted, shamanic world, covered over by a screen of modernity which made its survival and communication with the rest of the world possible.

On the surface, my impressions of China were similar to my first impressions of Japan. Its hectic economic and technological growth, its extraordinary practical energy, its highly rational and down-to-earth people with whom I find it so easy to communicate, made me feel I was again in a rapidly modernizing society, not too dissimilar to my own world. There were older features in the arts and ceremonies which told me that China was also, like Japan, highly aesthetic and sensitive, but I did not at first notice the enchantment.

Yet again the signs began to appear as I dug deeper. The Daoist philosophy is premised on enchantment. Like Shinto or much of Gurung religion, daoists believe that nature and culture are inseparable. Everything has meaning and is part of a larger pattern. The winds, waters, rocks, trees, directions, colours, written and spoken words are constantly fluctuating and not what they seem.

The same features can be seen in much of China's art and literature. I was amazed to see the fairy landscapes and plots of one of the two oldest forms of Chinese opera, *kun-cu*, which was systematized eight hundred years ago, but incorporates many much more ancient fragments. *Kun-cu* reminds me of Keats or Yeats and the Celtic folklore of the Andrew Lang fairy stories.

The same is true in the few great Chinese novels. The *Journey to the West* is about animals who are also human. *The Dream of the Red Mansion* is founded on a magic jade stone and wafts an air of enchantment.

The other great philosophy of China, Buddhism, is also enchanted, partly under the influence of the Daoism which shaped it. As described elsewhere, its extreme Zen-like form in Chan Buddhism dissolves all boundaries. Humans co-mingle with spirit, man with nature, there is no separate hard-and-fast physical reality. Everything has meaning and is connected. The mind can create and uncreate, all is possible. As Zen in Japan is part of its enchanted world, so Chan in China is not opposed to enchantment.

This is one of the great contrasts to that extreme form of disenchantment which Weber isolated in Protestant Christianity and Newtonian science. As I approach the last stretches of my life, I find a great delight in discovering that what I thought was the inevitable Wordsworthian tragedy, the loss of childhood enchantment, is not the case in the great civilisations of East Asia. China and Japan remain enchanted, and the re-enchantment of the world, which they may bring, may be among their chief gifts to us all.

God and His absence

I was brought up in a Christian household in the West. My uncle was devout and I went to religious camps as a boy where we were encouraged to ask Jesus into our hearts. Jesus seemed unenthusiastic about coming at my call, nevertheless I never really questioned my Christian faith through the ten years of my schooling where, each week we would study the bible, go to the Sunday services and say our prayers. I assumed that there was one God, who had created the world, was the source of all morality, was all powerful and all seeing, and who would be waiting for us in heaven when we died.

It was therefore a considerable shock to go to a Himalayan village and find this monotheistic system totally absent. There was a Sanskrit word for God, 'devta', but I soon discovered that a better translation of this would be 'godling'. For there were many godlings, they were both male and female, they shared the spiritual world with many other spirits, including witches and the souls of dead ancestors, and they had neither created the world, nor were they the source of morality. They were as far as possible from my childhood God.

Brought up in a world where much of my culture has been derived from a belief in a single God, I find it almost impossible to enter into a world where this whole foundation is missing. Much of the art, poetry, literature, philosophy, ethics and even language I have been surrounded with are absent. My world would disintegrate without God, even if I don't believe in Him.

It is God who unites the different parts of my life, my social, moral and even economic and political life is pinned onto him. For example, the Queen rules under God, the morality of the economic market is founded on Christian ethics, the way I behave and all my social life is influenced by the residue of the idea that God is like our parents. He cares for us, listens to us, guides us, punishes us for our failures, rewards us for our meritorious acts, watches our every move. He is always there, as He was for Robinson Crusoe on his desert island. We are never alone because He is always at our side. We are filled with guilt when we fail Him and we strive constantly through our life to please Him and to ascend to heaven to reside with him for ever. How can one live without this steady anchor, I sometimes wonder?

Yet it is clearly possible to do so, and indeed much of the world lives outside the monotheistic belt of Judaism, Christianity and Islam. And they seem perfectly happy without Him

*

In the West, we think of 'Religion' as being an institution where all of the major parts of a bundle are present – a Creator God, a dogma and set of beliefs about heaven, hell, sin, salvation, an ethical code, and a set of rituals by which we can approach and influence spiritual powers. If this total package is what we mean by 'Religion', then none of the three major philosophies in China individually, or even when put together, constitute a 'Religion' as an autonomous and separate sphere.

Confucianism provides some ethics and social rituals, but no God or dogma about a spiritual world. Taoism has some rituals but no ethics or God. Buddhism has some rituals, ethics and some dogma but there is no creator God.

Another approach would be to argue that a phenomenon

like 'religion' should be understood by setting up a set of possible features, and then seeing whether most of them (if not all) are present. If we do this, and include not only those noted above but also others, such as a belief in ghosts, the reverence due to ancestors, the power of certain sacred places or people, the sacredness of certain texts, then the Chinese have a 'family resemblance' to what we feel is 'religion' in the West.

Any visitor who has been to Shangri-La or the minority areas, or to the Confucian or Buddhist temples which are springing up in all their red and gold glory over China, will feel a sense of 'otherness'. We sense that some things are set apart from normal life, that people are aware of something larger than the individual, a power like electricity which runs through everything and hence requires geomancers to determine propitious days and directions.

So let us agree that, even before we allow for the now considerable presence of real religious sentiments in the minority areas (Tibetan Buddhism, Uighur Muslims) and now many Christians, China has many elements which seem roughly like certain aspects of religion in the West.

What it did not have was a dominant, evangelical, proselytizing, monotheistic creed with its attendant vast corpus of priests, except for a short period in the Tang dynasty with Buddhism. Religion played little part in education, unlike in the West, and the religious did not form a separate order, like the Brahmins or clergy elsewhere.

There were no religious legal courts and apart from social ethics, religion was not a separate force in the economy or politics. The Emperor was heaven's representative and to be revered just as the father or husband was to be revered, but he was not a God.

What strikes a westerner about China is how this-worldly and rational the Chinese are and have long been. To them, as with the Japanese, the huge influence of Judaism, Christianity or Islam in Western thought – in our philosophies, social life, even our economics and politics – is extraordinary. To them we seem very superstitious, God-soaked people. It is not surprising that, until recently, there has been no word for 'religion' in China. Even now, the word used, stresses veneration and obeying the rules of one's ancestors, rather than believing in a God. For many who live in the western world of fundamentalist conflicts, the heir to the Crusades and missionary endeavours, this can all seem refreshing, yet it has pervasive effects on China in many spheres.

*

One particular aspect of this, concerns our concepts of the afterlife. From my childhood onwards, I was brought up in the belief that when we die we go to some other world. There was no chance that we would return to this world, reborn as an animal or human. Our ancestors were dead and gone. As for what that other world was like, we were given a sketch in our Bible readings and in poetry and painting.

Heaven was vague, nebulous, a place above the earth and therefore above the clouds. There, on a throne, a smiling, bearded, God would be sitting surrounded by a heavenly host of angels and arch-angels. They would all be sitting playing musical instruments and adoring God. The entrance to this place was a gate where St Peter greeted the souls of the departed and interrogated them before they were allowed into heaven. It was not specified in any detail as to whether we would meet our family and friends in Heaven. Nor was it clear what we would look like or how we would spend all eternity, except in supposed bliss.

Hell was described much more carefully. There were numerous paintings and descriptions of the burning fires, the tortures, the frightful demons leaping about and Satan rejoicing in our everlasting miseries. Again, it was not clear whether we would meet people we knew or what, apart from being tortured, would occupy our days and nights.

I had always assumed that this frightful binary choice of Heaven and Hell was to be found in the same form in all of the monotheistic religions. Only much later did I find that all in the

Jewish and Islamic world who were practising their ritual duties would go to Heaven. The only ones who went to Hell were unbelievers or those who had abandoned their faith.

Later in life I came to see Christianity as a harsh and cruel religion in this respect. Especially as a Protestant, without the last-minute absolution of the Catholic church, you could never be certain that you would avoid perpetual torture for some sin or other. The thought that the majority of mankind was condemned to Hell, even if they had not heard of Christianity, seemed arrogant at best, and at worst horrific.

In China there is a thing called heaven, 'Tien', but it is very far from the Christian heaven. It just means some place high up and beyond human reach, a sky kingdom, where certain powers dwell. It is not crowded with the souls of the dead, there is no God there, nor angels.

Likewise, one of the four places a Buddhist soul may go is a kind of Hell which, in the painting to be found in Buddhist monasteries, looks rather like the Christian Hell, with devils cavorting, fire and torture. Yet most souls are either reborn into this world, or escape to a vague nothingness or erasure of all pain in Nirvana. Neither Daoism nor Confucianism has any idea of Heaven and Hell. It is all very different and the pressure towards moral behaviour to escape the infernal fires is much less. To me, nowadays, it appears to be a more humane view of human destiny after death.

8. The future of China: some guesses

People often ask me about the future of China given that I see it as a sympathetic outsider who has visited many areas, talked to many Chinese students and friends, and have read something of its history over a period of years. There are certain things which seem likely to happen. Probabilities are all that one can deal with in such an attempt at prophecy.

The first thing that seems pretty certain is that, putting aside the possible extermination of humanity, China will endure. It has survived massive attacks and revolutions and, for reasons I have tried to explain, come back each time. The present turmoils – huge growth in numbers of people and their redistributions and scientific, technological, educational and other changes – even though they look like something that could break a civilisation, are being dealt with calmly and rationally in China.

China went through the huge changes of industrialization and urbanization which took a hundred and fifty years in the West in just thirty years with less disruption, poverty, brutality and pollution. This happened even though it is twenty times as large a change as that which occurred in the West or in Japan. It was far faster and affected a population ten times the size of the other comparable industrial revolutions.

If China can cope with the urban and industrial revolution in this way and not fall apart, there is no reason to think it will do so in the future. It has gone through the vast change for much of its people who have left an agrarian world for the cities. Built on the structural cohesiveness which I describe in this book, China is immensely tough, extendable and efficient. It will survive and grow.

My guess is that China has only reached a small part of its potential and that in thirty years it will be (again) the most important economy and civilisation on the planet – reaching out and influencing lives all over this world.

As far as I can see, while it wants to create a reasonable life for its citizens, and also would like others to understand and appreciate its great traditions, it has no missionizing zeal to make others 'Chinese'. There is no interest in turning us all into Taoists, Confucianists, Communists, Buddhists, Mandarin-speakers or lovers of Beijing opera.

Here it is different from the Spanish, French, British and recently the American, civilisations which have tried to make those encountered conform to themselves – whether this was Christianity, capitalism, human rights or western-style democracy. China does not, and has never, believed that others can be forced to change at the point of a sword or with a gun. Even if they were to be 'converted', what would they be converted to? Playing mah jong, drinking tea, appreciating the ancient classics, calligraphy, a respect for parents and authority? This is the limit of the package to be exported.

I hope I am right about this. For if China had the zeal of a North Korea or Wahabi Saudi Arabia or even America at times, then given its huge economic potential, we should indeed tremble. It seems to me that China is not like this; it is not the Third Reich, or Stalin's Russia, or Philip II's Spain. Such analogies miss the point.

We do not have to buy Chinese goods, even if they are better and cheaper. We do not have to eat Chinese food, however delicious. We do not have to practice Chinese martial arts, calligraphy, opera, or painting. They are on offer but not backed up by sword and fire.

I suspect that what I see in Cambridge, which is a situation where things have changed hugely just in twelve years, will develop further. Sixteen years ago, the Department at Cambridge in which I worked had no mainland Chinese Ph.D. students. There were very few Chinese in the streets, scarcely any interest in Cambridge in the great cultural objects from China in our museums and libraries, no great interest in bringing Chinese culture to Cambridge. China was far away and hardly seemed to be influencing us. Now it is totally different.

The Chinese are buying houses in Cambridge and sending their children to school there. The University has numerous excellent Chinese students, the science parks are starting to build up joint ventures, the Backs are filled with Chinese visitors; exhibitions, prose, poetry and calligraphy seminars, summer schools are all bringing a taste of China. In return many Western students and scholars are going to China and contributing there. No doubt some feel threatened or irritated. Yet measured in terms of energy, growing mutual respect and understanding, creativity and cultural richness, I can only be amazed and delighted at the integration and exchanges.

Let me examine some possibilities for the future by comparing the four civilisations I have worked in, the Anglo-American, European, Japanese and Chinese.

Law

Starting with the law, we see a great divide. Traditionally, complex and instituted legal systems, criminal and civil, have been more or less absent in China whereas they have been highly developed in Europe and the Anglosphere. Although this is changing quite rapidly in China nowadays, the basic difference is still between two kinds of legal order.

In the past in China, law was not needed except at the margins. Peace, conflict resolution and civil disputes were largely dealt with by non-legal processes. The basic organization of the system was through family and interpersonal pressures. Reciprocity, reconciliation, mediation, arbitration, these were the keys in a situation of multi-stranded connections where formal law was thought to be too confrontational and divisive.

As China moved to a situation where the traditional closeness was partly undermined by rapid urbanization and where the Chinese hope to import many Western technologies, educational ideas, economic institutions, people are faced with the problem of how far to go down the road towards the litigation-soaked West.

How far China will move towards western legal systems is not yet certain. Certainly my visits to Chinese law courts and talking to judges gives me a sense so far that China will absorb much more of the Western framework. Yet I suspect that as time passes, it will evolve a new hybrid version – 'Western law with Chinese characteristics'.

For example, I am not sure that the jury system will ever take off in China – just as it has failed to take off in Japan. And I suspect that the huge ratio of lawyers to population which we find in America, or the obsession with prosecuting for money, or the strong assertion of 'human rights' without the counterbalancing 'human responsibilities' will only partly be transported to China. There will be much more of a family flavour to the law, encouraging respect and duties to relatives.

The 'rule of law', meaning that all are subject to the same legal process and that all matters are ultimately to be settled, if necessary, by law rather than by physical force, will develop much more – but again there may be limits. Things are changing so fast – 'improving' from a western point of view, that it is difficult to keep up. It is not easy to predict, but I suspect the Chinese law will be just as efficient, fair and responsible as that anywhere in the world within the next thirty years.

Politics

The political future of these four civilisations is clearly the great question. If there are serious clashes, it is all over for humanity. And even minor outbreaks of aggression, for example a war between China and Japan, could do terrible damage. It is also an important question since there is so much talk of democracy, human rights and so on.

Looking across the four examples, it is clear that until the last century, their political systems were totally different. The Chinese had an Imperial-bureaucratic centralised system. After brief experiments during the Republic, China then reverted for forty years to another form of absolutism – Communist Rule. Only within the last thirty years has there been a serious attempt to increase political participation, through the delegation of power to the provinces and autonomous regions. Given the recentness and the fragility of the form of delegated power – what of the future?

It is worth remembering here that democracy has two meanings. In the sense that Tocqueville used 'democracy' in his *Democracy in America*, it does not mean the people choosing representatives to Parliament. It means that individuals have control over their own lives at the local level – civil society, freedom of association, a sense of empowerment through local bodies, freedom from constraint both of others and material constraints of hunger and disease.

In this broader sense of democracy, there is every hope that as wealth, education and self-confidence increases, this kind of democracy can spread anywhere. It is not affected by scale, since the lower units which matter, the villages, towns, counties, provinces, and the proliferation of associational bodies within them (business, professional, universities, churches) can be multiplied indefinitely and even cover something as huge as the 1.4 billion Chinese.

This kind of bottom-up democracy is being constructed in China. I have observed it from our first anthropological visit in 2002, where we watched and discussed with villagers the setting up of new village councils. This was a system which was then extended to the cities.

We have been impressed by the independence and power of the Chinese regions. This province-level democracy seems to be the way ahead and makes sense when one realizes that each of the Chinese provinces is the size of an average nation in the West.

For example, the population of Jiangsu province in southern China is roughly the same as that of a united Germany and its total GDP is nearly equivalent to that of Russia or India. It obviously makes sense to give it greater power over education, business and transport. And this is what is happening. This power is then taken down to each sub unit, so that each township and village or ward in a city is increasingly given the right to elect its own government and officers through secret ballots – though the watchful eyes of the Party are still present in a parallel organization of Party Secretaries.

China could well end up, as Adam Smith imagined his 'night-watchman' state, with the central state only dealing with civilisation-level matters – defence, international trade and high-level communication infrastructure, where the regional and local issues are left to provincial, city and village government

*

The other aspect of politics concerns the widespread cry for more 'freedom'. That freedom – of speech, action, association, thought – is now asserted to be a 'human right', though people tend to forget that the idea was invented only a little over two centuries ago in the American and French Revolutions.

Nor do many people tend to remember that freedom, in Isaiah Berlin's well-known formulation, has two meanings – the negative and positive forms of liberty. Negative liberty is the freedom from fear, hunger, oppression of all kinds. It is a legal tradition in England going back to at least the 12th century, for example 'habeas corpus, 'I have a body' which is mine and cannot be threatened or imprisoned except after due process.

The negative rules of liberty are simple and defensible like the simple rules of a game such as football. Once they are recognised, it has to be accepted that they entail responsibilities – for we have to be careful and responsible in our treatment of others who also have their negative liberties. The Anglosphere tradition of negative liberty is one which China is rapidly introducing into its laws, reducing the areas where raw power can overwhelm an individual.

The other meaning of liberty, positive liberty, is the right to do things, to say what we like, do what we like, force others if necessary to conform to what we think is best for them, in other words to force others to be 'free'. It is the tradition well represented by the idea of the 'General Will' in Rousseau and in the seminal ideas in all Communist and Fascist regimes.

It is the right of the general body to enforce their views on the individual. This is a tradition which has been regarded with deep suspicion in the Anglosphere. Even its greatest theorist and supporter of central power, Thomas Hobbes, when faced with the question of whether the individual's negative liberty, the liberty to live, was superior to the state's right to force him or her to die, opted for negative liberty. The 'social contract' which released us from a life which was one of perpetual war and endless misery by instituting a Ruler and general rules did not bind us to lose our natural liberty to defend ourselves.

If the Chinese follow the path of negative liberty, of minimum rights and responsibilities which cannot be violated, then there is a good chance that this, blended with a Confucian tradition which does not have such an idea, except indirectly through the idea of respecting and supporting the other, could lead to a viable political outcome in China. It could move away from the period of the enforcement of a Western-derived Marxist 'positive liberty' within communism, toward something which, although based on a rather bleak, Hobbesian, view of human nature, has worked for many centuries to protect and encourage the individual.

Science, technology and material change.

There is a curious remark by Karl Jaspers to the effect that if there comes a time when Science comes to China, China will no longer be China and the Chinese will no longer be Chinese. What could he mean and can it be true?

My guess is that what he means, being a profound scholar and an expert who had written on the thought of Confucius, Laotze and Mencius, as well as many great thinkers in the West and elsewhere, is as follows.

The 'structural' core of China to which I have alluded means that people and things are treated as related. Everything has its meaning in the relation rather than the thing itself. This is the way of Chinese traditional thinking. On the other hand, the world of Descartes and Newton is an atomistic one, where we set out intending to proceed along chains of reasoning to understand things *in themselves*, their properties and tendencies, and then to link them to other things. If this atomistic way of thinking, which is necessary for example for particle physics, were to take hold at a deep level in China, then, Jaspers may be suggesting, the great tradition of China would melt away.

It is a fascinating idea, no doubt containing much truth. Yet it can be qualified in several ways. The first is that it seems to apply more to the physical than to the biological sciences. It is been pointed out that the holistic, interconnected, structural way of thinking of the world, where man and nature are unseparated and everything is in some kind of 'chain of being' is rather appropriate and apt for biology.

Such a premise is especially useful for the relatively new and important field of ecology, for example the Gaia theory. It does not seem too implausible to argue that the Chinese will make a special contribution to the natural sciences. The award of the first Nobel prize in medicine (creating *artemesian*) to a Chinese scientist in 2015 suggests this. It may also not be irrelevant that a number of the Japanese science laureates have also been in the natural sciences in particular medicine, where a holistic tradition is so important.

A second qualification concerns the shift in the deeper ideas of science precisely in the period when Jaspers was writing. The whole idea of an 'atomic' universe was being challenged, not just by the splitting of the atom and the discovery of sub-atomic particles such as electrons and neutrons, but even more so by the work to establish a quantum theory of science.

In the quantum world, of course, there are no indivisible or basic stable units since the smallest elements are highly unstable. Things, as with Schrodinger's cat, can both be present and absent at the same time. It is no longer a binary world of either/or, but of both/and. This is much closer to the ancient conception of Yin and Yang, which coexist as *both* separate *and* the same. Again, it may be that the ancient Confucian, organic, thought which recognizes that there is a permanent flux and flow, with everything lying in a relationship, will be highly compatible with the quantum world.

Of course, it may be that Jaspers was thinking more of the practical effects of science, that is its institutionalization in technology. Technology, the application of reliable knowledge (science) to a world of matter, the shifting of atoms, the 'traditional effective action' by which humans extend their bodies, has always been particularly powerful in China. As we saw, until the fourteenth century almost all of the great technologies in the world were invented in China. After that, however, the West took the technological lead with machines of all kinds.

And it may be that Jaspers felt that the inrush of the products of science – new machines of all kinds – would throw China into a state where its roots were dragged out of the ground. If he did mean that, which is unlikely, then it also seems unlikely to be the case.

Of course, technology is not only shaped by humans, but shapes them, and the various revolutions in technology which have swept across China, from housing to roads, trains and cars, factories and cities, the Internet and television have transformed people's lives. This is having a huge effect and impact. The young Chinese growing up in Shanghai or Beijing are living in a world which is many ways hundreds of years away from their grandparents back in the villages of ancient China.

At first, we might expect that this would change the character and ideas of the new city dwellers. As they chat on their cell-phones, catch the subway, pop into McDonald's, watch their televisions, how can they be the same Chinese as their grandparents raising pigs, ducks and rice in a remote village in central China?

All this is happening so fast and on such a scale that it is difficult to know whether it is the end of the 'old China'. I have watched the same phenomenon on a smaller scale over a period of nearly half a century in villages in Nepal, and particularly in a village where I have worked since 1968. I have seen people who grew rice and collected fodder from the forest migrate to the cities of Nepal, India, the Middle East, Europe and Hong Kong.

My impression of meeting my friends from Nepal in their new worlds is that while in terms of material life and technology, they have changed enormously and seem very much like my world, and their children, who go to city schools seem like English children, this is the surface. In many ways their character and views, even down to continuing to believe in witches and shamanic trances, and certainly in their attitudes to their family, food, space and many other things, have survived.

This has happened even when they are a small minority living in a mass society in Hong Kong or London. I suspect that in the context of the Chinese cities, where individuals are surrounded by others from similar backgrounds, a great deal survives under the surface of the material changes.

Indeed, this is one of the strange characteristics of our mobile world. Just as the British wandered their Empire for several centuries, yet mostly tended to remain British at heart, so I believe the Chinese diaspora will be similar.

This is a vast topic and I do not have the data or experience to back up my hunch. Yet I would guess that looking back in a hundred years' time, it will be found that shoots and cuttings taken off from the trees of different civilisations will root all over the world. Yet I guess that the ginkgo will remain a ginkgo, the oak an oak, even if it small and surrounded by other trees. The melting pot will only partly melt the huge movement of peoples. Sadly, I will not be here to see if I am right.

What China is and will be

It is now difficult to see what the situation is. Because of the amazing economic, technological, social, political and cultural changes of the last thirty years, a series of rapid and huge changes unparalleled in the history of the world, especially in such a short and peaceful way, there is much confusion. It is not easy to discern whether the deep structure has been destroyed, damaged, or merely overlain, waiting to be revived.

My guess is that when historians look back on the current period in a hundred years' time, as we can look back on the Manchus or the Opium Wars, they will conclude that, while the surface and certain elements may have changed hugely, the basic relational, structure has remained.

I have quizzed my younger Chinese friends about this problem, dazed by how fast their life and lifestyles are changing every day so that they tell me that they cannot understand people two or three years older or younger than themselves. I sense that while they feel very different from their parents, especially if they have been partially educated abroad, they quickly revert to the previous patterns as they grow older and especially if they return to live in China. They feel at one with other Chinese, and like to be with them and linked to them.

One reason for believing that China will remain the old China is because of China's immense bulk. It is like some great ocean liner which gets buffeted by gales and waves but ploughs on. Even

Chairman Mao could not destroy or redirect it at a deep level. Currently much of China's effort is to integrate useful outside things while paying increasing attention to the revival of the vast and valuable legacy of its ancient linguistic, artistic, cultural and social traditions.

China could be seen to lead the way. Its ancient and magnificent art, culture, technology and wealth were unparalleled up to the early nineteenth century. It lacked many of the disfiguring features of other worlds. China was often peaceful and in general less aggressive than western civilisations. The philosophy put a high premium on harmonious social relations. It was highly literate and respectful of knowledge. The Chinese people were, and are, hard-working, tolerant and rational, ingenious and humorous. In many respects it was not just the longest and largest civilisation in history, but the most estimable.

Lacking religious fundamentalism, striving to adapt to its ecology and environment to make a living for millions in an often difficult world, it has created a model for all of us. Now that we face the Chinese century ahead, with Chinese food, culture and people spreading very widely, it provides an alternative to various aggressive fundamentalisms elsewhere. Yet if we are to benefit from its lessons, we need to understand it.

People often ask me about the future of China, as I see it as a sympathetic outsider. There are certain things which seem likely to happen; probabilities are all that one can deal with in such an attempt at prophecy.

The first thing that seems pretty certain is that China will endure. It has survived myriad attacks and revolutions and recovered. The present turmoils – huge growth and redistributions and scientific, technological, educational and other changes – though they look like something that would break a civilisation are being dealt with.

China went through the huge changes of industrialization and urbanization in a generation, while the British achieved this in over a period of three generations. Yet the Chinese case has, in terms of the speed and size of what has happened, caused much less disruption, poverty, brutality and pollution relative to the size of the two populations. It was far faster and affected a population ten times the size of the other comparable industrial revolutions of Japan and Britain.

If China can cope with the urban and industrial revolution in this way and not fall apart, there is no reason to think it will do so in the future. It has gone through the huge trauma of leaving an agrarian world and now is sailing on calmer water, even though it faces other problems. Built on the structural cohesiveness which I described earlier, China is immensely tough, extendable and efficient. It will survive and grow. My guess is that China has only reached a small part of its potential and that in thirty years it will be (again) the most important economy and civilisation on the planet – reaching out and influencing lives all over this world.

As far as I can see, while it wants to create a reasonable life for its citizens, and also would like others to understand and appreciate its great traditions, it has no missionizing zeal to make others 'Chinese'. There is no interest in turning us all into Taoist, Confucian, Communists, Buddhists, Mandarin-speakers or lovers of Beijing opera.

Here it is different from the Spanish, French, British, American, civilisations which tried to make all those it encountered conform to themselves – whether this was Christianity, capitalism, human rights or western-style democracy. China does not, and has never, believed that others can be forced to change their culture at the point of a sword or with a gun. Even if they were to be 'converted', what is it to? Playing mah jong, drinking tea, appreciating the Ancient classics, calligraphy, a respect for parents and authority? This is the limit of the package to be exported.

Twenty books and ten films on China which I recommend

If I could take only twenty books on China to a desert island, this is my selection.

Etienne Balazs, *Chinese civilisation and bureaucracy* (1967)
J. Dyer Ball, *Things Chinese* (1903, 1989)
Ronald Coase and Ning Wang, *How China Became Capitalist* (2012)
G. Lowes Dickinson, *Letters from John Chinaman* (1902)
Jean-Baptiste Duhalde, *Description of China* (1735), 2 vols.
Mark Elvin, *The Pattern of the Chinese Past* (1973)
Fei Hsiao-Tung, *Peasant Life in China; A field study of country life in the Yangtze valley* (1939)
Jacques Gernet, *Daily Life in China on the Eve of the Mongol Invasion 1250-1276* (1962)
Amitav Ghosh, *Flood of Fire* (2015)
Marcel Granet, *Chinese Civilization* (1922, 1958)
Sir Robert Hart, *These from the Land of Sinim. Essays on the Chinese Question* (1903)
F. H. King, *Farmers of Forty Centuries* (1911)
Joseph Needham, *The Great Titration* (1969)
Rob Schmitz, *Street of Eternal Happiness; Big City Dreams along a Shanghai Road* (2016)
Jonathan D. Spence, *The Death of Woman Wang: Rural Life in China in the seventeenth century* (1978)
Arthur H. Smith, *Chinese Characteristics* (1900)
R.H. Tawney, *Land and Labour in China* (1932)
Max Weber, *The Religion of China* (1951)
S. Wells Williams, *The Middle Kingdom; A survey of the geography, government, literature, social life, arts, and history of the Chinese Empire and its inhabitants* ((1883) 2 vols.
Lin Yutang, *My Country and my People* (1941)

If I could take ten films, I would select:

'The Last Emperor' (1987), Bernardo Bertolucci
'To Live' (1994), Zhang Yimou
'Farewell my Concubine' (1993), Chen Kaige
'11 Flowers' (2010), Wang Xiaoshuai
'Balzac and the Little Chinese Seamstress (2001)
'Yellow Earth' (1984), Chen Kaige
'Crouching Tiger, Hidden Dragon' (1999), Ang Lee
'Hero' (2002), Zhang Yimou
'House of Flying Daggers' (2005), Zhang Yimou
'The story of China' (2016)), six part BBC documentary with Michael Wood

Books by Alan Macfarlane referred to in Understanding Chinese A-Z

The Origins of English Individualism (1978)
The Culture of Capitalism (1987)
The Savage Wars of Peace (1997)
The Riddle of the Modern World (2000)
The Making of the Modern World (2002)
Japan Through the Looking Glass (2008)
Encounters with Japan and the Japanese (Essays on Japan) (2013)
The Invention of the Modern World (2014)
I*ntelligent Machine*s (2018)
Yukichi Fukuzawa and the Making of the Modern World (2018)
Adam Smith and the Making of the Modern World (2018)

Acknowledgements

There are numerous people and organizations who have helped over the years in helping me to understand and visit China. I am enormously grateful to them all, but will just single out a very few who have read parts or all of the text and made enormously helpful comments. They are:

Sarah Harrison, Mark Turin, Wang Zilan, Li Shuo, Michael O'Sullivan, Kent Deng, Frances Wood, Xiong Ling, Xun Xiaoya,Wang Kelin, Wang Zichao and Jonathan Benthall.

I would like to thank Qin Yuchen for her help in various ways, including designing the book.

I have incorporated several paragraphs from my book *China, Japan, Europe and the Anglo-Sphere* (2018) in the text under the following headings:

The Bureaucratic Empire; Family, Confucianism and Power; Separation of Natural and Supernatural; Money and cities; what will China be.

[i] J Dyer Ball, *Things Chinese* (1903), 431

[ii] R. H. Tawney, *Land and Labour in China* (1932), 48

[iii] Reprinted in *Narratives of the Mission of George Bogle to Tibet and of the Journey of Thomas Manning to Lhasa*, ed. Clements R. Markham (Cosmo edn 1969),314. There are many references in Bogle's narrative of 1774 which show that Tibet was firmly in the possession of China at that point in time.

Printed in Great Britain
by Amazon

42112278R00249